WILFUL BLINDNESS

HOW A NETWORK OF NARCOS, TYCOONS AND CCP AGENTS INFILTRATED THE WEST

SAM COOPER

Wilful Blindness,
How a network of narcos, tycoons and CCP agents infiltrated the West

© Ottawa, 2021, Optimum Publishing International and Sam Cooper

First Edition

Published by Optimum Publishing International
a division of JF Moore Lithographers Inc.

Library and Archives Canada cataloguing in publication
Sam Cooper, 1974

ISBN: 978-0-88890-301-3

Hardcover Edition
ISBN 978- 088890-314-3

Digital Version of the book is also available
ISBN: 978-0-88890-302-0

Wilful Blindness, How a network of narcos, tycoons and CCP agents Infiltrated the
West . I. Title

Printed and bound in Canada
For information on rights or any submissions please write to Optimum

Optimum Publishing International
144 Rochester Avenue
Toronto, Ontario
M4N 1P1
Dean Baxendale, President
www.optimumpublishinginternational.com
Twitter @opibooks

Foreword | ix

1 | The Whales | 1

2 | Section 86 | 19

3 | Vancouver Model 1.0 | 29

4 | The Mission In Hong Kong | 47

5 | Triads Entering Canada | 57

6 | Project Fallout | 73

7 | The Casino Diaries | 89

8 | The PLA Whale | 101

9 | The Illegal Gaming Unit | 129

10 | Killing the Golden Goose | 165

11 | Narco City | 189

12 | Ockham's Razor | 209

13 | Silver and Gold | 249

14 | Known Knowns | 277

15 | Compromised Nodes | 311

16 | Strike Back Hard | 355

17 | Afterword: Infinite Connectivity | 373

Acknowledgments | 389

Index | 391

Appendix A | 401

Appendix B | 411

Appendix C | 425

Appendix D | 433

Appendix E | 437

WORLDWIDE ACCLAIM FOR WILFUL BLINDNESS

One of the more useful methodologies in investigative journalism can be reduced to a simple maxim: "follow the money." Journalists who undertake difficult and dangerous assignments of the type Sam has pursued in this book will sooner or later encounter an encumbrance to the purpose of revealing the truth that emerges from the work of uncovering facts, and it's this. Among the political vices, the thing about corruption is that the more widespread it is, and the higher up it goes in the political establishment, the less people want to talk about it.

This book is a testament to Sam's persistence and determination to follow the money - hundreds of millions of dollars in dirty drug money, trunkloads of $20 bills carried into casinos in hockey bags, money laundered from China by Beijing's "whale gambler" princelings and their back-alley go-betweens in Metro Vancouver. It's about the Canadian politicians who saw benefits in a seedy underground industry that outweighed whatever harm they noticed in sky-high real estate prices and the corpse heaps of dead fentanyl users.

It's a shocking story, told by a brave reporter who has forced a public conversation about corruption in Canada, how widespread it has become and how high up in the political establishment it has spread. It's also a ripping yarn.

Terry Glavin, *National Post*

Wilful Blindness reveals how Vancouver has become a global springboard for China into the world's most lucrative drug markets, including New York, Miami, Boston, Seattle, Los Angeles, San Francisco, and Las Vegas. These markets are supplied by not only Vancouver, but Richmond, Calgary, Winnipeg, and thousands of mini-drug labs in homes along the border of the US that are mixing illicit chemicals into pills for onward sale.

Tens of thousands of people die in these cities every year, from drug overdoses of illegal fentanyl, opium, heroin, ecstasy, and methamphetamines imported from Burma, through Singapore, Malaysia, Vietnam, Macau, Hong Kong, and China, by violent Triad gangs like the Big Circle Boys, Shui Fong, and 14K. The Triad gangs were started in the 17th century in China, and have fanned out globally, using a willing or unwilling Chinese diaspora, as the water in which they swim.

Anders Corr, PHD, Publisher of *the Journal of Political Risk*

"The transnational organized criminal networks are flourishing in Canada and elsewhere. With archaic legal systems, political indifference, and absent national strategy with siloed structures and systems, nations will continue to wake up to more dead kids, corrupt politicians and the rise of this 21st Century's most significant national and global security threat.

Vancouver and the rest of Canada have been a 'convergence zone' for Chinese, Middle Eastern, Mexican and Columbian Cartels for well over a decade as they sell and export their drugs, make their money and finance their related operations within Canada and the U.S.

Money laundering is merely a symptom of their crime and nefarious activities; the dirty money will find the cracks in the system just as water finds on all surfaces.

Sam Cooper has done what security officials have been hesitant to share until recently, Canada is a haven for nefarious national security and transnational organized crime networks, and our democracy is at risk".

Calvin Chrustie
Former officer in charge of major projects federal policing, RCMP, BC
Senior Advisor and Consultant, The Critical Risk Team

"This book reads like a thriller, and is stranger than fiction. Gripping, racy and exciting, it is difficult to put down. A tale of gambling, narcotics, tycoons, criminal gangs and Communists. And the shocking part is that it's not a novel, it is all true. Based on meticulous research, this aptly titled book exposes the naivety and corruption at the heart of western democracies which for too long have kowtowed to the Chinese Communist Party regime and their crime syndicates and as a result put the free world in jeopardy. This book is a wake-up call, and a must-read."

Benedict Rogers, co-founder and
Chief Executive of *Hong Kong Watch*

FOREWORD

Charles Burton

Senior Fellow, Macdonald-Laurier Institute and Non-Resident
Senior Fellow, European Values Center for Security Policy

Surrounded by majestic mountain vistas, set on the Pacific Ocean with clean, fresh sea air and sandy beaches, Vancouver enjoys a moderate climate with no extremes of heat or cold, a 'gardeners' paradise of lush peonies and flowering trees. Who would not want to live in such a paradise?

Since its founding, Vancouver has been a favoured destination for immigrants from China. Today, Vancouver has a larger share of Chinese residents than all other major Canadian or U.S. metro areas. 40% of the southeast Vancouver residents identify as ethnic Chinese, with over 50% Chinese in Richmond and about 20% over the Vancouver metro area as a whole. Through hard work and persistence against decades of systematized racism, including draconian measures to limit Chinese immigration and integration into mainstream society, ' 'Vancouver's Chinese community today thrives and prospers as citizens of Canada. Hospital wings, university buildings and institutions of arts and culture all over Vancouver proudly bear the Chinese-Canadian names of generous donors. But racial discrimination, misunderstanding and separateness continue to exist behind language and cultural barriers. There is a lot of work still to be done to overcome the shameful legacy of anti-Chinese bigotry. And more and more misidentification of the Canadian Chinese community with the Communist Party-led brutal, repressive and corrupt regime in 'China's 'People's Republic today. This is no more evident than in its dissembling over the origins of the COVID-19 pandemic and ugly tactic of hostage diplomacy to intimidate and coerce Canada, which means anti-Chinese racism is again on the rise in Canada.

This book looks at the opaque relationship between the Chinese Communist political élite and criminal triad gangs who trade in fentanyl, methamphetamines and opioids, money laundering through casinos, the escalating price of real estate in Vancouver and the Canadian officials, lawyers and law enforcement who may be complicit in murky illicit highly lucrative underground transactions. But we should be clear that this book is not about the ordinary honest, and hard-working members of the Chinese-Canadian community in Vancouver who are primarily the victims of all this dark depravity.

Much of *Wilful Blindness* is written in the first person. In addition to its revelations of malfeasance leading up to the most senior levels of Canadian political power, this book is also a personal story of an investigative reporter's quest over more than a decade, of the relentless painstaking work by journalist Sam Cooper to find the facts behind a complex web of circumstantial interconnection between the massive investments by families of 'China's Communist élite in Vancouver real estate, huge cash transactions in B.C. casinos and the recurring presence of senior officials of 'China's Communist regime and Canadian politicians photographed in the company of shadowy figures associated with transnational organized crime.

Vancouver is where the Huawei CFO, Meng Wanzhou, was arrested in 2019. She had seven passports in her possession when she was detained at the Vancouver Airport with indications that she had had an eighth official public purposes special PRC passport. Why so many passports, and why does she own two multi-million-dollar mansions in Vancouver when she is not even a resident of Canada? Why did Immigration Canada grant her husband and two children COVID-19 travel exemptions to visit Ms. Meng in Vancouver last year? Yet Canada got no reciprocal permission for the families of Michael Kovrig and Michael Spavor to see their loved ones in their Chinese prisons? It is the reason Canada now finds itself struggling with the Canada/China relations.

But these just scratch the surface of the many, many strange goings-on that Sam found hard to account for as he embarked on this journey of discovery back in 2009.

Moreover, considering that the Government of China has enacted strict controls limiting the export of foreign currency from China, how do the families of Chinese officials and their business associates transfer such enormous quantities of money to Canada? For so many Chinese Communist 'officials' families who have acquired real estate in Vancouver, the provenance of the vast amounts of Canadian dollars they used to pay for it is unclear. Especially as their Lamborghini and Ferrari lifestyles far exceed the range of their legitimate modest government salaries. But the relationship between the Communist Party and Triad criminals at all levels domestically and abroad are well established. From the thugs that rough up Chinese political dissidents and force impoverished farmers to give up their land pennies on the dollar for expropriation for lucrative development to the "respected captains of industry" in Chinese enterprises with established high level Triad associations whose stock in trade is tax evasion, massive official bribery and intimidation like Hollywood mafia dons because that is the only way to make a go of it in Xi' Jinping's China. There is no space in the CCP's system for an honest man.

So the idea that such people linked to Triads use illegal underground banks to get their both legitimate and ill-gotten gains to safety through luxurious bolt holes in Canada against the day they get on the wrong side of a Communist Party factional struggle is not unexpected. It turns out that it is based on reciprocity with Triads active in Canada, like the infamous Big Circle Boys, who make their profits in North America but need to source the product they are selling to drug addicts here from factories in China. The process is as simple as it is blatant. Some of the money derived from Communist Party official corruption is handed over to the Triads in China. Hockey bags packed with rolls of Canadian $20s, the proceeds of drug sales to Canadian downtrodden, are later transferred from the trunks of cars to B.C. casinos where they are exchanged for gambling chips used by Chinese gamblers to play baccarat at up to $100,000 a bet. The chips are then cashed in for cheques and deposited into Canadian Banks and given to lawyers to complete real estate purchases. But this tidy little scheme implicates Canadian banks, Canadian lawyers, Canadian real estate agents, the provincial regulators of casino gambling and the politicians who oversee them. The wilful blindness hangs on their pretence that if the Chinese money is not from illicit sources, they are not culpable under Canadian law. So, the hockey bags of bundled-up small bills are dismissed by the absurd logic that carrying around considerable sums in small bills is a Chinese cultural norm!

Sam Cooper has based a lot of this book on classified information leaked to him by brave RCMP officers, B.C. casino investigators, and intelligence sources outraged at the level of criminality going on in Canada, without those complicit in and enabling it to be made accountable for their crimes. These police officers and investigators are only too aware that they lack the linguistic expertise and resources to meet the challenge of such a large-scale sophisticated operation that evidently has the support of PRC consular officials in Canada. They are angry and frustrated that their internal reports back to Ottawa on what is going on with detailed recommendations for what should be done about it are consistently ignored. Some of these voices were heard in British Columbia as BC Attorney General David Eby has called a provincial inquiry to be headed by British Columbia Supreme Court Justice, Austin Cullen.

Sam Cooper in these pages speaks for all of them. This book is a call for further action!

Behind Vancouver's magnificent verdant beauty setting is the ugly avarice of greed and shadowy corruption in high places. After you read this book; you will understand that these operations go well beyond Canada's borders, reaching into the U.S., Australia, Japan and other western nations.

Thanks to Sam Cooper, we are starting to see the facts of this political and criminal depravity exposed to the light of public debate. Sam Cooper has done Canada a great service by finally getting the truth out. After all, sunshine is the best disinfectant.

"But everyone who hears these words of mine and does not put them into practice is like a foolish man who built his house on sand. The rain came down, the streams rose, and the winds blew and beat against that house, and it fell with a great crash."

ACCOUNTABILITY FIRST: HOLDING GOVERNMENTS TO ACCOUNT, SHOULD NOT BE CONFLATED WITH RACISM.

By Teng Biao

I was born and grew up in China and I still have a Chinese passport. My academic research and activism focuses on human rights, justice and politics in China. I have dedicated and sacrificed a lot to fight for a better China. I am against the Chinese Communist Party.

I support sanctioning Chinese corrupt officials and human rights abusers. I participated in the fight for Human Rights and freedom of the Uyghurs, Tibetans and Hongkongers. I proposed more scrutiny on the CCP operations in the West, such as the Confucius Institutes, the GONGOs and the propaganda media outlets directed by United Front Works Department operations linked to consulates around the world.

It is ridiculous to claim that criticizing the Chinese government is part of the racist narratives of anti-China or anti-Chinese. To a great extent, to love China or the Chinese people requires those outside of China to oppose the Chinese government or the CCP.

It's important for countries like the United States and Canada to remain open to the world, to welcome people from different cultures, religions and political systems. but that definitely doesn't mean a country should become a safe haven for money-laundering, corruption, and human trafficking. An open society must not be exploited by dictatorial regimes to monitor the diaspora communities and to spread its anti-democracy propaganda.

Two Canadian citizens Michael Spavor and Michael Kovrig were arbitrarily detained and cruelly treated by the Chinese Communist Party, as an obvious retaliation for the detention of Meng Wanzhou. If Canadians have been shocked by "the judicial blackmail", it is a wonderful opportunity to deepen their understanding of the characteristics of the regime by reading this book. The author's argument, as well as the value of the book, have been proved by the fact that the UFWD operatives were trying to file a vicious lawsuit against him.

After the Tiananmen Square Massacre in 1989, with the help of Western engagement, money, and technology, the CCP has established increasingly powerful and brutal totalitarianism domestically and has become more and more aggressive on the international stage and a threat to global freedom. Its extraterritorial laws and the long arm of enforcement overstretch in many different ways. For example, its control of Chinese immigrants, its economic coercion, and its abduction of refugees overseas, including dissidents, booksellers, Uyghurs, and businessmen. Its theft, bribery, and propaganda are institutionalized through the Asia Infrastructure Investment Bank (AIIB), One belt One Road(BRI), South China Sea aggression, international cyber attacks and espionage, manipulation of the UN human rights mechanisms, and the "Thousand Talents Program".

Now, China is demanding a rewriting of international norms, attempting to create a new international order in which the rule of law is manipulated, human dignity is debased, democracy is abused, and justice is denied. The free countries should re-examine their China policy and stand up to the CCP's infiltration, erosion and bullying, before it is too late. The Chinese people will sooner or later enjoy liberal democracy and fundamental human rights, but the world should support the suppressed people and the courageous freedom fighters.

Teng Biao 滕 彪

Pozen Visiting Professor, University of Chicago Grove Human Rights Scholar, Hunter College, CUNYPresident, China Against the Death Penalty

1
THE WHALES

For the cops at the summit, it was insane how these gamblers were allowed to lug bags of cash into the casinos every day of the week. All you had to do was watch the casino surveillance footage. Mind-blowing.

Ross Alderson woke early at his home in Richmond and told his wife he was going out for coffee before work. He sometimes talked to her about his job in the casinos. But he decided not to mention he was about to meet one of Canada's top drug cops. Alderson stepped into his black Ford Ranger and drove east along the Fraser River, passing the lowrise malls, warehouses and shipping containers. He turned north onto the Queensborough Bridge and drove over the port of New Westminster.

He slipped Pearl Jam's *Ten* into the CD player and turned the volume on low. Just enough sound to ease the nerves. He was thinking about the cryptic late-night text from Calvin Chrustie, a senior officer with Canada's Federal Serious and Organized Crime Unit. They had agreed to meet at the Cafe Artigiano on Hastings Street in Vancouver.

Alderson could only guess what Chrustie wanted to tell him, but it seemed big.

Just a few months into his new job as B.C. Lottery Corps anti-money-laundering director and Alderson felt like he was living a double-life. In some ways, it felt like he was back in Melbourne, Australia. Back to being a cop.

He turned on Marine Drive and drove west along the Fraser River, cutting across the southern slice of Burnaby, mostly fields of timber until you come up to the River District near Boundary Road. Alderson was amazed by how fast the luxury condo projects were stacking up beside the river. Small rooms and high prices. It's mostly offshore money, he thought to himself. He looked out his driver-side window and back across the river to Richmond. It was sprawling, chaotic, growing at a crazy pace.

The city had the largest population of Mainland China immigrants in the world. Incredible amounts of absentee property owners. Alderson's own family had been lucky. In 2009 they had bought a townhouse for $341,000. Six years later — in his dinky little suburban corner of east Richmond — you couldn't buy a house for less than $1-million.

****

Alderson turned north on Boundary Road — the dividing line between Vancouver and Burnaby — and powered his truck up the steep hill. His mind was circling around the evolving threats he faced in his new job. It was July 2015. In June, his first big task had been to organize a summit for leaders from British Columbia's casino industry. About 20 experts had gathered in the conference room at the Lottery Corps Vancouver headquarters. Calvin Chrustie and several RCMP leaders attended, along with leaders from the B.C. casino regulator, GPEB, some banking executives, and investigators from the Canada Revenue Agency and Canada Border Services Agency.

Alderson remembered that Chrustie — a broad-shouldered and blunt talking investigator who looked a bit like former Oakland Raiders linebacker Howie Long — had seemed skeptical about the Lottery Corps motives for holding the summit.

The correct answer to the summit's headline question — do B.C. casinos have a money-laundering problem — was obvious to most people there. But not everyone.

Everybody there knew the primary revenue driver for B.C. government casinos were visits from ultra-wealthy Chinese businessmen. At any given time, there were about 100 foreign 'VIP' patrons gambling at the Lottery Corp. casinos in Richmond, Vancouver, Burnaby, New Westminster and Coquitlam.

These visitors were among the richest and most powerful men in the world, industrialist tycoons and Chinese state, military and police officials who claimed to have amassed tremendous fortunes as real estate developers, miners, oil barons, shipbuilders and construction moguls.

Gambling is illegal in China, banned for the masses by the Chinese Communist Party. But betting is also deeply embedded in the country's underground culture. And from Alderson's point of view, gambling was permitted for China's elite through backdoor channels.

For these 'whale' gamblers, baccarat was the game of choice. And they travelled the world to play it. In some B.C. Lottery Corp. casinos, in private salons where the VIPs were treated like royalty, they could bet up to $100,000 per hand.

They won and lost obscene amounts of money at Richmond's River Rock Casino, the favourite destination in Canada for the Chinese whales, who also gambled in Macau, Las Vegas, and Melbourne. At the elite level — what the Lottery Corp. called 'VVIP' players — the gamblers bought chips with no less than $500,000 cash.

Alderson topped the hill on Boundary Road where Burnaby's skyline showed over the pines in Central Park. He stopped at Kingsway Road and looked east to the cranes and condo towers surrounding Burnaby's Metrotown mall. He knew Kingsway was thick with underground casinos tucked behind currency exchanges and in the back rooms of karaoke lounges. But trying to shut them down was like playing whack-a-mole. The locations changed so often. Alderson crossed Kingsway and continued north on Boundary Road.

He turned his thoughts back to the B.C. casino summit. Alderson knew that China's economy had to be considered in order to grasp what was happening in B.C. Lottery Corp. casinos.

He had arranged a presentation from Canadian foreign correspondent Jonathan Manthorpe, a veteran China-watcher. Manthorpe's point was that Canadian leaders — including the bankers and bureaucrats and casino brass at the summit — hadn't taken the first step to answer serious questions about funds pouring in from China and the impact on Canada.

"How much money is being spirited out illegally?" Manthorpe asked. "Why are China's wealthy hiding their money abroad? And how are they getting their money past China's strict currency controls?"

Manthorpe said that unimaginable private wealth had been created in the 1980s under the reforms of paramount Chinese Communist Party leader Deng Xiaoping. And now it was flooding cities like Vancouver, Seattle, and Melbourne. Figures from Chinese national banks predicted $320 billion in cash would flee China in 2015, Manthorpe said. Some analysts estimated much higher figures. And the corruption watchdog Global Financial Integrity had reported that $1.25 trillion in shady funds had rushed out of China from 2002 to 2012.

Almost all of the funds came from the top of the pyramid. "They are either senior members of the ruling Communist Party, or close to them, through family or business ties," Manthorpe said. "They're the elite who have benefited most from the economic revolution. Much of the wealth created in the last three decades, is now in the hands of a few families, attached to the Communist Party."

For Alderson the takeaway from Manthorpe's presentation was blunt. China's population was getting raped by its leaders. And Chinese state corruption was turning Vancouver's real estate market into an overpriced collection of lockboxes. But Manthorpe's research didn't address cash funneling into Lottery Corp. casinos.

The multi-billion-dollar question was how the offshore high rollers had acquired industrial loads of paper currency in Canada. It was not coming from Canadian banks.

For the cops at the summit, it was insane how these gamblers were allowed to lug bags of cash into the casinos every day of the week. All you had to do was watch the casino surveillance footage. Mind-blowing.

You had guys carrying big Louis Vuitton and Gucci leather totes, suitcases on wheels. And for the ultra-whales hockey bags stuffed with $20 bills. GPEB investigators had witnessed gamblers literally dragging hockey bags holding $1 million cash up the escalators to private cash cages. You would see a couple of guys rapidly unload the bricks of cash wrapped in elastic bands, and shove them across the counter to cashiers, who stacked the paper like hay bales and then fired the bills through electronic money counters. When the bills were tallied the cashiers passed the gamblers high-value betting chips. And the cash was immediately spirited from the cage down to the casino vault. And this happened night after night.

The way Alderson and the RCMP and GPEB investigators at the summit saw it, this was obviously incredibly suspicious.

But not for all of the Lottery Corp. executives. Brad Desmarais — a retired cop with years of experience leading RCMP anti-gang teams — had some funny explanations.

Desmarais theorized the Chinese high-rollers were flying into Vancouver International Airport with suitcases full of Canadian cash. But the GPEB investigators ridiculed this explanation — how the hell do you fly to Canada carrying a sack of $20 bills weighing about as much as an average-sized female? Not to mention that Canadian cash is disliked in China, and very seldom carried there. And on top of that, what legitimate businessman would fly across the Pacific Ocean with $1 million cash in a hockey bag, taking on the incredibly high odds of seizure or theft — just for a weekend of gambling in Vancouver?

It would be like risking your chips before even getting to the baccarat table. But when the airplanes-from-China theory got shot down, Desmarais had another explanation.

The VIPs were acquiring cash in Canada through legitimate underground banking, he explained. It wasn't Canada's problem that China barred its citizens from exporting more than $50,000 per year. And so, the Chinese community in Canada had established underground banking methods to facilitate trade. And this wasn't a bad thing. As ridiculous and blindered as this argument may have sounded to the cops in the room, it was basically unwritten policy for Canada's real estate and banking sectors.

And Desmarais had previously flown to Victoria and briefed B.C. Finance Minister Mike de Jong's office on the Lottery Corporation's surging cash transactions. He told de Jong's deputy, Cheryl Wenezenki-Yolland, that underground banking could explain the mystery money flooding into B.C. casinos and the provincial treasury.

So as the cash arguments heated up at the summit, Desmarais doubled down. For years, the RCMP had known that wealthy visitors from China were moving loads of cash around Vancouver, he said. But they'd never been able to prove this cash was criminal.

That's when Wayne Rideout, the highest-ranking RCMP officer, stepped in. It's silly to argue that bags of cash carried into B.C. casinos are not suspicious, Rideout told Desmarais.

Chrustie and Rideout had talked about this before the summit. Are we the king or the pawn at this table? Was the Lottery Corp. trying to play everyone else, building a narrative to justify revenue from Chinese capital flight? So on June 5, 2015 — the day after the summit — Chrustie emailed GPEB's director, Len Meilleur.

"It is a complex issue, but as stated yesterday, while the flight of capital issue is a key concern, we know China's financial elite have close ties to organized crime," Chrustie wrote. "And we also know the cartels are close to Chinese networks."

***

On the sidelines at the summit, Alderson had good talks with the RCMP leaders, and he suggested following up with private meetings.

The RCMP bosses agreed. A few days later, Alderson drove from Lottery Corp. headquarters in Vancouver across the Port Mann Bridge into Surrey and parked his Ranger outside the national force's high-security facility, Green Timbers.

Walking up to the massive white complex, Alderson felt his gut tighten. He turned his driver's licence in at a security desk behind a large glass wall, bullet-proof he guessed, and the officers handed him a visitor's pass. He was led through a turnstile and they walked him into a conference room. He was a bit awestruck. The $1-billion federal building, a collection of giant rectangles sprawled across a park, had bunkers within bunkers. There was an ultra-secure command and control centre where leaders would retreat and run B.C. during a major disaster or terror attack. There was a real-time intelligence centre where analysts monitored all manner of electronic records and signals.

It was intimidating sitting at the board table. Just try to hold your own, Alderson said to himself. He had been a police detective in Australia, yes. But this was the RCMP's top brass, intently looking at him. Most he recognized from the Lottery Corp. summit. But there were people he didn't know, like the man in a finely cut suit, an intelligence type, he guessed. After introductions, Alderson made it clear he sympathized with the RCMP. He said that B.C. casinos had a massive crime and dirty money problem. Alderson said he wouldn't apologize for what came before him inside B.C. casinos. But he was committed to cleaning up. And whatever the RCMP asked from him at the Lottery Corp., they'd get it.

Calvin Chrustie didn't have much to say in the boardroom. But afterwards, several officers from Chrustie's team brought Alderson into an operations room and excitedly introduced him to the file they called "Silver." They had maps all over the walls, photos of suspects that were linked to other suspects with pins and coloured threads. And the suspects were geolocated to businesses across Richmond and Vancouver, and also connected to various vehicles and private residences. There were lists of suspicious transactions and police investigations and incidents. Link charts and flow charts and hierarchy charts. And China's territory was a focal point for the RCMP.

The officers told Alderson the Silver file was really two major organized crime investigations running parallel. But they appeared to be converging. The file had started as a transnational drug-trafficking probe focused on a cartel based in Mainland China and strong around the world, especially in B.C., Macau and Hong Kong. In the beginning, the RCMP suspected links to B.C. casinos, but that wasn't the focus. But now undercover officers had identified what they believed was an illegal "cash house" in downtown Richmond. This was "Silver" — and Chrustie's team was starting to see connections between Silver and the network of casino loan sharks and whale baccarat players at River Rock Casino.

One of the primary targets pinned to the wall of the Silver ops room was a Richmond man named Paul King Jin. Alderson looked at Jin's photo. He was bald, muscular, had a strong jaw and thick lips. He looked like a fighter. Alderson recognized his mug shot from Lottery Corp. investigation files. They had a huge cache of casino security reports on Jin. He was a VIP gambler at River Rock Casino. But he was also reputed to be the biggest loan shark in B.C. casinos, and connected to lots of VIP gamblers from Mainland China and some B.C. casino staff.

Chrustie's team asked if Alderson could provide them his Lottery Corp. investigation unit's suspicious cash transaction reports.

Alderson said he could, and after the first visit to Green Timbers, he had returned about once a week, and also met with RCMP officers across Vancouver, at malls and coffee shops. They would show him photos of Silver targets and give him USB drives containing surveillance photos from inside Silver's "cash house." They asked Alderson if he recognized any of the people they showed him, from his own Lottery Corp. casino surveillance files. Yes, he told them. He did.

By this time, Alderson could guess why Chrustie's team had brought him inside their sanctum.

Alderson had the keys to B.C. Lottery Corp's kingdom. Secret information on the Chinese VIPs — how much they were gambling, what industries they claimed to be involved in, and who they associated with inside the casinos, including other gamblers, casino employees and managers, loan sharks, body guards, and politicians. And so he agreed to give Chrustie's team the VIPs they should watch. It was personal and confidential information.

These were the handful of mainland Chinese whales connected to hundreds of millions in suspicious cash transactions every year in B.C. The Canadian privacy laws that protect corporations, lawyers and investors are notoriously stringent, from a police perspective. Alderson knew he was putting himself out on a limb, providing this information to Chrustie's team. And he wasn't asking permission from his Lottery Corp. bosses. It was dangerous territory.

In some ways, Alderson was feeling greater allegiance to the police than the Lottery Corp. His access to corporate intelligence on suspicious gamblers and transactions — tightly guarded from public scrutiny by the Lottery Corp. — when combined with the RCMP's organized crime intelligence, made an extremely powerful investigative database.

But the tension was growing inside him. In basic terms, the job of a casino anti-money-laundering director was to identify and reject suspicious cash. But realistically, to turn away a 'VVIP' player carrying $500,000 in cash? That obviously had huge revenue impacts for the casinos, the Lottery Corp. and B.C.'s government. There would be pressure from all sides if you barred a billionaire industrialist.

* * *

In the windshield Alderson could see the North Shore mountains rising across the Burrard Inlet, and through his driver-side window in the distance, downtown Vancouver, a gleaming wall of glass. He was coming down Boundary Road through the Hastings-Sunrise area of East Vancouver, a lowrise blue-collar neighbourhood where a run-down 1,100-square-foot bungalow could sell for over $1.5 million. He had already driven past the Lottery Corporation Vancouver office at Renfrew and Broadway. No turning back, just a few minutes away from Caffe Artigiano, to meet Chrustie, again.

Was he trying to serve two masters? How much information could he share with the RCMP while still doing his job for B.C. Lottery Corp? It was stressful. And Alderson wasn't just weighing his relations with the RCMP.

I didn't know it yet. But Alderson was closely following my reporting for the *Vancouver Province*. I was filing story after story about Vancouver's insane real estate market and the mystery money from China. Alderson recognized some of the biggest whales in B.C. casinos were the exact same Mainland Chinese developers and corruption suspects I was writing about. And he was especially bothered by my March 2015 report, "Chinese Police Run Secret Operations in B.C. to Hunt Allegedly Corrupt Officials and Laundered Money."

Finally, in 2017, Alderson contacted me. We arranged to meet at an anti-money-laundering conference in Victoria. He decided to share confidential B.C. Lottery Corp. files, including a document naming dozens of River Rock Casino whales funded by Paul King Jin. It was the most sensitive record I have ever obtained, and the codebreaker I used to expose the criminal method now known as the 'Vancouver Model.'

* * *

Life had moved fast since Alderson was promoted as the Lottery Corps' new anti-money-laundering director, in April 2015. He and his wife had talked about his past and the expectations. He told her that if he did his job right, he would be going against the grain of a powerful industry. They also talked about his lingering regret from leaving policing. In a strange way, he told her, with this new casino job, he might be able to do more fighting organized crime than he had ever hoped to in Australia.

He was from New Zealand and growing up had always wanted to be a cop. He had some tough circumstances in his teens and had to move away from home and grow up fast. He was big and athletic — about 6-foot-3 and over 200 pounds. And he disliked bullies. It all drew him to policing. But it didn't happen until he moved to Australia. In his late 20s he was sworn in. He started working the street beat in Melbourne's Box Hill neighbourhood. It was one of Australia's largest Chinese communities, and very similar to Richmond and Vancouver in many ways, he thought. Lots of wealth pouring in from China via mysterious channels. An international resort casino in Melbourne filled with jetset Chinese highrollers. So much cash. Super cars, empty condos. All the red flags.

Alderson had moved up quickly from a junior constable position to a special enforcement team in Box Hill. He did well and won an award. It was an interesting place for a cop to learn the ropes. Several times he had pulled over flashy sports cars and been offered cash out the window.

He wanted to see more of the world, so he left his police job in Box Hill and came to Canada in 2008 and took a job with the Lottery Corp. interviewing prize winners.

When he decided to settle in British Columbia and married a woman from Richmond, he saw the flags again, but even bigger now. He liked to tell people that he knew the good and the bad of Chinese culture from his time in Box Hill.

He liked to eat Chinese for lunch at the Aberdeen Centre, right across from the Radisson Airport hotel on the bank of the Fraser River, a five-minute drive from River Rock Casino. The restaurants always asked for cash. In 2011 he was stationed in River Rock Casino in a security and surveillance job. Working for the B.C. government in casinos was a good gig. Perks at the Lottery Corp. were great. He had a company car right away, and a phone. He was well paid. But people had blinders on.

His first day in the Richmond casino, he thought, "Holy shit" — bags and bags and bags of cash coming in. The staff was completely blasé. No one was asking questions.

Alderson had read the security files. The top Lottery Corp. VIP baccarat player for the past ten years, Li Lin Sha, claimed to be a coal miner in China. He brought in hundreds of thousands almost nightly. He's legitimate, Alderson was told. Cash is lucky in China. Mr. Sha was a commercial real estate developer too, according to Alderson's bosses at the Lottery Corp. But he also happened to lend big money to Chinese immigrants, B.C. Court records showed me. And these cash loans were secured against Vancouver real estate.

For me he looked more like an underground banker of some kind than a coal miner. And when I found that a woman involved in Mr.

Sha's U.S. dollar loan network was also listed as RCMP Suspect 16 in a hierarchy chart that named Paul King Jin as Suspect 22 — my hunch about Mr. Sha looked right.

But back in the day when Alderson would press people about patrons like Mr. Sha — why can't you just ask the high-rollers where the cash is from? — they would say, "Because they lose face. They are very wealthy. It's not customer-friendly. It's invasive."

Did the fact that Mr. Sha once bet $3.1 million in a single month in B.C. casinos have anything to do with the lack of interest in where his cash came from? In Alderson's mind, there was no question.

As a cop in Australia, he had learned all about flight of capital from China and corrupt officials. But the staff in B.C. government casinos didn't want to hear it. Alderson felt the governments of Canada and Australia had different attitudes towards excessive offshore wealth. A memorable quote from a Melbourne cop put the national differences in perspective.

In 2013, after a 12-month operation targeting a super-cartel operating out of China, Hong Kong, Macau, Thailand, Malaysia, Vietnam, and Burma, Australian federal police seized 42 kilograms of heroin and methamphetamines, and $4 million in cash, plus luxury homes worth $5 million, $600,000 in gambling chips from Crown Casino resort in Melbourne, a Lamborghini, and 99 designer handbags.

This was one of the new, corporate-style drug syndicates run out of Asia — a sophisticated collective of untouchable figures from various Chinese gangs. International police were starting to believe these Asian supercartels were bigger than Pablo Escobar had ever been. There were natural limits to how much cocaine Colombia could produce each year. But the sky was the limit for chemical production in Chinese factories.

The *Age* newspaper quoted Federal Police Commander David Sharpe saying that the 27 people arrested were significant players in the Chinese syndicate, and the luxury items seized by police displayed "extravagance and arrogance."

"It's personally quite satisfying when you see these people live this sort of lifestyle, and you see them in tears when the handcuffs go on, and their Lamborghini is on the back of a truck being towed away," Sharpe said. Lots of Canadian police would agree with that comment.

But in the Canadian government, the statement would be seen as bad form. A bit too passionate and aggressive. A bit too gung-ho and American. From what I heard about Calvin Chrustie — an investigator who relished working with United States drug enforcement teams — the more aggressive policing style seemed to fit.

I was told that Chrustie came from Winnipeg and had seen the fatal damage drug addiction does to vulnerable communities, especially First Nations.

His international military service was also formative, and he saw Canada as a nation with blinders on, most of the population clueless about international criminals who were often secretly connected to foreign states.

In drug-trafficking investigations, Chrustie saw the world as a field of play, and he was fluid in his play-calling, not afraid to shove an active probe aside and respond quickly to source info. That's how you could intercept an incoming load of chemical precursors from Hong Kong or a shipping container from Brazil packed with Peruvian cocaine and Chinese fentanyl pills.

Chrustie's philosophy didn't always mesh with upper management in the RCMP. I heard he had fans and also a few critics. Some viewed him as too aggressive and blunt. But he was also seen as a person who would take the most challenging files without factoring in political calculations. And as one investigator with the Canada Revenue Agency in Ottawa once told me, with a shrug: "Say what you want, but no one is taking more drugs off the streets in British Columbia than Calvin Chrustie." It was fair to say that in July 2015, both Chrustie and Alderson were experiencing considerable institutional tensions.

* * *

There were a few Lottery Corp. colleagues that shared Alderson's aggressive instincts on the whale gamblers. But he had to be careful.

When he started asking questions about the mysterious billionaires flying in, it got back to him that a Lottery Corp. investigator who had also worked for River Rock Casino told people that Alderson was guilty of racially profiling Chinese casino patrons. And increasingly, he was butting heads with some staff in the Richmond casino.

Every day he would come in at 9 a.m. and start by reviewing surveillance tapes and casino security reports. Quite often, Alderson told me, important information from the videos was missing from the reports. Very incriminating stuff on suspicious transactions.

He could never prove that the security staff was pressured to sanitize their reports. But he did question them sometimes and once escalated a report to GPEB, suggesting they kick the tires on a staff integrity investigation. But GPEB, which was controlled by the same B.C. ministry that oversaw the Lottery Corp., apparently did not have executive support for such a probe, Alderson was told.

He would also look at the internal I-Trak reports filed by casino staff, records that logged suspicious transactions and associations. One case that stood out was a B.C. politician, Richard Ching Chang, a man from Taiwan elected as a municipal councillor in Burnaby.

Reading this man's files was incredibly telling. Any investigator at River Rock could have read those files and taken action. But Chang was still in the casino almost every night.

Chang would loiter around the VIP salon holding a man purse. He was passing casino chips to players, from what Alderson saw. To Alderson, he looked like a loan shark. Obviously. In the sanitized corporate language of B.C. Lottery Corp, a "banned lender" or "cash facilitator."

Someone who could reasonably be suspected to be laundering criminal proceeds in the casino.

One Lottery Corp. report that struck Alderson said that Chang drove a black Porsche Carrera, and surveillance footage showed him driving up to the Starlight Casino in New Westminster and making cash drops to Chinese VIPs.

This is while he is serving on Burnaby council, Alderson thought. With the power to make laws and greenlight condo zoning development permits. And councillors make about $60,000 per year. How could Chang afford a sports car worth over $100,000?

Alderson saw that Chang had been cited for an incident at River Rock Casino. So he wrote a summary report and banned him from all B.C. casinos.

But incredibly — Alderson told me — a manager at River Rock responded by vouching for Chang.

"He was a great guy" who had travelled with a River Rock Casino manager to China on business.

Alderson was amazed. What kind of business? Recruiting whales?

* * *

Alderson turned off Boundary Road and parked on Hastings Street. He walked into the Artigiano and sat down. Chrustie wasn't there yet. A few last minutes to gather his thoughts. Obviously, something had changed last night. Just a few days previously, Chrustie had told Alderson their Silver intel-sharing agreement had to end. And then Chrustie texted late at night asking to meet for coffee. Now here he was. They got coffees and sat down in a corner booth.

Chrustie got to the point.

Last night his unit had broken the case. The RCMP could now connect the bags of cash being dropped off at River Rock Casino for Chinese VIPs to drug-trafficking from a Mainland China crime cartel. The Richmond loan shark, Paul King Jin, was allegedly running an underground bank. It was a business located in a Richmond office tower, called Silver International, basically a criminal bank, unlicenced, operating in broad daylight. Drug dealers were delivering cash every day to the business — suitcases full of cash — and Paul Jin's gang was lending it out. In very basic terms it worked like this: Paul Jin travelled to Macau and China and recruited whale gamblers. The gamblers agreed to fly to Vancouver, and after landing at the airport in Richmond, they called or texted Jin on WeChat.

The whales would place orders for cash deliveries from Silver using coded WeChat messages. Jin would receive the coded orders, drive to Silver International and load up the cash in his white Lexus SUV, then drive the cash loads to the VIPs, waiting in parking lots near the Richmond casino. The VIPs would take delivery of hockey bags of cash from Jin, walk them into the casino and wash the money in casino chip purchases.

That was the basic transaction flow. Drug dealers from China shipped drugs to Vancouver. Gangsters across Canada sold the drugs. The drug cash was collected and deposited at Silver International. Jin's gang provided Silver's criminal cash deposits to whale gamblers. The money was washed in B.C. Lottery Corp. casinos.

After that, the transactions got more complex. Money was coming in from China, getting wired from Silver's accounts in Richmond to bank accounts in China in order to fund drug imports to B.C. Silver was bouncing wire transfers to banks offshore and covering bank wires with false trade invoices, and the funds were released in Venezuela, Peru, and Mexico, to ship cocaine to Canada. This was global drug crime at the highest echelons. All of it running through the underground bank in the Richmond office tower, and the Lottery Corp. VIP rooms.

Chrustie had one last bombshell for Alderson. He said RCMP transaction analysis indicated some terrorist financing entities in South America were linked to Silver and the Chinese underground banking network in Richmond.

Alderson was knocked out. It was almost too much to process. If B.C. Lottery Corp. had managers knowingly accepting cash connected to drug trafficking and terrorist financing, that could put government officials in jail.

Alderson got into his Ranger and drove west on East Hastings. He had to meet right away with BCLC's chief executive, Jim Lightbody.

2
SECTION 86

So, Alderson put a transcript of the interview into a suspicious transaction report to be filed with the RCMP, GPEB, and Fintrac, Canada's anti-money-laundering intelligence agency.

Alderson crossed Boundary Road and took a deep breath. His heartbeat was up. It was a shot of adrenaline. The vastness of the information Chrustie had downloaded on him. He was driving through the area that Vancouver Police call District Two, and through his windshield East Hastings was a long tunnel framing the bank and condo towers rising behind the Downtown Eastside housing projects.

It was a stark contrast — the beautiful twisting glass structures with units mostly sold unseen to offshore buyers and the desperate street corners below, like Main and Hastings, the epicentre of six blocks of addiction and death, the most impoverished neighbourhood in Canada.

Holy shit, Alderson kept saying to himself. This is big. This is very big. This changes everything. And I knew it. It had to be drug money. I knew it. Now he had a dilemma. The intel that Chrustie had provided was incredibly sensitive. Alderson didn't want to lose the trust of the RCMP. But he also had a legal obligation to officially report any suspected criminality to the B.C. casino regulator, GPEB. It was called a Section 86 report. In some ways, the Section 86 law was a promise to B.C. citizens. You, the people, will allow the government to administer casinos — businesses extremely prone to crime — if we transparently report on and act against crime within them.

Now, the way Alderson saw it, for the B.C. government, there was no more room for speculating or debating about mystery money from China. Calvin Chrustie had said the RCMP was in the middle of investigating criminals from China using B.C. casinos to launder cash. And not only that, evidently using River Rock Casino systematically.

The Lottery Corp. had to refuse the criminal proceeds or become a party to the offence of money-laundering. Alderson hit the steering wheel. And I told them this was happening, he said to himself.

He thought back to early 2012, a few months after he had banned the Burnaby city politician, Ching Chang. One morning, he logged into the River Rock Casino security system and started reviewing footage, and he saw one baccarat player buy-in for $100,000 and play for about an hour. The gambler from China had played a few hands but mostly just jiggled his chips in his pocket. The $100,000 in chips was never at risk. The gambler was acting. And then he abruptly cashed out. The gambler had bought his chips with bricks of $20s. But the casino cage paid him out in wads of $100s. A huge red flag for money-laundering, known in the casino industry as "refining" currency.

It allows drug traffickers to exchange $20s wrapped in elastic bands — the type of currency most often used in drug transactions — for $100s that come clean from the casino, wrapped to banking standards. Funds that are now endorsed by Canada's anti-money-laundering system.

In the simplest terms, refining is about reducing volume. Drug deals produce trailer truck-loads of $20 bills that are basically worthless, and dangerous for criminal organizations to warehouse. But narcos employ money launderers to reduce trailer loads of cash down to pickup truck loads, by refining the $20s in casinos and turning them into $100s or $1000s. Next, they can convert the smaller loads of bigger bills into bank drafts or cheques or wire transfers, by breaking $100,000 in $100 bills into ten or twenty parcels, and employing squads of 'smurfs' to deposit amounts of under $10,000 per person, into separate bank accounts.

Looking at this $100,000 baccarat refining transaction on tape at River Rock Casino, Alderson was pissed. The tape should have been flagged.

He ran up to the casino security office and checked a live camera, and he saw the same player at it again. Another buy-in for $100,000 in $20 bills. He called surveillance right away.

"You stop his play right now and give him his money back in $20s. I want to talk to him."

Within minutes the Richmond casino manager was on the phone, shouting. It was the same manager who had vouched for Ching Chang when Alderson banned the Burnaby politician for loan sharking. You don't tell my guys what to do, the casino manager had yelled at Alderson.

"This is my casino, not yours. And if I want to pay him back in $100s or a cheque, I will."

"OK, can I quote you on that in my suspicious transaction report?" Alderson fired back. "The player is refining."

This casino executive, Rick Duff, a manager with Great Canadian Gaming, the company that operated the Richmond casino, appeared to have a long history of conflict with front-line investigators who tried to bar Chinese VIPs at River Rock Casino.

One of those investigators was Mike Hiller, a former RCMP officer. Hiller was probably Canada's leading expert on Chinese transnational narcos and operatives like Paul King Jin.

Hiller and Duff had a dust-up in 2009. And the same problem was at the heart of Alderson's shouting match with Duff.

Hiller's investigation notebook said on July 3, 2009, Duff came into Hiller's office "upset about B.C. Lottery Corp. barrings for Large Cash Transaction players. Rick Duff also mentions that if that is how Lottery Corp. investigators are going to do business, then he will instruct surveillance to do things differently."

There it was. You don't tell my casino staff what to do. And a few days later Duff met with Hiller's boss, Gord Friesen. They discussed Hiller's five-year ban on a River Rock VIP. And the ban was rescinded, according to Hiller's notes. Alderson knew about this case. Pretty damning stuff, he told me.

Years later, Duff would testify that he didn't do anything wrong. But he did acknowledge he argued with Hiller and Alderson about VIPs, and told Alderson, "I thought your job was to report [suspicious transactions] and let the real police investigate."

In 2012, Alderson's heated conversation with Duff had ended abruptly. And Alderson filed the Lottery Corp. forms needed to suspend the gambler pending an interview on his source of funds.

The gambler had agreed to meet Alderson for an initial interview at River Rock. But Alderson didn't probe too deeply on that occasion, because the casino provided its own translator for Chinese VIP interviews. And Alderson didn't trust the scenario. One interesting thing the whale had said was that he traded goods with his associates in China, and in return they provided him $20s to buy-in with when he travelled to Richmond. Within a few days the player had contacted Alderson again, and agreed to a further interview at Lottery Corp. headquarters in Vancouver. The VIP wanted his gambling privileges back.

Alderson had a co-worker who spoke Cantonese interpret for the interview. He started with the simple question that no one in River Rock Casino wanted to ask the high-rollers.

So where did you get the $100,000 cash to gamble? Not from the bank, right?

The high-roller said he used WeChat, the Chinese text-messaging application, to connect with cash lenders in Richmond. A red flag right off the bat.

So Alderson had started asking more penetrating questions. Who are the lenders? Do you know where they get the money? What is your source of income?

The man didn't want to identify his lender. This guy is full of shit, Alderson's co-worker, the Cantonese interpreter, had said to Alderson in English. But the River Rock gambler kept talking, and he admitted to a stunning detail.

After connecting with his source on WeChat, the gambler was directed to a strip mall in Richmond. A car pulled up and flashed its headlights. And the VIP walked over to the trunk of the car. He was handed a bag of $20s — a $100,000 load — and he went straight to River Rock Casino.

Drug cops from Vancouver to Toronto to Montreal to Las Vegas would recognize this as a textbook narco-cash drop.

Drug-dealing transactions always have more people involved than most imagine — top-tier narcos insulated by middlemen and mules and front-line money launderers. And the cash exchanges almost always take place out of car trunks in strip mall lots.

This is fricking evidence of money-laundering, Alderson had thought to himself in the middle of the interview. Whether narcos hired the VIP to launder money in the casino, whether he was unwittingly laundering for narcos, or whether he was a narco himself, it didn't matter.

So Alderson put a transcript of the interview into a suspicious transaction report to be filed with the RCMP, GPEB, and Fintrac, Canada's anti-money-laundering intelligence agency.

Now Alderson was driving past the Pacific National Exhibition and the Hastings Racetrack, and he turned north on Renfrew Street. Just a couple minutes away from the Vancouver Lottery Corp. office. Thinking back to what happened after he grilled the VIP and clashed with the River Rock Casino manager really burned him now.

His currency refining report had gone up the chain to the compliance department. And a few days later, Alderson was called into Terry Towns' office. Towns was his boss, the Lottery Corp. director of compliance. Someone wasn't happy that Alderson had directed Richmond casino staff to toss out the Cantonese-speaking VIP. Alderson argued his case to Towns. The evidence clearly showed the gambler was laundering cash. He was refining. This was not legal gambling.

But Towns was exasperated. You aren't a cop anymore, Alderson had heard Towns say. You aren't at the casino to investigate money-laundering.

"Cut that shit out," Towns barked.

The message was simple. Don't approach VIPs at River Rock. Don't question them. Don't even walk into the VIP rooms.

Alderson's fellow investigators, Steve Beeksma and Stone Lee, were there too. Lee — a former Great Canadian employee who religiously took notes in his Lottery Corp. investigator's notebook — captured the dialogue for posterity.

And he wrote down that Towns had said it was Great Canadian's president, Rod Baker, who had called and complained that Lottery Corp. investigators were tossing VIPs out of River Rock's high-limit salon.

"It's my understanding we're being told to back off by our managers," Lee wrote in his April 2012 notebook entry. "When the meeting was over, had conversations over what was discussed in Terry's office. [Another manager] Gord Friesen stated that he agrees with what we're doing, but 'This is political, what you gonna do?'"

Years later, Towns denied ordering his staff to not question River Rock VIPs, and testified that he performed his compliance duties diligently, and B.C. casinos were not used for bulk cash money-laundering on his watch.

That night, after the dust-up with Terry Towns, Alderson and Beeksma and Lee went out to the Shark Club in Richmond. Screw this, Alderson had said, sipping at his Guinness Stout. I'm done with this. The next day in the River Rock Casino security office, Alderson and Lee and Beeksma put posters of the Three Monkeys on the wall. See no evil. Hear no evil. Speak no evil.

Every day that week he woke up thinking, Today's the day they fire me. But incredibly, the opposite happened. He was promoted off the floor at River Rock Casino and into Lottery Corp. headquarters in Vancouver, to work in the Internet gambling division. Monitoring casino surveillance tapes wasn't his job anymore.

The joke with his mates at work was: Say you want to get promoted out of casino security in Richmond and into a nice office job at Lottery Corp. headquarters. How do you do it? You just grab onto the cash cages at River Rock Casino and start rattling them like a bastard.

And now he was in the same office with the brass: a situation that complicated his cop instincts, big time. You had to play nice to move up in the corporation. You had to paper the trail when going after VIPs. It was a lot easier to toss a suspected gangster from the casino floor than head office. And now, it had all come to a head. Alderson turned off Renfrew and parked in front of the corporation's Vancouver headquarters.

He walked into his office and sat quietly for a bit. The Lottery Corp. executives were in all-day board meetings on the third floor. Alderson called the B.C. government in Victoria to get Len Meilleur, GPEB's executive director of compliance.

It was a brief call. Alderson told Meilleur he had just had a very disturbing conversation with Calvin Chrustie, and it was probably best that Meilleur call Chrustie right away.

Soon Meilleur called back. Alderson felt that Meilleur sounded quite shaken as he recounted the same information Alderson had already heard from Chrustie.

Meilleur told Alderson that he had just briefed the assistant deputy minister in charge of GPEB and that Chrustie's information was now going up to Finance Minister Mike de Jong, who was in charge of the Lottery Corp. and GPEB.

Meilleur told Alderson he should brief the Lottery Corp. executives before they got a call from de Jong's office.

And Meilleur said something else that would stick in Alderson's mind. GPEB's director of investigations, Larry Vander Graaf, had been fired in late 2014, after warning B.C.'s government about a "massive escalation" in money-laundering. Larry Vander Graaf was right all along, Meilleur said, without elaborating further.

Alderson went up to the third floor and spoke to Lottery Corp. CEO Jim Lightbody's personal assistant and said he had an urgent briefing to share. In a few minutes, Lightbody and Alderson's boss, vice president of compliance Brad Desmarais, walked out of the boardroom.

They all went into Lightbody's large, open-concept office. Lightbody was a 54-year-old former lacrosse player, lean and athletic, a popular leader with a salesman's charisma.

Alderson told them precisely what he had heard from Calvin Chrustie. Drug-traffickers were using Lottery Corp. casinos systematically to launder cash through whale gamblers from China.

Looking back at this briefing, Alderson told me he was surprised with how blunt Lightbody was. He remembers Lightbody's first words were: "I guess we shouldn't be surprised."

Next, Lightbody asked Alderson and Desmarais, What do we need to do? Everyone agreed the Lottery Corp. had to identify the VIPs linked to Silver International and Paul King Jin and either bar them from casinos or put tight restrictions on them, forcing them to prove their large cash buy-ins came from Canadian banks.

Alderson was asked to arrange meetings between the RCMP and provincial government to get started on identifying the VIPs connected to drug money, and he went back to his office and started making calls.

Driving home that night he was elated. He felt his job had become much easier. If he wanted to ban a VIP suspected of links to organized crime, he wouldn't be getting pushback from casino managers anymore.

The next day at 7:49 a.m. Len Meilleur emailed Alderson requesting a report on the Federal Serious and Organized Crime's investigation. "Good morning, Ross. I am requesting a Section 86 Report from BCLC which is to be sent directly to me (no distribution beyond that) outlining the following: The names and other descriptors, vehicles, addresses provided by BCLC to the investigative body; the names of all individuals at BCLC who are currently aware of this Project."

And Alderson wrote back.

"BCLC suspected potential criminal involvement in Feb 2015 involving Paul JIN. There was communication between BCLC and GPEB investigations alluding to intelligence around both JIN and possible illegal gaming in the Lower Mainland.

"On June 29, 2015, at 1300 hrs — BCLC Director AML Ross ALDERSON met with the Federal Serious and Organized Crime (FSOC) Operational team to discuss the JIN file. ALDERSON was advised that there were two concurrent investigations that may be linked, however that JIN was not the primary focus of their investigation and that the Casino involvement had not been looked at for some time.

"On July 20, 2015, at 1400 hrs — BCLC Director AML Ross ALDERSON met with FSOC Operational team to discuss any updates on the JIN file. ALDERSON was advised that FSOC had now established a direct link from an 'illegal cash' facility which involved illicit funds being involved in drops offs to Casino patrons at River Rock Casino Resort.

"On July 22, 2015, at 0800 hrs — BCLC Director AML Ross ALDERSON met with Inspector Cal CHRUSTIE to discuss the new information. ALDERSON was advised that the investigation had uncovered that potentially some of the funds linked to transnational drug trafficking and terrorist financing were directly related to casino activity. Also that several foreign law enforcement agencies were now involved. It was discussed how over several years, a number of investigative agencies had highlighted concerns about some of the funds entering Casinos and those investigations had not progressed."

And Alderson concluded his Section 86 report with a sentence that acknowledged the highly confidential nature of the information provided by Chrustie.

"ALDERSON was aware this was privileged information. However the information discussed could have a potentially devastating impact on the Casino industry should it be true or leaked out to media."

There was dramatic irony in the sentence, too. It foreshadowed Alderson's ultimate decision to share sensitive information with me, in a choice that altered his life.

And it did impact B.C.'s casino industry. Because when I obtained the "Jin" Section 86 report, the document gave me the protection to withstand legal attacks from the casino industry and report on the devastating impact of Silver International's underground banking operations.

It was a stunning and terrible operation, laundering more than $1 billion each year in Vancouver for Chinese, Mexican and Iranian crime cartels. To my mind, Silver took on the shape of a financial weapon, a toxic creation that systematically eroded Canada's economic foundations and the rule of law, while fulfilling the needs of transnational narcos and Chinese Communist Party oligarchs in elegantly balanced, symbiotic transactions — effortlessly shifting narco-dollars worldwide by leveraging massive reserves of corruption money seeking underground channels out of Mainland China.

3
VANCOUVER MODEL 1.0

*So, when I looked into Tam, I saw that he had
been ordered deported in the late 1990s. And yet,
he remained in Canada, gambling at River Rock
Casino and running a Macau-style junket operation
for mainland Chinese whales.*

On December 5, 1988, Kwok Chung Tam was about six miles above
the Pacific Ocean on a flight from Thailand. It was a good place for
Tam to flush travel and identification documents down the toilet.

The plane descended through fog and rain above Vancouver International Airport, a typical early winter day in Richmond, about 8
degrees Celsius. Tam was 30, thin and handsome with a childish side-part hairstyle. And walking towards the Canadian border officials,
he must have felt some nervousness. But also a reasonable degree
of confidence. His wife and infant daughter had already flown from
Thailand to Vancouver in July, and his wife had claimed refugee status
using false documents.

Tam was not the type of person you would imagine when picturing a
refugee. He wasn't poor and powerless. He was so well-connected that
while staying in Bangkok, he had been photographed meeting with
the King of Thailand.

Before flying into Bangkok, Tam had sold his three factories in
Guangzhou, the largest city of Guangdong, the booming southern
province of China.

Guangzhou, also known by its nickname the Big Circle, was immense and full of contrasts. Incredible urban masses gave way to parks full of trees and flowers, and Chinese temples rose over European boulevards in the old section of the city.

The green and grey murk hovering over Guangzhou's new skyscrapers pointed to a terrifying expanse of industrialization. And the city straddled the Pearl River, a sludgy tributary marked by giant algae blooms and floating pig carcasses, flowing down between vast blocks of factories towards Macau and Hong Kong, and the South China Sea.

Before leaving Guangzhou, Tam told everyone who owed him money to deposit the debts with his parents.

And somehow, although Chinese citizens are barred from sending more than $50,000 per year abroad, Tam had transferred as much as $5 million to his wife in Canada. The funds materialized from the mysterious underground banking channels that flow from Guangzhou to Hong Kong to Macau and into Vancouver. Transactions are underwritten by hidden pools of wealth worldwide, the adjusting of credit and debt in secret ledger books maintained between family members. A transaction paid out in Vancouver secures a return transaction in Hong Kong at a later date.

When Tam walked through customs in Vancouver, he admitted to sending funds to his wife in a B.C. bank account through a "friend" in Hong Kong. And for border officials, tracking Tam's flights to Vancouver was just like trying to unwind his underground fund transfers. He had taken a trip on Korean Air after arriving in Thailand, and possibly a side flight to Hong Kong, border officials believed. But after boarding a Singapore Airlines flight from Bangkok to Vancouver, he "lost" his travel records.

It didn't matter, though. Tam knew that in Canada, you didn't need any supporting documents to declare yourself a refugee. And so he launched into his myth. He told Canadian officials he had printed over 1,000 pro-democracy T-shirts at one of his garment factories in Guangzhou. And so the Communists saw him as an enemy, he said. But Tam didn't seem to put much effort into the story. It's not like he was claiming to have run from the tanks in Tiananmen Square. He said his only real problem in China was paying high taxes. "I had to come to Canada because it's a good country," Tam told the officials sitting with him. "I think I'm a refugee because I have nowhere to go. And I have sold my businesses and given up my licences. But I had a good life in China. Only they charge me so much because I'm rich."

* * *

Kwok Chung Tam was an underworld entrepreneur, a heavyweight with the Big Circle Boys, the cartel of Mainland China criminals that since the 1980s has flourished internationally in conjunction with the exponential growth of China Inc.

Tam was identified as among the most significant Big Circle Boys who hit Canada in waves from about 1986 to 1990, one of the elite gangsters that Dr. Alex Chung of the University College of London, in his 2019 study Chinese criminal entrepreneurs in Canada, called "a decentralized network of career criminals comprised of illegal immigrants from Guangzhou, China."

Tam and his Big Circle associates exploited gaping weaknesses in Canada's border controls, citizenship and criminal justice systems, to establish a beachhead in Vancouver from which to dominate North American drug markets.

More than any crime syndicate in Canada, and the world, the Big Circle Boys have perfected casino infiltration and money-laundering, by importing Macau-style underground banking to Vancouver.

In the process the Big Circle Boys have become the factor most responsible for transforming large portions of British Columbia's casino and real estate industries into narco-economies. And from their power bases in Vancouver and Toronto, they have turned Canada into a springboard to access the most lucrative United States drug markets — New York, Boston, Seattle, Miami, Los Angeles, Las Vegas and San Francisco — where they have operatives and underground casinos.

In the 1990s the cartel had about two times as many members in Toronto compared to Vancouver, according to a report by the Federal

Research Division of the U.S. Library of Congress. But their impact in Vancouver, the smaller Canadian city, is proportionately much greater.

There is no dispute among criminologists about the cartel's profound influence in Vancouver's conversion into a hub for transnational crime. A 2015 report prepared by Canada's anti-money-laundering agency Fintrac says: "Vancouver is a critical money-laundering hub for: international drug money; dirty money from China (drugs, corruption, tax evasion.) Transnational criminal organizations and local drug money." The report says Vancouver is especially vulnerable to money-laundering because of its proximity to China and the U.S., its hot real estate market, and its busy marine port, which has been stripped of regulation by provincial and federal government funding cuts.

The 2003 U.S. Library of Congress report lays some of the blame for deregulation of ports on the federal Liberal government of Jean Chrétien, in the early 1990s, when Canada was targeting investment from Asia. "Organized crime groups reportedly exercise great control over Canadian ports and were cited as major conduits for drug smuggling, the export and import of stolen automobiles, and the theft of cargo," the report says, citing Canadian senate committee findings. "The committee additionally reported that the Chrétien government had been receiving warnings on the state of Canada's ports for six years, but continued to ignore the advice of law enforcement officials."

Of all the transnational narcos that operate in Canada — Sicilian and Calabrian mafias, Middle Eastern and European mobs, and the surging Mexican cartels — Chinese organized crime is the most significant criminal threat, according to Canadian and United States intelligence reports. And the Big Circle Boys are the super-predators. Senior bosses of the cartel from Guangzhou are now believed to be more wealthy and powerful than Pablo Escobar ever was.

So how did the Big Circle Boys rise so quickly in North America, and especially in Vancouver? To understand their dominance and criminalization of B.C. casinos, I found Tam's life story incredibly illuminating.

* * *

Tam first came onto my radar in 2017. Even though court records said Tam had been barred numerous times from B.C. Lottery Corp. casinos, I learned that Ross Alderson was forced to confront him in Richmond's River Rock Casino VIP room in 2011.

In Alderson's recollection, it was time to send a message to the gambling kingpins. Tam was at a table with a young woman playing baccarat, and Alderson served him ban papers. He escorted the couple down an escalator to the ground floor, where punters work the slot machines.

Tam didn't have anything to say, but his female friend did.

You're making a big mistake, she told Alderson.

So when I looked into Tam, I saw that he had been ordered deported in the late 1990s. And yet, he remained in Canada, gambling at River Rock Casino and running a Macau-style junket operation for mainland Chinese whales. Tam was living the high life, and from what I could see, was impervious to the many, many investigations against him.

I had to know why.

So I questioned immigration officials about Tam's case. They gave me nothing. In Canada, privacy laws are cited extremely broadly by the government.

So I shared Tam's case with Brian Hill, a Global News colleague who studies immigration cases.

He contacted a valuable source.

This government employee had already helped me to confirm an interesting fact. Several River Rock Casino VIPs investigated by Alderson for their connections to Paul King Jin and Kwok Chung Tam had obtained permanent residency through the largest immigration-investment fraud case in Canadian history.

In that case, a Richmond immigration broker named Xun Sunny Wang was convicted in 2015 for helping over 1,000 investors from China to cheat their way into Canada with fake passports, fake job offers, and fake Canadian home addresses.

The government source came back to us in 2019 with a federal court file. It was an incredible record of Tam's history in Canada, thousands of pages gathering dust in the volumes of immigration files warehoused in Ottawa. These were records that Tam disclosed in his lengthy court battles fighting deportation to China.

They included many unreported allegations, some of them shedding light on how the Vancouver Model took root.

I knew of estimations counting up to 1,000 Big Circle Boys operating in Canada in the 1990s. You only had to isolate a few pages in Tam's file to see that for Canadian investigators, he stood out like a killer whale in a bathtub.

By 1991, Vancouver police had pegged Tam as a major player. He and four other Chinese refugee claimants were arrested in a "massive strike" by officers. A report said Tam's cell was terrorizing wealthy Chinese-Canadian families with violent home invasions.

"There is no doubt that all five arrested are involved in organized crime in Vancouver," a Canadian immigration manager wrote.

Also, in the early 1990s, Vancouver gang squad officer Doug Spencer warned Canada Border Services Agency officers that "Tam could get almost any ID" he wanted, including documents in the names of other Chinese citizens.

A record from Spencer meant something in British Columbia policing. He was respected by his fellow officers — and hardened gangsters too. His colleagues told me that Spencer had more underworld sources than anyone else in Vancouver; he knew gang affiliations and hierarchies like the creases of his hands and could locate a target within thirty minutes, after making three or four phone calls. And many people agreed with Spencer about Tam's prominence and criminal resources.

Court records showed me that Canadian immigration officials chose to name only Tam in a massive international heroin-trafficking investigation that resulted in the arrest of 28 Big Circle Boys. The case included two other bosses described by police informants as "untouchable" in Mainland China and Hong Kong.

These were the Chinese businessmen who controlled worldwide drug shipping routes, financed heroin exports to Vancouver and moved the cash proceeds worldwide. And in the early days, Tam was considered a step below them.

But in 1999, when police seized 70 kilograms of heroin from a storage locker in Richmond not far from the River Rock Casino — it was Tam who most fascinated the Canada Border Services Agency (CBSA).

"The Asian Crime cartel was so powerful that police said it could stockpile heroin and dictate the street price of the drug in North America," a CBSA intelligence file said. "Its members had connections to underground banks in Hong Kong and the poppy fields of Burma. They did not hesitate to eliminate obstructions. One of them, a loan shark banned from B.C. casinos [Kwok Chung Tam] was also brazen enough to have his picture taken with the former [B.C.] premier, Glen Clark while seeking to open a casino."

This particular photo had legendary status in Vancouver's police force. And Doug Spencer was there during the raid of Tam's Burnaby home in 1998. Vancouver gang cop Murray Phillips had spotted the portrait sitting on Tam's living room mantle.

"Hey, Doug, come here," Phillips had called. "Remember I told you these guys are connected, up above?"

Spencer's jaw dropped. And then he had to stop himself from laughing. It was a giant portrait of Tam and Clark, basically arm-in-arm.

The context of the CBSA's report citing the photo of Tam and Clark was the RCMP's so-called Casinogate investigation. It was alleged that several Vancouver business people sought to influence Clark and his NDP government to approve a Burnaby casino licence application. Clark was forced to step down in 1999. But Clark has always denied wrongdoing in Casinogate, and he was acquitted of all charges in 2002.

Casinogate is seen as ancient history in B.C. gambling lore. But the allegation that Kwok Chung Tam was involved in the Burnaby casino licence application had never been revealed publicly. Tam was never named, never even hinted at among those accused of making approaches to Glen Clark and the NDP. So this was a new and relevant clue — one of those rewarding moments at work when I feel a bit like an archaeologist. Had the Big Circle Boys tried to own a B.C. casino? Had they tried more than once? Did existing B.C. casinos have any secret backers lurking behind supposedly legit owners? The Tam file raised a lot of questions for me. And the file also showed that Cheryl Shapka — a bulldog CBSA investigator in Vancouver — was fascinated with Tam's frequent proximity to political leaders.

"VPD found and seized a whole bunch of photographs taken of Tam, including one where he was shaking Clark's hand in his office, and one where Tam was shaking hands or standing with the King of Thailand," an email from Shapka to Vancouver police said. "I know a lot of other people saw the photos. Do you know what happened to them?"

In 2021 I asked Clark about his photo with Tam, and he said: "Zero relationship with this man. Zero discussion of casinos. Never actually heard of the man until recent news stories."

* * *

It is not just CBSA documents that attest to the power of Kwok Chung Tam and the Big Circle Boys.

According to U.S. government intelligence reports, police first detected the spread of the Guangzhou cartel in the late 1980s, "and by the early 1990s it had established criminal cells throughout Canada where it has come to dominate the heroin trade within the country." The United States-Canada Border Drug Threat Assessment of December 2001 estimated that 95 percent of all heroin entering Canada originates from the Golden Triangle region — where the borders of Thailand, Laos and Myanmar meet — which is controlled by the Big Circle Boys. And the cartel ships the opioids from southern China and Hong Kong into Vancouver, where they warehouse and distribute the supply across North America, controlling price swings and collecting cash in major cities. According to that 2003 report by the Federal Research Division of the U.S. Library of Congress, "worrisome" factors in Canada allowed the Big Circle Boys to infiltrate North America.

"Faced with the likely spread of Asian organized crime groups and given border porosity and immigration laws, for the foreseeable future, Canada will continue to serve as an ideal transit point for crime groups to gain a foothold in the United States," the report says. "Several factors continue to support these criminal and terrorist groups' use of Canada."

The report underlined the loophole exploited by Tam's family and all Big Circle Boys in the 1980s and 1990s.

Canada's refugee policy "has been very welcoming since the mid-80s," when the Canadian Supreme Court guaranteed a hearing for anyone entering the country claiming to be a refugee, even if that person could provide no documentation.

Prior to 2000, the report said, as many as 60 percent of all refugee claimants in Canada possessed insufficient documentation — or no documentation at all.

And this weakness meant the Big Circle Boys could scale up lucrative human-smuggling schemes because Canada relied only on paper identification for immigrants — "forged versions of which are available on the black market for roughly $1,000."

This policy also allowed the Big Circle Boys to traffic women from Asia and run "sex slave rings based in the United States that have apparent links to such activities in Toronto."

Most Canadians want their government to have humanitarian immigration policies.

But the flip side of a porous immigration vetting system is a society in which Asian women are forced into selling their bodies in underground casinos and bawdy houses in big North American cities. They are victims paying extortionate debts to Big Circle Boy loan sharks. And Toronto and Vancouver are the hubs of this human trafficking, used to supply gangs in the United States with sex slaves.

* * *

When Tam responded to questions from Global News regarding our 2019 report on his case file, he denied connections to the Big Circle Boys and, through his lawyer, cautioned us. And Tam wrote in an affidavit in July 2016, "I am not now nor have I ever been a member of a gang, Triad or criminal organization."

But thousands of pages of Canadian records say the opposite. And that warning from Doug Spencer — that Tam could get any ID — raises a question that often surfaces in major Chinese organized crime figures' files.

The kingpins from Gaungzhou would habitually claim they were enemies of the Chinese Communist Party — and they would suffer if they were returned to China. But many repeatedly travelled back and forth between Canada and China. And Tam's file reads like a book of Chinese state connections. Police found a business card for China's consul general in Tam's home. They also seized the business card of the vice-president of China Poly Technologies, a murky arms-trading and military-industrial company that is owned by Red Princelings of the People's Liberation Army.

And the B.C. NDP premier Glen Clark wasn't the only Canadian politician whom Tam approached. His RCMP file shows that in 1992, Tam signed up as member No. 650 for the Vancouver Society in Support of

Democratic Movement, a group run by Raymond Chan, a Richmond politician elected as a Liberal MP in 1993. Chan became Canada's minister of multiculturalism, a rainmaker fundraiser for the Liberal Party in the Chinese business community, and an associate of billionaire migrants from China, such as Vancouver real estate developer Muyang "Michael" Cheng. Cheng is the son of the former governor and Communist Party chief of China's Hebei province, Weigao Cheng.

Chan has not responded to my questions about his fundraising for the Liberals and Tam's membership in Chan's pro-democracy society. But while Tam was rubbing shoulders with Raymond Chan in the early 1990s, police were already asking fundamental questions about Tam's source of wealth — the types of questions that I would hammer on after 2010, when I started reporting on Vancouver's insane real estate prices.

"In Canada less than four years as a refugee claimant — owns [three homes in Vancouver and a Vancouver luxury auto-sales business] mortgage-free — even though he has not worked and declared no wealth," a Tam immigration memo in 1991 said. And RCMP files that year alleged Tam was involved in illegal gambling, heroin importation and dealing, alien smuggling, credit card fraud, and weapons trafficking. The questions about Tam's wealth never went away.

"The applicant is currently unemployed," another immigration official wrote in 2004. "The applicant has not provided me with an explanation of how he supported himself or his family during this period [1999 to 2004]."

Vancouver police also believed that Tam's wife was forging identity documents and passports in the family's Burnaby home during the 1990s. And yet Tam seemed utterly immune to criminal charges until 1998. Tam's violent loan-sharking operations in Vancouver and Richmond casinos finally led police to raid his Burnaby home. They found Walther PPK and Ruger semi-automatic pistols complete with silencers and ammunition, plus "a pound of raw heroin and caches used to stamp heroin for sale stating it was 100 percent pure," an email from Cheryl Shapka said. In the loan-sharking complaint that triggered the raid, a 60-year-old woman named Mrs.

Chow said she had borrowed $19,000 from Tam to gamble but lost her bets. She had signed her Mercedes-Benz over to Tam — but it still wasn't enough to satisfy him. So Tam's wife and a man named Huo Quin Zheng went to Mrs. Chow's Vancouver home. Tam's wife told her she owed the "boss" money. Mrs. Chow refused to open her door. So Huo Quin Zheng hired a locksmith. The gangsters forced their way in. And Huo Quin Zheng threatened to kill Mrs. Chow unless she signed over all of her furniture. Mrs. Chow signed the papers, and the Big Circle Boys sent a moving truck over. But Mrs. Chow decided to go to the police — a rarity in Vancouver loan-sharking cases.

There was some debate among Canadian immigration officials in the late 1990s about whether there was enough evidence to deport Tam's family. The Burnaby raid changed that conversation.

One day in 1998, Dave Quartermain of the CBSA summarized Tam's file to a colleague this way: "Tam is a heavyweight in the Big Circle Boys. He has multiple outstanding charges and is likely to be convicted. I can remove both husband and his wife, but I'm going to wait for his convictions."

But an official named Bob Benger seemed less convinced: "Judging by his occupation, the thought of transporting stolen autos to the PRC immediately came to mind. Thought he might be 'one of the gang.' So far, I don't see any redeeming features to this case. But I have to give them their opportunity."

Quartermain fired back with a flood of details that left nothing to the imagination. "Subject owns a car dealership. His cars supplied by extortion. He and his minions hand out [cash] at casinos and approach fellow Chinese who need $$$ for betting and give them loans at loan-shark rates. Then when they cannot pay — collects their cars, and in one case, the house. Was recently arrested for extortion — basically, they took a car and then brought a moving truck in and cleaned out the house of ALL furniture. He was also in possession of an improperly obtained PRC passport — confirmed obtained from the PRC consulate in Vancouver under a different name. In recent search warrant of house: a cache of weapons found; 7 ounces raw opium/heroin; $270,000 worth of cheques made out to Tam from alleged extortions; stolen jewellery and buckets of cash. In a search of storage locker warehouse, mountains of Oriental furniture.

"Convictions look good on this one," Quartermain concluded. "Wife also implicated. Want him convicted before removals take place." But Quartermain had misplaced confidence in Canada's legal system.

Tam's wife pleaded guilty to possession of property through extortion. And Tam faced the same loan-sharking charge, plus weapons charges. Some of the charges evaporated after Tam's wife pleaded guilty, a ruling says. And the remaining charges against Tam were dropped because the case was adjourned so many times. The delays were caused because Tam's wife claimed to be too ill to appear in court.

In a ruling that seems sympathetic to Tam, the judge found that "none of the adjournments can be laid at the feet of Mr. Tam."

The judge also seemed open to Tam's explanation for the "7 ounces raw opium/heroin" found in his home. "He arrived in Canada in 1988, seeking refugee status," the judge wrote in 2002. "He has a wife and children. He was introduced to the smoking of heroin not long after he arrived in this country and became addicted to it. In early 1998, he was ordered deported; for some reason, this order has not been executed."

So Tam wasn't convicted and deported in the loan-sharking case. Meanwhile, violence followed him like a curse.

Police records say Tam was shot outside his Vancouver home, the "result of extortion carried out by Mr. Tam on other Asian organized crime members."

But Tam refused to talk with police and shrugged off his bullet wound.

* * *

In the 1999 case that led to the arrest of 28 Big Circle Boys, Tam was charged with conspiracy to import and traffic heroin. He was acquitted of these charges in 2002 because a judge found wiretap evidence in the case was inadmissible.

But confidential informant records filed in the case explained a lot about the Big Circle Boys' international narco-smuggling methods. When I matched records like Dave Quartermain's emails on Tam with these informant records, it connected all the pieces of the Vancouver Model 1.0 puzzle.

There have been many technological advances in the model since 1999. But the cyclical flow of cash and contraband is the same. Opioids or chemical precursors come from corrupted Asian ports and into Richmond and Vancouver ports to be released across North America. And the criminal proceeds are shipped back to Richmond and warehoused, where the cash is diffused into Vancouver's economy and ultimately transferred back to China.

"One of the methods of heroin importation used by 'Big Circle Boys' was the use of human couriers using air transportation," the 1999 case informant files say. "It would cost [amount redacted by judge] to pay off people to help bring the heroin onto an aircraft in Thailand."

But the massive loads of narcotics were hidden in the bowels of ships from Guangzhou or Shenzhen, sometimes in shipping containers with false bottoms, and sometimes in packages disguised as containers of soy sauce and rice noodles.

And drug cash warehoused in Vancouver ultimately had to go back to Hong Kong and China, to fund more drug exports. "All heroin proceeds generally go back to southeast Asia, specifically China. As Canadian currency is not liked in China, it is generally transferred to Hong Kong and converted to Hong Kong currency," the informant files say. "From Hong Kong, the money is transferred to China." There were many methods to move cash back to China, some simple and some complex. "The heroin importers generally ship Canadian cash in suitcases to Hong Kong. They use human couriers to do this," the files say. "Another method for moving money from Canada to Hong Kong was through Canadian companies which also had connections to Hong Kong. Cash would be given to cooperating businesses in

Canada, and taken out in Hong Kong." The latter method, a form of trade-based money-laundering, expanded year by year, and allowed the Big Circle Boys' corruption to expand into broader portions of Canada's economy.

But the Vancouver Model couldn't function without the blessing of officials inside China.

"Not just anyone can put a heroin load together. To do so, one had to have the contacts in China with a set group of people," the 1999 case files said. And in the 1990s, two families in the Big Circle Boys had the best contacts. Both were seen as a step above Kwok Chung Tam's family at that time.

Kwok "Ah Chut" Chan, Kwok "Chester" Chan, and Kwok Hung Chan led one group. The eldest brother, Kwok Hung Chan, controlled the cell from Hong Kong, running its banking operations, moving drug cash worldwide, and brokering heroin shipments. Ah Chut and Chester operated in Toronto and Vancouver. In 1999 it was "Ah Chut" who had organized a 70-kilogram shipment of heroin that police found stashed in a mini-storage locker at 8520 Cambie Road in Richmond. "Ah Chut was well established in China among high ranking police and government officials," informants told police, and "he was untouchable in China." The other cell that controlled North American heroin markets was led by a man named See Chun Lee in Vancouver. Informants said he loved to bet big in Macau casinos, and it was his cell that smuggled "several boatloads of Chinese migrants that arrived off the coast of British Columbia late in the summer of 1999." See Chun Lee's cell was controlled by his uncle in Hong Kong — a man called Ng Yat — and informants said they were "involved in the monthly shipments destined for Vancouver, Toronto and New York that continually flooded the market."

The informants said Ng Yat "was an international crime figure who was very wealthy and had lots of property," and he was "untouchable by the law enforcement authorities."

Informants told police these cells laundered money out of restaurants in Vancouver and Toronto — establishments that were bought with

Hong Kong drug money — and cartel members were seen at all hours of the night travelling between these restaurants, government casinos, and underground betting houses.

But the B.C. government casinos had a special purpose. They were used to give drug deals the stamp of official business.

"These drug traffickers liked to conduct money exchanges in casinos," informants said. "The drug trafficker could then have the casino as an explanation for the money if stopped by the police."

So police gathered a massive cache of intel in the case against the 28 Big Circle Boys. But they struck out in Canadian courts. It's interesting to consider how the history of opioid trafficking may have changed in Canada if this major investigation could have knocked the Big Circle Boys off stride. For Tam and other cartel bosses, the Canadian court victories came at a pivotal time. Prices for heroin in North America and Australia crashed in 2000. It's not clear why. Maybe the cartel bosses wanted it that way. In any case, they were ready to shift into chemical narcotics, especially ecstasy and methamphetamines. They only had to transfer supply chains from the poppy fields of Burma to factories churning out chemical precursors in remote regions of the Golden Triangle or the industrial expanses of Guangdong.

And in British Columbia, mini drug labs proliferated in many homes near the U.S. border. The cartel shipped chemicals from China into Richmond and Vancouver, following the same routes as heroin, and then mixed and pressed the precursors into pills in basement labs before moving them in car and truckloads down the west coast to Seattle, San Francisco and Los Angeles, and east to Calgary and Winnipeg. And they sent pill shipments out of Vancouver to Australia and Japan. Once the Big Circle Boys had mastered the pill business they had the template in place for fentanyl distribution.

And in the mid-2000s, Kwok Chung Tam would set up a family drug lab in Richmond. Police raided it, leading to one of the few minor criminal charges that ever stuck to Tam. The case didn't lead to his deportation and didn't keep him out of River Rock Casino. But it created a paper trail in Tam's immigration file that led to a major break in my Vancouver Model investigation. I found that a law firm run by a federal Liberal MP was involved in condo development for Tam and family members charged in the drug lab bust. The Big Circle Boys were dominating the global drug trade because they had political connections in China and Hong Kong. But it looked like they had powerful friends in Canada too.

4
THE MISSION IN HONG KONG

*But at least one more enormous pan of the scope is
needed to track the full circle in relations between
the Triads and China's rulers, and the present
consequences for the West.*

In the early 1990s, Garry Clement made friends with a Macau police officer who introduced him to the less travelled regions of Stanley Ho's casinos. It was something like a set of Russian nesting dolls. The cavernous gambling rooms packed with tourists were merely facades enveloping multiple layers of darker business tucked deeper inside the glittering buildings.

When Clement walked down the quiet hallways and passed the restricted gambling partitions rented out to the Sun Yee On Triad, he could almost feel the eyes of the men posted by the doorways stabbing at him. Clement was the RCMP liaison officer in Canada's Hong Kong Commission. He'd been in Hong Kong long enough to know Sun Yee On was a ruthlessly efficient organization. If the order came down, some thug with a meat cleaver would ritualistically administer a thousand slashes to the person who pissed off the Triad dragon-head.

It was in the private VIP baccarat rooms — just one or two little betting tables but decorated in palatial style — where Sociedade de Turismo e Diversões de Macau, a corporation of Hong Kong tycoons that held a monopoly on Macau casinos, raked in about two-thirds of its casino revenue.

Clement knew that the tycoons, including Stanley Ho and Cheng Yu Tung, dealt with the Triads so that junket-operators laundering funds for Chinese narcos could lend cash to the Asian whales who bet ridiculous sums in the Macau casinos, some of them losing tens of millions in single nights of debauchery.

And the decadence didn't end there. Clement's Macau police source also walked him past the fishbowls — glass-walled rooms where scantily dressed girls were displayed like delicacies on a tray, waiting patiently to be selected and led into private rooms in the underground regions of the casino.

Clement knew that the Triads, tycoons, People's Liberation Army princelings and corrupt Communist Party officials had longstanding and mutually beneficial arrangements in Macau, and that Stanley Ho brokered incredible power among them. Ho was tall and dapper, of Eurasian ancestry, with a taste for ballroom dancing, champion racehorses and beautiful young women. He was very tight with the leaders of North Korea, Iran and China, involved in state-level trade with these authoritarian regimes, and he looked like a statesman himself, chauffeured in Macau, Hong Kong and Shenzhen in his majestic blue Rolls-Royce.

But this was Macau in the 1990s. How does it relate to my investigations into the perfected machine of money-laundering that Silver International and the Big Circle Boys constructed in British Columbia, finally exploding into public view in the fall of 2017, with my reports in the *Vancouver Sun*? Because the misery of the opioid death crisis that is wracking North America, stems from the geography and players that Clement encountered in Macau and Hong Kong in the early 1990s.

He and a handful of ex-Canadian officials know the golden path for men like Paul King Jin was paved through Canada's Hong Kong embassy. At the time, Clement understood that many of Hong Kong's richest men, the multi-billionaire tycoons who were buying incredible amounts of real estate in Vancouver and Toronto, were tied to the Triads. It was rumoured among Clement's Hong Kong police sources that some of the tycoons themselves were dragon-heads.

With the Hong Kong tycoons, it was almost always a rags-to-riches story, Clement told me: a journey from Guangdong to Hong Kong as a young man, a job in a factory, an incredibly shrewd ability to trade in some or other commodities — steel, rubber, gold, arms, heroin — and all of a sudden a fortune magically appearing in real estate, hotels, casinos, banks and transportation.

When Clement discussed the tycoons with British ex-pats from the Hong Kong police, the euphemism was: "Well, it's fair to say that he didn't make his fortune in the traditional way."

But there was an irony in that comment for the British ex-pats. Really, what was the traditional way? In the 1830s, it was the Scottish gentleman traders Jardine and Matheson, who made their careers exporting tea from China but made their *fortunes* importing opium to Guangzhou through Chinese merchants and smugglers, and bribing Chinese officials to turn a blind eye.

Eventually, the Chinese could not ignore the growing ranks of listless opium addicts in Guangzhou, Hong Kong and Macau. They moved to seize and destroy whole shipments of opium from the Scottish gentlemen, dumping their "black dirt" into the Hong Kong bay, and causing Jardine and Matheson to lobby for an armed response from Britain.

The result was the First Opium War and Hong Kong's surrender and colonization, a scar on the national psyche that Communist Party propaganda still refers to as China's 100 years of humiliation to the West. So for my visual way of thinking, to get at the root of Vancouver's money-laundering and fentanyl overdose crises — to understand the Vancouver Model of transnational crime — was something like Clement's gradual journey of discovery inside Stanley Ho's casinos.

You can zoom in on certain times and people and then pull back to a wider frame and let the kaleidoscopic images clear and settle. And when the picture finally clears, you dig deeper and end up finding more answers. You finally recognize that a massive dose of history and politics as big as Mainland China itself, pressurized like a syringe through the needlepoint of Hong Kong, is bursting back at the West now. Or as an RCMP source once told me: "It's like the Opium Wars, but in reverse."

Pick a year and a place. Was the Vancouver Model of money-laundering birthed in 1988, when cartel heavyweights like Kwok Chung Tam first landed in Vancouver and Tam's fellow Big Circle Boy, Chi Lop Tse, arrived in Toronto? Both men arrived as refugees and were quickly recognized by Canadian police as mid-level drug traffickers. But look where they are now. Especially Chi Lop Tse.

According to a 2019 Reuters investigation, Chi Lop Tse is now seen by police worldwide as the Pablo Escobar of methamphetamine in the Golden Triangle, a man who allegedly heads a merged syndicate of Chinese Triads "conservatively" estimated to clear $8 billion per year in meth sales. Another mind-blowing figure? Reuters reported that Chi Lop Tse is so enormously rich that he could shrug off a loss of $66 million in one night in a Macau casino.

But if you focus on 1988, you have to zoom further back, all the way to China's bloody Cultural Revolution and the year 1967, when overly aggressive members of Chairman Mao's paratrooper Red Guards were purged and detained in Guangzhou.

It was in these internment camps that the Red paratroopers formed a new Triad-like society, the Big Circle Gang, and the prisoners eventually escaped to Hong Kong, where they made a violent impression on the original Triads that had already fled to Hong Kong and Macau in the 1950s and 1960s, after losing bloody battles with Mao and the Communists.

But at least one more enormous pan of the scope is needed to track the full circle in relations between the Triads and China's rulers, and the present consequences for the West.

In Canadian federal court records regarding Triad infiltration of Canada's immigration system, the Hong Kong police force's leading Triad expert, Stanley Ip, is cited explaining the ancient roots of these secret societies.

According to Ip, governments in China have, to various degrees, confronted the Triads since 1674 — when leaders from China's Han ethnic groups formed sects to buck the authority of the Manchurian Qing dynasty. The Triads functioned like shadow governments, evolving into powerful criminal societies controlling underground channels of finance and trade, and enforcing contracts through *guanxi* (relationships) and violence.

In the 1900s, secretive relations between national leaders and criminal leaders continued, Ip says, until Mao and the Communists firmly gained the upper hand and vanquished the Triads.

But in the early 1980s, as negotiations progressed between the United Kingdom and China for the handover of Hong Kong, the pragmatic paramount leader Deng Xiaopeng had a new arrangement in mind.

* * *

Garry Clement had always wanted to wear the Mountie's iconic Red Serge, so much that some of his earliest memories involved pinning Royal Canadian Mounted Police postcards to his bedroom wall.

His first RCMP posting was to Langley, a detachment in the Fraser Valley to the east of Vancouver. He quickly caught a promotion to the undercover drug unit, a post that would take most officers years longer. Clement was one of the best at cultivating informants and developing criminal intelligence. He mastered the art of creating a persona and casually inserting himself into big drug deals.

It was the 1970s, before Canada's Charter of Rights came in, and you could gather evidence aggressively to take out big players. In organized crime investigations, you had to be fearless and willing to walk up to the line, and Clement became 100 percent efficient at doing that, coming into dark rooms with a suitcase of cash, looking at the guys across the table and knowing they were packing guns, making the deal and walking out calmly with their drugs.

Early in his career, he learned that anyone could be turned, especially with big narco dollars. His undercover drug unit partner Patrick Kelly was very corrupt, so bad that he was jailed for life in 1984 after throwing his wife off the balcony of a 17th-floor apartment in Toronto.

Another thing that Clement quickly learned that good drug cops did the meaningful work, balancing risk and reward, putting their lives on the line. They spent all their time putting killers in jail. Meanwhile, it was the hot shots in Vancouver commercial crime units who got RCMP promotions. Clement was convinced they spent more of their time getting business degrees than pushing cases through. And no joke, the white-collar crime team in Vancouver headquarters actually had "suit of the week" contests.

In Clement's mind, these guys looked golden because they wouldn't take risks. They stayed away from controversy and politically sensitive files. They were more like politicians and academics than cops. And year after year, they moved up in the national force.

It was no wonder, he thought, that the RCMP was turning into a politicized bureaucracy.

Before arriving in Hong Kong, Clement was asked to do a study. The RCMP wanted to know why Canada's Commission in Hong Kong was so uncooperative.

Clement found that officers in Toronto and Vancouver said they wouldn't even bother sending information requests to the Commission. They knew that staff wouldn't follow up on it. The result: the Hong Kong RCMP liaison office was seen as nothing more than a glorified post office. And this was the posting with jurisdiction over all of Hong Kong, Macau and Southeast Asia.

Think about that. Canada's enforcement presence in the area of the world with the most numerous, powerful and sophisticated transnational drug cartels was zero.

So when Clement arrived in the Canadian Commission in 1991, he decided to shake things up. Sumptuous dinners with Hong Kong's white-shirt officers and the diplomat set were out. Instead, Clement spent his nights ingratiating himself with the inspectors who ran vice ops for the Royal Hong Kong Police. He started to work with the Triad Bureau and the economic crime and anti-corruption units.

After a while, he felt like he was a member of the Hong Kong force. The officers he gained trust with told him they had spent little time with the RCMP previously, but his interest in their files was a welcome change. And meanwhile, Clement was learning the secretive power relationships of Hong Kong's government.

He realized that to penetrate this insulated and ancient culture, he needed a friend and mentor. He found one in an elderly Hong Kong gentleman, the son of one of the original dragons, who started to teach Clement about the enormously wealthy men who ran Hong Kong, Macau and China.

At the same time, a veteran Canadian foreign affairs officer named Brian McAdam was looking for a colleague he could trust. McAdam was posted to the Hong Kong Commission in 1989. And as the immigration control officer in a glorified post office, he had quickly become frustrated and isolated. He was a detail-oriented man, a voracious reader and compiler of intelligence, and also a student of Chinese history.

Soon after Clement arrived in Hong Kong, he sat down for a long talk with McAdam in his office.

Month by month, McAdam increasingly felt something was wrong in the Commission. He wrote many intelligence briefs, he told Clement, but his files seemed completely unwelcome to his superiors in Hong Kong and Ottawa. It seemed there was an immigration fraud-ring, and Ottawa was turning a blind eye.

McAdam couldn't understand it because this was after Canada's immigration department had been put on notice in 1975 with the scandal of Lui Lok, an elite Hong Kong police commander and secretly a Triad member.

Lui had made up to $500 million taking bribes from heroin traffickers, but as Hong Kong corruption investigators closed in, he and his family obtained Canadian visas and fled to Vancouver.

The case was so alarming that all Canadian officials handling immigration from Hong Kong and China were put on alert.

"As a result of this incident, the Department issued to all Canadian immigration offices outside of Canada instructions and procedures on the handling of the applications submitted by residents of Hong Kong because of the Triad threat," an affidavit filed in Canadian federal court says.

And Lui Lok's case had become widely known in Canada. In 1977 *Maclean's* published an exposé on Lui and his conspirators — the so-called Five Dragons — titled "Whoever Said 'Crime Does Not Pay' Never Hung Out with a Hong Kong Cop."

The story opened with an anecdote about the symbolic greeting that seasoned Royal Hong Kong Police Force officers shared with young officers arriving from Britain: "You can jump on the bus, you can run alongside it, or you can stand in the road and try to stop it."

The bus represented bribes flowing throughout Hong Kong's vice districts. The story explained how Lui and four elite officers had escaped a special corruption probe and somehow were allowed to immigrate to Canada after contributing to the opioid crisis ravaging Hong Kong, where "100,000 addicts spent vast sums each day to support their habit."

And according to the story, Canadians were outraged by "suggestions that some former Hong Kong policemen who emigrated to Vancouver and Toronto had been able to finance the heroin trade with their kickback money."

But now, ten years after the Five Dragons scandal, McAdam told Clement he was stunned to find elite Triad officers appeared to be very friendly with elite staff in Canada's Commission. They talked about Hong Kong's immigration chief, Lawrence Leung. There was strong intelligence that suggested Leung was a member of a Triad, and also connected to China's military and espionage networks.

And McAdam told Clement about the Hong Kong steel tycoon seeking a Canadian passport. He also was in a Triad. And the billionaire would visit the Canadian Commission and give the staff "red envelopes" with cash to gamble in his private box at the Hong Kong Jockey

Club. McAdam said numerous other tycoons visited the Commission while seeking visas for themselves and their families and also lobbying for their associates and their investments. They would take the Canadians out for decadent yacht cruises in Hong Kong bay.

Clement told McAdam what he was saying made a lot of sense. Already Clement had ruffled feathers in the Commission for turning down red envelopes. And this caused a loss of face for some tycoons, an egregious insult in Chinese culture. Clement told McAdam about one quiet standoff in the Commission. When Clement was introduced by a Canadian official to Cheng Yu Tung, the Macau casino tycoon, Cheng had icily refused to shake Clement's hand and walked away. Clement told McAdam he took it as a badge of honour.

They agreed it was impossible for Canadian officials to rub shoulders with the tycoons and not have these powerful men come back to collect. The cash gifts were not free. So McAdam and Clement agreed to file unequivocal warnings to Ottawa before another Five Dragons scandal rocked the Commission.

5

TRIADS ENTERING CANADA

Dawson told me all of these questions swirling
around Gordon Fu and Chrétien occurred while
Fu and his brother were under investigation for
allegedly offering $50,000 cash apiece to two senior
Canadian immigration officials.

By the end of 1991, Brian McAdam had seen enough. A woman from Hong Kong who wanted to immigrate to B.C. had called McAdam making serious allegations. She said two women in the Commission had offered to move her to the front of the line for Canadian visas if she paid them each $10,000 cash.

So McAdam put the two Hong Kong staffers under surveillance. The probe netted an accomplice. The two women and the wife of a Canadian official were tracked to a Hong Kong bank and observed depositing large amounts of cash.

McAdam's internal investigation also found that fake Canadian visa stamps were hidden in the desk of a fourth employee in the Commission. And there were troubling signs that someone in the mission was working to fast-track Canadian visas for a giant immigration-investment consulting firm in Taiwan run by a man named Gordon Fu.

As the suspicions mounted, McAdam and Clement finally discovered direct evidence of a stunning national security breach. Somehow, the Hong Kong Triads had hacked into the Canadian Commission's computer network. The network incursion would let gangsters see sensitive Canadian intelligence records and enable them to delete red flags in Immigration Canada's organized crime watchlists. This would allow Triad thugs to migrate into Canada undetected.

So McAdam and Clement filed a report requesting a criminal investigation to RCMP headquarters in Ottawa.

McAdam believed there was concrete evidence to prove serious neglignce at least and likely serious corruption in Canada's Hong Kong mission. But there was something strange in Hong Kong that was possibly worse than the network hack. McAdam told Clement he suspected inappropriate connections between some Hong Kong tycoons and some elite Canadian bureaucrats and politicians.

Clement and McAdam boiled down what they'd learned and agreed on the core intelligence. A group of Hong Kong applicants for Canadian immigrant visas were among the world's most ruthless criminals. It was the duty of Commission officials to stop these Triad bosses from importing violence and corruption to Canada.

But the problem was that gang bosses often didn't have criminal records. They were insulated by thousands of subordinates and decades of money-laundering.

So McAdam and Clement came up with a solution. They decided to write Triad intelligence manuals to help Canadian officials profile and identify Triad associates seeking to immigrate to Canada and invest massive sums in Vancouver and Toronto real estate.

One of Clement's first intelligence cables to Ottawa put it like this: "Cheng Yu Tung, through Sociedade de Turismo e Diversões de Macau, is in direct partnership with Stanley HO, YIP Hon and FOK Ying Tung. Within the enforcement community, there are many allegations relative to Stanley HO and his partners in connection to Sociedade de Turismo e Diversões de Macau. Most of these allegations pertain to the control exercised by this group over the gambling industry in Macau. And more to the point their frequent association with well-documented Triad office bearers."

Clement warned his RCMP bosses that some of his sources suspected Cheng Yu Tung's development company was "one of the legitimate corporations used for co-mingling of illegal assets." And Hong Kong police intel had confirmed that Cheng's real estate conglomerate hosted meetings for some of the world's biggest gangsters.

"New World is frequently the venue for meetings involving well-known Triad figures. One such meeting was the United World Chinese Association, headed by CHING Men Ky, which was attended by many well-documented Triad personalities from around the world. In addition, New World is the venue of choice for Stanley HO."

Clement would send almost two books' worth of similar intelligence reports to Ottawa. And McAdam wrote even more. But the reports were buried by Canada's government until an unorthodox investigative reporter from Southeast Asia travelled to Ottawa and came across Brian McAdam's explosive dossier.

* * *

When I arrived in the *Vancouver Province* newsroom in 2009, Fabian Dawson was something of a legend. He had migrated to Canada from Malaysia in the 1980s and scrapped his way into the business with shoe-leather reporting skills that were rapidly becoming a thing of the past in modern newsrooms.

And he succeeded — as he would tell me over lagers at the Lions Pub near the *Province*'s downtown office — at a time when few Asian reporters were hired in Canada. To call Dawson old-school would be an understatement.

He hated to sit at his desk and look at the computer. He was more like an intelligence officer, and he got his scoops by spending late nights talking to cops and underworld sources in gritty Vancouver bars.

He was known to disappear from the *Province* newsroom for weeks, chasing down leads in exotic countries. He scored terrific stories with his uncanny capacity to get businessmen with ambiguous backgrounds chatting freely with him.

The classic example was Dawson's 2009 interview of David Kwok Ho, the billionaire scion of a Hong Kong tobacco dynasty. Ho moved to Vancouver in the 1980s and immediately bought a golf course, a shipping company, a Rolls-Royce dealership, and copious amounts of real estate. He also forged connections with B.C. governments by making big donations and even landed a spot on Vancouver's Police Board. That was before his crack-smoking and abuse of drug-addicted prostitutes was exposed in 2008. Ho was charged for unlawfully confining a woman at his Vancouver mansion and possessing an unregistered Glock semi-automatic pistol. But he told Dawson that his crack-fueled sex parties with impoverished prostitutes occurred because of his humanitarian trips to the heroin-scarred Downtown Eastside.

"I'm addicted to helping them," Ho was quoted as saying in Dawson's 2009 *Vancouver Province* scoop. "It's worse when it rains ... that's when I get into the car and go looking for them." As a rookie reporter at the *Province*, if I was running into roadblocks on a story, editors would tell me to go see Fabian.

Usually, the issue would be finding good sources. That's a big challenge for young reporters. I remember that I would explain my cases to Fabian while he leaned back with arms crossed, blank-faced, giving the impression he'd much rather be somewhere else. He would periodically mutter a question and offer a few comments. And then he would break into a grin and abruptly rattle off about ten names and phone numbers.

In Vancouver in the 1990s — because of Dawson's international sources and understanding of politics and business in Asia — he was first to grasp the scale of real estate money-laundering in Canada.

Dawson took the Five Dragons scandal to the next level when he obtained a covert study from B.C. Co-ordinated Law Enforcement Unit's (CLEU) Asian Organized Crime division. He reported that one of the Five Dragons, Hon Kwing-shum, had bought at least 11 residential and commercial properties in Vancouver's wealthiest neighbourhoods. The study showed that up to 44 dirty Hong Kong cops had followed the Five Dragons to Canada, using their children and concubines to make major real estate investments in Vancouver and Toronto.

CLEU believed these heroin-trafficking cops bought blocks worth of prime property in Vancouver. "It is not exactly understood how much influence or power these former police officials possess regarding Chinese criminal activities in North America," Dawson quoted, from the CLEU study. "But, because of past ties, former influence, possible triad connections and money illegally obtained, they definitely could influence Chinese criminal patterns as we know them today."

As Dawson continued to probe Asian organized crime, he travelled east to Ottawa to meet with contacts from the Criminal Intelligence Service of Canada. Everyone told Dawson about McAdam and his dossier. They said McAdam's career had ended when he was recalled from Hong Kong to Ottawa in 1993. Some in the Criminal Intelligence Service told Dawson they thought McAdam had pointed to powerful figures in Canada without adequate evidence. But others believed McAdam's dossier contained solid reports that made him a target for people with lots to lose.

Dawson decided to look McAdam up, and they agreed to meet in Dawson's hotel near Parliament Hill. As McAdam told his story, Dawson flipped through the Hong Kong dossier. The writing was packed with details and sourcing. Right away, Dawson understood it was probably too much for the average Ottawa bureaucrat to digest, let alone believe. But for an investigative reporter who understood corruption in Southeast Asia, the material was plausible. Here were the names of the Hong Kong juggernauts that had purchased about 20 percent of Vancouver's prime real estate during the 1980s in blockbuster transactions, including the Expo '86 land deal.

Dawson recognized a handful of bombshell stories in the dossier. He saw the names of top Canadian consular officials and staff, Hong Kong legislative assembly leaders, Canadian politicians, and alleged Chinese spies. He saw a shady Taiwanese immigration-consulting business funneling incredible amounts of money into Quebec's immigration program, and directly into the riding of Prime Minister Jean Chrétien.

And McAdam's dossier crossed over with names that Dawson recognized from his own files. So he flew back to Vancouver with the dossier and started to track down the Canadian diplomats and RCMP officers cited as sources in McAdam's work.

And in 1999, he began to break major stories that suggested a cover -up in Ottawa.

* * *

Dawson reported that RCMP Cpl. Robert Read had been tasked with investigating McAdam's allegations that staff in the Canadian embassy had received bribes. Some of the allegations related to 30 Canadian officials who had accepted gambling cash from tycoons McAdam believed were Triad figures. Dawson reported the RCMP was preparing criminal charges, but in 1999 RCMP brass abruptly decided to abandon the bribery probe.

Read had been so disappointed with the decision that he leaked several records to Dawson.

Dawson reported that names of the Canadian officials who had faced criminal charges in the abandoned probe "have been ordered to be kept secret, [but these people] have since gone on to become senior government officials after only minor reprimands."

But after Dawson broke Read's whistleblower stories, the RCMP fired Read. And this led to an RCMP tribunal hearing in Ottawa.

Dawson covered the hearing and learned a second RCMP officer assigned to review Read's immigration fraud probe in Hong Kong was "shocked beyond belief" that Immigration Canada had tried to bury Read's investigation.

An RCMP memo revealed that an RCMP liaison officer in Hong Kong had warned his superiors that Canada's ambassador would "be screaming at the highest political levels" if the RCMP continued investigating McAdam and Read's bribery allegations.

Dawson reported the Royal Canadian Mounted Police External Review Committee found that the RCMP had dropped Read's politically sensitive probe because it didn't want to anger the Canadian Department of Foreign Affairs.

"What is at issue was a deliberate choice made by the RCMP not to pursue an investigation into possible criminal wrongdoing," the review found, "even though numerous examples had been drawn to the RCMP's attention of incidents that suggested that an immigration fraud ring was operating within the [Commission] and possibly involved employees of the government of Canada."

* * *

Looking back almost 20 years after he dissected the McAdam and Read files, Fabian Dawson told me he could draw several key inferences.

First, the names disclosed in McAdam's files included some of the most powerful men in China, Hong Kong, and Canada.

Dawson told me he firmly believes too much money and power was involved in McAdam's files and Robert Read's criminal probe. That's why the RCMP couldn't follow the Hong Kong probe to its logical conclusions.

So Dawson did what the media is supposed to do in such circumstances.

He published key documents and names from the reports filed to Ottawa in the early 1990s by McAdam and Clement.

It was these intelligence reports that would ultimately trigger a secret RCMP and CSIS study — code-named Sidewinder — that alleged Triads and tycoons and Chinese intelligence operatives had corrupted Canada's institutions and markets.

I obtained a copy of one of these reports, called "Triads Entering Canada."

It was a powerful national security warning that should have put Ottawa on notice.

"We have identified a sample of 16 crime figures that are among the world's most ruthless, vicious criminals who have sought or are seeking admission to Canada," the report said, "in order to highlight the threat that Triad societies, whose members form close-knit criminal organizations, many times larger and more powerful than the Mafia, pose to the security of Canadian society."

In Dawson's media reports for the *Province* and *Asian Pacific Post*, McAdam's files to Ottawa were broadly called "the Hong Kong probe."

Dawson reported the probe focused on Hong Kong's wealthiest tycoons, Li Ka Shing, Stanley Ho, and Cheng Yu Tung. In one probe document cited by Dawson, Hong Kong police investigators had requested assistance from Canada to investigate Li Ka Shing's growing acquisitions of Canadian real estate and corporate assets. But the Commission had refused to cooperate.

Dawson also reported on a memo filed by Garry Clement that warned Stanley Ho and Cheng Yu Tung were frequent guests at the Canadian Commission.

"In Hong Kong, it is a way of life for the legitimate Hong Kong society and the Triads to ingratiate themselves with charitable organizations, foreign missions and government officials," the memo said. "[Stanley Ho and Cheng Yu Tung] are known to be associated to many documented triads ... and they have been major Canadian investors."

And Dawson's reports identified Hong Kong probe targets Albert Yeung and movie mogul Charles Heung. Both have been named in U.S. and Canadian government records as alleged leaders of the Sun Yee On, one of the world's largest heroin-trafficking syndicates.

The Hong Kong probe documents also detailed several instances of Triad figures approaching Canadian leaders. In the 1990s, B.C. NDP premier Mike Harcourt "was hosted by a known Triad associate, Henry Fok, whose son was arrested in the United States for arms smuggling," Dawson reported.

Another example was when Vancouver mayor Gordon Campbell, who later became B.C. Liberal premier, met with the son of a Hong Kong politician who was identified as a senior Sun Yee On gangster.

And in another case, probe documents alleged that Ottawa had refused to assist Hong Kong police in the fraud investigation of Imperial Consultants, a Taiwanese firm owned by tycoon Gordon Fu. Fu was a significant player in Quebec's immigration investment programs. And Fu was connected in Canadian media reports to a proposal for investment in a money-losing hotel in the Quebec riding of Shawinigan. This was Prime Minister Chrétien's riding. And Chrétien had a business interest in the hotel.

"Gordon Fu's entree to the Prime Minister's Office came through Montreal-based Lévesque Beaubien Geoffrion, one of the largest Quebec-based investment firms dealing with business immigration," *Maclean's* reported, in a piece called "Citizenship on Sale." "Fu took the highly unusual step of personally handing Chrétien a letter asking that the Prime Minister speed up his application for permanent residency in Canada."

Chrétien's political opponents continued to ask questions about his efforts in 1996 and 1997 to secure Canadian government business loans for the Quebec hotel. This was around the time when he and Gordon Fu discussed investing in the Shawinigan hotel. But in 2001, Chrétien defended himself in Parliamentary debates, saying, "I never had any conflict of interest."

Dawson told me all of these questions swirling around Gordon Fu and Chrétien occurred while Fu and his brother were under investigation for allegedly offering $50,000 cash apiece to two senior Canadian immigration officials who were looking into Gordon Fu's immigration-investment fund in Quebec. But the RCMP dropped the bribery allegations against the Fu brothers.

Dawson told me he believes the Fu case was too politically sensitive to proceed. But in hindsight, questions raised by McAdam's Hong Kong probe turned out to be accurate. The stench of fraud surrounding immigration-investment programs caused Canada's program to be cancelled in 2014 and Quebec's program to be suspended in 2020.

But there is one unresolved case in McAdam's dossier that I think highlights the extreme dangers to Canada's national security.

It is the case of Lawrence Leung, the former immigration chief in Hong Kong.

In the early 1990s, the RCMP looked into allegations that Leung was an agent of the People's Republic of China. He was suspected of using his status with the Canadian Commission to facilitate immigration into Canada for Chinese spies and tycoons with Triad connections.

McAdam's dossier says that two Immigration Canada officers were sent to Hong Kong to determine whether Leung was an agent of China's intelligence services. The Canadians tracked Leung to a lunch meeting with a Triad boss.

At the time, Britain was also probing allegations that Leung was working with Beijing to share sensitive information about Hong Kong citizens seeking to migrate to the United Kingdom. Leung abruptly resigned from his job in July 1996 under a cloud of suspicion.

But his family had already migrated to Vancouver, with deadly consequences. In 1993 Leung's 22-year-old daughter Silvia, an aspiring entertainer, was murdered with an arrow fired from a crossbow. She was walking from a class at the B.C. Institute of Technology in Burnaby. She approached her parked car but struggled with the door while the shooter took aim. Police found the door handle had been glued shut. And before the murder, her family in Vancouver had been targeted in a number of fire-bombing attacks. It all had the marks of Triad warnings.

McAdam's dossier had linked Lawrence Leung to several elite Triad figures and a tycoon involved in Chinese-state corporations that were cited for shipping weapons to Iran. So Ottawa immigration officials had all this information. But somehow, Leung was allowed to immigrate to Canada in a process that "circumvented normal immigration rules," the *Independent* reported in July 1997. Why would a suspected Chinese agent be allowed to immigrate to Canada? Some-one in Ottawa must be able to answer that question. But Canadian immigration officials have stonewalled my legal applications seeking records from Leung's file.

* * *

Brian McAdam and Robert Read were not the only Canadians who believed Ottawa was covering up corruption in Hong Kong.

Project Sidewinder, the confidential RCMP-CSIS investigation trig-gered by McAdam's reporting from Hong Kong, was completed in 1997.

Sidewinder concluded that Canada faced a growing national security threat of economic infiltration driven by a network of allies from the Chinese Communist Party, Triads and Hong Kong tycoons — all work-ing together with Chinese intelligence services.

And there was a shocking thesis: ahead of the conversion of Hong Kong from British rule, the CCP had forged a truce with the Triads in order to secure Hong Kong's stability.

On May 23, 1982, Xiaoping Deng met with Li Ka Shing and Henry Fok in Beijing, Sidewinder says. They bartered on the future of Hong Kong and China. Hong Kong would soon be under CCP control. And Deng asked for cooperation and business advice from the Hong Kong tycoons. He wanted to smoothly adjust China's economy to capital-ism. In return, Beijing would give the tycoons privileged access to China's markets.

Two years later, Deng publicly stated that "not all Triads are bad, and many of the secret societies are patriotic."

Garry Clement told me he firmly believes that Li Ka Shing and Henry Fok were influential in Deng's statement.

But the dark alliance didn't just flow organically from Deng's pub-lic support for Triads. Sidewinder says that throughout the 1980s, Western intelligence agencies recognized increasing activity in

Hong Kong from one of China's foreign intelligence arms, the United Front Work Department. United Front agents were responsible for fostering business ties between the CCP and Triads. Bonds were forged with United Front shell companies that enabled Triad leaders to run businesses in Mainland China with elite military and revolutionary families.

"As early as 1992, Western intelligence services knew that Wong Man Fong, formerly Head of the New China News Agency, was instructed to inform the Triad bosses that if they agreed not to jeopardize the transition process and the normal business in Hong Kong, Beijing would assure them that they will be allowed to pursue their illegal activities without interference," Sidewinder said.

The Sun Yee On did especially well, according to Triad intelligence reports that I dug up in Canadian federal court files. They set up a nightclub in Beijing with Deng's Public Security Bureau chief Tao Siju, and also ran a number of similar clubs in Shanghai in partnership with People's Liberation Army officers.

The allegations are shocking. But several media and academic reports have corroborated the secret deals between Beijing and Triad bosses.

Notably, in his July 1997 piece "Partners in Crime," U.S. author Fredric Dannen cited his interview with alleged Sun Yee On boss Albert Yeung, one of the key figures cited in McAdam's 1990s dossier. According to Dannen, Albert Yeung and Chinese officials partnered in many Mainland China businesses after the Tiananmen Square massacre of June 4, 1989.

"China is in very bad shape. Nobody wanted to be their friend. But we go there, one of the big tycoon from Hong Kong, and start to make friends with the top people, and invest money there," Albert Yeung was quoted in the piece. "And they appreciate this."

And in his 2010 study "Beyond Social Capital," Hong Kong criminologist T. Wing Lo reiterated Sidewinder's findings on business ties between the Chinese Communist Party and Hong Kong Triads.

Lo's most fascinating case study focused on the 1993 grand opening of an entertainment business in Hong Kong. The company was run by film producers Charles and Jimmy Heung, alleged to be elite Sun Yee On officers. And the guest of honour was the governor of Guangdong, Ye Xuanping. Lo's study included a photo of Ye standing with the Heung brothers. And he argued that in China's system, this photograph essentially gave Sun Yee On licence to do business in Mainland China.

To understand Lo's argument, you have to understand Ye's place in China's power structure. The Ye's are one of the most powerful Red Army Princeling clans, controlling vast military and industrial conglomerates. And they are known to be backers of Chinese leader Xi Jinping.

* * *

The Sidewinder report also dealt with the former Hong Kong immigration boss Lawrence Leung.

"Even before Hong Kong's official return to the Communists, it was established by several Western agencies that their national immigration systems had been affected by illegal Chinese intelligence service and Triad interference," a Sidewinder file said. "Laurence Leung Ming-Yen, a former director of the Hong Kong immigration service, is still under investigation after he had to resign under the pressure of allegations of corruption and illegally disclosing confidential information about residents of the peninsula."

The Sidewinder report called for more intensive study of China's infiltration of Canadian institutions. And the first report would have remained classified if Ottawa had taken it seriously. But the draft was buried and then leaked to Canadian media. Critics jumped on a few flaws in the report, which was years ahead of its time and incredible in every sense of the word.

"It came out much too early," one Canadian intelligence source familiar with Sidewinder's authors told me. "But I also took away from Sidewinder that, yes, China is very active in Canada. And there is very little light between Chinese organized crime and the Chinese Communist Party."

But Sidewinder's core allegations look more prescient, year after year.

The Lawrence Leung case is a great example. He eventually died in 2008. And Hong Kong's government continued to deny the allegations surrounding him.

But in 2019, the *South China Morning Post* obtained declassified Hong Kong Independent Commission Against Corruption reports.

Leung was forced to step down in 1997, when corruption investigators proved his ties to at least two Triad bosses, the documents said. The records showed an integrity probe in 1993 had discovered a Hong Kong Immigration Tribunal judge had wired HK$750,000 to Leung from an offshore company jointly owned by Leung and the immigration judge.

And the offshore company was linked to a Chinese heroin-trafficking syndicate. It struck me that 1993 was the same year Leung's daughter was murdered in Vancouver. Perhaps a warning that Leung had better keep his mouth shut?

"Leung showed reluctance to initially name a person known to be involved in organized crime in Hong Kong and overseas, whom he admitted to being a close friend whose two sons [Leung] nominated for membership of a local institution," the records obtained by *South China Morning Post* say. "This person is documented as being widely and actively involved in organized crime."

The files also showed Leung had a full membership in the Hong Kong Jockey Club. And it occurred to me that according to McAdam's dossier, this was the playground where Triads and tycoons sought to influence Canadian immigration officials.

* * *

Garry Clement fared better than Robert Read and Brian McAdam after returning from Hong Kong. He became one of the RCMP's top experts on money-laundering and financial crimes. But in retirement he sometimes reads his Hong Kong files and shakes his head. He used to believe no one is above the law. Not after Hong Kong.

"I had a ton of intel. And I shared almost two books with Ottawa," Clement told me. "We could file affidavits based on that intelligence and stop people from going into Canada. Politics won the day, though."

Brian McAdam still has his files on the tycoons and Triads. And he is still in contact with former colleagues from CSIS and the RCMP. McAdam's files and hierarchy charts indicate the Sun Yee On Triad's elderly leader is a name that could shock global banking communities. But this type of information will almost certainly never be proven in court.

McAdam has struggled with health issues related to his ruined career in Canada's government. But he continues to follow my investigations into money-laundering in Canada's real estate and casino industries. He says the transnational narcotics cartels laundering money in Canada are executing the same playbook that he spelled out for Ottawa in about 30 reports from Hong Kong.

I obtained an unofficial report that McAdam wrote in 2018, in which he explains the sourcing and verification behind his Commission files, and questions who in Ottawa is ultimately responsible for ignoring his dire warnings.

The files were compiled from Western intelligence agencies, national security experts at the missions of Western allies in Hong Kong, the Royal Hong Kong Triad Bureau, the Hong Kong Independent Commission Against Corruption, and the Royal Hong Kong Drug Squad, McAdam's 2018 report says.

"We tried to convey to others that the Chinese intelligence working in conjunction with the Triads made unrelenting, determined efforts to suborn foreign diplomats, using money and sex as entrapments," McAdam wrote in 2018. "No one wanted to listen to Garry Clement nor myself when we made it very well-known that the Macau casinos, where many staff took trips paid for by a Triad leader, were owned by Triads and persons who were agents of the Communist Chinese Government."

In his 2018 report McAdam questioned the fate of a specific 1990s report — "Triads and Other Asian Organized Crime Groups" — that he filed from Hong Kong so that Canadian border officials could block immigration applications from Triad bosses.

"We discovered among the files a number were Triad leaders with many thousands of followers involved in credit-card fraud, criminal intimidation, extortion, wounding, blackmail, prostitution, gambling, and money-laundering," McAdam wrote in his 2018 report. "Garry Clement managed to have over 8,000 copies [of the Triad guide] sent to the RCMP and widely distributed. But [Canadian official name redacted] allegedly arranged ... that it would never be circulated in Foreign Affairs, Immigration, or to Canada's Security and Intelligence Service, by having it destroyed."

McAdam's 2018 report concludes by pointing to one of the 30 Canadian officials that reportedly avoided charges in Robert Read's RCMP probe and rapidly ascended to some of Ottawa's most influential positions, ultimately advising prime ministers on foreign affairs, trade, and national security.

"If [Canadian official name redacted] did destroy these reports, did he contribute to the Triad and Chinese Communist invasion of Canada ... knowingly withholding and allegedly destroying extremely critical intelligence information intended to ensure persons inadmissible under the Canadian Immigration Act would be refused admission to Canada?"

For my investigation into the Vancouver Model this question can't be ignored. Brian McAdam's unofficial 2018 report is about a cold case. It points to decades of corruption in Ottawa. And the information should be part of a national inquiry into fentanyl trafficking, real estate money-laundering, and Chinese foreign influence operations in Canada.

6
PROJECT FALLOUT

Peter Li had to do the wiretap equivalent of stripping naked and standing in a public square. He was forced to explain at length that Chipped Tooth Koi and Tong Sang Lai — who were rumoured to be childhood friends in Macau but now enemies to the death — had taken out contracts on each other.

In January 1994, Tong Sang Lai visited Canada's Commission in Hong Kong. He wanted to become a Canadian permanent resident by applying to Quebec's immigrant investor program. So in March that year, Lai transferred the standard fee in Quebec's program, C$350,000, into account #89-17AA-4 at Lévesque Beaubien Geoffrion, a Montreal immigration-investment firm connected in business and immigration dealings to Prime Minister Jean Chrétien. At the time, Lévesque Beaubien Geoffrion was lobbying Chrétien to expand Quebec's millionaire migrant scheme, and throughout the 1990s, the firm would flood Asian investment into Chrétien's Shawinigan riding. This was the backdrop behind thousands of applications from Hong Kong. But Tong Sang Lai was a very special case — a Macau Triad dragon and VIP room operator in a Macau casino.

Lai was born in Guangdong in 1955 and had little education, but had risen quickly in the Shui Fong Triad. Unlike the Hong Kong tycoons with their English-tailored suits and statesman-like auras, Lai had a hard, cadaverous look and the dark eyes of a killer. With his stake in Macau's casino trade, he was positioned to issue death orders and broker with Chinese officials.

He owned a junket company that operated out of Casino Pelota Basca — one of Stanley Ho's nine Macau casinos — and he ran the Fortuna VIP room, taking a big cut of Sociedade de Turismo e Diversões de Macau's baccarat rake. In Macau, Lai also owned real estate development, construction, automobile and import-export firms that benefited his "money-laundering activities," according to police.

But Lai's trade extended far beyond Macau. Police said he sold "Chinese-made arsenal to Zaire" and imported illegal labour and electrical products from the People's Republic of China. He even owned a cigarette brand in China and used his Shui Fong muscle to persuade retailers that didn't carry his tobacco.

He also contracted for fire-bombings and tenant eviction via arson, and provided debt-collection services for other casino VIP room operators and chip lenders. It was estimated that Lai had thousands of Triad soldiers at his command in Asia.

But he also had his eye on British Columbia's expanding casino industry. There was too much money in the Chinese-Canadian community to ignore. From 1990 to 1997, over 200,000 citizens migrated to Canada from Hong Kong, including about 70,000 in the 'investor' and 'entrepreneur' categories. Most of the migrants were from hard-working families. But Canadian intelligence found a very significant portion of gangsters in the investor stream. And while Macau had become the Las Vegas of the East, the Triads wanted Vancouver to be the Macau of the West.

Lai had a problem, though. In the Hong Kong Commission, a visa control officer named Jean-Paul Delisle was on his case. Delisle was in Canada's embassy in Jamaica in the 1970s, when Canada's government sent out confidential warnings on the Lui Lok and Five Dragons corruption cases. Using the gangster-vetting system designed by Garry Clement and Brian McAdam, Delisle flagged Lai in a few categories: he was uneducated but claimed a high net worth; he was in the construction business in Macau.

Lai had lots of charges related to Triad activity but no convictions. So Delisle needed more intel to complete his profile.

He reached out to a few untouchables in Macau police, officers that he knew could not be corrupted. Delisle's sources connected Lai to all the vice rackets in Macau: heroin smuggling, prostitution, illegal gambling, loan sharking, extortion.

As Delisle gathered intelligence on him in Hong Kong, Lai's immigration plan was stalled in Quebec. So Lai started to look for different routes into Canada and surveyed points of weakness on the west coast. British Columbia — a natural resource and real-estate economy as hungry for Asian investment as Quebec — was a no-brainer.

According to a report cited in Lai's Canada federal court immigration file, in July 1994 — despite Delisle's ongoing investigations into his Triad associations in Hong Kong — Lai was able to lead a trade delegation of 16 Macau casino personnel into Vancouver with his entourage, including the "special inspector of the Macau gaming control board."

Citing confidential records and a *Vancouver Sun* report, the federal court records say Lai's Macau gambling mission entered British Columbia "as the province was conducting a review of its gaming policy."

"Among Lai's entourage on a July 12 [1994] visit were three known Triad members and two people with criminal records," the records say. "Lai may have had some interest in gambling opportunities in British Columbia."

Meanwhile, regulatory changes were on the horizon in Macau casinos. In January 1995, the Triads started to count down the months until China would retake Hong Kong and Macau. And growing uncertainty on the future of Asian criminal markets triggered a race to secure shares of the Macau VIP rooms before Beijing took control. In August 1995, representatives of the four Macau-based Triads, including 14K, Shui Fong, and Big Circle Boys, formed a compact called the Four Pacificals — to stand united against incursions from the Hong Kong-based Triads.

Lai was elected treasurer of the Four Pacificals, giving him a 5 percent cut in all Macau casino VIP rooms and junket-lending operations for Chinese whale gamblers.

But the temporary peace started to unravel in 1996. Lai and the Macau 14K boss — a flamboyantly violent Lamborghini-driving thug named Chipped Tooth Koi — clashed over VIP room control.

And in an odd twist, Vancouver police happened to be listening in on several Triad wires, giving Canadian intelligence a front-row seat on Macau's turmoil. Canadian police learned that the November 1996 attempted murder of Lieut. Col. Manuel Antonio Apolinario, the Macanese government's chief of gambling security, triggered a historically bloody war for Macau's multi-billion-dollar underground economy. In a busy Macau intersection, two men on a motorcycle had raced towards Apolinario; a Big Circle Boy gunman blasted him twice in the face, lodging one bullet in his jaw and sending the second bullet through his body, narrowly missing his spine. Police suspected the shooters had fled quickly to China. Apolinario survived, and a deal was brokered — by someone unidentified by Canadian police intelligence, but evidently with tremendous influence over Macau's casinos — to settle the conflict between Lai and Chipped Tooth Koi: ten days of bloodshed would be allowed, and the winner would take all VIP rooms in Stanley Ho's casinos.

That's how it was supposed to happen. But after two weeks, the fighting just continued. In the early stages, the 14K were winning. But there was too much criminal money at stake for the Shui Fong to bow out. Already many Macau police officers were on Triad payrolls. And so Lai just hired more officers to side with him and turned the tables on 14K.

Macau descended into chaos, streets rocked by grenade attacks, fire bombings, machete choppings and drive-by motorcycle shootings. Police often found Chinese People's Liberation Army bullet casings on the ground, pointing to Big Circle Boys assassins. In a few months, 14 people had died, including a nurse coming off her shift at a Macau hospital.

But here is the twist that, for my Vancouver Model investigation, best illustrates the blindness and corruption of Canada's immigration system in the 1990s. Tong Sang Lai was ordering the hits in Macau. But from a safe distance. In 1995, when Lai learned his application in Canada's Hong Kong mission was stalled due to Jean-Paul Delisle's anti-Triad vetting, he formally withdrew it. In May 1996, he flew to Los

Angeles and walked into Canada's consulate. There he made another immigrant investor proposal, but this time through British Columbia's program. To support his application, Lai and a number of men from China wired funds from Hong Kong into a shell company in Richmond, purportedly for a mining venture in Canada.

And in a massive breach of national security, Lai's application through the Los Angeles consulate was approved in September 1996, after just three months. Ottawa claimed that Los Angeles staff had not even checked for red flags from Deslisle's vetting of Lai in the Hong Kong Commission.

I researched Lai's court records in Ottawa, and they show that a Canadian official stamped approvals on Lai's Los Angeles consulate application documents, and Lai became a landed immigrant in British Columbia in October 1996.

He was ready for battle — but 10,000 kilometres from the war zone — living with his wife and young children in the East Vancouver home that he had bought in 1994, for $515,000. And in November 1996 — armed with just his cell phone — he called in his orders.

In May 1997, after six months of war, in the evening rush hour on Macau's packed Rua da Praia Grand, a squad of motorcycles buzzed around a small turquoise sedan, and shooters wearing dark-visored helmets and seated back to back with their motorcycle pilots, sprayed the small car from all sides, smashing out three windows. They had slaughtered three 14k heavyweights. Two men were slumped over in the front seat. And in the back, left hanging forward into his seatbelt, was Chipped Tooth Koi's bodyguard, the 14K's No. 2 in Macau. In a two-year war that would kill dozens of gangsters, police and government officials, and innocents, this hit was the singular bloodbath that caused Macau's casino wars to spill into the streets and VIP baccarat rooms of Metro Vancouver.

* * *

Detective Constable Patrick Fogarty got at least three lucky breaks. In 1997 cars were disappearing from the streets of Vancouver like a strange twist on the biblical plagues. Fogarty was a smart detective with sandy red hair and a thick jaw. He looked like the type who might play the bad guy in an interview room, banging tables to get suspects talking. But he was just the opposite. He always found you got better information by talking quietly to people.

Fogarty was learning that Chinese criminals were taking over in western Canada. They had mastered drug importation and distribution. They had connections and routes worldwide. In B.C., they worked with the Vietnamese, the Persians, the Hells Angels and the new multi-cultural dial-a-doper gangs, the United Nations and Red Scorpions. Some of the bikers were still doing well. But they didn't run Vancouver anymore. Fogarty knew of men with an HA patch on their back sleeping on park benches.

The Chinese gangsters had reached another level of wealth and sophistication. And for the most part, they didn't walk around giving off the steroid-popping, thug-and-bling aura. It was often some quiet businesslike guy driving a Toyota Corolla pulling the strings. Their only problem in the 1990s was where to put the heroin proceeds. The drugs were easy to conceal and fast-moving, tight and compact. The cash was gargantuan and slow. Once Fogarty had raided a Vancouver home and seized a stack of $4 million in $20 bills.

But year by year, he saw his targets getting better at moving narco-dollars around the world. Sending it out of Canada in stolen car exports, layering it into casino and hotel developments in Vietnam and Cambodia, building towers in Mainland China, selling real estate across Asia, wiring the funds back into Canada through import-export companies, mixing it into casino chips and homes in Vancouver and Richmond and Burnaby. They bought cheap tear-down properties and built the crap out of the lots, building monster homes or multi-family townhouses.

Fogarty and some of the Vancouver gang officers who understood money-laundering knew that whole blocks of homes in some neighbourhoods were built with drug cash. And each year, the gangs improved the narco-infrastructure, weaving the heroin money deeper into B.C.'s legitimate economy.

So while Fogarty got his head around the plumbing of this rapidly evolving international laundromat, he was working his way up through the Asian organized crime section of the B.C. Coordinated Law Enforcement Unit. And in 1997, he got the chance to start Project Bamboo, his car theft and trade-based money-laundering case.

It started the way good operations always started for Fogarty, with good warrants. He got judicial approval to 'go up' on three phone lines from the crew he believed was running British Columbia. It was North America's western branch of a cartel with worldwide ties, a Triad he believed was affiliated to 14K out of Hong Kong and Macau. His targets were stealing multiple cars every day and shipping them out of Vancouver's crime-soaked ports and across the Pacific to Hong Kong.

Wilson Wong was the No. 3 on Fogarty's charts. And above him was his boss, Simon Chow, a man Fogarty knew to be a brilliant capitalist who ran pool halls in Vancouver. It was an oddly small and simple business line for a man who was constantly travelling to the United States, Hong Kong, China, Macau, Cambodia and Vietnam.

But Fogarty knew Simon Chow was really into big-time heroin importation, underground gambling in Vancouver and casino junkets in Las Vegas and Miami. He had extensive loan-sharking networks in B.C. Lottery Corporation's Richmond casino, ran large-scale weapons trafficking and massive credit card fraud, and had business lines in Los Angeles and San Francisco. He had interests all across Southeast Asia.

And he had a Vancouver lawyer at his beck and call.

Fogarty was working on Project Bamboo when a call came in from Hong Kong in early June 1997. It was an unidentified man asking Wilson Wong for Simon Chow.

Fogarty wasn't authorized to go up on Chow's phone yet. So his first lucky break was that the man from Hong Kong had to call Wilson Wong, only because he couldn't directly reach Simon Chow. The caller from Hong Kong was a Cantonese speaker and obviously highly respected. But he was speaking for people well above his pay-grade.

And right away, another huge break for Fogarty. Wilson Wong wasn't well-informed on the Macau situation. The Hong Kong man — identified in June 1997 as Peter Sum Li, an elite Big Circle Boy — asked Wong if the phone was safe. And Wong said that it was. Big break number three.

Peter Li got comfortable on the line, asked Wong if he knew what was going on in the Macau casinos. Wong said he didn't. But in the most blatant way imaginable. He actually said, "What war in Macau?"

When the Cantonese-speaking gangsters talked about criminal matters such as trading guns, they liked to use code words like "little black guys."

But for Peter Li, explaining Macau's epic gang war wasn't something you could do in code words.

Wong's ignorance of major events in Asia meant that Peter Li had to do the wiretap equivalent of stripping naked and standing in a public square. He was forced to explain at length that Chipped Tooth Koi and Tong Sang Lai — who were rumoured to be childhood friends in Macau but now enemies to the death — had taken out contracts on each other.

Wilson, you don't even read the news from Hong Kong, Fogarty said to himself. You made a huge mistake. Thanks very much.

So with the Macau situation thoroughly explained, Peter Li told Wilson Wong that he had to get a hold of Simon Chow urgently because there was a contract out of Hong Kong that the "boss" would want part of.

Tong Sang Lai was somewhere in Vancouver. All they had in Hong Kong was a few digits from the Shui Fong boss's Vancouver cell phone number. If the Big Circle Boys in Vancouver could find Lai and execute the contract, Peter Li said, someone very high-level in the Asian casino world would pay Chow HK$1 million. And beyond that, it would be very good for the outlook of the Big Circle Boys.

In the second week of June 1997, Fogarty read up on Ottawa's intelligence reports and the RCMP Commission liaison in Hong Kong. It was confirmed: 14k and Shui Fong were in a massive war, and Chipped Tooth Koi planned to wipe Shui Fong out of Macau. It was further confirmed that Lai had "circumvented Canada's immigration system."

Fogarty talked to Cheryl Shapka, the Triad expert from the Canada Border Services Agency. Shapka's boss was apoplectic. Someone in Immigration Canada had messed up royally, or worse, opened the door to Lai in the Los Angeles consulate despite Lai's red-flagged application in Hong Kong. It appeared to be corruption, Fogarty thought. There was some suggestion that someone in Canada got paid off. But that was an issue for someone else.

Now it was confirmed Lai and his family were in Vancouver. Dark forces in Hong Kong wanted Lai dead, and possibly his family too. Fogarty had a duty to warn Lai his family was in danger and prevent Macau casino bloodshed in Vancouver. And he now had evidence to go up on Simon Chow's phone and Tong Sang Lai's. Project Bamboo was on the side burner, and Project Fallout was underway.

It was a police intelligence gold mine. Fogarty was listening to the world's largest criminal organization's command structure hashing out the next steps in a gang war with geopolitical and trade implications. He would learn how high tentacles of the Triads directed from China and Hong Kong reached into Canada, the United States, and beyond.

Phone taps showed the first order of operations for Wilson Wong was to track down Simon Chow, who was doing business in Las Vegas. Simon Chow accepted the contract on Lai, Fogarty's intercepts showed, and Chow ordered Wilson Wong to use all means needed to track down Lai's residence.

This was a sobering moment for Fogarty, still a relatively young Canadian cop.

He was surprised to find Wilson Wong had moles in a number of Canadian travel agencies and phone companies, and apparently even government offices. It was no problem for the Chinese cartel to look into Canadian driving licence records. The Big Circle Boys were able to peer into Canadian residents' lives and travel schedules and track them down if they wanted to. Still, by the end of June 1997, the Big Circle Boys had not yet found Lai in Vancouver.

And then some mind-blowing phone calls occurred. As the war raged in Macau and its economy started to suffer, the Chinese government appeared to take an interest.

On June 30, at 11:05 p.m. in Vancouver, Tong Sang Lai called a "Mr. Kwok" in Mainland China.

"Kwok appears to be the mediator between the two Triads," Fogarty wrote in his Project Fallout report. "Lai is very respectful towards Kwok. Lai has ordered his men not to take any action until after July 10."

In Fogarty's mind, Mr. Kwok was obviously a person of immense influence. It was something that citizens in the U.S. and Canada just couldn't grasp. China's government was directing the gangs.

There were thousands of people involved in this gang fight, and someone in Beijing had decided enough was enough. It would be like the White House brokering with the Five Families to quell Italian mafia disputes in New York, or Ottawa making deals with the Hells Angels and Rock Machine in Montreal to end the Quebec biker wars.

As Fogarty listened, he heard Mr. Kwok tell Tong Sang Lai that there was a person who Lai must call. Mr. Kwok said that Lai had to talk to this unidentified person — a new leader rising in the 14K — every two or three days.

The next day, three Shui Fong Triad members flew to Vancouver to join Lai. Fogarty knew that these were bodyguards. And he made sure they were flagged and rejected by Immigration Canada.

In response, Lai made calls to the United States looking for more men. One thug was on the way to San Francisco for business. And two others were working in Las Vegas. A customer in an unidentified Las Vegas casino owed the Shui Fong $10 million, Lai's men informed him. So Lai told them not to bother coming to Vancouver but to stay in Las Vegas and collect the debt.

And in early July 1997, there was another shocking call for Fogarty. Lai called to a source that Fogarty believed was a mole in the Macau police headquarters.

Lai was checking into the reasons Immigration Canada had rejected his soldiers at the Vancouver airport.

Fogarty believed that in Lai's own case, he was able to get red flags erased from his name in Macau using his contacts in the police and judiciary.

But something in Lai's corruption web had gone wrong. His mole had found that a book of Triad hierarchies that should have been erased was still in use by untouchables in Macau police Triad units.

"Everyone is there; there are 2,800 odd pages. Anyone who is slightly connected is in there," the source told Lai. "One after one. No one is missed."

"So troublesome," Lai sighed, before hanging up.

* * *

The contract on Lai's head was in flux. It wasn't clear to Fogarty whether the final order from Hong Kong would be for Lai's death, a kidnapping of his wife and children, a fire-bombing on his home, or something less lethal. But negotiations in Hong Kong, China, and Macau appeared to favour Lai's continued existence.

Simon Chow was waiting for a photo to arrive from Hong Kong that would identify Lai's home. And meanwhile the *Vancouver Province* scored a front-page scoop. The newspaper revealed the scandal of Lai's passage into Canada through the Los Angeles consulate, even printing a photo of Lai's East Vancouver residence. Wilson Wong believed the media heat would make the contract on Lai harder to execute.

But Simon Chow was zeroing in. Fogarty and his team started to pick up calls between Chow and a gravelly-voiced man named "George." They traced George's phone to a Vancouver apartment building, and Fogarty put surveillance on him. Fogarty talked to the building manager, who pointed to a suspicious Caucasian man, a guy who lived with a woman in the apartment and liked to sit in his unit's street-facing balcony in his underwear.

Fogarty reviewed his team's surveillance notes: George was fat, 35 years old, about 220 pounds with brown receding hair and a tattoo on his upper arms. In mid-July, Chow and George were seen sitting in a car in front of the apartment building talking for a long time. And they also talked on the phone about "two things" and some "little black guys."

"One is a '47 with a pistol grip, and one is a Tec 22," George said.

"OK, can you get, like, the shorter?" Chow said.

Fogarty almost had to laugh when he read the transcripts of calls between George and Simon Chow. It was so clearly a dumb guy talking with a smart guy. George was a perfect example of the knuckle-dragging thug who lived and died by the gun. He wouldn't last. But Simon Chow was entirely different. He was always evolving himself and recreating. It was like watching the organized crime version of a butterfly coming out of a cocoon. Chow exemplified a rare type: an extremely intelligent transnational gangster in the middle of his transformation into a tycoon.

The last week of July, Peter Sum Li called Chow from Hong Kong. "The person" had ordered that Lai would live, with a warning, Li said. A fire bomb or stray bullets would do the trick.

And, Peter Li added to Chow, "the person" will be travelling to Cambodia, and had said if any of the younger Big Circle Boys had problems with police in Vancouver, they could be sent to work in his Cambodia casinos and hotels.

So that was that. Hong Kong had given the final order and the exit strategy.

On July 25 at 3 a.m., the Vancouver Police Department dispatcher reported a drive-by shooting at Lai's home, 2205 Fraserview Drive. There were four shots. But Lai's family was not inside the house.

At 3:38 a.m. Simon Chow called George.

"Hi, how many tequila you drink?"

"Four."

"Quick pop?"

"Yeah, quick shot," George said. "Fuck, that hit me real good."

Both Simon and George laughed.

"So. Everything fine, right?" Chow asked.

"Yeah, um. I'm going to get rid of the worm in the bottle. You know the bottle?"

"Yeah, George."

"You know what I mean?"

"Yeah, George. That's fine."

And minutes later, Simon Chow called Peter Li in Hong Kong.

"It's done."

"It's done already?"

"I thought that's the place. But just to make sure, drank four glasses."

* * *

For Fogarty, there was still the question of whether Hong Kong would call in a more deadly follow-up. The contract was hanging. It seemed that payment was not coming to Simon Chow in Vancouver. And the person that Fogarty called "Mr. Big" was not easy to track down. After Lai's Vancouver home was shot up, the unidentified man behind the contract had travelled to Shenzhen. And on August 4, he was in Vietnam. Peter Li told Simon Chow to be patient. On August 6, Mr. Big's son would be holding a grand opening for a new casino in Vietnam.

"I told him people on the other side have been waiting [for money]," Peter Li said to Chow. "He says he will get it from the casino when the casino begins business."

But the Macau gang wars seemed to be winding down.

Canadian federal court records on Tong Sang Lai's case cite a cryptic report in the *Vancouver Sun*. It said on August 7, 1997, Stanley Ho informed Hong Kong media "the wars would end in three weeks."

And Fogarty's Project Fallout files concluded with some stunning insights.

In Macau, a new leader for the 14K — "Market Wai" — had been installed to replace Chipped Tooth Koi. Koi's penchant for high-visibility gang hits was bringing way too much heat on Macau.

"Wai has openly criticized Koi and has arranged to work with both the Shui Fong and the Sun Yee On Triad in an attempt to end the battle in Macau," Fogarty's report says. "This has been done with the support of the Chinese government."

Fogarty concluded: "Due to the intervention of Market Wai and his cooperation with the Shui Fong Triad, and the Chinese government, it would not be in the best interest to have Lai and his family killed."

So for my Vancouver Model investigation, Project Fallout provided powerful evidence of direct connections between China's government, the Macau casino tycoons, and the Triads.

And again, I have to hammer this point. Assessments from the Sidewinder report that were scorned in Ottawa power circles are supported by Canadian police wiretaps. China's government is in fact controlling drug cartels.

In the aftermath of Project Fallout, Simon Chow and his hitman George were eventually convicted in the 1998 murder of a man named Vikash Chand. Chand was shot seven times while changing Chow's licence plate at a Vancouver car lot.

And media reports continued to see Simon Chow as the key player in the 14K's hunt for Tong Sang Lai.

But my investigation of Kwok Chung Tam's immigration file pointed to a different interpretation. Simon Chow was the No. 2 for the Big Circle Boys. And Tam was the boss.

"The interesting fact I learned in this whole thing is that Tam is the one who allegedly tried to do Lai," Cheryl Shapka, the Canada Border Services Triad investigator, wrote in an email to Vancouver Police. "Tam is Big Circle Boys, as you know."

7
THE CASINO DIARIES

*Labine's handwritten notes described senior Big
Circle Boys who were deeply feared. She looked at
associations and rivalries. Her journal assigned
nicknames and code-names to the bosses.*

"We have decided to keep this journal to record the events that are
transpiring in our casino. We are all concerned for our safety, and
we feel we need to document these activities for our own well-being.
The 'Boys' have been working the tables for months now. The action
continues to increase and the clients are spending more money
every day. We feel the baccarat pit is getting out of hand and that the
casino is ignoring our warnings. Staff are becoming more aware of
the gangs that are now working amongst us. Supervisors are feeling
intimidated and overwhelmed. The population of $500 players has
grown substantially over the last few months. We have been looking
into different crime units. The Combined Forces Asian Crime Investigation Unit, and the Canadian Secret Service. We decided that we
should know who they are, but it is unlikely that we will turn to them
as this is big business involving gangs. We are not sure how long this
is going to last. We hope the casino will at least try to stop them."

* * *

In May 1997, Muriel Labine knew that she was seeing momentous
changes in Richmond's Great Canadian Gaming casino. She was a
supervisor of dealers, a sharp-eyed grandmother from the suburbs
of Vancouver. Her workplace seemed to be undergoing something
like a merger. Or possibly a takeover. All that Labine really knew was
it was becoming perilous at work. Customers were coming in with

black eyes. Some high-rollers seemed to be concealing guns. A VIP gangster had threatened to kill a dealer. Some of the reasons for the arrival of this new violent clientele could be guessed at. But some were too deep to fathom. Labine had no idea that she was on the frontlines of a major geopolitical shift.

In 1997, China took Hong Kong back from the British. Since 1984, when Prime Minister Margaret Thatcher had announced the handover, there was a flood of migration to the West, accelerated by the Tiananmen Square massacre in 1989. And China would take Macau too, in 1999. As a result of the epochal shift, from 1996 to 1998, a bloody turf war raged in Macau. No one was safe there. Dozens of gangsters, government officials and innocent bystanders died.

In a poetically tragic irony, in May 1997 — the same month that the hit on Chipped Tooth Koi's right-hand man caused Macau's casino violence to arrive in British Columbia — the provincial government enacted a major shift in gambling policy. In that month, the NDP introduced baccarat tables for the first time, extended gambling hours, and increased bet limits. Overnight the maximum bet had jumped from $25 to $500 per hand, a 1,900 percent increase. At some level, and for some reason — could it be related to the Shui Fong boss's gambling trade mission in 1994 to B.C., or Stanley Ho's wooing of B.C. politicians, or the major real estate investments by the Hong Kong tycoons and the Five Dragons? — the government decided to bring Macau-style gambling to Canada. And days later, Muriel Labine noticed the arrival of youthful gangsters that she dubbed 'the Boys.'

To my mind, it seems that through greed, naivety, wilful blindness, or possibly corruption, Canadian politicians and businessmen had imported Macau's shady economy and its deadly gang war.

Whatever the reasons, it was an incredibly profitable market disruption.

Just three months after baccarat tables were introduced, revenue at the Richmond casino had nearly doubled. Labine saw that most of the cash coming across the tables was in $20s. They were wrapped in elastic and carried in bundles of $1,000 or $2,000. Labine had worked at a bank before coming to the Richmond casino in 1992.

She knew what legitimate funds coming into and going out of banks were supposed to look like.

And most of the baccarat cash coming into the casino did not appear to be coming from banks. It was coming from loan sharks.

So Labine decided to dig deeper. She collected casino revenue sheets and matched them against the shady transactions she saw with her own eyes.

In May 1997, before the baccarat changes took effect, the Richmond casino's total revenue was $1,617,000. Most of it went to the B.C. government, and Great Canadian Gaming's share was $647,000. In June, after baccarat was introduced, the Richmond casino's win surged to $2,490,000. And in July, the casino's take exploded to $3,035,000. Great Canadian's share was $1,214,000.

You could not mistake it. The loan sharks were now a primary economic driver. Staff started to call these young men, who spent 10-hour days inside the casino, human ATMs. And Labine realized they had essentially become her co-workers.

But upper management did not seem to care. Labine was starting to suspect they were in on it. And so she started to gather evidence and create records. She hoped to make a case so compelling that authorities would have to clean house. Like so many truth-tellers after in B.C.'s casino industry, she failed. But in the process, Labine provided perhaps the most detailed account of how the Big Circle Boys infiltrated a significant portion of Canada's economy. And twenty years later, her records would make a difference. Labine agreed to share her records and story with me. And according to sources with knowledge of B.C. government decisions, my reporting for Global News on Labine's "Casino Diaries" along with my colleague John Hua, was the factor that finally persuaded the B.C. NDP government to launch a money-laundering Commission of Inquiry.

At first, it was a mystery for Labine how cash magically arrived inside the casino and was converted into $1,000 betting chips in the hands of baccarat VIPs. Management repeatedly told the floor staff that what they were witnessing was a unique cultural practice in the Asian community. It was not loan sharking. It was relatives and friends lending money to relatives and friends. But Labine's detailed journal notes destroyed this corrupt rationalization.

"We are aware that there is more than one gang operating the tables. The Asian dealers and the casino security have slowly been feeding us this information. The 'Boys' have their own clients which they are catering to exclusively. They sit with the clients, providing anything they want, but mostly handing them large quantities of cash or chips when they run out of money. An average buy-in from one of the Boys appears to be about $5,000. The shark carries $1,000 chips around with him, until one of his clients requires them. We have been wondering where they manage to find these massive amounts of twenty dollar bills. The well, it never seems to dry up."

But occasionally, as on August 2, 1998, the well did dry up. That day, Labine recorded an unusual series of interactions between the Boys and their clients

> "The Boys are short on cash today. They seem to be scrambling to find money to give the clients. The players are having a bad day today. The house is cleaning them out faster than they can get their hands on it."

> 3:30 p.m.

> "The Boys' cell phones are ringing away. They seem to be trying to find more money."

> 4 p.m.

> "Elvis, a head loan shark who has been operating for quite some time at our casino, comes in. He is carrying a grocery bag full of money. He signals the other 'Boys' to join him. They all stand at the concession stand and Elvis opens the bag, and begins to pass out bundles of twenty dollar bills. The 'Boys' bring the cash back to the tables to begin the transactions."
> 6:45 p.m.

"Some of the Boys have gathered at the concession counter to tabulate transactions on the slip of paper. They leave the paper on the counter, and return to work. We manage to get a hold of the card. It has Chinese characters on the left side, and dollar amounts on the right side. The amounts read in quantities of $5,000, $2,000, $1,000. With the help of a Chinese dealer, we were able to determine the Chinese characters read, 'The Iranian,' and 'The Japanese.' Clearly characters that owe money. We alerted the casino's chief of security, and he promptly requested the papers."

* * *

Once Labine understood how the loan distribution networks worked she wanted to know more. What was the hierarchy of these criminal operators? Where did the gangs come from?

She confirmed the answer on August 27, 1998.

"Security informs us that one of the gangs is the Big Circle Boys. We confirm it with another member of security. We are still trying to figure out who the top individuals are. They seem to be shrouded by the others and always remain in the background."

Labine's handwritten notes described senior Big Circle Boys who were deeply feared. She looked at associations and rivalries. Her journal assigned nicknames and code-names to the bosses. Labine and her co-workers were too afraid to refer to these men by their real Chinese names.

"Plainly a top boss. Staff fear Columbo greatly, especially Asian staff. We were told by senior casino management months ago to 'Lay off him. He is not someone you want to deal with.' He recently disappeared. Rumour has it that he was arrested for counterfeiting in the United States. He stood only about five feet high, was balding, in his fifties and had the most sinister look one could ever imagine. He was the only shark that was given free cigarettes. He was once seen shaking hands and engaged in long conversations with the vice-president of the casino. Most of the staff seemed highly intimidated. He was obviously one of the most respected sharks among the gangs. This was noticed by the treatment he received from the other Boys."

The question that Labine pondered was, where did the never-ending piles of cash come from?

> "The staff are becoming more aware of the amount of currency the Boys are generating for the casino. The drops are in the hundreds of thousands, and it never seems to let up. It has certainly benefited the casino by having the sharks operating the tables. It is common now to see men carrying handbags full of cash and others who feel it is safe to carry the money in a plain, brown lunch bag."

Labine strongly suspected the loan sharks were laundering drug money. And other employees claimed to have direct knowledge.

> "[Name redacted] feels strongly that heroin, not extortion, is the major source of income for the sharks. According to him, deals occur all the time, and are visible if you are paying attention. In public washrooms, according to him, on several occasions, [he] was witness to drug deals by the 'Boys.'"

This was an observation that was later corroborated in B.C. Supreme Court records. Confidential informants told police the Big Circle Boys preferred to make drug transactions inside casinos, because if police caught them they could claim the drug cash was gambling proceeds.

Labine had already noted that senior sharks brought grocery bags stuffed with bundles of cash into the casino and distributed the funds to junior sharks, who then bought chips for their VIP clients. They did this by exchanging $20s handed to them by the senior sharks for $100s at the casino cash cage. And then they used the $100s to buy-in for $1,000 chips at the baccarat tables. This transaction pro-cedure is known to money-laundering investigators as refining or "colouring up" currency because $20 bills used in drug transactions are exchanged for $100 bills, which are more acceptable for large banking transactions. And win or lose, the gamblers have to pay back the loan sharks, with personal cheques or property, including homes and cars.

Labine continued to dig, trying to trace the hierarchy of the drug-cash networks.

Her journal says that according to a co-worker who was close to a senior loan shark, the gangster had claimed that a high-ranking Big Circle Boy would have the responsibility of laundering $5 million per month for the cartel's heroin-traffickers. And a senior shark would have 40 to 50 boys working as "runners" to distribute heroin cash to high-rollers. His task for the cartel was to return $3 million in laundered funds per month. But he was allowed $2 million in "overhead" for gambling losses. If this was true — and the information has not been tested in court — it suggests the Big Circle gang knew it would "lose" about half of its drug cash to the B.C. government and its casino operators.

The runners working for senior loan sharks, according to Labine's journal entry, earned about $10,000 per month.

But with all this drug cash sloshing through the casino, violence had to follow.

September 1998

"We have become more confident discussing the Boys with various members of security. Another member of security confesses he fears confrontation with the Boys. He says he is positive that they are carrying weapons. He states quite frankly, 'I wish they would kill each other off.'"

The security staff in the Richmond casino were tough men. Many of them had come to Canada from Yugoslavia, and some had military backgrounds. So if they feared the gangsters, the female baccarat dealers lived in absolute terror. According to Labine's journal and my interviews with other Richmond casino staff, it was especially staff from the Chinese-Canadian community who faced harassment and threats of violence.

"A pit supervisor, was threatened by a baccarat player, known simply as the Fat Man. The Fat Man is a high-roller who associates with gangs. Certain members of management have informed us of their desire to remove him, however higher management, out of fear, and/or out of greed for the man's money, have opted not to. The threat that was uttered to the pit supervisor was, 'I'm going to put a bullet between your eyes.' The staff are outraged!"

September 5, 1998.

"The Fat Man wins $30,000 today. Mr. Money, another excessive high-roller, loses over $30,000 in roughly 30 minutes today. The Lottery Corporation seems to still be unaware of the gangs. It was always our understanding that they are supposed to be the first ones to know about this kind of crime. We are not about to risk our jobs to inform them."

* * *

In just under two years, Muriel Labine and her circle of trusted co-workers had gathered an incredible pool of intelligence, seeing the gangs operate firsthand. In some ways, it felt like they were living in a parallel reality. Working with the gangsters, in a strange way, had become normalized. Some of the loan sharks were friendly and humorous. Some you wouldn't even glance at because they looked like they could kill in a second. But life went on inside the casino. Sometimes clients came in looking bruised up. Sometimes you saw gambling addicts shaken down or heard of clients robbed for their cash. Characters came and went, and you wondered if they were still alive. But you went to work and brought home your paycheque. You sometimes felt a little bad inside when you went to sleep, but you woke up and went to work again. Did the outside world have any idea of the rapidly growing narco-economy that B.C.'s government was taking a cut from?

The Richmond casino's secrets finally became a mainstream reality when a Big Circle Boy named Pretty Boy Meng was shot by another loan shark from the casino. The attempted murder unfolded in the

back room of a Chinese restaurant in Vancouver, as a table of gangsters
played a mah-jong game with stakes in the tens of thousands.

November 1998

"The news articles roamed freely among the staff and were
read by almost everyone during their breaks. Some of them
were immensely overjoyed by the news. But we all feared that
we would have to face this killer again, should he return to
the casino. We are now concerned at the potential for retaliation by the rival gangs. The news article allowed us an eerie
glimpse into some of the private life of Scarface. We learned
that he was 35, married and resided in a cozy neighbourhood nearby. Much the same kind of neighbourhood we all
strive to raise a family in, here was a gangster living a normal,
wealthy life, right under our noses. A fact that placed a reality
check in our minds. These kinds of criminals are everywhere.
We have to stand around hoping and praying that we are safe
from harm. We are in the line of fire more than any other
individual in this predicament."

The *Vancouver Sun* covered the case, opening a series of stories with
this line: "An attempted murder trial in B.C. Supreme Court this week
has offered an unusual glimpse into the shadowy world of gambling
and loan-sharking among a small segment of the Lower Mainland's
Asian refugee community."

The *Sun* reported that famed Vancouver criminal lawyer Russ
Chamberlain defended Hoi San Yim, the man called Scarface in
Labine's journal. Chamberlain probed Pretty Boy Meng sarcasti-
cally. He asked Meng how he could afford a $65,000 car when he
only claimed income of $3,000 to $6,000 per year from working
in a kitchen and mowing lawns. Meng responded that his mother
in China was in the car business, and she had provided him with
a downpayment.

Chamberlain suggested to Meng that he was a heroin dealer and
loan shark for the Big Circle Boys and that he had used Vietnamese

henchman to collect a debt from a victim at a Chinese restaurant near the Richmond casino.

Meng denied being a Big Circle Boy but admitted that he he arrived in Canada on a flight from Hong Kong in 1993 and that he went through customs with no identification papers. Meng said he claimed asylum in Canada because he had written some political slogans in Guangzhou, where he worked at a bakery.

A witness to the mah-jong shooting named Kat Hai Chan acknowledged during the trial that he had arrived in Vancouver and claimed refugee status after destroying his immigration papers during the flight to Canada. But he denied that he had owed $200,000 to another loan shark at the Richmond casino, or that he had once lost $360,000 in a gambling den in Vancouver's Chinatown.

He told Chamberlain he didn't know what a Big Circle Boy was.

"It's a criminal enterprise in Richmond and elsewhere involved in prostitution, drug trafficking, loan sharking," Chamberlain said. "One of the objects of the Big Circle gang is to smuggle people."

The star witness, though, was a woman named Betty "Big Sister" Yan. Yan testified that she saw Hoe San Yim curse in the middle of the mah-jong game and shoot Pretty Boy Meng, whom she knew as a loan shark with Vietnamese bodyguards.

Yan recanted her earlier testimony that Pretty Boy Meng owed her $10,000 prior to the shooting. And she denied that she was a loan shark and Big Circle gang member. But the trial heard about her path to Canada fom Guangzhou and the familiar Big Circle gang autobiography.

Upon arriving in Vancouver in 1995, she claimed refugee status, telling Canadian authorities that her father was a democracy activist who was politically persecuted.

Chamberlain noted, though, that despite Yan's supposed fear of the Chinese Communist Party, she had worked for the Chinese government as a customs officer. And Chamberlain also got Yan to admit that while collecting welfare in Canada, she somehow had the means to wear a $25,000 Piaget watch.

Surprisingly, Yan's notoriety from the *Sun*'s reports in 1999 did nothing to stop her meteoric rise in Vancouver's establishment. While laundering money for transnational narcos and testifying in an attempted murder trial, she was embraced at Vancouver's West Point Grey school, the elite academy where future prime minister Justin Trudeau was teaching French at the time of the Pretty Boy Meng trial.

Reportedly, Yan's popularity at the school was due to her facilitating incredibly lucrative business with international students from Mainland China. And other elite Big Circle Boys had children in the school, as well.

Big Sister Betty would still have a much larger part to play in Canada, though. She had a role in a major diplomatic stand-off with China, the case of Lai "Fat Man" Changxing, a billionaire baccarat player and Big Circle Boy associate who fled from a corruption probe carrying the secrets of China's most powerful men.

Yan's stunning life as a triple-agent with connections to China's foreign intelligence operations in Canada would only become clear ten years later, when she was shot dead while sitting in her Mercedes in a barren strip-mall parking lot outside an underground casino in Richmond. Fabian Dawson, the *Province* editor, got the scoop that laid Yan's ties to international espionage networks bare.

In the Richmond casino, though, by 1999, Muriel Labine had seen enough. The spotlight caused by Pretty Boy Meng's shooting quickly faded, and it was back to business as usual.

January 1999

"As we expected, the Boys are back. As they begin to multiply again, it would almost seem hopeless for the police to intervene at all. The sharks have their own agenda and way of handling the element called police. They seem to know that after a few weeks the entire house cleaning project will cease, and it will be business as usual. In fact, at the rate they are returning, we will have more than we started with by month's end. We almost feel sorry for the police at this point. They seem to be helpless. The whole problem is far beyond our ability to cope with."

8

THE PLA WHALE

*Transferring his wealth between Hong Kong and
Canada was as easy as rolling the dice at B.C.
government baccarat tables.*

Lai Changxing had a simple motto.

"I'm not afraid of government officials," he would say. "I'm only afraid
of government officials who don't have hobbies."

By hobbies, Lai meant women and money. He was born in September
1958 in Fujian, the coastal province bordered by Guangdong to
the south and the Taiwan strait to the east. He only reached third
grade, and though barely literate, Lai rose in a time and place in
China's history, a surreal time and place, when a unique blend
of brazenness, cunning and charm could turn a smuggler into
an oligarch.

Like the tycoons of Hong Kong, Lai had his rags-to-riches story. He
was one of eight children in a family of peasant farmers in Xiamen.
And under China's laws, he should have stayed where he was born,
scratching at the land. But Lai was bigger than that. In his creation
myth, it all started when he collected $150 from family and friends to
open a small auto parts business.

China was in rapid transition in the 1980s, especially in the special
economic zones of Guangdong and Fujian, where privatization of
state assets and promotion of international trade moved forward at
light-speed under Deng Xiaoping's reforms.

In charge of the Fujian economic liberalization — a fast-rising Communist Party princeling named Xi Jinping, who was trying to emulate his father, the revolutionary hero Xi Zhongxun. The elder Xi had successfully implemented privatization in Guangdong, with the backing of governor Ye Xuanping.

As for Lai, with nothing but $150 in startup funds, as if by black magic, he multiplied his manufacturing operations year after year, collecting factories in textiles, garments, print and machinery. By 1991 he was a multi-millionaire.

"The businesses paid taxes as required and were held up as a model of the evolving Chinese economy by central Chinese political officials, who would come to visit," Lai would testify years later. "I was encouraged at this time by the deputy minister of the Fujian department of national security to move to Hong Kong, where he said I would enjoy more business activities."

Once in Hong Kong, Lai started a real estate development and trading conglomerate called Yuan Hua Co. In Hong Kong, he could access international markets and ship foreign goods into the Mainland.

By 1995, Yuan Hua had eight business limbs in Hong Kong and on the Mainland, including shipping container businesses in Shanghai. At the same time, the People's Liberation Army (PLA) and Chinese intelligence arms were planting trading companies in Hong Kong, in efforts, according to Western intelligence analysts, to prepare for the 1997 handover. Lai's growing empire in Hong Kong was deeply intertwined with these Chinese intelligence business fronts.

Back in Fujian, the amiable peasant boy called "Fatty" Lai had become a billionaire and hero of China's modernization. He funded schools and playgrounds in Xiamen, bought the city's soccer team, and started construction on an 88-storey tower.

Just how big was he? In Xiamen, Lai had a seven-storey palace called the Red Mansion — a compound leased from China's Public Security Bureau — and beside it, a boxing facility for his personal phalanx of military guards.

At the height of his power, Lai was chauffeured in a bullet-proof black Mercedes-Benz sedan. He reportedly purchased the vehicle for $1.5 million, after it was used in 1997 by President Jiang Zemin for the ceremonial handover of Hong Kong.

And it was said that Lai never travelled in his armoured Mercedes without a bag of diamonds and a trailing guard of two Mercedes 600 sedans, trunks stuffed with loads of U.S. dollars and Rolex watches.

Lai, in essence, was the port of Xiamen. Yuan Hua produced more GDP than all other regional businesses combined. He was able to dictate prices in China's oil trade, reportedly earning about US$35 million from crude oil shipments per day. But Lai was not a Communist Party princeling. He was a peasant. So there was nowhere to go but down.

Lai's empire's secrets finally started to drip out in March 1999, when the son of an elite PLA official mailed a dossier stacked with evidence to Beijing. The case landed on the desk of China's premier, Zhu Rongji, a member of the Politburo Standing Committee. According to reports from China that are filed in Canadian federal court, the PLA princeling had incurred a Macau casino loan-sharking debt that could not possibly be paid.

And the debtor had turned on Lai.

The evidence was so damning the Politburo had to act. But carefully. There were fears that Lai's corruption touched the highest echelons of the Party, and possibly even Jiang Zemin's top aides.

So on April 20, 1999, Zhu Rongji carved out a special team within the Public Security Bureau, called the 420 Investigation Task Force, and they started to probe Lai's operation.

Lai had purchased eyes and ears everywhere in China and Hong Kong. By the time murmurs of the 420 investigations reached him in mid-1999, his family was already in Hong Kong, and Lai's wife filed fraudulent Canadian investor immigrant applications through Yuan Hua.

Meanwhile, Lai still had a card to play. A meeting was arranged, and he offered Zhu Rongji a $2-billion yuan bribe — about $350 million — to call off the 420 team, according to Canadian court records. But Zhu refused.

On August 13, an incredibly humid day in Xiamen, Lai got a call from "a friend" — the head of Hong Kong's immigration investigation section. The man said he had been ordered to arrest Lai, and the 420 team was about to raid the Red Mansion. Lai could flee or face execution.

But Lai's mole in Hong Kong had a plan.

"He urged me to go to Canada, from where, he said, perhaps I could work something out," Lai later testified.

That night Lai boarded a speed boat from Xiamen and raced across the dark waters to Hong Kong, and within hours his family was flying to Vancouver. They held fraudulent Hong Kong exit documents and used fake Canadian visitor visas, but cleared Canadian Customs and Immigration.

A friend from Hong Kong had a mansion in South Granville, an area of Vancouver popular with Chinese real estate investors, and Lai's family was given the home. And immediately, Lai hooked up with his Macau money-laundering network, including "Big Sister" Betty Yan, Kwok Chung Tam, and the Big Circle Boys.

Transferring his wealth between Hong Kong and Canada was as easy as rolling the dice at B.C. government baccarat tables.

***

For Lai, the Red Mansion was a double-edged sword.

The bottom floors held four decadent dining rooms where Lai would serve his visitors from Beijing shark fin soup, abalone shipped from Africa and the most expensive of European wines. On the third-floor, Communist cadres and PLA generals sweated off culinary delights in massage rooms and Jacuzzis. On the fourth floor were several dance halls and a movie theatre.

The Public Security Bureau had an office on the top floor.

And on the fifth and sixth floors were private bedrooms. Here, Lai pressed money and prostitutes into the arms of his visitors, while the hidden video cameras rolled tape.

The tapes provided invaluable leverage for Lai's empire — but they were turned against him when 420 detectives marched out with boxes of evidence.

What the 420 team found was stunning, even by China's standards of corruption. Lai was running a global smuggling ring, Red Mansion records showed.

He had bribed thousands of civilian officials to lubricate his trade, starting with the 'flies' and rising to the 'tigers'.

From 1996 to 1999, Lai made at least $US6.4 billion, records in the Red Mansion showed.

In 1997 alone, Lai's cartel had shipped 3,588 stolen Mercedes-Benz, BMWs and Lexus vehicles through the ports of Hong Kong and Xiamen.

Lai and his "underground society thugs" traded raw chemicals, computers, telecommunications, rubber, cigarettes, diesel, vast containers of crude, and more, according to 420 evidence.

"There were no limitations on the goods they smuggled, as long as they could make money," one conspirator testified.

It was organized crime at the state level. The investigations in China, not surprisingly, failed to publicize Lai's shipments of weapons and narcotics, which are described in a 2003 U.S. Library of Congress report on Lai Changxing's case.

The 420 Task Force investigation also did not detail Lai's Triad ventures in Macau casinos. But like cash and women, Macau casino junkets, loan sharking and extortion greased the wheels of Lai's schemes. And after fleeing to Canada, Lai continued where he left off in Hong Kong. "The [420 Task Force] material indicates that Mr. Lai may have been involved in obtaining video-taped information of compromising activities by government officials to assist in the ultimate objectives of smuggling," a Canadian government lawyer said in November 2000, after Lai sought asylum in Canada. "And I was provided information regarding some degree of continuation of similar activities in Canada."

***

When he landed in Vancouver, if Lai was concerned about his problems with the Politburo, he didn't show it. He had run from at least 11 homes in China, a partially constructed 88-storey tower, and a multibillion-dollar business. But he also had been moving funds from China into Hong Kong for at least a decade, and he knew that underground banking channels between Hong Kong, Macau and Vancouver were primed and pumping.

Three months after illegally entering Canada, although he didn't have a Canadian bank account, Lai's family purchased a $1.3 million property in a south Vancouver neighbourhood. Lai's wife was on the title. The home, while not extravagant by Vancouver standards, was a good investment: in 2017, its assessed value was $4.3 million

Vancouver police were secretly following Lai from the start. He drove around at all hours of the night, and police would park outside while he spent hours inside mansions in South Granville, the even pricier Shaughnessy area, or sprawling compounds on Richmond farmland.

Police quickly noticed that Lai and Betty Yan were tied at the hip.

They were in underground casinos and the Richmond and Vancouver Lottery Corp. casinos almost every day.

In 1999, the first time police connected them, Lai was in the passenger seat of his blue Range Rover, and Yan was driving.

"Ms. YAN stated they had been at a casino together in explanation of the significant amount of cash she had in her purse," a Canada Border Services report said. "When the vehicle pulled away, the police officer who interviewed her found a fake Canadian Citizenship Card laying on the road right beside where LAI had been sitting in the vehicle, and the card had LAI's picture on it."

Lai knew he was being watched. Sometimes he would switch cars when he exited a home. He had many cars, in many people's names, and many drivers. Officers noticed that Lai would park in alleys outside expensive Japanese restaurants, leaving his car running, while young men would pull up and jump into Lai's car, and then drive away.

"There are constant meets with other people in very expensive vehicles," one Canada Border Services agent said years later, in a hearing. "There was Mercedes, Lexus, BMWs. He went into very expensive homes, million-dollar homes, in Shaughnessy, Surrey, Richmond, with sophisticated surveillance equipment."

And if Lai really had to slip away, he had the means.

"In my training, we term it counter-surveillance," the border services agent said at Lai's hearing. "There's about five vehicles parked outside [a South Granville mansion run as a Big Circle Boys casino], and there were approximately 20 to 25 people that exited the house at the same time, including Mr. Lai. And an unknown Asian female got into the BMW, and she blocked our lead car from following Mr. Lai."

There were uncountable illegal casinos in Vancouver like this one, and they had to have an impact on real estate prices. The mansion Lai was seen leaving was sold for $1.7 million in 2007. And it was sold for $5.95 million in 2017, B.C. land titles show.

There is no way to calculate how many tens of millions Lai and his crew laundered through B.C. Lottery casinos and Vancouver mansions.

But Lai was cleaning big-time drug money.

Records showed, for example, that he put a $500,000 mortgage on one of his Richmond mansions in order to secure a gambling debt owed to a Chinese narco who the DEA said was supplying ecstasy to Big Circle Boys cells in Los Angeles.

Like it is done in Macau, Lai leveraged his criminal wealth offshore, using it as a collateral pool, and borrowing against it in Vancouver.

The transactions worked like this: in the casinos, Lai made calls for bags of drug cash from his Big Circle associates; the cash arrived and he used it to buy baccarat chips and laundered the funds out of casino cash cages through high-value chips, $100 bills, and casino cheques.

Lai could then loan these laundered funds out to fellow gamblers in his own illegal casinos throughout Vancouver and get repaid in cheques and other forms of currency, real estate, or luxury vehicles. And he could pay back his own gambling cash loans in other jurisdictions, including China and Macau and Hong Kong, where his wealth was hidden in underground banks or assets.

All of these transactions would serve a few key purposes, including ultimately moving funds to jurisdictions such as Hong Kong or Guangdong or Burma, where the Big Circle Boys produce heroin, ecstasy and fentanyl.

But the first objective was simpler: to obscure the blood-soaked path of $20 bills taken out of the hands of impoverished heroin junkies in Vancouver's Downtown Eastside, transferred into the hands of low-level drug-dealers, then stored and redistributed into the hands of loan sharks, and next loaned into the hands of VIP gamblers and transferred into casino cash cages.

On paper, at least, B.C. Lottery records establish that Lai made 69 transactions of $10,000 or more at government casinos in Richmond and Vancouver from September 1999 to March 2000.

And at the same time, he made 30 trips to Ontario's Casino Niagara, where he was a valued VIP. He gambled $3 million in the Ontario casino in a few months, court records say, and lost $500,000.

Lai's travelling companion for the Casino Niagara junkets, an alleged Vancouver Big Circle Boy associate named Billy Chen, later testified that Ontario casino managers had comped his and Lai's flights to Toronto, and paid for their hotels and more.

Police also said that Lai visited various casinos in Ontario with members of the Kung Lok Triad in Toronto, including gangsters known as Black Ghost Ming and Stupid Ricky. Lai was also connected to Big Circle Boys active in gambling, prostitution, and drug trafficking in Saskatchewan.

But it was in the Richmond casino where Lai's betting habits were so gargantuan and brazen, that he first attracted attention from security staff.

One security manager, a man named Proka Avramovic, told me that Lai wanted to bet in the range of $1 million per night. Another security manager told me that Lai asked staff to let him store $500,000 cash in a casino vault for his convenience.

Avramovic says he was deeply concerned that some staff in the casino were counselling others to turn a blind eye to heavyweights like Betty Yan and Lai Changxing. So he started to secretly forward evidence to a B.C. Lottery Corp. investigator. And Avramovic wasn't alone in his suspicions about casino managers.

Doug Spencer, a Vancouver gang squad officer, recalled the case of one high-roller who took wads of cash from young Asian men before he was beaten with pieces of metal rebar.

"He had his legs broken and was kicked several times in the head," Spencer told me. "I identified these young men as well as their boss, an older Asian female named 'Big Sister' — real name, Betty Yan."

Spencer went to the Richmond casino to find and arrest Betty Yan for extortion. "I located the manager and asked her if she had seen Betty around lately. The manager said no. I literally looked over [her] shoulder and see Betty seated. I walked up, arrested her and handcuffed her. On the way out, I told the manager I would be back and arrest her for obstruction."

According to Spencer, his boss was happy with the Betty Yan bust but told him it was better to leave the casino manager alone.

Spencer came away thinking that senior police didn't want "the headache" with B.C. government leaders.

"There are loan sharks all over the casinos and have been as far back as I can remember," Spencer said. "The politicians turn a blind eye."

***

Records show that in early 2000, a Lottery Corp. investigator named Gordon Board had placed surveillance on Lai and Betty Yan in Great Canadian's Vancouver and Richmond casino locations.

Board's investigation found that Lai's whale operation was facilitated by many Big Circle Boys inside the casinos. They were loan sharks and drug dealers, cash deliverers, chip passers, and "gofers" who could front Lai's transactions.

One roll of videotape showed the cash coming in.

"The Richmond casino where Mr. Lai was observed playing at a table, it was obvious he ran out of cash to do any further buy-ins," Board testified, in 2001. "He made a cellular phone call, a short one, put the phone away and just sat there occupying a place at the table. Ten minutes later, [a Big Circle Boy] showed up and handed over an amount of cash to Mr. Lai."

And another video, in Great Canadian's Vancouver casino, showed the chips going out.

While taking a break from the baccarat tables, Lai would relax in a smoking room and wait for a gofer named Stephen Chow to sit down and chat. Lai would shovel handfuls of chips to Chow, tapes showed, and Chow would go and cash the chips out for Lai. It meant that Lai's transactions were completely invisible to Canada's anti-money-laundering reporting system. He had small armies of gangsters, relatives, and whales handling his chips in B.C. casinos, allowing him to anonymously launder incalculable drug-dealing funds.

Stone Lee — then a surveillance manager for Great Canadian — remembered watching Lai throwing down $20,000 bets at baccarat tables. Lee knew that Lai was China's most wanted fugitive. And he informed his managers. But nothing was done, Lee said.

Finally, in March 2000, based on Gordon Board's investigations, B.C. Lottery Corp. had to act on Lai and his loan sharks.

"Betty YAN and LAI were involved in an incident in February 2000 at a casino in B.C., wherein they were observed by security making suspicious financial transactions and chip-passing that resulted in both of them being barred from casinos in B.C. for two years," Lottery Corp. records say. "It is suspected that this group is involved in loan sharking activities in and around casinos."

But Lai returned the banning letter unopened, and simply continued to gamble at the Royal Diamond, a downtown Vancouver casino owned by a man named Gary Jackson.

"Did Mr. Jackson agree to support the ban?" Gordon Board was asked by a Canadian government lawyer in 2001, in Lai's refugee hearing.

"To the contrary. He did not want to comply," Board said. "This is why this high-level meeting had to take place."

The issue of chip-passing was so serious, Board explained, that for the Lottery Corp. or casino managers to knowingly turn a blind eye to it could mean criminal charges.

The reason is transactions of over $10,000 per day by one gambler in any casino had to be recorded so Canadian regulators could flag money-laundering. But if one whale gambler had ten gangsters cashing in and cashing out for him, he could bet ten times the amount required to be recorded.

In his testimony, the Royal Diamond casino owner, Jackson, explained why he was resistant to Gordon Board's directive.

Lai was just one of about 30 similar whales at the Royal Diamond, Jackson claimed, whereas other B.C. casinos had hundreds of whales who could have been flagged for similar transactions.

And finally, Jackson said he had received legal advice that the Canadian Charter of Rights could protect high-rollers from casino bans.

"My concern with what BCLC was trying to impose was a banning of players, based on suspicion. I felt that it was not in the best interests of either party or the government to act in that fashion."

To my mind, these answers highlighted the self-serving reasoning that would be repeated over and again in B.C.'s casino industry, until Ross Alderson met with Calvin Chrustie in July 2015, and warned his Lottery Corp. bosses that a massive RCMP investigation would raise the possibility of criminal charges on casino managers.

Meanwhile, at Lai's refugee board hearing in 2001, a government lawyer said even after Lai's casino bans, "he felt secure, comfortable, and confident that there was little if any possibility his family would be removed from Canada."

But Lai didn't know that the 420 Task Force had a loan-sharking spy inside the Richmond and Vancouver casinos.

***

Betty Yan was playing for so many sides, it was hard to keep the wires straight. She was an informant for the RCMP's Richmond bureau, flipping her handlers intel on the Triads. And in 2000, when Yan was faced with deportation to China, she decided it was a good time to let Canadian police know that her father worked for China's Public Security Bureau. She said that while running her Big Circle Boys' operation out of Vancouver casinos, she had also been spying for China.

And when Lai Changxing arrived in August 1999, her value in Beijing had shot through the roof. China's leaders were terrified that Lai would spill state secrets. So Yan was asked to get next to Lai and soften him up for the 420 Task Force.

This was according to a Canadian intelligence official who was a primary source for Fabian Dawson.

"Betty was a player with the gangs, with us, and some think with Chinese intelligence," Dawson quoted the RCMP official in a 2009 report for the *Province*.

According to Dawson's source, Betty Yan facilitated negotiations between 420 team agents and Lai, initially by setting up phone calls between Vancouver and China.

Lai knew that Beijing badly wanted him. After he fled from Hong Kong, some of his family had been beaten and jailed. But Lai also knew he held powerful secrets, which gave him some leverage. And he knew that his conspirators were getting executed in the Yuan Hua take-down, and Chinese agents didn't see international borders as an impediment.

China had many ways to insert its spies. Just as the Chinese Communist Party had planted uncountable "window" companies in Hong Kong — usually import-export firms — they also had many state-sponsored "accessory" companies in Vancouver.

Two of these companies were Top Glory, a tiny storefront on East Hastings in Chinatown, and Tricell Forest Products, an office located in Canada Place, a prominent international trade and tourism centre on Vancouver's downtown waterfront.

Both companies were subsidiaries of state-owned corporations in Beijing, Canadian court records say.

On May 16, 2000, Canada's embassy in China got a letter from a Beijing company calling itself China Light Industrial Products Import-Export, announcing a trade mission to Vancouver, sponsored by Tricell.

"Respectfully requesting entry visas to be issued to three persons comprising Lai Shui Qiang [Lai Changxing's brother] and so on, belonging to the trade group, for the purpose of entering your noble country," the message said.

Another letter, from the China Grain Oil Foods Import-Export group, said: "Three persons of our company will depart Beijing to visit your noble country at the invitation of Top-Glory Company."

The visas were approved. And that's how three 420 team spies entered Canada through Vancouver airport on May 31, falsely declaring themselves as businessmen and bringing Lai Changxing's brother with them.

Betty Yan continued to earn her *guanxi* from all sides. She set up the first meeting between Lai and the 420 agents at the Delta hotel in Richmond, where Lai also rented a room for himself, in preparation for negotiations.

And Yan notified the RCMP too.

"That hotel meeting in Richmond, Betty set that up," Fabian Dawson told me, citing his RCMP sources. "She set Lai up. And she also told RCMP about the meeting. And Special 'O' (the RCMP's surveillance unit) trailed Betty and Lai there, to the Delta."

Lai met with the 420 agents three times in June. And the first meeting was so cordial that Lai helped the spies find a more comfortable hotel and paid for their rooms.

According to Lai, the 420 team put six issues on the table. Beijing had to bring him back. That was never negotiable. And they wanted information on certain elite officials. They would allow Lai to keep a portion of his fortune if he voluntarily returned. And they would return Chinese identity cards to Lai's relatives and give them lighter sentences if Lai would come voluntarily. And unlike some of his con-spirators, Lai would escape the death sentence.

But after a week, Lai broke off talks, and he walked into a government office in Vancouver to declare asylum. His refugee claim was allowed to proceed while secret discussions between Beijing and Ottawa were occurring in the background, RCMP sources told me.

The RCMP finally stepped in on orders from Ottawa, and on November 23, 2000, Lai was arrested while gambling at Casino Niagara.

After eleven years of legal wrangling and the production of thousands of court records, Lai was finally extradited in 2011. And the evidence Lai left behind gave me a paper trail to map the network of Chinese gangsters, gamblers, soldiers and spies who are endangering the West.

One of the best examples is this: by searching Chinese government records online I found that Top Glory and Tricell — the front com-panies used by Chinese agents — were on the same list of state 'acces-sory' companies in B.C. as Water Cube, the Richmond massage spa run by Paul King Jin.

***

One of the first orders of business in Lai's refugee case was for Canadian lawyers to decide whether the 420 Task Force's accusation — that Lai was the kingpin of China's largest organized crime smuggling ring since 1949 — had any merit.

Lai characterized his bribes as loans rather than pay-offs. But there was too much credible testimony from the officials he enriched for Lai to claim innocence.

And he described why it was impossible to count every person he had bought.

Officials from across China preparing to travel to Canada or the United States would visit Lai first, in Hong Kong. If they were big enough, Lai would meet them himself and dole out stacks of U.S. dollars for spending abroad. If they weren't that important, Lai would just send emissaries.

"Some of them, I don't even know them," Lai testified. "Some of them were government officials referred to me by my friends. They would say, 'Hey, if you go to Hong Kong, you can go look for Lai Changxing.' This is a kind of tradition that Chinese people keep."

Lai's bribes greased national security officials in ports throughout China so that he could run his ships of contraband inland. A Canadian government investigator travelled to China to interview some of the highest officials in Lai's network.

The Canadian transcripts show that one conspirator, the director-general of customs in Xiamen, admitted Lai had visited his office and told him it was not proper for a Chinese official to be driving a shabby car. So Lai left him a black Lexus 400 and a tiger pelt for his office, which Lai said "would ward off bad spirits."

Closer to the top of Lai's payroll was China's deputy security chief, Li Jizhou, who directed the nation's police and controlled its borders.

Li Jizhou acknowledged that in one case, Lai had called him and requested intervention when one of Li's subordinates had seized some of Lai's oil tankers.

The bribes that Li acknowledged taking included a gift of $121,000 from Lai to Li's wife to open up a restaurant in Beijing. And Lai had wired $500,000 to Li's daughter in San Francisco, where Li's family had "substantial business dealings."

This was the type of 'loan' that resembled Lai's wiring of $250,000 to the son of Xiamen's vice-mayor, who was in Australia and wanted some financing to construct a home.

Li Jizhou said that Lai Changxing was generous with smaller amounts of spending money, too. He told Canadian investigators about the time he visited Lai, who was staying in the presidential suite of the Palace Hotel in Beijing. Li was sitting in the back seat of his sedan, and Lai approached the vehicle, opened the door, and left a stack of thousands of dollars on the back seat.

***

There was never a question about Lai's bribes. But Canadian courts had to decide if Lai could possibly be what he said — just a persecuted businessman caught up in an espionage power struggle.

So Lai was allowed to tell his story, starting with his reasons for relocating to Hong Kong in the first place.

According to Lai, in 1991, in the aftermath of the Tiananmen Square massacre, China's Ministry of National Security tasked him with spying on students and pro-democracy groups in Hong Kong.

Fujian's deputy director of foreign affairs had asked Lai to meet, and "he said I was too famous [in Xiamen]," Lai testified. "[He said] if they ask me to go to Hong Kong and do things for them? And I ask him, 'What kind of thing you like me to do?' At that time there was June 4th [Tiananmen Square commemoration democracy] movement. A lot of student movements. So they want me to go check for this."

So according to Lai, while running Yuan Hua, he monitored Hong Kong citizens and bureaucrats and transferred intelligence back to Beijing.

And as the 1997 handover approached, Lai moved higher in China's national security ranks — obtaining a card to travel anywhere in China and the power to order arrests — as a reward for recruiting and paying the salaries of 16 Taiwanese double-agents in Hong Kong.

"I was asked to provide intelligence on Taiwan — for example, the location of Taiwanese intelligence stations in Hong Kong and PRC," Lai testified, "and the types of weapons purchases Taiwan sought to make."

Lai was also moving deeper into networks of intelligence trading, where spies circled each other in Hong Kong's underground and arranged to meet in Macau casinos and exchange information in return for massive amounts of cash.

One of Lai's more stunning claims was that he successfully turned Taiwan's head of military intelligence in Hong Kong, and facilitated the transfer of five "major pieces of secret military information" to Beijing.

Lai said that his Taiwanese military source, for example, knew that a People's Liberation Army general had sold secrets in Macau for US$500,000.

"One of the pieces of information was that in 1996, when PRC was threatening to launch missiles against Taiwan, Taiwan was aware that Beijing had determined not to arm the missiles," Lai testified in an affidavit.

According to Lai, when Beijing sent an agent named Mr. Deng to Lai's Red Mansion in Xiamen, in order to vet the Taiwanese military intelligence source's evidence, Mr. Deng responded by abruptly arresting Lai's source. And this triggered the national security power struggle that ultimately forced Lai to flee to Canada, he claimed.

But strangely, when Lai arrived in Vancouver, it was Mr. Deng, the agent from Beijing, who sold his own South Granville property to Lai's wife and provided Lai with bags of cash to gamble.

Mr. Deng reluctantly testified in Lai's refugee case in Canada and admitted to dealing with Lai in China and also providing Lai gambling cash in Vancouver. But Mr. Deng denied being a Chinese spy.

China also downplayed Lai's espionage claims.

"Lai Changxing provided some information regarding the circumstances of Hong Kong and Taiwan to the Chinese state security authority," Chinese government lawyers asserted in Lai's refugee case. "Lai was not asked to be a member of the Chinese State Security Authority."

***

April 15, 2009. At 4:20 a.m., B.C. Integrated Homicide Investigation Team got the call from dispatchers, and detectives pulled up to a dreary industrial complex on Shell Road, beside the Fraser River in Richmond.

Big Sister was slumped in the driver's seat of her gray Mercedes-Benz, shot dead. She was parked in front of the Dynasty Club, a Big Circle Boys' underground casino.

"It was only a matter of time," Fabian Dawson wrote in the *Province*, quoting a Vancouver police source.

"She was a violent woman who has been using her own kids as human shields when she felt there was a hit out on her," the source said. "The list of people who wanted her dead is long, and large."

Affidavits filed in Canadian federal court show how closely Betty Yan's and Lai's operations were intertwined from the time Lai landed in Vancouver.

But more crucially for me — to understand how China's organized crime and espionage hub established a beachhead on Canada's west coast — the records show that Canada's legal and immigration systems allowed Lai to roam free for a decade, using computers to run virtual Macau casino operations, selling young women to whale gamblers, laundering Big Circle Boy drug cash into real estate with absolute impunity, and using an army of straw-buyers to launder funds in B.C. government casinos.

Lai's central bail release condition, all the way back to 2001, was that he could not associate with the Big Circle Boys and the Kung Lok Triad in Vancouver and Toronto, and specifically, Big Circle bosses Betty Yan and Kwok Chung Tam.

But in a 2011 sworn statement seeking to have Lai jailed, Canada Border Services Agency investigator Cheryl Shapka showed that Lai had constantly breached these conditions. And Shapka said she had started a new investigation of Lai in March 2009.

She looked into Lai's string of properties in Vancouver and Richmond, and his extensive contacts with Big Circle Boys active in major narco networks running from Toronto to Los Angeles to Vancouver.

One of Lai's properties, a gated mansion in central Richmond, was purchased in the name of his girlfriend 'Ping Ping' in August 2008. This was several months after a female Big Circle Boy working for Lai was banned from a B.C. Lottery casino in Coquitlam for her involvement in suspicious transactions and chip-passing incidents.

The Richmond mansion had a $500,000 mortgage on it from a Big Circle Boy named Henry Ting. And Ting was often in contact with Lai via a cell phone number that Ting had used to receive 116 phone calls from suspects in the RCMP's investigation of a cocaine importation ring active in California and Ontario.

Shapka said Ting's mortgage was a standard method of loan shark real estate financing.

"[Ting] claims he supports his family by loan-sharking, and he charges interest rate to patrons in casinos, specifically the River Rock Casino in Richmond," Shapka wrote.

According to Shapka, Henry Ting and many other Big Circle Boys often visited one of Lai's more opulent properties. It was a 3,500-square-foot rancher on a secluded 1.72-acre farmland lot on Gilbert Road in the south-west corner of Richmond, right beside the ocean and surrounded by tall cedar hedges.

Lai bought the mansion in October 2008. The same month Ping Ping and Lai's son had "cashed out $150,000 worth of gambling chips for a third individual," at the Starlight Casino, a B.C. Lottery casino in the suburb of New Westminster.

The custom rancher on Gilbert Road cost over $250,000 to renovate, with new oak floors, granite countertops, a 600-square-foot gourmet kitchen, and a master bedroom with a jacuzzi. Lai also constructed a detached garage, and paved over most of the farmland on the property, to build a parking lot with more than 16 stalls.

The garage housed six separate bedrooms "that each contained a bed and computer."

"Lai paid the construction workers in cash," Shapka's affidavit said, "and based on their description the bills may have been Chinese yuan."

So now Lai had built a mansion with Big Circle Boy narco dollars and turned into a transnational money-laundering instrument.

"The RCMP have advised me that they conducted surveillance on the property on a number of occasions and confirmed they observed LAI along with numerous other individuals," Shapka wrote. "The RCMP had source information stating that LAI was running a private illegal gambling club on the premises, and the rooms in the garage were used by young females to entertain customers privately."

Visitors to Lai's casino included Kwok Chung Tam and Betty Yan, according to Shapka's intelligence sources.

And Lai had computer terminals that were linked live to an unidentified casino in Macau.

"People would come to the residence to play baccarat on the computers against other players who were playing in Macau," the police sources said. "The gambling and betting was facilitated at the residence, with the game occurring in Macau. And Mr. Lai guaranteed that the money bet by players at the [Richmond] residence would be paid in the game in Macau."

In other words, Lai Changxing and unidentified Macau VIP room operators were running a China-Canada underground bank and casino.

If a gambler at Lai's virtual baccarat table won against the players in the Macau casino, he would be paid out by Lai's criminal casino-bank in the Richmond mansion. "But if a player lost money he would pay the money he lost to Mr. Lai. And Mr. Lai was then responsible for paying the operators of the game in Macau."

This evidence was extremely illuminating for my understanding of the Vancouver Model. It means that the Big Circle Boys are running borderless Chinese casinos in Canada, using virtual technology.

And Lai's VIPs could enjoy the same luxuries that Stanley Ho's casinos in Macau offered.

"Mr. Lai had a private chef and masseuses available to the players while they gambled," an affidavit says.

And of course Lai's casino was funded by Big Circle Boys loan sharks.

"Betty Yan had entered into an agreement with Mr. Lai wherein she would be permitted to provide loan shark services at the residence," an affidavit says. "In exchange for being permitted to provide this service, Betty Yan provided a portion of the profit from the usurious loans to Mr. Lai. And Mr. Lai arranged for players to borrow money from Betty Yan, to continue gambling."

But the agreement was short-lived for Big Sister.

Police sources believe that Lai had been looking at Yan with suspicion for some time. And when they disagreed over lending arrangements at Lai's casino, Yan's reputation suffered.

"In flyers posted all over Richmond, Betty Yan was implicated in the murder on 15 September 2002 of her alleged boss," Shapka's affidavit says. "The RCMP advised me that her alleged boss had been the leader of a Big Circle Boys cell and that Betty Yan was a member of his cell. Subsequent to his death, they believe she assumed leadership of her own Big Circle Boys cell."

And Shapka's affidavit pointed at Yan's dispute with Lai before her execution.

"Betty Yan was in frequent contact with Lai in the months preceding her murder," Shapka wrote. "Prior to her murder, she and her husband attended Lai's [Gilbert Road casino] for dinner with Lai and Ping Ping. Betty Yan's husband also advised the RCMP that Lai owed her $300,000. But the RCMP confirmed Lai told them he owed Betty Yan $150,000."

Betty Yan's murder remains unsolved.

But all of this shocking detail about Chinese transnational crime failed to impress the Canadian Immigration and Refugee Board. In early July 2011, an adjudicator found that Lai was not a flight risk, and his association with Betty Yan wasn't a big problem.

In one particularly absurd passage, the adjudicator reasoned that Betty Yan was bonded to Vancouver's upper crust. So if well-known Vancouverites could associate with Big Sister, couldn't Lai Changxing too?

"Ms. Yan was treated very well by the headmaster of West Point Grey Academy, and other parents at the school were friendly with Ms. Yan, were aware of her wealth and her lifestyle, and had no reason to disconnect their ties with her," the adjudicator wrote, citing a *Maclean's* article. "There certainly seems to be information in the article that these people deny having known Yan was a 'loanshark.' It leads me to the question of how or why Lai could have known that Ms. Yan, about whether she was a big underworld criminal or a Big Circle Boy."

It was typical of many strange legal decisions in Lai's refugee case.

***

Lai was deported in July 2011 and jailed for life in China.

The Politburo Standing Committee suffered deep embarrassment in Lai's Canadian court battle but also snuffed out a fire at its gate.

Evidently, because of Ottawa's lack of interest in getting to the bottom of Lai Changxing's case, the eight Politburo men who ruled China were spared the intense scrutiny they might have faced. And Canadians missed an opportunity to peer into the true nature of China's economic system.

Just how high did Lai's corruption reach?

The answer is unlikely to ever be known outside a very small circle in Beijing.

But Jia Qingling, an ally of Jiang Zemin and the CCP boss in Fujian during Lai's heyday, was implicated in the 420 probes. And his wife was accused of taking bribes from Lai.

Jia Qingling, however, was officially cleared. And based on his ties to Jiang Zemin, Jia was promoted to the Politburo Standing Committee in 2007. "Dogged by corruption charges, China's fourth most powerful Communist Party leader, Jia Qinglin, has been seen as proof that in the Communist Party's murky politics, connections trump clean hands," is how Reuters summarized Jia's magical promotion.

The second most powerful Communist Party official in Fujian during Lai's crime spree, deputy governor Xi Jinping, fared even better.

While Xi was advancing towards China's presidency in 2011, it was reported he was summoned to Beijing to explain Lai's case. And some media reports in China suggest that Xi himself may have been viewed as a suspect. But in 2012 the *South China Morning Post* reported: "Several people who worked under Xi in Fujian said it was hard to notice any flaws with him, even as the controversial Yuanhua smuggling case ensnared at least 700 central government and local officials."

The story quoted an anonymous source "close to" the Fujian government.

"No evidence shows Xi, Fujian's No. 2 leader after Jia Qinglin, had a connection with A-Xing [Lai]," the source said. "Almost all the provincial government officials, including our party head, Jia, were so proud of making friends with A-Xing. But Xi was a rare senior official who tried to keep his distance from A-Xing."

So the official line from Beijing is that Xi remained completely above Lai's corruption of Xiamen's special economic zone, the project for privatizing state assets that Xi was directly responsible for overseeing.

Fair enough.

But there are remaining questions from Lai's case that highlight national security risks for the West that have not yet been understood in Canada.

What did the Yuan Hua case really entail? Was it about bribery, actually? More likely, it seems to be a textbook example of China's so-called white gloves system and the Chinese Communist Party's leveraging of criminals to gather intelligence.

Lai was allowed to monopolize China's oil trade with his access to the country's military vessels and ports. He robbed China's communist economy and paid the dividends to himself and its leaders. But corruption of this scale can't occur unless extremely powerful leaders pull the strings. This is the white gloves system.

In order to conceal their ownership of privatized state assets, Red Princelings use the 'white gloves' of People's Liberation Army figures like Lai. In fact, after Lai fled to Canada, a young Fujian man named Ye Jianming who is believed to have Chinese intelligence connections, "bought" Lai's oil assets at auction and built a transnational oil conglomerate worth about US$40 billion. That was before Ye was disappeared in March 2018, after a United Nations corruption case surfaced, with direct connections to a Macau casino tycoon named Ng Lap Seng. I'll come back to that case in this book's final chapters.

But what about Lai's claims of involvement in military intelligence and foreign espionage? A Canadian judge said they were not credible. But the judge obviously didn't understand how organized crime, espionage and corruption converge in China's system. And recall that Lai himself said it was a Chinese security official who told him to take his racket to Hong Kong and report back on Taiwanese intelligence.

It is a textbook example of how the Chinese Communist Party co-opts organized crime.

Dr. James Mulvenon, a Chinese military and espionage expert who has testified before a U.S. Senate Judiciary Committee, explains Lai's place in China's security apparatus in his report "To Get Rich Is Unprofessional."

"From the beginning of the Yuan Hua scandal, rumours swirled about the central participation of the PLA in the smuggling racket," Mulvenon wrote in 2003. "There were widespread reports of rampant smuggling by the military of crude oil, petrochemical products, plastics, telecommunications equipment, guns, ammunition, chemical raw materials, steel, computers, cars, semiconductors, counterfeit money, drugs, cigarettes, electronics, and food."

Mulvenon also noted — contrary to Beijing's responses in Lai's refugee case — that Lai had the markers of elite military and intelligence positions. This included white plates on his bullet-proof Mercedes-Benz bearing the Chinese character "Jia in red, which usually signifies that the PLA General Staff Department owns a vehicle."

Another sign of Lai's ties to espionage networks, Mulvenon wrote, was the "prosecution of former General Staff Department intelligence chief General Ji Shengde on multiple counts of corruption..."

General Ji, as head of military intelligence, had access to large amounts of money for intelligence operations and control over the department's front companies," Mulvenon's report says.

And Lai's smuggling operation included family members of Admiral Liu Huaqing, then China's top general. Mulvenon noted that prior to the Yuan Hua scandal, "General Ji Shengde had been accused of funnelling $300,000" to several of Admiral Liu Huaqing's daughters in the United States.

The $300,000 was ultimately forwarded to Chinese agents and Macau casino bosses involved in fundraising for President Bill Clinton in the 1996 Clinton-Gore reelection effort.

Back to Lai's extradition case. I think the evidence suggests that Lai's adventures in Canada involve a great deal more than inveterate gambling and drug trafficking.

And there are still more indications of international intrigue hovering over Lai's case.

One example is China's new most wanted man, Miles Guo, the controversial billionaire real estate developer who fled China in 2014. Like Lai, Guo has been visited by Chinese agents who claimed to be businessmen. The *Wall Street Journal* has reported the FBI unsuccessfully tried to cultivate Guo as a counterintelligence informant. And Guo now faces FBI fraud charges for his strange media and fundraising activities.

Guo has continued to broadcast allegations against China's princelings from the safety of his New York City residence, a 5th Avenue penthouse worth about $70 million. Some of his claims have proven true. But many seem to be self-serving hyperbole. Whether it's true or not, Guo claims to know Lai and his network.

"Lai Changxing, before getting rich, his boss was (PLA General Staff Department intelligence chief) Ji Shengde," Guo claimed in a media post in 2018. "At that time, Ji Shengde was very good with me."

But we don't have to rely on Guo's claims to establish the PLA's interest in Lai Changing.

In 2011 an elite cyberwar team operated from the PLA General Staff Department in Shanghai was monitored by U.S. investigators while mounting persistent attacks on corporate and national security assets in the United States and Canada. The team, called Unit 61398, is directed by the Chinese Communist Party's most elite leaders. It hacked into U.S. nuclear assets, United Nations computers, Canadian and U.S. government offices, and critical telecommunications infrastructure.

Unit 61398 also hacked into a Canadian Immigration and Refugee Board adjudicator's computer. This was the adjudicator handling Lai's case. The impact of the hack is unknown. Obviously, though, the hack was important for China.

Unit 61398's other famous target in Canada was Nortel, the world's dominant Internet technology provider, until it collapsed in 2009 and China's 5G champion Huawei rose in its place.

9
THE ILLEGAL GAMING UNIT

*Rich Coleman did not respond to my repeated
interview requests.*

It was a complete shitshow in the B.C. Lottery casinos.

In 2002, RCMP Staff Sargeant Fred Pinnock took command of the force's human source unit, handling informants, police agents, and witnesses.

The position gave Pinnock complete visibility on the best intelligence files from the most connected crime bosses.

As he was getting his head around the files, an epiphany hit him. B.C. casinos were out of control — a 'shitshow,' as one of his sources put it.

Other than federal prisons, Pinnock believed, the Metro Vancouver casinos had the highest concentration of gangsters in the province. It was like turning over a boulder and seeing a hissing vault of rattlesnakes.

And his commanding officers in the RCMP knew it.

The crazy thing was the force had no plan, literally zero, to target organized crime in the casinos. Pinnock could not understand it. It was like giving the enemy the high ground, a licence to bank narco-proceeds. It went against his every instinct in policing.

He was a third-generation officer. His grandfather was a Boston city cop. And his father was a Mountie in Ottawa. Pinnock would some-times think about growing up in Canada's icy capital.

He was a chubby bookworm in grade school, spent a lot of time alone, and the bullies would tail him after school. When they cornered you, they would toss your books into the snowbanks, sweep away your legs, pin your arms back and rub crusty snowballs in your face. There was nothing you could do. Just absorb the abuse until they tired of the game.

But he remembered lying on his back in the snow thinking, When I get bigger, I'm going to do stuff to guys like this. And he did.

In high school, he packed on muscle, and he joined the football team. By college, he was 5'8, 210 pounds, built like a bowling ball.

He was an excellent running back, good enough to try out with the Toronto Argonauts, good at making people miss, good at taking punishment, but not fast enough to stick in the Canadian Football League.

Some friends convinced him to try policing. What better job in the world to go after bullies?

So he joined the RCMP. Right away, he was drawn into the excitement of the Vancouver drug units, undercover ops and infiltrating organized crime. To call B.C. a target-rich environment was an understatement.

Around 1986 the loads of heroin coming into Vancouver surged, purity soared, prices plummeted, and people started dropping like flies in the Downtown Eastside.

And B.C. bud yielded billions of dollars annually. Gangs produced incredible supplies of marijuana on mountainsides across the province and in residential grow-ops across Metro Vancouver. This gave the Hells Angels, Vietnamese gangs and the Big Circle Boys surplus commodity to trade with cocaine syndicates in Mexico.

Pinnock gained a reputation as a capable handler of high-level sources. He had no reluctance approaching senior gang members and trying to bring them into his stable of informants. It was a fascinating world, with intoxicating tradecraft.

Sources would provide intel on the location of drug stashes, who was combining on an import, how the domestic and international routes worked, who was beefing, who was going to die, who knew where the bones were.

A great source could keep a drug unit busy for decades. And almost invariably, they were kingpins, eager to break down competitors by tipping police on incoming shipments.

Pinnock worked the Hells Angels, the Calabrian and Sicilian mafias, the Persian syndicates in North Vancouver, the Russians. One of his best sources was a senior Chinese organized crime figure who did lots of business with the Hells Angels and also the 'unaffiliated importers' — Vancouver businessmen with high-priced lawyers and connections for cocaine in Mexico and southern California.

It burned him, too, seeing some prominent and politically connected lawyers in Vancouver getting rich with the cartels. Setting up shell companies offshore and advising on financial structures. Pinnock wasn't above dropping a bug in the leather wingback chairs in the backroom of a certain posh restaurant near the Supreme Court in downtown Vancouver.

It was like the United Nations of crime in Vancouver. All the biggest cartels in the world had a seat at the table. And it was a constant source of amazement how they co-invested on incoming loads, traded meth from China for coke from Mexico for strains of Purple Kush grown in B.C. mountain towns like Nelson. And the mountains of cash piled up in warehouses, and everyone was happy until someone ripped someone else's supply. And then it was spates of shootings for weeks and bloody headlines in the Vancouver newspapers.

That's exactly what one of Pinnock's informants — one of the biggest Chinese-Canadian narcos in Vancouver — would say when he wanted someone gone. Put him on the front page.

So after three years of running the RCMP's informant unit, Pinnock had digested all the intelligence, and he came to a simple conclusion.

Holy crap, this all runs through the casinos. When Calvin Chrustie told him a command position for the RCMP's anti-illegal gaming unit was coming open, he didn't think twice. He had enormous respect for Chrustie. It was time to shine a light inside B.C. Lottery Corp. casinos.

***

Madame Szeto and her boys did not want to walk through the metal detectors to board Great Canadian Gaming's floating casino, the *China Sea Discovery*. And the ship's security detail knew they did not have to — and for good reason.

She was nicknamed the Big Sister of Macau, the first VIP room operator inside Stanley Ho's original Lisboa casino in the 1980s, and Madame Szeto was highly respected, actually feared, in Hong Kong. Her office was in the Shun Tak Centre, the building owned by Cheng Yu Tung and Stanley Ho, where the Hong Kong tycoons ran many private real estate, transportation, and tourism businesses. Many of the companies were intertwined, and most were connected to the Macau casinos in one way or another. The Shun Tak ferry — for example — carried gamblers to and from Macau.

Proka Avramovic was head of security for Great Canadian Gaming's journey into the dark heart of gambling junkets in the South China Seas in 2001.

It was here, Avramovic believes, Great Canadian Gaming staff learned important lessons on what he called the "no hassle" Macau gambling method that would overtake B.C. Lottery casinos in the years to come.

Great Canadian, former managers told me, had recognized the sky was the limit with Chinese VIP baccarat players. An executive named Walter Soo — an intelligent, discreet former card dealer with a good head for numbers — had risen quickly in Great Canadian's corporate structure. He was the company's vice-president of player development. This made him something like a rainmaker in the world of whales such as Lai Changxing. As Avramovic saw it, Walter

Soo appeared to be an architect of VIP baccarat gambling in Canada and the "Chinese arm" of Great Canadian.

There was so much more money to be had in China than in Vancouver. The $500 bet limits in B.C. Lottery baccarat pits were an impediment. Gambling, of course, was illegal in China. And if you wanted to get closer to the fountains of Chinese cash, you couldn't break into Stanley Ho's Macau casino monopoly. As Walter Soo noted on his Twitter account many years later, there was a solution.

Gambling was not illegal if you were floating on the South China Sea. You just needed a ship and the right plan.

You could set up the baccarat tables and run from Hong Kong, sailing right past Macau to the Chinese island of Hainan and on to Vietnam, before returning to Hong Kong again.

And the company could mint fortunes.

"We had $500 limits in B.C., and we wanted to do $10,000 bets," one former Great Canadian Gaming manager told me in an interview.

"Soo is the guy that put everything together," is how another former Great Canadian executive named Boki Sikimic put it in court testimony. "He's walking around with a piece of paper with all the numbers. Here we are going to make $80, $100 million. That was his baby."

But to get the Chinese whales on board, it wasn't as easy as docking in Hong Kong and hanging a casino sign off your ship. The VIPs literally had to be carried out in small boats called tenders. And that meant dealing with junket operators.

Avramovic says he and his staff would be shown pictures of the junket agents and their VIP gamblers.

"I was briefed that some important people will come through the security and we shouldn't really check them because they are junket players," Avramovic told me. "I was instructed those players and their entourage are probably armed and have lots of cash. So they won't be going through the metal detectors. They have bodyguards. I was briefed that those people are decent, and junkets are smooth. They won't cause a scene. So just turn my head when they come up to the metal detector, and they won't go through."

This was the "no hassle" method.

And that allegation alone — which Avramovic made in a Texas court deposition in 2004 — underlined the extreme rewards and risks at the centre of Great Canadian's South China Sea adventure.

But the casino cruise backfired spectacularly. And legal transcripts stemming from the venture would help me corroborate allegations of regulatory corruption — and the shitshow in B.C. casinos — that Fred Pinnock's police reports would also provide.

***

The *China Sea Discovery* was a partnership between Great Canadian, an investment bank from Texas called Allegiance Capital, and Hong Kong real estate tycoon Charles Ming, a director of Great Canadian and partner of company founder Ross McLeod, corporate and legal records show.

The parties invested $15 million in a rickety cruise ship, according to court records that say Walter Soo and Charles Ming were the key minds for the casino cruise and that Ming planned to draw investors in Hong Kong.

According to a *Wall Street Journal* story, the floating casino would run through Charles Ming's Hong Kong travel company, Kamhon.

But court records and the *Journal*'s story didn't point to the man standing behind Ming and Kamhon: Macau casino magnate Cheng Yu Tung.

Cheng Yu Tung, according to former Great Canadian employees and reports from Hong Kong, was Ming's best friend, a partner with Ming in horse racing, and from my review of corporate filings, the ultimate controller of Kamhon, which was a subsidiary of Cheng's New World Development conglomerate.

Former Great Canadian employees remembered feeling the glorious recognition of "face" — as Chinese people call it — standing shoulder-to-shoulder with Ming and Cheng in the winner's circle at the Hong Kong race track. Cheng was seen as "royalty" in Hong Kong, they said, along with men like Lee Shau-kee, Hong Kong's second wealthiest real estate tycoon, who was co-owner of the racehorse Yellow Diamond, with Cheng and Ming.

The expectation from Great Canadian was that powers that be in Asian gambling would bless the *China Sea Discovery* and allow the ship to access Cheng's Shun Tak Centre ports.

But Cheng preferred to stay under the radar.

Maybe he didn't want to anger his fellow tycoons by openly competing with his own Macau casino conglomerate.

Or possibly, there was concern over the confidential RCMP files — written by officers like Garry Clement — that alleged Cheng's associations to Triads in Macau and Hong Kong.

Another factor might have been the U.S. intelligence that would lead New Jersey's casino regulator to bar Cheng Yu Tung from casino ownership in 2009, because he allegedly ran three VIP rooms "that are notorious for Triad activities" in Stanley Ho's Macau casinos.

Whatever the case, as far as former Great Canadian employees know, Cheng was a key backer.

"Cheng was an original partner, all the way through," one former Great Canadian employee, who asked not to be named for fear of being sued, told me in an interview for a Global News story.

"But there was no access to any of Cheng's infrastructure, and that was kind of disappointing to Great Canadian. Because you think you are partnering with a substantial player in Asia, and then you get there, and it is almost like they didn't really want to be seen being in the gambling business."

Until my 2018 story for Global News — "An Alleged Partnership of a Canadian Casino Company with a Gambling Tycoon Could Trigger a New Investigation." — Cheng's alleged involvement in Great Canadian's offshore venture remained hidden.

But my story raised uncomfortable questions for the B.C. casino industry.

What had B.C. regulators known about Cheng's involvement in the *China Sea Discovery*? And furthermore, what did they know about the Hong Kong real estate tycoon Charles Ming — who was Cheng's business partner — and Ming's investments in Great Canadian Gaming?

A statement from B.C. attorney general David Eby, in response to my Global News story, said significant investors involved with B.C. registered casino companies must be vetted for suitability and integrity by B.C.'s government. Eby's ministry confirmed that Cheng Yu Tung had not been registered to participate in B.C.-based gambling businesses.

Cheng's business partner Stanley Ho and Ho's family have twice been rejected as suitable investors in B.C. casino companies, Eby's office confirmed to me. But Cheng Yu Tung's alleged partnership with Great Canadian in the Hong Kong casino cruise appears to have been undetected.

"Allegations of unregistered individuals participating in companies that deliver gaming services in British Columbia are serious," Eby said in a statement.

And yet, successive B.C. governments apparently have done nothing about the allegations.

For example, my questions about a privately held numbered company incorporated in 2002 by Charles Ming and Great Canadian founder Ross McLeod — called No. 179 — remain unanswered by

B.C.'s government. And the government's redactions have hindered my document searches regarding this company.

What I do know is that Charles Ming died in 2008, and McLeod died in 2011.

And in 2015, B.C.'s securities regulator permitted the controllers of No. 179 — which beneficially owned 3.4 million Great Canadian Gaming shares — to sell the shares back to Great Canadian Gaming.

It was combing through transcripts of court depositions in Texas — especially statements by Proka Avramovic and his boss, Boki Sikimic — that led me to extensive interviews with former Great Canadian employees, who in turn led me to information about Charles Ming and Cheng Yu Tung.

The records also showed me that Charles Ming's involvement with Great Canadian Gaming and Ross McLeod was not just a Canadian casino licensing story.

In 1999, when Ross McLeod and Charles Ming applied for a gambling licence in Washington state, Ming's "personal/criminal history" statement revealed he was charged twice for corruption in Hong Kong.

The licensing disclosures said Ming was a director and significant stockholder for Great Canadian Gaming, and in 1980 he was charged for bribing a Hong Kong public works official by offering "a supply of complimentary ferry passages to Macau and hotel accommodation in Macau to a Mr. Anthony Brian Lawrence."

And in December 1979, Ming "offered an advantage, namely an all-expenses paid trip to the United States of America, to a Mr. Edward Trevor Kennard, a public servant," the statement says. This was to reward the Hong Kong official for performing "an act in his capacity as a public servant by the giving of advice in relation to the development of a building site in Hong Kong."

Ming pleaded not guilty on both charges, and the Hong Kong prosecutors offered to drop the Macau ferry and hotel benefits case. They proceeded with charges on the U.S. vacation benefits case.

Ming was found guilty in that case. But he appealed, and the Hong Kong appeals court overturned his conviction.

And Great Canadian Gaming was able to expand in the United States in 2004, obtaining 100 percent control of four Washington State casinos.

***

In the aftermath of their shambolic joint venture, Allegiance Capital accused Great Canadian of fraud, and the bank's attorneys attempted to discover how money flowed through the *China Sea Discovery*.

Avramovic testified that in 2001 he received a $900,000 cheque from a Great Canadian executive at Vancouver's YVR airport and was asked to pass the cheque to other executives at a hotel in Hong Kong. Boki Sikimic testified that the transaction followed an emergency meeting of Great Canadian executives in Richmond.

"The cost is huge. All the time they ask for money," Sikimic testified.

Sikimic had been receiving terrifying reports from the Chinese territory of Hainan, a tropical island off the coast of Vietnam and governed from the capital of Haikou, a city of 500,000 people. His staff reported that a junket operator known only as Mr. Y had taken control of the *China Sea Discovery* and had detained Great Canadian's staff.

He was not like other junket operators, though. Mr. Y ran spas and karaokes in Hong Kong, one of the detainees told me. He also governed Hainan and commanded armed forces. Whether his power was officially sanctioned by China or not is unclear. But he certainly controlled immigration, police, military and resource allocation for the 30,000-square-kilometre island with eight million inhabitants, former Great Canadian Gaming managers told me.

In court, Boki Sikimic and Proka Avramovic outlined Mr. Y's power.

"I know that's in Hainan when we have to send money to pay," Sikimic testified. "Somebody took the ship and — the reports that I receive, they're running away [with] all money to Hong Kong. They owe money to China. They been paid some Mr. Y. He wants to take the ship. I remember guys sending reports there was guns on the ship. Everybody is, you know, running scared for their lives from operation."

Avramovic was one of the staff sending reports back to Sikimic in Canada.

"We had real trouble with Mr. Y, that mob guy, because he's been threatening some of the Great Canadian employees there — to be more specific, Walter Soo," Avramovic testified. "Mr. Y was making some demands about the money that he invest. And Walter Soo tried to resolve the issues. But Mr. Y wanted money back in order to free the ship from China. Right after that meeting, the whole Great Canadian Gaming crew just disappear, like ran off [the ship.]"

The lawyer questioning Avramovic wasn't sure what he meant.

"They literally did what? I'm sorry."

"Like, ran off the ship."

"They ran off the ship?"

"Yeah."

"Because of Mr. Y?"

Avramovic nodded.

"The only guys who's staying on the ship were myself and my assistant."

It was an illuminating lesson for Great Canadian management on the mysterious nature of business and power in China.

"It was very, very obvious to me that Mr. Y is a very, very powerful person in China when he can control the customs and police and the sale of fuel in Hainan," Avramovic recalled.

The standard reports on junket gambling in Macau explain that junket agents arrange deals with Chinese border officials. This is so Chinese VIPs can covertly transfer cash out of China, avoiding capital export controls, and receive the cash or betting chips in private casino rooms.

Or the junket provides cash loans or chips on credit outside of China. And Big Circle Boys enforcers make sure the loans are repaid inside China. Call it the Macau model, the Vancouver Model, the Chinese transnational crime banking model. Whatever you call it, this is how corruption money flees China and funds drug trafficking.

In any case the junkets are associated with Chinese organized crime. But the case of Mr. Y suggests the de facto governor of Hainan can also be a junket boss.

He doesn't have to pay off Chinese customs. Because he is Chinese customs.

Unlike Proka Avramovic, not everyone saw Mr. Y as a "mob guy."

"Mr. Y was a tiny guy. I didn't see him as a gangster," another former Great Canadian employee told me. "I saw him more as high-level politically connected. We heard Mr. Y's father was one of the revolutionary guys in China. But we never knew that for sure."

There was no disagreement that Mr. Y had the power to deliver Chinese whales to Great Canadian. And he wanted a big piece of the action in return.

"There were bad people trying to control what we did, and they could control immigration in China," a former employee said. "Mr. Y wanted a stake in the casino because he could bring on the players, and he knew there was a lot of money to be made. He was the king of that island, and what he said went."

In the Texas case, although Great Canadian's lawyer objected strenuously to the testimony, Boki Sikimic spoke about Chinese junket operations.

"Did you observe any activities that you would consider to be irregular in regards to these junkets?" a lawyer asked.

Sikimic said yes, and explained how it worked.

"Say you're the junket, you bring me on the ship. If I buy $100,000 in chips — you get $5,000 or $10,000. My guy send me a report that there's so many of them don't play. They just grab the $10,000 profit or $5,000 — I don't know what was the percentage. And they don't play, or they just go play a few hands and they leave."

Obviously, under Canadian anti-money-laundering law, these transactions are problematic. They are so-called third-party transactions — a hidden buyer behind a transaction. These transactions are flags for dirty money, according to Fintrac, Canada's anti-money-laundering-watchdog.

But you don't have to be an expert in Fintrac's technicalities to understand that if armed men ushering bags of cash onto a ship were ignored by the ship's security, it would not be a kosher business model in British Columbia.

In court, Great Canadian's lawyer cross-examined Avramovic, and told him there was no proof that Mr. Y or anyone else on the *China Sea Discovery* was armed.

But I found that credible reports from a shipping history site corroborated claims that Great Canadian Gaming staff were threatened by armed junket operators in China.

"Onboard during the maiden voyage, there were three representatives of the charter company, and it was discovered that they were armed, one being the 'top dog for the police in Haikou,'" a report attributed to a senior crew member on the *China Sea Discovery* said. The report said that Charles Ming and others were threatened that "personal consequences could be severe" if they did not follow the orders issued from Haikou.

But the conflict was resolved. According to Avramovic, Mr. Y and Great Canadian came to an agreement.

I have never been able to reach Walter Soo to ask questions about the *China Sea Discovery* and Soo's role building VIP gambling at River Rock Casino. Through his lawyer, Soo has claimed that my reports naming him as an executive at River Rock Casino have defamed him.

And in testimony for the Cullen Commission in 2021, Soo claimed that Ross McLeod tasked him with building River Rock's Chinese VIP business, and his superiors tossed him under the bus after I started reporting on casino money-laundering.

"Media reporting about issues related to money-laundering at River Rock Casino intensified around September 2017," Soo wrote in an affidavit for the inquiry. "Great Canadian had just been awarded a contract … to operate casinos in the Greater Toronto Area. There was a concern with Great Canadian's senior executive group that this media coverage might jeopardize this contract … [They] began to distance themselves from me."

Soo also testified that he never met Cheng Yu Tung, and he "never had a relationship with Paul King Jin … and had no awareness of Mr. Jin's activities."

But numerous records filed with the inquiry showed that Soo and other Great Canadian executives repeatedly wrote confidential business plans aimed at juicing River Rock's revenue via the Macau VIP market, including seeking VIP bet limits up to $150,000 and proposing deals with "player agents" that would deliver Chinese VIPs to River Rock for fees.

One of Soo's confidential memos, filed in October 2014, proposed expanding River Rock's VIP tables into an area formerly housing security staff, and building an "inner sanctum" that would be "more appealing to the Chinese [and] Macau VIPs."

The logic of Soo's business case was stunning.

"China Central Government's anti-corruption and flight capital campaign will escalate in 2015 thus diverting a fair portion of VIP Baccarat play from Macau to River Rock Casino ... the effect of this action will divert affluent Chinese travelers to the Vancouver region to avoid unwanted profile in their home country ... [and] the United States' campaign against illicit money-laundering ... will continue to intensify its investigation into governance of Las Vegas companies operating in Macau ... [therefore] PRC VIPs will encounter more restrictions in Macau and Las Vegas ... diverting their play to River Rock Casino."

If this memo doesn't prove some form of wilful blindness, I don't know what will.

In a prepared response to my questions for Global News on the *China Sea Discovery* investigation, Great Canadian did not answer specific questions about Cheng Yu Tung's alleged involvement with Great Canadian, or directly address claims made by former employees.

"Any attempt to extrapolate from this business venture, while relying on the comments of former Great Canadian employees or innuendo, significantly risks doing a disservice to your readers," Great Canadian stated in 2018, adding the company was a minority partner in the short-lived *China Sea Discovery* venture.

***

It was entirely irrelevant for the *China Sea Discovery* case, according to Great Canadian's lawyer. But Proka Avramovic wanted to talk about loan sharking in B.C. casinos. His testimony, for me, supported allegations of potential regulatory corruption in B.C.'s government, contained in an RCMP report later filed by Fred Pinnock's unit.

Avramovic was asked why he had left his job with Great Canadian in 2003.

"The main purpose of me leaving Great Canadian Casino was I didn't want to get involved in some stuff that they were illegal," Avramovic said. "Loan sharks activities, and selected barring of loan sharks."

Selected barring of loan sharks? Avramovic was asked what that meant.

"Well, I notice that the company and some people at the head office, including my director, were very selective who they're going to bar," Avramovic said. "One of the security and surveillance managers meeting, I've been advised by my director, who was Boki Sikimic, that I supposed to direct my people to turn their heads the other way when they see those big loan sharks around. Because that's good for business. So some loan sharks were allowed to stay, and some small-timer loan sharks were asked to leave."

Following Avramovic's testimony that day in Texas, Sikimic, Great Canadian Gaming's former top security official, corroborated the jarring claim.

Management turned a blind eye to loan sharks and B.C.'s government knew it.

"I was afraid for my life, and the life of my family, if I go further," Sikimic said. "Everything dealing with loan sharks. The activity, it's the biggest problem. Government is — they know what's going on."

Allegiance's lawyer asked Sikimic to explain how loan sharks operated.

"I give you $10,000 and tomorrow you're going to give me $11,000. Next week it's $15,000. Two weeks after that, it's your car. Doesn't matter if it's Mercedes, BMW or whatever. You sign the car, we lend the money, and if you don't pay? We probably go break your legs or do something else. There was shooting. There was people found dead in the car. And everything was connected to the loan sharks. So it's not a group of people that you would mess with."

Sikimic was asked whether he reported the loan sharks to his managers.

"I did report and they knew," he said. "The first [report] they actually barred 19 people from loan sharking. But you bar 19, the top three stays there. And they bring another 15 runners and they keep doing that. It's just — it's a part of the casino."

Sikimic was asked how a casino could benefit by allowing loan sharks to operate. Simple, he said. Revenue.

"If you don't have money with you, you stop playing."

Allegiance's lawyer pressed Sikimic on the chain of command. "You said there was someone else that told you to leave the loan sharking alone," the lawyer said. "What I'm asking you is what the name of that person is. And what position that person held with the company, please."

Sikimic named Great Canadian Gaming's Richmond casino manager, Adrian Thomas.

"On the way we discuss that," Sikimic said. "And yes. We leave some of them alone, we kick some of them out."

Great Canadian's lawyer objected to Sikimic's answer, calling it "totally incomprehensible."

So Allegiance's lawyer tried again.

"Okay. When you said [Adrian Thomas] told you to kick some of them out and leave some of them alone, what do you mean by that?"

"So we're going to go and we're going to kick John and Peter, because they're small times, to show everybody that we are doing something," Sikimic answered. "And we're going to leave Mike and Al alone. Because they're big-timers."

Great Canadian Gaming's lawyer objected to Sikimic's statements about loan sharks. And the allegations were not proven in a trial.

But in a 2004 sworn statement, Nebojsa Kalajdzic, another member of Sikimic's security team, claimed: "It is well known among the employees of Great Canadian Gaming who work at the casinos that loan sharking in and around the casinos is widespread and that it is tolerated by management."

"I have been told by my supervisor and others at Great Canadian to 'look the other way' when I see loan sharking activities take place," Kalajdzic's statement alleged. "I also know that some staff members and supervisors at Great Canadian Casinos assist loan sharks by telling them which customers have been losing and how much they lost. Loan sharking increases the revenues."

Kalajdzic also claimed that in 2002, he was assigned to evict some loan sharks from Great Canadian's Richmond and Vancouver casinos, because there were "as many loan sharks as players at the tables."

"When we arrived at the Richmond casino and informed the casino manager ... what we were intending to do, we were told to ignore certain known loan sharks who were in the casino and only to evict others," Kalajdzic alleged.

For me, these statements corroborated some of the allegations made in Muriel Labine's "casino diary" records, which were filed as evidence in B.C.'s money-laundering inquiry after Global News told Labine's story.

According to Labine, when she took workplace safety concerns about loan sharks and gangs to Adrian Thomas her complaints were brushed aside. Eventually, Thomas asked for a private meeting in the Richmond casino, Labine said. And Thomas asked Labine if she was concerned about safety.

"I said yes, I was. I knew there were gangs in the casino, and this was no longer a safe place to work," Labine told me. "He said: 'You have nothing to worry about. These are only Asian gangs.'"

Labine said she was stunned, but Thomas said something that bothered her even more.

"He then said to me: 'I have made a deal. They won't shit in their own nest.'"

"I couldn't believe what I was hearing," Labine told me. "He said he had made a deal with the other casino gangs, too, that there were at other locations. I was totally shocked. This was my workplace, and he tells me they won't shit in their nest. When did my workplace become their nest?"

In interviews with me, Adrian Thomas denied Labine's allegations and said she had an axe to grind with him.

But Thomas says the meeting with Labine did occur, and "shit in their own nest" is probably a comment he made. The language was familiar to me, too.

In a previous interview, Adrian Thomas had told me that he personally issued a strong message to Lai Changxing, the associate of Big Circle Boys Betty Yan and Kwok Chung Tam.

"I told him this is our business and we don't want any problems with his boys," Thomas recalled. "We had security and backup. These guys don't shit in their nest."

But there was never any deal made with Asian gangs, Thomas repeatedly stressed to me.

"If anybody comes out and says that, I will demand to know who it is and I will have them in goddamn court and I will prove it," Thomas told me. "Absolute bullshit. I didn't have any dealings, and nor did anyone at the company, as far as I know, have any dealings with any bad guys or any gangs. Certainly not to do with drugs or money lending."

***

In the 2004 Texas court case, Avramovic also alleged that casino staff were coached on how not to report loan sharking. Avramovic pointed directly to a former B.C. Gaming Policy Enforcement Branch (GPEB) employee who took a job with Great Canadian Gaming.

"He's been explaining how to avoid to report everything to the authorities," Avramovic testified.

Avramovic testified, and also told me, that he reported many corruption allegations to B.C. Lottery Corp. and GPEB, including the allegation that Lai Changxing had raped the relative of a prominent Great Canadian Gaming employee.

"I've been told by both agencies that information is going to be processed [but] right now it's not good time because it's expansion of the gaming industry."

In cross-examination, Great Canadian's lawyer challenged Avramovic's testimony. Great Canadian denied wrongdoing in the case, and it has been settled out of court.

But Avramovic was left believing B.C.'s government purposely ignored the red flags he raised in the early 2000s. That's why he decided to go public in 2004, and revealed his allegations about loan sharking in an interview broadcast by the CBC.

"Upon my arrival back from China[from the *China Sea Discovery*], I felt that I had to do something more regarding loan sharks in Lower Mainland casinos," Avramovic told me in 2018. "Because I saw some of the familiar faces, from the time sailing on the casino ship in the China Sea."

His reward for blowing the whistle in 2004, according to Avramovic, was that the minister responsible for B.C. Lottery casinos, Solicitor-General Rich Coleman, harshly discredited him.

***

The Gaming Policy Enforcement Branch was set up in 2002 by Rich Coleman, after his B.C. Liberal government reviewed the casino expansion that was started under NDP premier Glen Clark, who lost his job in the late 1990s casino-gate licensing scandal.

GPEB was staffed with accomplished former RCMP officers, investigators familiar with serious crimes, drug-trafficking, and gangs. Under B.C.'s new Gaming Control Act, GPEB was supposed to have seven investigators in Metro Vancouver casinos. But from the start, they were woefully understaffed.

They were given oversight of B.C. Lottery Corp., technically, but didn't have the same powers as police. And the Lottery Corp. executives seemed to lord it over them. Right away, GPEB leaders couldn't help noticing the elephant in the room. Solicitor-General Rich Coleman oversaw both arms, the casino administrator and the regulator. He was a hulking man, about 6'4" and built like an NFL lineman. He was a former RCMP officer turned real estate developer turned politician. And people who have disagreed with him say he has little time for disagreements.

It was a huge conflict of interest, the money-making machine and the regulatory arm serving the same master, GPEB's leaders felt. They also felt B.C. Lottery executives had better access to Coleman than GPEB's brass.

A B.C. ombudsman's report in 2007 was the first warning of systemic problems between GPEB and the Lottery Corp. as B.C.'s money-printing machine rocketed skyward.

"The British Columbia Lottery Corporation is big business. The business is legal gaming in British Columbia, and the biggest 'winner' since 1985 has been consecutive provincial governments," the report said. Total revenues for 2006 were $2.26 billion, the report said, and most of the revenue came from several Vancouver-area casinos.

The report found that Lottery Corp. retailers were winning lotteries at inexplicably higher rates than consumers, and that senior Lottery Corp. managers knew about complaints of corruption but failed to audit for systemic problems. Furthermore, the Lottery Corp. was supposed to forward all reports of suspected criminal activity to GPEB, in Section 86 Gaming Control Act reports. But they weren't doing it.

The ombudsman didn't look at casinos in the 2007 report. But the failure to share Section 86 reports with GPEB is extremely problematic. Some in GPEB felt this could have allowed the deadly cancer of loan sharking to grow in B.C. casinos.

And it wasn't a big mental leap for GPEB investigators to believe that damaging reports on loan sharking were buried by the Lottery Corp.

***

Fred Pinnock took over the B.C. Integrated Illegal Gaming Enforcement Team (IIGET) in 2005. The unit was set up in 2003 because the RCMP's robust illegal gambling contingent from the 1970s had dwindled to just one gambling expert in B.C. by the 1990s.

But the unit wasn't getting traction. A couple of commanding officers rotated out before Pinnock took over.

His first official act was attending a joint conference with GPEB's leaders at a resort in Kelowna. From his three years overseeing the B.C. RCMP confidential informant unit, he knew that transnational and domestic organized crime was deep inside Canadian casinos.

But GPEB wasn't targeting casinos from the top of the criminal food-chain.

They were competent but focused on the low-hanging fruit, Pinnock felt. And IIGET — as far as Pinnock understood the circumstances — had no mandate to enter B.C. Lottery Corp. casinos. The deal with Rich Coleman's ministry was IIGET only touched illegal gaming.

It was insane when you turned it over in your mind. RCMP's special gambling enforcement unit was barred from entering government casinos. But big loan sharks were not.

So Pinnock stood up in Kelowna and said it point blank: "We need to target crime in gambling from a higher level than we have been so far. And we need to target inside the Lottery Corp. casinos."

The call to arms didn't have the effect of what Pinnock expected. You could hear a pin drop. After a few seconds, there was a derisive guffaw.

Looking back, for Pinnock, this was the start of the end of his policing career.

The way that Solicitor-General Rich Coleman had set IIGET up was B.C. Lottery Corp. would fund IIGET's costs, for about $1.5 million per year. And in practice there was no deviating from the unit's founding mission. IIGET was only to target underground casinos, illegal lotteries, pyramid schemes, illegal internet gambling and esoteric crimes like cockfighting.

The consulting board responsible for the unit's direction included the B.C. Lottery Corp. chief executive, the head of RCMP's federal police in B.C., and the manager of GPEB.

Right there in the mandate — the funding, the oversight — Pinnock and some GPEB officers felt there was something strange.

There was one story about a board meeting, where the Lottery Corp. representative barked, "What am I getting for my money!"

The story rang true. I had read internal documents where a Lottery Corp. executive had reiterated to GPEB brass that his staff had identified a big illegal casino in Richmond. What was GPEB doing about it?

Pinnock was feeling this weirdness directly. He knew his first official statement as IIGET boss made him unpopular. He was feeling the vibe from his commanders, like 'stay in your lane Pinnock, what's wrong with you?'

And some comments started filtering down that blew his mind.

The vision for IIGET was for you to kick over some common gaming houses so that these guys would come into the casinos, Pinnock recalled hearing once.

What?

There were many underground casinos in Burnaby and East Vancouver, run by Big Circle Boys and also some Italian mafia and Hells Angels. This was big business. The Asian and Italian mobs were running sports betting books too. You had to be blind or stupid to miss the connection. Organized crime didn't see divisions between legal and illegal casinos.

But the message settling in Pinnock's mind — and it felt like sacrilege to think it — was B.C.'s government wanted to crush the illegal casinos just for the sake of diverting criminal proceeds into Lottery Corp. casinos. There was no high moral purpose of fighting crime.

Someone even told him outright. The feeling from upper regions in Victoria was IIGET needed to eradicate the underground casinos in Burnaby and East Vancouver, "so the gambling addicts can be directed into legal casinos, where we have programs to help gambling addiction."

Bullshit, Pinnock thought. The government just wants that revenue.

But you would have to be crazy to think B.C.'s government coveted the dirty cash running through illegal casinos, wouldn't you?

The answer was no. Other people were wondering the same thing.

As Pinnock continued to bang his head into walls with his unit, there was an independent review of IIGET's effectiveness and mandate in 2007.

And it said Lottery Corp. funding of IIGET looked like a conflict of interest.

"Some interviewed for this review question BCLC's role in funding IIGET, which focuses on illegal gaming that occurs away from legal gaming venues," the review said. "Some people also raised a concern about the appropriateness of BCLC presence at IIGET consultative board meetings where confidential information regarding investigations is presented."

It was spelled out even more clearly by Larry Vander Graaf, director of the GPEB investigations division. In his official response to the

IIGET mandate review, he said the B.C. government and the Lottery Corp. had it wrong if they thought they could improve the integrity of legal gambling by targeting illegal casinos.

"How illegal gaming enforcement could affect legal gaming, other than possibly from a revenue standpoint in legal gaming, cannot be envisioned," he wrote. "Protecting the assets or revenue in legal gaming by eliminating competition in illegal gaming is not an integrity issue. We believe that may even be perceived as a conflict of interest."

And Vander Graaf left no guessing at his meaning with this conclusion.

"Our investigators, as witnesses giving evidence on the stand, have been accused of being a government enforcement body set up solely to eliminate competition for government controlled legalized gaming venues."

***

Pinnock believed he had accomplished something impossible in a supposed country of law like Canada. For having the temerity to suggest the RCMP should target organized crime in B.C. Lottery Corp. casinos, he'd become the whipping boy of B.C.'s justice establishment.

He felt he was on a collision course with Rich Coleman's deputies.

The tension came to a head when one of them demanded that Pinnock share stats on RCMP take-downs of illegal casinos.

"Statistical analyses of criminal code activity within the realm of illegal gaming will remain the responsibility of the police and not GPEB," Pinnock wrote to Coleman's deputy in March 2006. "Given the nature of our relationship with [B.C.] government, it is incumbent upon me to protect our IIGET operations from the appearance of political interference at all costs. It is inappropriate for GPEB to be commenting upon policing matters."

The emails and comments that came back made Pinnock feel he'd infuriated B.C.'s government. And several of Pinnock's commanders were responsible for handling the RCMP's B.C. provincial policing contract. They dealt directly with Coleman's deputies.

Pinnock felt sure his RCMP bosses were now getting angry calls about his stance on IIGET's mandate.

He was tired of banging his head against the wall. Conflicts with GPEB, conflicts with RCMP brass, conflicts with Coleman's deputies. It was starting to feel again like his childhood in Ottawa. The little bookworm getting his face rubbed in the snow. All because I'm refusing to play the game, he thought. I've stepped in the path of the gravy train.

But he was used to taking punishment. Instead of backing down, he went all in.

He submitted a new strategic vision for IIGET's consulting board, complete with recommendations he believed could make a serious dent in Canada's money-laundering problems.

His unit was down to three people. He said he needed about 25 officers to cover illegal casinos and legal casinos, systematically, all at once.

Because at the highest levels — the evidence was clear — legal and illegal casinos were the same economy. The same loan sharks, the same gangs, the same whales, the same cash flowing between Lottery Corp. baccarat tables and the hidden tables in luxurious Vancouver mansions. Even the same bloody Lottery Corp. casino chips and the same card dealers. It really was that simple.

So he laid it all out.

And Pinnock's findings combined with those of a new IIGET unit commander, Wayne Holland, were filed with B.C.'s government in a confidential January 2009 report.

"Illegal and legal gaming share the same issues, such as loan sharking, extortions, assaults, kidnappings and murders," the IIGET report said. "And besides sharing some of the same criminal issues, illegal and legal gaming have been interlinked when, in some cases, casino staff have directed patrons to loan sharks or to common gaming houses. Some casino staff have also been known to act as card dealers in common gaming houses."

It was the same type of allegation that Proka Avramovic said he had secretly reported to B.C.'s government in the early 2000s. Loan sharks approached casino staff, Avramovic and one of his colleagues told me, and offered to bribe them and work with them.

And the January 2009 IIGET report made it clear — if there was any doubt — that money-laundering between legal and illegal casinos was a serious integrity concern for B.C.'s government.

"The organized crime section of this report emphasizes the potential for serious problems regarding legal and illegal gaming in B.C.," the report says. "Illegal gaming can be a source of income for criminal organizations and, through the infiltration of legitimate gaming venues, they can also launder, and transfer money easily."

The report contains one passage with two stunning allegations. In my investigation, the importance of these allegations can't be exaggerated. When I finally obtained this confidential IIGET report in late 2019, after years of legal applications, this specific paragraph felt to me like the final puzzle piece in my collection of thousands of casino money-laundering records.

It was a smoking gun.

I recognized this crucial passage could connect to my investigation of the *China Sea Discovery* fiasco. It could connect to Garry Clement's and Brian McAdam's corruption investigations in Macau and Hong Kong in the 1990s. I felt that it had to connect with some information I had received — from an RCMP source — about undisclosed RCMP investigations in Hong Kong and Macau in the early 2000s.

The RCMP source had contacted me after an independent review of money-laundering in B.C. casinos was released in 2018. The source said the review by former RCMP executive Peter German didn't even get close to the bottom of Canada's casino problems.

"There were direct links from Macau to B.C. casinos to Las Vegas," the source told me. He said a team of investigators travelled to Macau and looked at "the set of casinos in Macau and the role different Chinese organized crime gangs played in owning the various parts of the casinos."

In my analysis, the smoking gun paragraph in the IIGET report meant this: a man connected to Chinese organized crime had owned a portion of a B.C. Lottery casino; B.C.'s government had been in business with organized crime; and the government was potentially involved in regulatory corruption.

"A conflict of interest or perception of corruption undermines the integrity of gaming in British Columbia," the 2009 IIGET report warned. "One subject, connected to Asian Organized Crime, was allowed to buy into a casino. Open-source information indicates that he is now dead, but his casino business associates also have Asian Organized Crime connections. The regulatory investigator involved in the share transfer process is alleged to have known about these connections when this subject originally bought into a casino. The regulatory investigator is now retired from the provincial government. However, he still appears to be involved in the legitimate gaming industry."

For my investigation, it becomes much easier to understand how VIPs from China were allowed to carry hockey bags of cash into Metro Vancouver casinos if the explosive facts alleged in this passage are true.

The reason is obvious. Organized crime loan sharks, organized crime whales, organized crime casino investors? Money-laundering of narco-dollars going into the casino via gangsters. And money-laundering going out of the casino and into Canadian bank vaults and casino stock shares. Organized crime clipping both sides of the coupon. Like Las Vegas casinos in the 1940s.

The IIGET report is a "protected A" version that redacts the identity of the alleged Asian organized crime figure, the B.C. casino that he reportedly bought a piece of, and the GPEB investigator who allegedly turned a blind eye before retiring from government and taking a job with a B.C. casino company.

There are good clues about the identities of the alleged players.

But at the time of this book's publishing, my efforts to learn their names in documents have been blocked by Canada's privacy laws. I do not have the powers of justice officials — or the Cullen Commission into money-laundering in B.C. — to subpoena the documents that will reveal their names. And I can't obtain cabinet-privileged documents from the B.C. Liberal or NDP governments that could answer my questions.

But I believe the Cullen Commission must discover all facts related to the Asian organized crime casino ownership allegations. If the commission doesn't, it will have failed in its mandate to probe whether regulatory corruption allowed organized crime and money-laundering to drive B.C.'s economy.

***

The IIGET report contained many more stunning cases that underlined why Fred Pinnock believed the unit's mandate had to be altered.

Chinese organized crime was the main player in illegal casinos. In one 12-block strip of Kingsway Avenue there were at least nine underground casinos.

But the locations shuffled so frequently and ownership of the properties was so slippery, they were hard to shut down. The number of casinos located in otherwise uninhabited luxury homes in Metro Vancouver was not even addressed.

But in one South Granville home operated as an illegal casino, IIGET found that eight Malaysian women were working as prostitutes. One was selling her body in Vancouver to pay off gambling debts in Asia. As I reported for Global News, former Crown prosecutor and prominent B.C. casino industry critic Sandy Garrossino believed the IIGET report connected Asian organized crime in B.C. casinos to human trafficking and sex slavery in Asia.

But it is the report's detailing of vicious loan-sharking rings and massive money-laundering with connections between casinos and banksthat made IIGET's call for increased resources to attack gangs in Lottery Corp. casinos a slam dunk.

There were at least seven major loan-sharking rings operating in Metro Vancouver casinos — about 50 known loan sharks — and they perpetrated horrific violence.

In May 2006, "the eight-year-old daughter and the six-year-old son of a common gaming house operator were abducted at gun-point," the report says. "The children were told by the kidnapper that their father owed $300,000. A neighbour saw the children climb out of the trunk of a stolen vehicle, and called police. They were recovered safely."

In another case, an illegal casino employee was abducted outside his Vancouver home, thrown into a car with a hood over his face, pistol whipped and stabbed repeatedly, then dumped beside a forest road in Coquitlam. He was told he would be killed next time if he didn't pay a $30,000 debt.

Also in May 2006, Richmond loan shark Rong Lilly Li was murdered outside River Rock Casino. She was a government registered River Rock employee and also a loan shark inside the casino, and was last seen alive on security camera footage walking out of River Rock's grand entrance.

She was lured into a gold-coloured van by two high-rollers who believed she would have up to $300,000 in her purse.

When Li sat down, the killer, Chu Ming Feng, and his accomplice, Guo Wei Liang, whipped a black leather belt around her neck and pulled it tight.

"Why are you doing this — I only have one daughter," were her last choked words. The murderers found only $2,000 in casino chips and $500 cash in her purse, and they dumped her in a shallow grave at a

Vancouver beach. Chu Ming Feng was convicted of murder, but his accomplice, Liang, was never found.

In another case, a woman borrowed $500,000 to gamble at River Rock Casino.

"She was able to pay $200,000 back by using her house as collateral to borrow money from the bank, but she still owed $300,000," the report says. "The loan shark threatened that if she did not come up with the money, her place of business and her house would be burned down, and she would be killed."

There was another murder and an attempted murder at two Vancouver underground casinos in 2007.

Also in 2007, the report said, the owner of a Richmond online gambling company, Po Ho Cheung, was found shot to death in his Cadillac, parked outside his east Vancouver home. His gambling company was linked to Nevada, Costa Rica, and the United Kingdom.

Cheung had been charged in 2001 with laundering hundreds of thousands in drug money. But federal prosecutors dropped the charges because they were focused on the drug traffickers he was working for rather than casino money-laundering.

He was facilitating currency refining.

He was able to deliver stacks of $20s from drug traffickers to his many whale gambler associates, and the high-rollers could exchange the dirty $20s for clean $1,000 bills.

"A lot of criminal organizations have colossal amounts of cash, mostly small bills, in their possession," the IIGET report explained. "The purpose of refining is to decrease the bulk of large quantities of cash by exchanging small denominations for larger ones, in order to more easily introduce the illegally-gained funds into the financial system. This initial step also serves to distance the dirty money from its initial source by trading bills that are often filthy, torn and sometimes contaminated, for new ones."

And the report pointed to numerous examples of these bulk cash transactions in B.C. Lottery casinos.

In one case, in just one year, a Vancouver bank employee bought chips with cash at four Metro Vancouver casinos, for a total of $4.9 million.

"In June 2007 alone, he purchased casino chips worth $3.287 million."

Another man who frequented the River Rock Casino, the Starlight Casino in New Westminster, the Edgewater Casino in Vancouver, and the Gateway Casino in Burnaby logged 285 large cash transaction reports, for a total of C$8.7 million and US$62,000.

And the RCMP knew this wasn't just a B.C. problem. The report said, "Many investigations across the country have shown that members of organized crime also use casinos for loan sharking and money-laundering and that some of these criminal elements have successfully infiltrated the industry."

The report said illegal sports betting was also believed to be a massive business connected to legal and illegal casinos. IIGET had received a request from Hong Kong police to identify a Vancouver phone number believed to be connected to a Chinese bookmaking ring. One Chinese bookie reportedly took bets of up to $200,000. The Sicilian and Calabrian mafias were involved in casinos and bookmaking too.

In 2001, an investigation "surfaced bets of $4 million per week, the whole operation driven by the Rizzuto Organized Crime group out of Montreal."

Targets in Quebec were charged, but there were no charges in B.C., probably because the RCMP had no illegal gambling experts, the report said.

Aside from providing mind-blowing evidence of criminality in B.C. casinos, the report indicated that Canada's anti-money-laundering system was a sham.

Fintrac had provided B.C. police with evidence of $40 million in suspected casino money-laundering transactions in several years.

In Canada's dirty money reporting system, which the Ministry of Finance administered in Ottawa, police can't directly access Fintrac's data for privacy reasons. But they are supposed to follow up on Fintrac's criminal case disclosures.

But the report found that "police managers have suggested that because of other resources and lack of resources at this time, nothing is being done to investigate these situations."

The January 2009 report concluded with a number of recommendations, including instituting the type of racketeering laws that enabled the United States government to weaken Italian mafia families that had held jurisdictions such as New York City in a stranglehold.

Recommendations included:

- Use other charges such as criminal organization charges, conspiracy charges, proceeds of crime legislation or civil forfeiture to combat illegal gaming.

- Use Revenue Canada to investigate offenders and take the profit out of illegal gaming.

- Use immigration laws for the deportation of certain offenders.

- That IIGET be the central database for all gaming-related criminal information in B.C. (Gaming-related criminal activities are handled by many different police jurisdictions, which serves to fragment operations and is not intelligence-led policing.)

- That IIGET would follow a similar system to Ontario's provincially funded Organized Crime Section Illegal Gambling Unit, which offers services to all police agencies in Ontario.

- That IIGET will lead a province-wide co-ordinated attack on organized crime in B.C. illegal gaming.

- IIGET will have a significant increase in resources with 25 full-time officers supported by analysts.

- A dedicated B.C. Crown prosecutor trained in illegal gaming and money-laundering would be assigned to handle IIGET charges.

- There will be mandatory illegal gaming training for all police officers trained in RCMP federal programs and B.C. police training programs.

But the recommendations were ignored.

***

Fred Pinnock tried to keep his hands on the steering wheel as his heart raced and stabs of pain rocked him against the driver seat. He made it only two blocks. He eased over to the curb and braced himself. I'm having a damn heart attack, he said.

He had just left IIGET's semi-annual meeting with GPEB and RCMP brass. His boss — the man directly responsible for maintaining the RCMP's provincial contract with Rich Coleman's ministry — had wrenched around in a chair and started screaming at him in front of everyone.

Pinnock sat in his car and caught his breath. Just then another commanding officer called him. Pinnock, it just isn't working. The best thing is to fall on your sword. He drove home and decided to leave the force. But his plan to expand IIGET was pressed forward by his successor in late 2008.

A review of the unit's effectiveness had been completed.

"A decision to discontinue IIGET at this point does not seem appropriate," the review had said.

But in April 2009, B.C.'s government did disband IIGET, citing funding pressures at B.C. Lottery Corp., the money machine that took in about $2.6 billion per year and forwarded over $1 billion in revenue to the government.

Pinnock was so disturbed by the decision that he burned his police files. One thing that helped him through the pain was the hope that someday, there would be a public inquiry into B.C. casino money-laundering.

Pinnock knew what he'd say if called to testify. He had concluded that his bosses didn't care about public safety. They didn't care about fighting organized crime, about gambling addicts, about murders, about kids tossed into cars at gunpoint, about thousands of heroin and fentanyl addicts dying in the Downtown Eastside, about money laundered into Vancouver's glass towers.

Inside, he knew it. There was no way the RCMP's leaders in B.C. would anger their masters in Ottawa by conflicting with B.C.'s government and endangering the provincial policing contract.

These guys don't give a shit about public safety, he told himself. It was all designed to maximize revenues.

These accusations were difficult to prove. But Pinnock had a way to test his theory.

He sent an emissary — his girlfriend, MLA Naomi Yamamoto — to convey a message to Rich Coleman.

He had to know whether his reporting at IIGET had made it up to Coleman's desk. He had to know — with the damning evidence IIGET put forward in January 2009 — how any government could choose to disband the unit.

And so Yamamoto passed the message: Fred Pinnock wants you to know there are major criminal problems in our government casinos. He wants to meet with you to discuss this.

Due to BC Liberal party rules, Yamamoto couldn't inform Pinnock what Coleman had said when she approached him in a cabinet meeting.

But she characterized Coleman's response as brutal, dismissive and embarrassing to her, Pinnock says. Coleman was furious, Pinnock concluded, because he didn't want the cabinet to see him being informed of gangs in B.C. Lottery casinos. So the shitshow would continue.

For my story with Global News on the 2009 IIGET report, the former B.C. prosecutor Sandy Garossino reviewed the report's details.

"It is stunning to me that any government official would be provided this information, and the solicitor general's response was, rather than to grant police the resources they were seeking, to do the reverse and disband this unit," Garossino said. "Children were kidnapped and murders took place in the pursuit of money, and the provincial government knew it. You have every appearance of human trafficking and women forced into prostitution. It's not just that they did nothing, but they actively disbanded this unit. So it is as if that is an intervention in making the police stop from looking at the corruption they wanted to probe."

And Denis Meunier, former deputy director of Fintrac, also reviewed the report for me. He called the revelations explosive.

"For licensing, casinos are expected to conduct due diligence on the owners, the employees and any associates to ensure criminals and their associates are nowhere near casino ownership or operations," Meunier said. "In my view, if [the criminal casino ownership allegations] were reported to anyone [in B.C. government and RCMP] and they were not further investigated, there is a breach. Because there is a fiduciary or legal responsibility to the public. This is shocking."

Rich Coleman did not respond to my repeated interview requests.

But he provided this statement in January 2020: "As you know, Justice Austin Cullen is expected to begin his inquiry into these matters this spring. I have full confidence that Justice Cullen will do his work thoroughly, and as I've stated previously, I will cooperate with him should I be requested to. I will also say that as Minister, I carried out my fiduciary and legal duties and to insinuate otherwise would be incorrect."

10
KILLING THE GOLDEN GOOSE

"He loses his chips and stalks around like a caged tiger
for a minute and then rushes out of the casino."

In 2010, while Canada celebrated the Winter Olympics in Vancouver and the city was heralded as a global model of prosperity and livability — a small group of GPEB and RCMP investigators were in a different mood. The way Calvin Chrustie saw it, Vancouver was sort of like one of those exotically colored tropical fish. On the surface, it's beautiful. But the flesh is toxic. So in Vancouver, under the sparkling veneer of wealth and health, torrents of dark money from China were flooding the casinos and empty condo towers. A new financial system based on secretive transactions had become the city's economic centre of gravity. The two dominant sources of liquidity at opposite poles: drug money and capital flight from Mainland China.

In a November 24, 2010, letter to the Lottery Corp. executives, GPEB's director of casino investigations, Derek Dickson, wrote that he was very concerned by a "dramatic increase" in suspicious cash transactions involving numerous patrons at Vancouver-area casinos.

"It typically involves well-known LCT [large cash transaction] patrons that play baccarat and arrive with cash as a buy-in," Dickson wrote. "We believe BCLC needs to seek solutions to the obvious, and increasing, money-laundering that is occurring, particularly involving the flood of small denomination currency, within B.C. casinos."

Dickson pointed to one particular high-roller, Li Lin Sha, who completed $3.9 million in cash buy-ins in just eight weeks.

Sha, who was supposed to own coal mines in China, was one of the Jin network's all-time top clients. In the two-month binge, Sha used almost all $20s. Night after night, he brought in about $200,000 cash — wrapped in rubber bands in bricks of $10,000 — stashed in gym bags. In one case, Sha quickly lost $330,000 playing baccarat.

A GPEB investigator who viewed the incriminating surveillance tape couldn't get over the imagery.

"He loses his chips and stalks around like a caged tiger for a minute and then rushes out of the casino."

Li Lin Sha was immediately met by a car at the casino's front door and handed "an object" from the trunk. And he walked back inside to gamble with the contents of the bag — $325,000 in casino chips.

In his letter, Dickson informed the Lottery Corp. that he and GPEB director Joe Schalk had met with Inspector Barry Baxter of the RCMP's Integrated Proceeds of Crime (IPOC) team, "and they are well aware of the issue and are seriously concerned that the casinos are being used as a method to launder large sums of money for organized crime groups."

But the Lottery Corp. refused to accept this view.

As long as these foreign baccarat high-rollers presented a picture I.D., claimed to be involved in a business of some sort, and had some history of gambling in B.C. government casinos, the Lottery Corp. considered the cash clean. No questions asked.

And in an argument that particularly galled GPEB, the Lottery Corp. asserted that Chinese VIPs had a cultural preference for gambling with bags of cash — for them, cash was lucky — so it was inappropriate to invade their privacy and view duffel bags of cash with suspicion.

This was the kind of stupidity that burned Joe Schalk, a former RCMP officer. Schalk and his GPEB colleagues were getting the feeling that B.C.'s government actually welcomed dirty money from visitors who claimed to be 'industrialists.'

"There could or may be a significant difference between what a person 'states' and what is real. Financial institutions do not simply go by way of what a person 'states,'" Schalk wrote to Lottery Corp. executives.

"B.C. Lottery Corp. has stated for years they are instituting a 'rigorous anti-money-laundering strategy.' However, over just the past ten months, reported incidents of suspicious currency transactions and money-laundering have more than tripled over the previous year."

Meanwhile, Fintrac records showed the Lottery Corp. had made 37,000 large cash transaction reports — casino chip purchases of at least $10,000 per transaction — in 2009. The large transaction reports would surge to 70,000 in 2012. And Lottery Corp's. casinos would rake in $1.6 billion in gross revenue. It was almost all cash, almost all from the "upstairs" private baccarat rooms in a few casinos around Richmond and Vancouver, and the lion's share was coming from an extremely small portion of Chinese whales.

But you could almost set your watch to it.

Every five years or so, a scandalous B.C. Lottery Corp. story would surface, and the government would have to respond to the waves of media attention.

In January 2011, a CBC story exposed the sharp divide between Dickson, Schalk and Baxter on one side and the senior B.C. officials that Fred Pinnock had already clashed with on the other.

In just three months in 2010 there were 90 large cash transactions at the River Rock Casino in Richmond and the Starlight in New Westminster, CBC reported, for a total of $8 million.

And while the dollar value of suspicious transactions had tripled in B.C. Lottery Corp. casinos in 2010, the stats had dropped or remained the same in casinos across the rest of Canada.

In the Starlight Casino, in the spring of 2010, GPEB reports showed that a man carrying a bag with $1.2 million in casino chips walked in and immediately asked staff to convert the chips to cash.

The VIP — Yu Xiang Zhang — wanted to fly to a Montreal casino but he was concerned that customs officials would be suspicious of his luggage — about 115 pounds worth of paper bills. He was the biggest gambler in B.C. at the time, according to GPEB's report. So he requested a confirmation letter from the casino saying the money was a casino payout. And the staff gave the man his letter. And here's the stunner. Senior casino staff knew Zhang was supplied by a barred loan shark, Ms. Lo. She was a suspect in Kwok Tam and Paul Jin's Big Circle Boys network, linked to cash deliveries and underground banking with the biggest baccarat players in Richmond. And an RCMP officer later looked at Dickson's case and said the casino had effectively handed Yu Xiang Zhang a "get out of jail free card" if the police tried to investigate him for money-laundering.

Days later, a gambler walked into River Rock Casino with $460,000 in $20 bills and bought chips. The casino reported the large cash transaction, but noted "none of [the man's] actions are suspicious."

The CBC went to River Rock Casino spokesman Howard Blank for comment. And Blank said it was not unusual for gamblers to walk into the casino with bags of $20s, and the summer was unusually busy at the Richmond casino with "a lot of influx of tourism from Southeast Asia, from Mainland China."

"A lot of that money is people who have businesses here, who are taking the money out of their business, and they're coming in, and they're gambling," Blank said.

For GPEB and police experts, this explanation was laughable.

The CBC tracked down Insp. Barry Baxter of IPOC for comment. There was a big problem in B.C. casinos, Baxter said, when the bags of $20s flooding in were recorded as large transactions rather than suspicious transactions.

"We're suspicious that it's dirty money," Baxter said. "The casino industry, in general, was targeted during that time period for what may well be some very sophisticated money-laundering activities by organized crime."

But Baxter's highly public comments made B.C. solicitor-general Rich Coleman livid.

"Yeah, I know what he said, and I don't agree with him, and neither do all the superiors of his in the RCMP," Coleman told the CBC.

This was not true. Baxter's superiors were aware of his comments, and they were approved. Baxter had seen videos of VIPs bringing stacks of cash into private casino cash cages. The GPEB investigators had trailed these VIPs from the casinos to nearby restaurants, luxury vehicles, and parking lots where they took delivery of bags of cash.

And Baxter's superiors knew this.

So in January 2011, the provincial government was in a dilemma.

The latest wave of media stories had come at the most inconvenient time. Coleman's ministry and the RCMP were in the middle of negotiations for the provincial policing contract, due for renewal in early 2012.

Baxter's straight-talk had thrown a wrench in the works. Would the RCMP brass in Ottawa allow a mid-level B.C. officer's words to demonstrate that the RCMP was ready to bite the hand that was feeding it?

Evidently not. A message of some sort was conveyed between the B.C. government and RCMP executives.

"Inspector Baxter was cautioned within the RCMP regarding his comments," an independent review found a number of years later. "Baxter's remarks would be the last public comment by an RCMP officer on any matter related to B.C. casinos for several years."

But silencing casino critics in the RCMP wasn't the only problem. Public outrage was gaining political traction, and Coleman was catching major heat.

"Dear Mr. Coleman, I would like to express my concern regarding recent media reports of suspicious gaming transactions, totalling some $8 million, taking place over a three-month period in 2010 at two Lottery Corp. casinos," one critic wrote in January 2011. "Of serious concern is why did it take the news media to expose these suspicious transactions at casinos before you took action?"

The critic, whose name is redacted in B.C. government records, asked why B.C. casinos couldn't follow the Ontario model, which relied on provincial police officers.

"Organized crime is part and parcel of B.C.'s casino operations and a serious problem at that. Why is there not a police presence right in our casinos to deal immediately and effectively with any suspicious gaming activity? In the province of Ontario, for example, there are plainclothes police in each casino. Why can't we adopt the same procedure in our province?"

The reason, the writer said, was obvious.

"Gaming enforcement is wilfully lacking in our Province's casinos, and it is clear to me that they are being targeted by organized crime groups looking to launder drug money."

And the writer showed that some had paid attention to the disappearance of Fred Pinnock's anti-illegal gaming unit.

"These recent suspicious money transactions also point to the folly of your decision in 2009 to disband the RCMP's integrated illegal gaming enforcement unit. Its demise makes one wonder if your government is really committed to meaningful illegal gaming investigations."

But Coleman countered the writer's observations.

"My ministry regulates all gaming in the province, ensures the integrity of gaming companies, people and equipment," Coleman wrote back. "Despite what is being reported in the media, there are several checks and balances in place to deter criminal activity in casinos. All suspicious transactions of any amount are reported and investigated by my ministry and or local police authorities."

This was not true. As the January 2009 IIGET report filed to Coleman's ministry showed, Fintrac was referring tens of millions' worth of casino money-laundering cases to police in B.C. But no one was investigating.

Yet B.C.'s government had to respond in some way, and quickly, with the clock ticking on the RCMP provincial contract renewal.

So Coleman called on a senior official from his own ministry, B.C.'s civil forfeiture director Rob Kroeker, to complete a review and "identify areas for improvement with regard to the handling of cash transactions."

Kroeker, a lawyer and former RCMP officer, was given until February 2011 to file his report.

Realistically, was Coleman's ministry going to review itself in under two months? I don't think so. But internal documents show that a public relations response was a big part of the plan.

"Potential benefits: This report will respond to high-profile criticism of the Province's efforts to prevent money-laundering in gaming facilities, in media reports starting in January 2011."

The strategic records laid bare the challenges for Coleman's ministry — especially the flameout with Barry Baxter — triggered by media reports that said "the RCMP suspect 'mystery money' transactions may represent drug money-laundering operations."

"The *Vancouver Sun*, among others, reported on differences of opinion between RCMP Insp. Barry Baxter and Solicitor General Rich Coleman," the government records say. "Baxter expressed concern about some casino transactions being reported as 'large' rather than 'suspicious,' asking: 'What is not suspicious about $250,000 in twenties? The average person on the street would go: 'There's something stinky about that.' So why would that be a large transaction and not a suspicious transaction?'"

"But Coleman indicated that Baxter's position was not aligned with that of his RCMP superiors," the government records explained, which was "a position [by Coleman] brought into question later with the release of RCMP documents under the force's freedom-of-information process."

Meanwhile, the communications documents noted, rival politicians were on the attack. In one media report, "opposition NDP critic Shane Simpson found it 'unacceptable' for people to enter casinos with large amounts of $20 bills without arousing suspicions." Even Christy Clark — the federal Liberal politician who was running for B.C. Liberal leadership — was slamming the party, the records said. "We can't have illegal activity going on in British Columbia's casinos," Clark said in one interview. "Part of the reason that casinos work in B.C. and that the public is willing to accept them as part of the revenue generation for government is because they believe, I hope quite rightly, that they're run with ethics and integrity."

So Coleman's casino review would help put these public relations challenges to rest. And his ministry was ready to counter criticism that the review was a hasty inside job.

"Given the high-profile discussion around money-laundering in January, and the sensitive nature of the matters at hand, we wanted to act quickly to strengthen the integrity of gaming as necessary," the ministry's policy records say. "That's why we drew upon staff within the ministry."

Kroeker's review was released in the summer of 2011. And he found that B.C. Lottery Corp. had sufficient anti-money-laundering protections in casinos. But the review acknowledged what was blatantly obvious.

"Gaming is almost entirely a cash business in B.C.," and "this presents opportunities for organized crime."

The report did not estimate the scale of money-laundering in B.C. casinos or recommend the simple remedy that GPEB was asking BCLC to implement: capping VIP buy-ins with $20 bills — the denomination associated with drug trafficking — to under $10,000 per transaction.

Instead, Kroeker recommended that B.C. casinos study ways to transition to electronic funds transactions.

And Coleman's ministry summed up its back-to-business conclusion: "The gaming industry will prevent money-laundering in gaming by moving from a cash-based industry as quickly as possible and scrutinizing the remaining cash for appropriate action. This shift will respect or enhance our responsible gaming practices and the health of the industry."

Anyone who had followed the history of casinos in B.C. would have been skeptical. And internal records indicated Coleman's ministry was worried that Kroeker's review found that GPEB didn't have the same powers to investigate money-laundering in casinos that the RCMP did. In other words, after Coleman's ministry disbanded Fred Pinnock's anti-illegal gaming unit, literally no one was investigating casino money-laundering.

"Without changes," the Kroeker review said, "money-laundering will infrequently rise sufficiently in priority, to warrant investigation by police."

So, Coleman's ministry was prepared for questions, in case reporters asked, "Is it possible for the province to eliminate some of these barriers for GPEB's investigators? Will you make it happen?"

The answer was no.

"Certain investigative abilities rightly fall to the RCMP," strategic communications records say. "As such, I don't foresee expanding the investigative powers of GPEB at this time."

And Coleman was also prepared if any reporter caught on to the Kroeker review sentence that said, "money-laundering will infrequently warrant investigation by police" — and asked Coleman whether that statement "implies that RCMP Proceeds of Crime unit are not taking suspected money-laundering at casinos seriously? Is this an issue you will raise with the RCMP as part of [provincial policing] contract negotiations?"

Coleman's prepared answer was no. Increasing RCMP policing of casinos would certainly not be part of the upcoming provincial policing contract negotiations.

"I am confident the RCMP takes money-laundering investigations seriously," was Coleman's prepared answer.

Finally, there was the lingering question about B.C. casino governance and the conflict between revenue generation and enforcement. In a 2007 audit of corruption in B.C. lottery payouts, an independent reviewer recommended the Lottery Corp. and GPEB be split into different ministries. In other words, the money-maker and regulator should not be serving the same master.

But Coleman's ministry was ready if a reporter noticed the Kroeker review had not made this recommendation and asked: "How can we be assured that government revenue goals won't trump improvements to casino security and compliance?"

The ministry's prepared answer was concisely Orwellian: "The governance model for gaming in B.C. ensures decisions are made in an open and transparent manner and are free from influence."

So no changes would come out of the ministry's review of its B.C. casino revenue machine.

The RCMP would not target organized crime in B.C. Lottery casinos. GPEB investigators would not be given the powers to tackle transnational loan-sharking rings. Criminality in B.C. casinos would be studied, supposedly. But not enforced. Hockey bags of $20s would not be rejected. The shitshow would continue and the RCMP and British Columbia would renew their provincial policing contract for 20 years, in early 2012. The non-policing of B.C. Lottery casinos had evidently not been a sticking point. And B.C. gained more control of the federal force.

"Through the new agreement, British Columbia will have increased input into issues affecting the cost, quality and standards of Contract Policing before decisions are made at the federal level," Canada's federal government announced in a March 2012 statement.

Meanwhile, later in 2012, the B.C. government would announce that Robert Kroeker had retired from public service. With little fanfare,

Kroeker was hired as director of compliance with Great Canadian Gaming in its flagship operation, River Rock Casino in Richmond.

Barry Baxter was out of the picture too. In late 2011, the RCMP's IPOC unit was defunded. In Ottawa, the rationale was that federal policing had to focus on terrorist threats. Money-laundering — the lifeblood of transnational organized crime, but also of narco-terror networks such as Hezbollah — would now be completely ignored by Canada's national force.

And it was tragic. Because in late 2011, IPOC and GPEB worked together to investigate the Mainland China loan-sharking network servicing VIPs at River Rock Casino. Paul King Jin and Kwok Chung Tam were finally serious targets for the RCMP. But the investigation died with IPOC's demise because GPEB was not empowered to investigate money-laundering in B.C. Lottery Corp. casinos.

The reason: Chinese transnational gangs had become so powerful inside a few Vancouver casinos, especially River Rock that GPEB staff judged any money-laundering investigations would threaten their personal safety. They knew that the loan-sharking gangs were violent. And these narcos possessed restricted weapons, even owned gun shops.

So it was open season inside Lottery Corp. casinos. Drug money-laundering was growing exponentially.

* * *

On February 28, 2011, GPEB's director of investigations, Joe Schalk, had written again to BCLC, warning that monstrous bulk cash loads involving a "significantly large number of patrons using large quantities of $20s for buy-ins" were trending higher and higher.

"This threat will increase into the future if something is not done," Schalk wrote. Not all of the Chinese VIPs were believed to be criminals, the letter said. But almost all were knowingly dealing with organized crime loan sharks. And they didn't have to win at baccarat to launder money, contrary to BCLC's blindered arguments.

"Regardless of whether they win or lose all of the money they buy-in with — we believe in many cases these patrons are at the very least FACILITATING the transfer of and laundering of proceeds of crime." Schalk wrote that the money-laundering occurred when the VIPs paid back their criminal cash lenders, whether through cheques, wires, ownership transfers of houses or vehicles.

But BCLC didn't want to hear it. So throughout 2011, the GPEB-IPOC investigation was the only thing standing between Silver International's nascent underground banking network and the Lottery Corporation's bulk cash refining laundromats. After IPOC was wound down, in early 2012, the Silver network's supernode, Paul King Jin, was first flagged for suspicious transactions at River Rock Casino, as a VIP high-roller. On November 5, 2012, the Lottery Corp. banned Jin from all its casinos for five years for alleged loan-sharking violations, a report filed with Fintrac says. The Fintrac report says Lottery Corp. money-laundering investigators considered Jin "to present an extreme risk to BCLC and its gaming service providers." But the ban turned out to be meaningless.

Jin and his legion of runners continued for years to deliver cash to Silver's Chinese VIP clients at River Rock Casino.

How was this happening? What about the government's promise that "the gaming industry will prevent money-laundering in gaming by moving from a cash-based industry as quickly as possible and scrutinizing the remaining cash for appropriate action"?

On paper, records show the government's supposed electronic transaction study groups "continually emphasized progress in this area."

But frontline GPEB and BCLC investigators saw no progress. In fact, the opposite was happening. As baccarat bet limits were raised, the flood of suspicious cash, of course, increased.

Ross Alderson, who was on the River Rock Casino floor in 2012, believed the VIP room was full of cash-facilitators, and his testimony about this was later reflected in B.C.'s 2018 independent review into casino money-laundering. Alderson also told the review he felt questionable friendships had bloomed between some senior managers at River Rock and some major VIPs.

So in 2012, Jin and his gang were operating unimpeded.

So a hard-bitten, sarcastic brand of humour started circulating in GPEB's Burnaby office.

"We know the cartels in Mexico also have warehouses of cash just waiting to be moved," the investigators would joke. "And we have no problem with bulk cash from China in our casinos. Why don't we just put up signs at the border, 'B.C. casinos open for money-laundering'?"

It was just a joke, but at the time, GPEB had no idea how right they were. The Chinese underground banking networks actually had taken over the so-called black market peso exchange from Colombian and Mexican money launderers. Jin and his gang were one piece of an incredibly complex shadow banking system that leveraged drug cash and international trade to launder Latin American cartel money from B.C. to China and back to Mexico and beyond. They were moving almost all of the cocaine, heroin, methamphetamine and fentanyl proceeds on the west coast of North America.

And as far-fetched as the premise of the joke — B.C. actually welcomes drug cash — GPEB and BCLC investigators had heard senior officials express similar thoughts.

It was very seductive reasoning. The thinking was: crime and money-laundering will happen whether the government is running legal casinos or organized crime is running underground casinos. All societies have crime. You can't stop people from gambling. So, the officials argued, the government should crack down on illegal casinos, and divert criminals into legal casinos, and vacuum up the dirty money, just like a tax. With the criminal proceeds reclaimed by government casinos, 'profits' could be used to pay for schools, hospitals and social programs. In other words, government casinos would become the ultimate money-laundering machine. In a banana republic narco state economy. It was insane.

* * *

On October 25, 2011, at 5:35 p.m., a black Rolls-Royce Phantom pulled up to the Starlight Casino in New Westminster. The owner — a Chinese industrialist named Guo Tai Shi who owned at least $30 million worth of properties in Vancouver and Richmond — carried a bag with 7,500 $20 bills into the VIP room. The bricks of cash were all wrapped in rubber bands. The cashier gave Shi $150,000 of high-value chips, and he sat to play baccarat. Shi was reportedly a pretty good gambler. But it wasn't his night. He had lost all his chips by 7:30 p.m. So he got up to make a call and walked down to the lobby. Paul King Jin had many beautiful cars, including a Bentley. But there was a fleet Jin used specifically for casino parking lot cash drops. Soon after Shi made his call, Jin arrived at the Starlight with his silver Lexus SUV. He had a passenger and a bag with $150,000 in cash, which he delivered to Shi. Jin was already a barred loan shark. He had been caught at River Rock Casino but continued to deliver cash personally, and through his many runners, to Starlight and River Rock. Unfortunately for Jin, Mike Hiller was the investigator reviewing footage at the Starlight in October 2012. Hiller barred Jin for five years for delivering cash to Shi. Jin, always brazen, made a B.C. Lottery consumer complaint. He told Hiller that Shi was his boss and that Jin had not even entered the Starlight. Right, you transferred the cash in the parking lot, Hiller replied. Jin accepted the explanation and hung up the phone. The workaround was simple, though. Just avoid casino parking lots.

Internal emails exchanged between BCLC investigators in 2014 explained how Jin's network continued to flood tens of millions into VIP rooms.

"Attached to this email is a collection of the Top-10 money facilitators that work out of the Lower Mainland casinos with the majority devoted to River Rock patrons," one email leaked to me says. "Of course, Paul JIN is the #1 target and is currently banned but is extremely active and has numerous people working for him."

But there is no explanation that I have found in documents — aside from the B.C. government's revenue-generation objectives — why BCLC management allowed the flood of loan-sharking cash to continue.

The GPEB investigators were standing by, almost helpless. At the least, they hoped to limit suspicious cash by keeping a lid on betting limits for baccarat, the game that ushered big-time Macau money-laundering into Vancouver casinos in 1997, when bet limits were raised from $25 per hand to $500 and increased exponentially ever since.

Finally, the conflict between BCLC and GPEB over baccarat VIPs came to a head.

A complaint letter sent December 19, 2013, from then BCLC chief executive Michael Graydon to John Mazure, the bureaucrat in charge of GPEB, said that in September 2013, BCLC had requested to raise VIP betting limits for baccarat again, to $100,000 per hand, in time for Chinese New Year, "particularly" at Richmond's River Rock Casino and Vancouver's Edgewater Casino.

The raised baccarat limits were needed to "provide greater player convenience during a peak period for casino visitation and revenue," Graydon's December 19, 2013, letter says. But Graydon had been angered by the regulator's temerity.

"BCLC was informed that GPEB would need to approve any change to table limits," his letter said.

GPEB, of course, had concerns. Baccarat was the primary channel for money-laundering in B.C. casinos. If you raised bet limits, you just opened the flood-gates wider and attracted the world's biggest money launderers.

A briefing note was escalated to Mike de Jong — the B.C. Liberal finance minister who took over BCLC and GPEB from Rich Coleman after the Barry Baxter controversy. The GPEB note informed de Jong of "integrity of gaming" concerns if baccarat betting limits were raised to $100,000 per hand.

"We have the right to set policy and issue a directive if we have concerns," a GPEB official explained to de Jong's staff. "We do have some related to money-laundering."

The briefing note showed that B.C. casinos were an extreme outlier in Canada for high-limit games.

But the minister was required to intervene with a "signed directive" to overrule GPEB's anti-money-laundering directive. And the Lottery Corp. got its way.

However, by choosing to write a domineering letter to GPEB, Graydon created a critical paper trail that eventually helped me prove how the government's greed had trumped money-laundering warnings.

"A very simple decision took 13 weeks to resolve, and if not for senior-level intervention, BCLC and the Province of B.C. would miss out on an important incremental revenue opportunity," Graydon concluded, in his December 2013 letter.

The records were revealed only because then-NDP casino critic David Eby filed a legal appeal over the Lottery Corps' failure to release documents. Eby was probing whether Graydon, who retired from the Lottery Corp. in 2014 and jumped into a job with Vancouver's Edgewater Casino, was in a conflict of interest.

"It is evident from the records that Mr. Graydon advocated — despite the concerns of the Gaming Policy Enforcement Branch — for an increase in the maximum bet limit," Eby's letter to the B.C. records disclosure office said.

And the final piece of the puzzle for me came in a B.C. legislature debate. Under questioning from Eby — on the record — de Jong denied that Graydon had personally benefited from the government's decision to raise baccarat limits.

According to de Jong, his ministry's intervention to approve $100,000 baccarat bets was made "in the public interest" — in order to maximize casino revenue.

For me, this was sufficient evidence. In B.C., revenue trumped money laundering concerns. However, in stunning testimony during the Cullen Commission in 2021, Graydon said in hindsight, the Lottery Corp. was fulfilling its mandate to maximize revenue and also monitor for money-laundering by accepting and reporting massive suspicious transactions. He was asked by a commission lawyer if he could give any good reason to take in $200,000 in $20 bills, bundled in elastic bands and delivered to a casino cash cage in a grocery bag, late at night.

Graydon acknowledged such transactions were obviously suspicious. But Fintrac actually wanted the Lottery Corp. to accept these transactions so they could be reported to police and then investigated, he said.

"My concern was we continued to work with our regulator and stake-holders."

But Fintrac vehemently denied Graydon's answer, saying the federal regulator would never tell a business to accept a bulk cash buy-in. And in cross-examination at the inquiry, Graydon backpedalled and said he was very likely mistaken.

And of course, as we now know, for some reason the RCMP wasn't investigating casino money-laundering files in B.C. referred to police by Fintrac.

The changes directed by de Jong took effect in January 2014, upping the maximum aggregate bet limit in BCLC VIP rooms — meaning one gambler's total combined bets on the baccarat table — from $45,000 to $100,000. (See River Rock VIP renovation plan, Appendix A)

Also in January 2014, coincidentally, the underground bank Silver International Investment was registered in B.C. It was located in a Richmond office tower, seven minutes by car from River Rock Casino.

In the aftermath of the Finance Ministry directive, Lottery Corp. revenue immediately spiked. One year later, the Lottery Corp. reported that "exceptional performance" in high-limit baccarat games drove a record $1.25 billion profit.

But at the same time the impact that GPEB warned of — an unprecedented flood of money-laundering—was unleashed.

Suspicious transactions in Lottery Corp. casinos had surged from 459 in 2011 to 1,013 in 2013. None of these suspicious transaction reports were investigated by the RCMP. And in 2014, apparently because GPEB was on the warpath, Lottery Corp. investigators reached out to B.C.'s combined forces anti-gang unit to share information about Paul King Jin and "undesirable gaming patrons."

"Just as an FYI, our main target at River Rock has been extremely active of late and has actually been on the property several times making deliveries of cash himself!" investigator Daryl Tottenham emailed in July 2014. "Their main vehicle is a white SUV that parks on River Road, avoiding our Licence-Plate-Recognition system most times. Last week Jin dropped two loads of a half-million per load to the same guy and a few smaller loads of $200-300 K each, so he is a busy boy."

Another email of the top-ten loan sharks working out of Vancouver-area casinos showed almost all were Jin associates, "with the majority devoted to River Rock patrons."

In the fall of 2014 the underground bank from China was pumping at historic highs, and the floodgates burst in Lottery Corp. casinos, with monthly suspicious cash transactions averaging $20 million. And in October 2014, Joe Schalk and his GPEB colleagues recognized that one of Jin's alleged River Rock VIP room clients, Kesi Wei — a Chinese national who had just bought a $10 million Vancouver home — took a cash delivery of $645,105 in small bills and entered River Rock Casino. It was just one of many "extremely large cash buy-ins" seen by investigators that month.

For some in GPEB, this was the straw that broke the camel's back. They complained about Kesi Wei and Jin's network to the Lottery Corp., triggering an internal investigation. And Lottery Corp. investigators started to directly question VIPs at River Rock Casino.

But at the same time, River Rock Casino managers were concerned that Lottery Corp. investigators were questioning the Chinese VIPs.

Lottery Corp. records leaked to me say a meeting was arranged at "River Rock with Rob Kroeker and several managers to discuss the approach of VIPs and the related issues of cash deliveries, chips leaving the casino and the amount of extremely large cash buy-ins that we are seeing recently."

"There was concern from River Rock staff that if we are going to be (questioning VIPs), they would like to be able to have staff bring the patron to a private room and be involved in the process ... and be given the opportunity when possible to deal directly with the patron."

A conference call was arranged between BCLC vice-president of compliance Brad Desmarais, Great Canadian Gaming and River Rock Casino security and compliance director Rob Kroeker, Great Canadian Gaming vice-president Walter Soo, and Great Canadian Gaming chief operating officer Terrance Doyle.

"Conference call to discuss patron Kesi Wei's recent use of large volumes of un-sourced cash and casino value chips at River Rock Casino," one meeting record said. "This has attracted the attention of the provincial regulator GPEB. GCGC Walter SOO advised that Kesi Wei is in Canada on a 10-year visitor visa and that he has significant assets in general as well as acquired assets in the Shaughnessy area of Vancouver."

According to the meeting notes Desmarais told the River Rock managers, "the message also needs to be communicated not only to K.W. but all his associates, that they must stop using cash and or un-sourced chips from individuals such as JIN and QIN."

But if Paul Jin was feeling any pressure, he didn't show it. Business at Silver's cash house was booming. And the management was not taking chances on security. In court records, I found that in November 2014, Silver International Investment sued a Richmond contractor in small claims court because the glass entrance installed in their downtown Richmond office was "not bullet resistant ... [and] it was a material term of the contract that the glass must be bullet-resistant ... so Silver has received a quote and contracted another company to replace the existing glass, with bullet-resistant glass."

Meanwhile, in December 2014, B.C.'s government fired GPEB's director and executive director of investigation, Joe Schalk and Larry Vander Graaf.

Vander Graaf had just escalated a stunning report to his bosses detailing a Kesi Wei buy-in of $1 million at River Rock. Wei had lost $50,000, made a call and got into a black Mercedes SUV outside the casino. He quickly returned and bought in with $500,000 from Paul Jin "bundled and secured with elastic bands inside silver plastic bags."

But he lost everything in almost an hour, made another call, walked outside and got into a light-coloured Range Rover. None other than Kwok Chung Tam — who was barred from casinos for public safety reasons — was seated inside. They pulled up to the casino entrance and Wei walked into the VIP room with a suitcase that held $500,000 in $20 bills, bundled in silver plastic bags. Wei would later claim to Lottery Corp. and River Rock casino staff he didn't even know who was giving him this cash. They warned Wei to be careful, records filed in the Cullen Commission say, because Paul Jin was involved in criminality, and Wei was laundering Jin's cash with casino chips and paying Jin back with cheques. Wei's answer? When he wanted cash in River Rock he made a call directly to Macau. And then someone delivered the cash. That was all he knew.

"Wei is a recent arrival from China, involved in numerous suspicious cash transactions," Vander Graaf's report said. "TAM is currently prohibited from BC casino as a result of suspected loan sharking activities. He is an associate of Paul Jing JIN."

And Vander Graaf added a handwritten note: "Paul Jin: known loan shark associated Chinese organized crime activities."

The report went straight to GPEB general manager John Mazure. Vander Graaf warned B.C. casino owners could be facilitating money-laundering. And GPEB could be failing in its moral duty to ensure the integrity of B.C. casinos.

Vander Graaf believed the regulator needed to act immediately and cap the flow of $20s any casino could accept during a 24-hour period. Many gangs were active in several big casinos. Violence was rising.

There had just been a contracted killing, he warned his bosses. And GPEB estimated suspected drug-money-laundering at almost $200 million annually in Lottery Corp. casinos.

But Mazure didn't respond to the report. In the Cullen Commission, he testified that Schalk and Vander Graaf were not fired for urgently pressing B.C.'s government to crack down on hundreds of millions of suspicous $20 bills, but rather, an audit of GPEB had turned up problems. However, Schalk and Vander Graaf and all their subordinate investigators still believe they were fired for blowing the whistle on the B.C. government laundromat, the commission heard in 2021.

"It is my belief and my knowledge that this was allowed to happen," Schalk told me. "BCLC could have stopped this. The service providers could have stopped this. This was not unwitting. So if you look at it with an investigative mind, there is complicity. And if it is deliberately allowed, the next question is, Where does the conspiracy start and end? And what different groups could be involved?"

And as I reported for Global News, during 2015 — after River Rock management had been directly warned about Jin and VIPs such as Kesi Wei, staff at Richmond's River Rock Casino are alleged to have "knowingly accepted" about $4 million in suspicious cash buy-ins from Jin, according to the allegations in GPEB documents that I obtained through freedom of information.

The records said Jin continued to deliver cash to Chinese VIP clients at River Rock Casino "in areas visible by surveillance."

In response to my questions for the Global News story, Great Canadian Gaming's chief operating officer, Terrance Doyle, said: "I'm unaware of any employees knowingly accepting cash transactions from banned customers during any period of time."

And when I asked about Paul Jin's alleged cash delivery network, the company said that "Great Canadian initially detected this suspicious activity at River Rock in 2012, and our comprehensive and ongoing monitoring and reporting to BCLC was, in fact, crucial to identifying these individuals to the authorities."

Finally, in February 2015, members of BCLC's anti-money-laundering team met with the RCMP to "lodge a complaint about cash drop-offs at Casinos involving a male by the name of Paul 'King' JIN who was believed to be associated to organized crime."

But that same month, the Lottery Corp's new CEO, Jim Lightbody, didn't seem at all concerned about risks presented by Jin and his VIP clients.

In a *Victoria Times Colonist* report headlined, "High Rollers, Betting $100,000 a Hand, Boost Revenue for B.C. Casinos." the newspaper reported BCLC expected to boost profits in 2015 "thanks to an influx of high-rolling gamblers from mainland China."

Lightbody said with lottery sales softening, "the Crown corporation and its partner casinos on the Lower Mainland have focused on attracting wealthy 'industrialists and businessmen' keen to play baccarat for up to $100,000 a hand."

And the strategy enabled BCLC to surpass its target of $1.2 billion in net income from March 2014 to March 2015, "due to an increase in high-limit table revenue."

"Lightbody said casinos have increased the number of private rooms or 'salons' and raised table limits to $100,000 from $5,000 a hand," the *Times Colonist* reported. Lightbody said the baccarat salons mostly catered to Chinese VIPs who commonly bought in for $200,000 per casino visit and "prefer dealing in cash."

"So they do come in with bags full of money for their buy-ins," Lightbody was quoted. "We know them very well. We know their source of wealth. We know all their personal information; they need to share that with us for regulatory reasons. These people are multimillionaires and, in some cases, billionaires." And Lightbody was similarly effusive in a speech to staff at Lottery Corp. headquarters in Kamloops.

It didn't sit well with Mike Hiller, who was not shy about speaking truth to power. Since the 1990s, very few Canadian investigators have had a better handle on North America's heroin and fentanyl kingpins.

Hiller was there for the major heroin importation busts in the 1990s in Vancouver and Victoria. He was there in Thailand, acting as a police liaison for investigations of the Canadian Big Circle Boys who would become bigger than El Chapo. And Hiller knew Paul King Jin. The $150,000 delivery from Paul King Jin to Guo Tai Shi in October 2012 would lead directly to Hiller's bombshell I-Trak report in 2014.

Hiller based his internal report on confidential sources from Big Circle Boys networks. They told him the major loan sharks operating out of Vancouver casinos supplied almost all the VIP gamblers. And in almost all cases, the cash loans were repaid in China with a commission. And the loan sharks were major drug traffickers. Hiller had nailed the Vancouver Model and escalated the report to his bosses.

And so, sitting there in Kamloops, he couldn't stand hearing Lightbody brag about skyrocketing profits from Chinese VIP baccarat players. (Lightbody would later testify in B.C.'s money-laundering inquiry that he had full confidence in his compliance managers, including Terry Towns and later Brad Desmarais, to monitor and report on suspicious casino transactions.)

So Hiller wrote an email to his direct boss, Brad Desmarais, the former RCMP anti-gang officer. He believed that Desmarais and his superiors were looking for "alternative" explanations for the loan shark cash — rather than drug proceeds — and he had written to Desmarais about it before.

"I wasn't surprised during our meeting in Kamloops to hear that we experienced greater profits last year from high stakes table games," Hiller wrote on March 24, 2015. "This seems to be directly related to the increase in large cash buy-ins and suspicious transactions that I noticed for table games during the same period."

The subject line of Hiller's email cited his 2014 I-Trak report. Always the diligent investigator, he referred Desmarais to the evidence. The seminal report explained exactly where Paul King Jin and Kwok Chung Tam and the whales got their cash and how it was repaid in China.

"All but one of the Asian persons mentioned in the report have been the targets of a series of major drug investigations since the 1990s," Hiller wrote to Desmarais. "I believe the persons mentioned in this report are responsible for an abundance of cash being supplied to our VIP players. They, and likely many more like them, have connections with our Asian VIP players on both sides of the Pacific. The familiar names we know to be delivering cash to our casinos are merely runners who are easily replaced. The volume of cash deliveries is a huge reputational risk."

And Desmarais replied that he had read Hiller's 2014 I-Trak report.

"Thanks, Mike. I do recall reading this before. Obviously, the drug connection is a huge concern, and we are attempting to engage a police response with respect to the main players in your report."

"But I am resistant to branding all-cash facilitators as dealing in proceeds of crime," Desmarais continued. "In my past life, we encountered many underground bankers who used other sources of cash. The purchase of real estate, luxury goods and cars is accelerating in the Lower Mainland, not diminishing."

The conclusion was obvious. Desmarais and his bosses did not want to confront the suspected source of funds in Chinese underground banking. They were looking at the scales of the exotic fish, dazzled by its beauty. They ignored the poisoned flesh inside.

II

NARCO CITY

Reuters reported in 2019 that four of the 19 Sam Gor syndicate members, including Chi Lop Tse, are Canadian citizens. The cell of elite members from the Big Circle Boys, 14K and Sun Yee On Triads is believed to earn $8 billion to $15 billion per year dealing heroin, methamphetamine, ecstasy and fentanyl.

It was a place that reflected the dark imagery of Psalm 23. "In the valley of the shadow of death" — six city blocks ruthlessly segregated from Vancouver's luxury towers. Heroin, crack, and fentanyl ruled. Sex workers disappeared without a trace. Many thousands of addicts populated it: bent, wasted figures staggering from needle to needle wearing torn and muddied clothing. Hustlers exchanged cash and drugs in broad daylight. Addicts huddled in alleys injecting and smoking. This place robbed everyone of humanity: the junkies, narcos, pimps — even the cops. You got desensitized to the endless brutality of the Downtown Eastside. It was the place where Vancouver police officer Kal Dosanjh found a woman curled in a fetal position on a public washroom floor. Her hands were bound in ropes, and she was half-naked, bruised and lying in filth. She had failed to pay her heroin debts. So a gang of drug dealers raped her for six hours straight. Dosanjh knew how the Eastside debt collectors worked. They shaved women's heads and made them into walking advertisements. It was symbolism. The dealers wanted to signify what happened to clients who didn't pay up fast.

But Dosanjh would never forget this woman in the public washroom. It was the worst drug violence he'd seen, short of death. Please tell me who did this to you, he said. I'm sorry, she told him. They're here every day. And you aren't. But we can get you out of here, he told her. No, she said, you can't.

For Dosanjh, working the Eastside, it felt like shovelling water. Many of the addicts were Indigenous boys and girls coming from deep poverty. The place was a magnet for misery. New addicts arrived constantly. The supply of drugs was seemingly bottomless. You could put one dealer in jail, and ten street kids were waiting to fill his spot. The narcos had no fear because Vancouver's prevailing laws and social attitudes were slanted towards them. So the cops and gangsters faced off every day, almost like punching the clock. And they got so familiar, they knew each other by name. Like Stan, the 6-foot-4, 260-pound man who commanded 80 soldiers in his chapter of Redd Alert, a First Nations gang that enforced Eastside drug debts and got supply from the Hells Angels.

Sometimes Stan and Dosanjh would stand toe-to-toe and Dosanjh would try to get into Stan's head.

Dosanjh could bench press 415 pounds, so he wasn't going to be intimidated. More importantly, he kept his cool, and he was open to dialogue. Sometimes he would try an angle with Stan. He would point to a crowd of drug-crippled women on the corner at Main and Hastings. The bones of their faces were shrunken and twisted from daily heroin abuse. You may have daughters one day, Dosanjh told him. You stay in this life, and it's coming back at you. Your children will end up out here. And to his surprise, years later, Stan called back and asked Dosanjh for help getting out.

It was one of those milestone events that underlined what Dosanjh knew about the Eastside. The justice system had little or no influence on it. The hole was far too deep. The Eastside was governed only by supply and demand.

Another case that Dosanjh would never forget was that of Pete Hodson. A promising recruit from the affluent suburb of White

Rock, Hodson had been a University of B.C. basketball star. He was well-known in White Rock's Christian community. The kind of officer who should have rocketed through Vancouver Police Department ranks. But he fell in with hardened Eastside beat cops, the kind who saw addicts as "just fucking junkies."

Hodson started tailgating with these officers after shifts, drinking from beer cases in squad car trunks, trying to decompress the Eastside's relentless entropy. But it sucked him in, and he spiralled so far, so fast that he started dealing drugs himself. Using his status and his badge and gun and Vancouver police databases, he ran an efficient operation, even recruiting a crack addict to sell marijuana for him.

When I covered Hodson's sentencing for the *Vancouver Province*, the addict, a man named Tyson Pappas, told me the Eastside must have triggered something in Hodson. He was an officer who could be warm and friendly with addicts, Pappas said. But he could turn cold and vicious, threatening torture sessions on Pappas, if he lost a supply of drugs.

"I've been on the street longer than he's been alive," Pappas told me after a judge handed Hodson three years in federal prison. "You can't go from a well-off home, good family, sports, smart, police officer, to suddenly [dealing drugs]. There's another guy inside. And he just started to come out."

But the officers who survived the illogic of the Eastside came away with hard-earned wisdom. Doug Spencer was one of the Vancouver Police Department colleagues that Dosanjh really respected, partly because Spencer was the force's criminal intel specialist. Spencer had a phone bill three times bigger than the force's chiefs because he was talking to sources day and night.

Dosanjh and Spencer had the same compassion for addicts, the same willingness to dialogue with gangsters, and the same clear-eyed view of the Eastside. This was a place created by negligence and greed in high offices. Dosanjh and Spencer agreed that you couldn't arrest your way out of the Eastside's narco-chasm in a million years.

Spencer joined the Vancouver Police Department in 1988, the same year that Kwok Chung Tam and Chi Lop Tse landed in Canada. Spencer's dad was on the drug squad for many years, and Spencer always liked how he tried to help people on his beat, handing out his card and trying to get addicts into rehab.

So Spencer decided to try the job himself. He started working in the wire room and quickly built his criminal intelligence files. Right away, he learned about high-level corruption. One of his early wiretaps was listening to the boss from an elite 'Ndrangheta mafia clan in north Toronto trying to make inroads with officials in a big B.C. union.

Soon Spencer joined Vancouver's gang unit, and he started developing informants in the south Vancouver district. Gangs were all over the city. But the action was in the Downtown Eastside. All of these people struggling with addictions and the gangsters fighting to feed them. After Vancouver's Expo 86 world's fair — when Hong Kong investment began flooding the city — the heroin arriving in Vancouver ports started going exponential. The addicts loved China White. It was highly pure and much cheaper than Mexican Brown.

Overdoses started to soar, and HIV infections caused by addicts sharing needles in the Eastside approached rates seen only in sub-Saharan Africa.

The Eastside wasn't just pavement and tenements. You could see the third-world conditions in sharp relief in small parks and greenspaces. There were masses of people laying out in the grass amid tattered makeshift tents and rusted shopping carts, hustlers and traders haggling over stolen goods, addicts shooting up, and alcoholics drinking from jugs of hand sanitizer.

It looked like a warzone refugee camp. And literally, the paramedics who came to work in the Eastside received warzone training. It was the best approximation for the deadly conditions they would encounter.

It was the perfect contained environment for 24/7 industrial-scale drug dealing. More high-grade heroin and cocaine was coming into Vancouver ports than anywhere else in North America. Police had given up arresting addicts for drug possession. The courts couldn't even handle the drug dealer cases, for the most part. Spencer felt the politicians in B.C. had essentially legalized hard drugs.

Meanwhile, police started to see interesting indicators in other areas of Vancouver. A surge in empty condo towers and luxury cars. The signals that DEA agents are taught to recognize in places like Miami and Panama, as evidence of narco-economies.

And by the early 1990s, it was becoming clear the top players were getting more international. The Hells Angels had dominated B.C.'s multi-billion-dollar marijuana market before 1990. But by 1995, Vietnamese gangs controlled the market. And these gangs morphed into the United Nations, a violent dial-a-dope gang that started dealing directly with the Mexican cartels, trading B.C. bud for cocaine, pound for pound. It was a massive, mutually beneficial trade because B.C. had a massive surplus of potent weed and Colombia had a massive coke surplus.

At the same time, Spencer recognized the Big Circle Boys were playing in a different league — ten times more corporate and connected than anyone else.

They had almost no overhead because they sourced China White — aka #4 heroin — in northern Thailand. One unit, about 1.5 pounds, cost about $5,000 US raw. Once it was shipped to Hong Kong, it cost $11,000 per unit. In Vancouver it was sold for $50,000 US to the Vietnamese gangs the Big Circle used as distributors. And for distributors in New York and Toronto, it cost about $100,000.

In B.C., Spencer was looking at players like Kwok Chung Tam and Sui Hung Mok. If you ever wanted to find them, you just went to the Richmond casino. No one else came close in casino crime and heroin imports. And almost all the businesses in Chinatown were paying the Big Circle Boys protection tax. They were great at recruiting young kids to collect their debts and put drugs on the street. And that's how Spencer started to learn the hierarchy. He was dealing with the street kids in east and south Vancouver and working his way up. Big Circle Boys were always looking to insulate further and further away from the streets. Yeah, they acted like gangsters in their 20s and 30s. But the smart ones, if they made it to 40, they started to look very businesslike. They were much better at blending into society than the Hells Angels and even the Calabrians and Sicilians. And they got a pass because most police in Canada didn't understand Asian organized crime. You had a 270-pound guy on a Harley Davidson wearing a skull patch on his leather jacket, and you had a 155-pound guy with a Mr. Rogers haircut driving his kids to piano lessons and looking like an accountant. Who was going to draw police attention?

But as Toronto Asian crime unit detective Ken Yates presciently told a U.S. Senate committee in 1992, after arriving in 1988, the Big Circle Boys were already recognized as "criminally brilliant" in Canada and making other Triads look "like amateurs" while using the country's "lax" immigration laws to "springboard" heroin into New York City, San Francisco and Los Angeles. Yates told the committee one unidentified Toronto Big Circle Boy — a refugee claimant from Guangzhou— was arrested with ledgers showing he had imported between 800 and 1,200 pounds of heroin to New York between 1988 and 1990, making wholesale profits of $72 million, "most of which was transferred back to the Far East."

Yates also warned that Canadian intelligence indicated many more Triad leaders were planning to immigrate to Canada before Hong Kong converted to Chinese rule in 1997, and that Canadian laws were mostly powerless to stop this. On the bright side, at least one alleged Sun Ye On boss — Hong Kong movie mogul Heung Wah-keung — had his Canadian visa rejected due to efforts in the Hong Kong Commission, the Senate committee heard.

Meanwhile, in Vancouver, Spencer was learning that to really understand the Big Circle Boys, it was useful to look beyond their dominance of money-laundering in casinos — anyone could see that —and dig their high-tech skills.

Vancouver police would raid some mouldy, rain-sogged monster home in East Vancouver and find 1,000 fraudulent credit cards. Each with a $10,000 limit. Agents came up from Los Angeles once and asked to examine an embossing machine that Vancouver police had seized from a Big Circle Boy lab. Two weeks later, they returned and told Spencer this single card-printing machine was tied to $100 million in credit card fraud in California.

Another time, Spencer was contacted by the U.S. Secret Service in California. They told him that Sui Hung Mok — the elite Richmond casino loan shark — was allegedly connected to a $10-million counterfeit currency case. Yeah, the Big Circle Boys were the leaders in bringing heroin and human trafficking and sex slavery to North America. But they were also cannibalizing financial institutions and passing massive fraud insurance costs on to everyone else.

Another thing that amazed Spencer with the Big Circle Boys: killing was merely a financial transaction. There was no passion or anger in it. They talked on the wires about death threats to Canadian judges, lawyers and cops. Anyone could be eliminated by paying a gunman $50,000. And for high-value internal targets — like Betty Yan or her former boss, Hong Chao "Raymond" Huang — chances of solving the case were slim and none. They'd fly someone in from Hong Kong and hand him a gun in a Richmond parking lot, and he'd be on a flight back to China before police zipped up the body bag.

The most mind-blowing factor was the political ties in China.

Spencer was mentored in B.C. by Asian-organized crime experts like Pat Fogarty and Murray Rankin. He was always hearing how connected the people like Mok and Tam were. Spencer was taught that the Red Army roots of the Big Circle Boys — coupled with corruption in the People's Liberation Army and Chinese Communist Party — meant elite gangsters had a range of incredibly powerful sponsors. But it was hard to believe it until you saw it yourself. Spencer finally grasped it after arresting three men from China in a big extortion case. They had been threatening a Vancouver businessman over a debt in Hong Kong. They sent him a repayment demand and included the address of his daughter's school in Vancouver. When police followed the targets to a congee shop in Chinatown, Spencer had to rub his eyes and look twice at the cars that pulled up. One of the suspects got out of a sedan with Chinese consulate diplomatic plates. Someone pretty powerful in China appeared to be serious about collecting his debt in Hong Kong. Years of observations like this meant cops like Spencer and Fogarty in Vancouver and Yates in Toronto were well ahead of Western criminal intelligence that became more widely known after 2017, with my reports on the Vancouver Model of underground banking, reports on similar Chinese casino money-laundering networks in Australia, and also revelations about the Sam Gor syndicate.

Reuters reported in 2019 that four of the 19 Sam Gor syndicate members, including Chi Lop Tse, are Canadian citizens. The cell of elite members from the Big Circle Boys, 14K and Sun Yee On Triads is believed to earn $8 billion to $15 billion per year dealing heroin, methamphetamine, Ecstasy and fentanyl out of China, Vietnam, Hong Kong, Macau, Myanmar, Singapore and Malaysia. Using Vancouver and Toronto to infiltrate the West, they've become as wealthy as the Sinaloa and Medellín cartels ever were, but with more sophistication and less notoriety.

"The crime groups in Southeast Asia and the Far East operate with seamless efficiency," Reuters quoted one police official familiar with Sam Gor. "They function like a global corporation."

The introduction of fentanyl and easy access to factory infrastructure in China and the Golden Triangle, along with deep underground banking capacity in diaspora communities worldwide, made the Chinese syndicates many times more lethal than the Colombian and Mexican cartels.

"When fentanyl came in, I just said, 'Woah,'" Spencer told me. "They now had no overhead. You can bring in a shoebox of fentanyl for about $17,000. And you can turn that into millions on the street."

After Reuters broke the Sam Gor story I started to hear more about Chi Lop Tse from my sources. Only a select few Canadians knew it, but Chi Lop Tse and his deputies had an extremely powerful base in Markham, Ontario.

And my network investigations showed his 'global corporation' could always be traced back to the gambling, real estate and construction businesses in Macau and Hong Kong and the casino gangsters in Vancouver and Toronto. I also found that Sam Gor was financially tied to the elite tycoons that Garry Clement and Bryan MacAdam ID'ed for the Canadian Commission in the early 1990s.

This is a good example.

In 2020, Washington, D.C., corporate due diligence firm Sayari Labs identified that Chi Lop Tse's wife holds shares in a Macao company licensed to run gambling junkets, an "industry known to be dominated by Triads."

And the couple are also connected to a conglomerate of construction and real estate investment companies in Hong Kong. I found the Chi Lop Tse company identified by Sayari Labs receives financing from the Hong Kong-Macau banking conglomerate built by Stanley Ho and Cheng Yu Tung. The particular bank was also investigated by U.S. law enforcement in the early 2000s for facilitating illegal narcotics and weapons transactions for North Korea and various state actors in Macau.

"Criminal syndicates working with the government of North Korea are flooding the U.S., Japan and other countries with counterfeit currency, fake cigarettes and methamphetamines," the *Wall Street Journal* reported in 2005, citing a U.S. Secret Service probe against the Hong Kong-Macau bank.

The network patterns were significant. Casinos, narcos, tycoons, real estate developers, bankers, weapons traffickers and state actors. All linked underground to Mainland China.

* * *

The thing that Pat Fogarty couldn't understand was that police could clearly see in the 1990s how Vancouver was evolving from a relatively small, law-abiding city into a drug capital with the corporate leadership to control global narco-dollars. The casinos were used by the

Triads and used easily. Vancouver real estate was becoming not just a lockbox for drug money but a dynamic high-tech, international drug-money transfer node. But there was no counter-punch from B.C.'s establishment.

The way Fogarty saw it: all the murders and violence in Vancouver were just by-products of organized crime battling for laundering infrastructure in B.C. casinos and real estate. In his analogy, organized crime was a big ship. The homicides were leaks in the hull. And Canadian police were just chasing the murders, just bailing water and patching holes. They weren't looking at the ship and how it runs.

Fogarty would tell people organized crime doesn't exist on drugs. It exists on money. Drugs are just the path of least resistance to making money fast. But you have to recycle it to use it. And thus, the profession of money-laundering — an extraordinary economy employing thousands of Vancouverites — was born.

The casinos were just the most apparent laundering machine. Like the broad-daylight drug deals in the Downtown Eastside, you could actually see the criminal transactions. But the banks were used big time. The Big Circle Boys used prepaid instabank cards to move funds into Canada and back to China. Banks in Hong Kong with branches in Canada were instrumental. The gangsters would load 40 bank cards with $9,000. And then fly someone into Vancouver to withdraw the funds, using 'runners' to hit up different bank branches. You sent ten gangsters armed with 40 bank cards each, and those ten gangsters recruited teams of 'smurfs' to make withdrawals. And suddenly, you have about $500,000 in Vancouver to buy ten units of heroin. Now you move it east across Canada or south into Seattle and down to California to double your money. Or instead, you could buy a home and build an ecstasy lab in Richmond, Burnaby or East Vancouver. You sell the drugs, collect the cash, lend it out at casinos, and get it back in cheques or instabank cards. Use your smurf bank accounts to deposit the funds in various Canadian banks, and smurf it back to Chinese bank accounts in wire transfers of under $10,000 to fund more drug imports.

Or you aggregate the funds in shell company accounts in Vancouver and wire it into Richmond legal trusts to buy more homes in Vancouver. Launder more drug cash into these homes with monthly mortgage payments, and use these homes as collateral to take out more loans to develop bigger homes or townhouse units in Vancouver. Repeat this cycle enough times? Now you are funding mid-rise condo developments in the outer Vancouver suburbs.

In the 1980s — the ancient Vancouver Model era — you started as a narco and casino loan shark in B.C., physically sending drug cash back to China with money mules. Or you did a bit of refining, got your volume down for the flight to Hong Kong with bags of diamonds and jade.

You worked your way up to laundering drug cash into stolen sports cars and shipped them to China to sell at big markups. You slipped out of a few heroin conspiracy cases in Canada and ran to Vietnam to work in a Triad hotel if it got too hot. You just avoided getting done in the United States, at all costs.

But even Chi Lop Tse — convicted by New York City's tough prosecutors for running heroin from Toronto into New York — got released early, returned to Canada, and just set up again in Asia. That was until Australia finally took him down with a stunning extradition case in December 2020. I'll come back to that case. It says everything about how badly Canada has been infiltrated.

Back to the early days of the Vancouver Model. You kept at it, and you kept recycling the drug imports through Vancouver and Toronto. And voila: you came back to Canada in your 50s or 60s with a bag of golf clubs on one arm and a Hong Kong starlet on the other.

Now you're not even a hidden investor with the old school Hong Kong tycoons and the Vancouver condo developers. You've got a construction company tied to Macau hotels and many directorships in Hong Kong-listed companies. You're openly developing luxury condo units in Vancouver and selling blocks of presales in Hong Kong, Singapore and Mainland China. A perfect way to co-mingle drug money and condo presale money into your Macau property holding shell companies. And you have transfers coming on paper from companies registered in the Cayman Islands or the British Virgin Islands into legal trusts in Vancouver, allowing you to co-invest in more luxury towers. And guess what? When your new Coal Harbour tower gets an upzoning permit, allowing you to build 50 floors into Vancouver's precious skyline, city hall is effectively laundering about $50 million of your funds. How does it work?

You are buying upzoning to build more condo units and the city is taking something called 'community amenities contributions' in exchange. These funds pay for Vancouver's beautiful public art displays and parks and daycares. Think about that once more. Your laundered drug money is going into Vancouver's community-building fund to pay for statues and cobble-stoned squares and daycares. They might as well put your name on the park. Vancouver Model city building. It was no exaggeration. Police saw the drug money coming out of the Downtown Eastside and into cheap single-family homes in East Vancouver and circling the world and coming back in mansions, townhouses and empty condo towers. So yeah, Fogarty did believe this narco infrastructure, to a significant extent, had formed the bedrock of Vancouver's 'real' economy.

There were some cases that became emblematic in his mind. There was a big building used by a money exchanger, a prominent guy in Vancouver. He shipped massive amounts of weed to the United States and had truckers hauling U.S. dollars back across the border. They needed to change the funds back to Canadian, so they got the building and registered a currency exchange. This was systematic, casino-level money-laundering—a blatant currency refinery. Fogarty's team made the case to seize the money-changing business as proceeds of crime. It was a nice little win. But still totally reflective of Canada's piece-meal policing. And the interesting twist? The narco-trafficker had been renting this building from B.C.'s government. It became clear to Fogarty that some high-ups in Victoria didn't want that fact to come out.

Fogarty remembered all kinds of similar conversations about money-laundering with high-level people in B.C. For some reason, he couldn't interest these justice officials in a concerted attack on the professional money-laundering infrastructure. The deliverables, in the eyes of certain people, just weren't worth it. And again, the casinos were the most obvious example.

Nobody in Victoria wanted to address it. Fogarty couldn't remember how many times he talked about the gangsters bringing cash in hockey bags into the casinos. His teams laughed at it. It was just common sense. This was dirty money.

You could take any jury off the street, show them tapes of criminals coming in every night with loads of cash. No qualifications for their incomes, calling themselves import-export industrialists. Okay, fine. You tell me that. But that duffel bag in your hands. Where is that $300,000 cash coming from? And Mr. Big could never answer that question. So just stop there and think about it.

Any layperson would say something is wrong here, especially when you compare this unexplainable cash to the prominent movement of drugs in Vancouver. So the next question in a responsible jurisdiction would be: What do we do about it?

And the sad truth in B.C. was nothing. The government, the police, the prosecutors, the judges, the developers, the bankers, the realtors and lawyers and accountants did nothing.

It was beyond wilful blindness, Fogarty thought. It was almost criminal. Canadian leaders evidently didn't deal with criminals or mediate in Macau-casino battles, as Fogarty had seen in the case of Tong Sang Lai and the Water Room Triad vs. Chipped Tooth Koi and the 14K and Big Circle Boys. But on the other hand, B.C. officials did nothing to stop the infiltration of Macau-style money-laundering. You can't just allow narcos to buy up Canadian land with no regulatory response. But they did.

So in Fogarty's analogy of the Vancouver Model, money was the root of all evil. Everyone was making money in the casinos, making money in real estate, making money selling luxury cars, building city parks with upzoning fees from Hong Kong tycoons and Panama Papers condo developers. And the provincial tax revenue was floating everyone's boat. The good guys are making money and the bad guys are making money, so what's the harm?

* * *

Like so much about the Downtown Eastside, the harm was easy to ignore if you averted your gaze from the contained killing zone surrounding Main and Hastings. But like horrific images that refuse to stay buried in a guilty conscience, the bone fragments and DNA of dozens of drug-addicted sex workers slaughtered on a pig farm just outside of Vancouver came back to haunt B.C.'s establishment in February 2002.

Since the 1980s, a serial killer named Robert Pickton had been scouring the Eastside for prostitutes with impunity. He lured these vulnerable women to his rural property, where he and a circle of criminals had a makeshift dancehall. And when the drug parties ended and guests left, Pickton would choose his target and end her life, sometimes using handcuffs and a knife and sometimes offering a syringe of heroin that actually contained anti-freeze.

He would run the bodies through a meat-grinder that he used to slaughter his pigs. Pickton and his accomplices operated in a moral vacuum because police leaders had paid little or no attention to the scores of women vanishing from the Eastside, a transient place that drew vulnerable girls from across Canada, many from First Nations reserves. And although Pickton had been on a list of suspects after an investigation into the Eastside's missing women was finally started in 1998, his spree continued until a rookie RCMP officer executed a search warrant on Pickton's acreage. Police eventually found the DNA of 33 women on the farm. But before he was convicted on six of those murders, he admitted to an undercover officer in prison that he had killed 49 women.

In 2005, when I was studying journalism at Langara College in Vancouver, this story — the victims, the drugs, the unfathomable institutional failings that allowed the Downtown Eastside to thrive — was the one that stayed with me.

I interviewed Maggie de Vries, the sister of one of Pickton's victims, Sarah de Vries. Sarah was a young black woman who was adopted into a well-off westside Vancouver family. Perhaps she felt misplaced despite a loving home. She gravitated to a life of heroin and sex work in the Eastside. She was last seen in April 1998 at Princess and Hastings, a five-minute walk from Main and Hastings. Sarah was aware of the dangers surrounding her, and she had left behind a journal of poems and warnings to other Eastside women, begging them to escape before heroin addiction devoured them. Vancouver police called Maggie de Vries in August 2002.

The quote from Maggie that stayed with me underlined the life-altering pain that families of murder victims experience. Everything changed, Maggie told me, when police said they'd found Sarah's DNA in a soil sample on Pickton's farm.

Eventually, when B.C. held a commission of inquiry into the uncountable cases of missing and murdered women across the province, for me, the testimony of one former Vancouver police officer stood out. Det. Const. Lorimer Shenher was given the whole job of investigating the women missing from the Downtown Eastside in 1998. Shenher had never investigated a murder or led a major investigation.

As I reported for the *Vancouver Province* in 2012, Shenher could never understand why the justice system discarded evidence from the one victim who had escaped Robert Pickton. Shenher's first big tip came from a man named Bill Hiscox, who had worked for Pickton. Hiscox said Pickton had killed Sarah de Vries, and she was just one of many prostitutes delivered to parties at the pig farm. Pickton had tried in 1997 to kill another Vancouver Downtown Eastside prostitute and was still trying to hire people to bring her back to be killed, Hiscox told Shenher. The woman had broken free from handcuffs at Pickton's trailer and escaped after a knife fight with him.

The woman reported Pickton's attempted murder. And RCMP had collected Pickton's blood-spattered clothing, a condom, handcuffs and bandages. But the evidence wasn't tested for DNA, and prosecutors dropped the charges. Shenher found the woman and interviewed her in July 1998. And according to Shenher, the woman said prosecutors and police dropped her case because "they told me I wasn't credible ... on account of me being an addict."

"I felt it incredibly frustrating that her evidence wasn't heard," Shenher testified in 2012.

* * *

As a journalism student, I felt drawn to the Downtown Eastside. It just didn't make sense for this place to exist in a city of great wealth, and a country that I had been taught was just. At the time, Vancouver's mayor was Larry Campbell, a former Vancouver-area drug-cop and B.C. chief coroner. He was a forcefully charismatic and persuasive man, so compelling that TV writers used him as a model for the lead character in several CBC dramas. Campbell's city hall had liberalized drug policy. The aim was to contain drug dealing and addicts within the Downtown Eastside and provide "harm reduction" by supplying clean needles, social housing and income and medical support. Police enforcement was supposed to be a "pillar" of this policy. But in reality, street-level drug dealing was ignored.

Another story that resonated for me at Langara College was when our municipal politics class hosted Peter Ladner, a city councillor and former *Vancouver Sun* reporter. I asked him how Vancouver's leaders could tolerate the Eastside's vast illegal drug market.

"That's the billion-dollar question," Ladner responded, before rolling into an attack on Larry Campbell's policies and those of his right-hand man Jim Green. Jim Green was responsible for promoting harm-reduction services in the Eastside along with the real estate development model of building luxury condos that included social housing units. Basically, building taller buildings with 80 percent of units sold on the market and 20 percent set aside for addicts and low-income earners.

Ladner said Campbell and Green's policies had effectively built an industry around poverty and drug addiction in Vancouver. He used the inflammatory words 'poverty pimps,' and I quoted him on it. Green read my story in the *Langara Voice* student newspaper and called me threatening a defamation case. It was my first indication that I was starting to hit a nerve on the politics of real estate development and drug policy in Vancouver.

The other city hall story that stayed with me was the fractious debate in late 2004 over slot machines at the Hastings Park racetrack in east Vancouver. Great Canadian Gaming wanted the slots. But the majority of Campbell's left-wing party was against the plan. In 2004 Great Canadian Gaming had opened its flagship River Rock Casino in Richmond, and the company was increasingly influential in B.C. politics.

Another major force in Vancouver politics, condo developer Bruno Wall, lined up behind the Hastings Park slot machine application. Campbell and several pro-developer colleagues, including Jim Green, split from their left-wing party, throwing full support behind casino and developer interests. It turned out that Campbell's vote for Great Canadian Gaming's gambling application at Hastings Park broke a deadlocked council. In the aftermath, Campbell formed his own party, Vision Vancouver. But at the height of his power in 2005, he decided to leave city hall. In 2007 he was made a Canadian senator by Liberal prime minister Paul Martin. And in 2008, Campbell was quietly appointed to the Great Canadian Gaming board, where he would be richly compensated for overseeing anti-money-laundering compliance while collecting his salary as an unelected senator.

B.C. citizens would see little of Campbell after these appointments. He continued to advocate for drug liberalization in Ottawa and also got involved in the medical marijuana business. But was Campbell's harm-reduction policy working out for Vancouver? It depends on how you look at it.

When I joined the *Vancouver Province* in 2009, the newspaper was in the middle of a year-long investigation into the Downtown Eastside's social, economic, and public health costs. My colleagues found that $259 million was spent annually on 260 groups involved in caring for and housing addicts. Certainly, these programs saved or prolonged some lives. HIV-infection rates dropped because of clean needles and supervised injections. It seemed the exponential curve of drug overdose deaths since the 1980s was levelling off.

But the programs did nothing to curb the Downtown Eastside's magnetic death pull. They possibly did the opposite.

The *Vancouver Sun* found that in 2013, $360 million was spent by 260 social agencies and housing providers in the Downtown Eastside to support roughly 6,500 people, most with addictions and mental health concerns. So $1 million per day was poured into the wasteland, with at least 75 percent coming from taxpayers. And this was before fentanyl hit.

In April 2013, a *Vancouver Province* editor told me that B.C.'s provincial health officer, Perry Kendall, had sent out an alert about some new "bad heroin" causing a rash of O.D.'s in the Eastside. I walked from our newsroom at 200 Granville and through Vancouver's tourist-friendly Gastown towards Main and Hastings. It was a ten-minute trip I often took for reporting assignments. It never ceased to amaze me. Every step towards Main and Hastings you could see the growing entropy, the devolution from an orderly corporate district to a cash-in-hand drug market

I stood on the sidewalk outside the East Hastings supervised injection site, and I interviewed some addicts. I met a young man from Newfoundland who had been living in the Eastside for nine months. He wore a baseball hat, and he still looked relatively healthy and strong. In contrast to most of the people passing on the crowded sidewalk, he wasn't flinching or scratching at needle sores.

This was the first time I'd heard of fentanyl's devastating power.

So I started my story with a quote that reflected exactly that.

"I heard it's something like 100 times stronger than heroin," says Michael Kennelly, a Downtown Eastside drug user. "About ten or 15 people here told me they OD'ed on fentanyl."

I also interviewed an expert, Dr. Kendall, and he told me fentanyl stolen from pharmacies had been recognized before in Vancouver. But something very new was happening. Police were finding street labs producing illicit fentanyl, and it wasn't just going to heroin addicts. Gangs were mixing it into drugs like ecstasy and methamphetamine. Unsuspecting teens were ingesting potentially deadly party pills.

Kendall told me in 2012, there had been only 20 fentanyl deaths in B.C. But in the first four months of 2013, there were already 23 fentanyl deaths.

"If we continue at this pace we could see a fourfold increase in deaths," Kendall said. And it happened. The fentanyl death rate started rising exponentially. And a B.C. public health emergency was declared in 2016. From 2016 through 2018 over 3,600 people overdosed in B.C., mostly in the Downtown Eastside.

"Driven by an increasingly toxic drug supply contaminated by fentanyl, carfentanil, and other contaminants, Vancouver is at the epicentre of this public health emergency," a 2019 B.C. public health report based on coroner's data said.

The report was full of tragic statistics and noted that Indigenous people were dying in disproportionate numbers. For me, one fact underlined the absurdity of B.C.'s systemic problems. Fentanyl overdose deaths roughly doubled on the days when addicts received their social assistance. Addicts were immediately converting welfare cheques into cash for drug binges — and dying. And in the process, Canadian tax dollars were transferred directly into the hands of the Big Circle Boys, who could launder the drug money in casinos and real estate, and transfer funds back to chemical factories in China through underground banks in order to produce and import more fentanyl to Vancouver, causing more overdose deaths. The Vicious Circle Boys was more like it.

But back in 2013, I hadn't yet made the connection. The Downtown Eastside never made sense to me. And Vancouver real estate prices didn't make sense either. In isolation, they were illogical. But when you put them together. Voila. I was following the money from China, though. It was like walking into a dark cave. And each story was a flash of illumination. As the stories added up, the big picture became more apparent. And some people in government, policing, real estate development, and U.S. financial markets were starting to take notice. One of them, legendary New York City hedge fund short-seller Marc Cohodes, messaged me on Twitter in early 2015: "Hey, something seems to be happening in Vancouver!"

I knew that Marc had played a role in exposing bank frauds in the U.S. subprime mortgage crisis in 2008. He had his own chapter in *New York Times* reporter Gretchen Morgenson's book on the crisis, *Reckless Endangerment*. Now he was living on a compound in the wine country outside San Francisco and looking for the next big short. So we started to share notes. And Marc's experience in detecting major frauds helped sharpen my analysis.

We were both seeing Vancouver's real estate bubble as a massive scam similar in some ways to the 2008 U.S. housing bubble. But on Canada's west coast, the major factor wasn't a toxic mishmash of leveraged debt built upon fraudulent mortgage loans issued to no-income-no-job borrowers. It was a mishmash of big bank and alternative-lender and loan shark mortgages mixed with organized crime, foreign corruption, and money-laundering. Vancouver's real estate bubble was sub-crime lending.

"When you write fraudulent loans, the money goes to Goldman Sachs and Wall Street," Cohodes told me years later, when we looked back at my Vancouver real estate investigations. "But in B.C., it went right to hardened criminals. People involved in murders, corrupted politicians, fentanyl, kiddie porn. It's all bad."

12
OCKHAM'S RAZOR

The law enforcement officers I interviewed told us agencies, including the RCMP and Canada Border Services Agency, were aware of investigations in China concerning Kevin Sun and a SunCom executive. But despite this, SunCom was incredibly active in B.C. land deals. And I later found through multiple sources with direct knowledge that after B.C.'s government cracked down on offshore investors, the Sun network was quickly expanding into Toronto land deals.

On a dead-end street that ran to the forest's edge in a Vancouver neighbourhood, Jason Edward Lee was found dead in his car's trunk. The young Chinese-Canadian money mule had been gambling with his life for a while. He travelled between China, Las Vegas and Vancouver, maintaining his gambling addiction while hustling real estate loans and transnational cash deliveries. He also owed casino loan sharks lots of money. In 2009, Jason had forged a power of attorney for his aunt, a hotel worker, and cashed a fraudulent loan for $265,000 against her Vancouver home. Jason's family claimed they didn't know what he did with the money. But they knew he was in trouble. In early May 2010, he had walked into his mother's home disheveled, claiming that thugs had kidnapped him, drugged him, and left him unconscious in a Vancouver park. He was running out of time. The last time his mother saw him was on June 7, 2010. And she called police on June 17 to report Jason missing.

She told police that some Vietnamese men had visited her home. They said that Jason would die if he didn't pay his bills soon. Police found Jason's car on June 19 and opened the trunk. It was a bizarre death. Jason was fully dressed and flat on his back with his head resting on a stuffed teddy bear. There was a plastic bag pulled over his head, and his hands and feet were bound with zap straps. Two used heroin needles were found lying beside the car's tires. Jason's family said he had no history of heroin use. The coroner found that he had died of heroin toxicity and suffocation. But they couldn't determine Jason's cause of death. Police believed that because Jason was a gambling addict in way over his head, he had killed himself and staged it to look like a hit, hoping to win his family an insurance payout. In other words, for an inveterate fraudster, one final desperate act of fraud.

The theory didn't make a lot of sense to me. Maybe Jason had decided to take his own life before someone else did. And perhaps he hoped to pay his mother back for fraudulent real estate loans he had saddled her with.

But to me, it was similar to the jumble of facts surrounding the botched Las Vegas cash transfer that Jason undertook with a prominent Vancouver realtor, shortly before his bizarre demise. The known facts raised as many questions as answers.

Looking back, I know one thing. My September 2015 *Vancouver Province* story about these cases — "Inside the World of B.C.'s Top Realtor: A Deep Pool of Mainland Chinese Buyers, a Dead Fraudster and a Forfeited Licence" — assembled many of the big Vancouver Model puzzle pieces that I would fit together in September 2017.

I had stumbled onto Jason Lee's case when a tip came in that Julia Lau, a realtor making enormous fees selling luxury homes to Chinese buyers, had quietly forfeited her real estate licence in 2015. I already knew that Julia Lau was big. She had come from Hong Kong and started selling real estate in 2005. By 2008 she was making $400,000 per year.

After 2010, as cash from China flooded in, she was reportedly selling over 100 luxury homes per year. These were mansions that often cost well over $10 million. In one interview, Lau had told me her Chinese clients were flying into Vancouver for Chinese New Year every January and driving prices higher. They did not need mortgage loans, she aid, because they bought homes with cash. So I searched B.C. courts looking for Lau's name.

One 2012 federal court file was a goldmine. Julia Lau had sued Canada's public safety minister for the return of $130,000 in cash seized from Jason Lee at the Vancouver airport as suspected proceeds of crime. But the federal judge upheld the Canadian government's anti-money-laundering seizure.

"Given the totality of the background of this case, it is hardly surprising that the Minister had suspicions as to the source of funds and the flow of monies," the judge wrote. "There is a clear and rational basis for the Minister's concern."

Julia Lau's battle with Canada's anti-money-laundering officials started in April 2010, the judge wrote, when she hired Jason Lee to buy a used 2008 Porsche Turbo Cabriolet in Florida. According to Lau's version of events, Jason Lee was to be paid $10,000 to buy the yellow Porsche in the United States and ship it into Vancouver.

But Lau's legal filings — which showed she'd claimed $690,000 in income in 2009 — provided no explanation of why she wired US$133,000 Bank of Nevada account at the Wynn Casino in Las Vegas, in order to facilitate Jason Lee's contract to buy a used Porsche in Florida.

"Curiously, the money was to go into a casino cage depository," the judge wrote.

Julia Lau's banking records showed she had indeed wired US funds into the Las Vegas casino account. But it is not clear what happened to this money next. According to Julia Lau, Jason Lee claimed he had purchased and shipped a Porsche 911 to her with his own money. And so he had wire transferred Lau's $133,000 back to her. It turned out that neither the Porsche nor the $133,000 in funds arrived in Vancouver.

But for unexplained reasons, Julia Lau took another $100,000 cash from her American Security lockbox and gave it to Lee. And she obtained a $50,000 cash loan on April 28 in Vancouver from a man named Mailin Chen. Chen was a pharmaceutical and real estate development tycoon from Guangdong, who happened to be making major real estate investments in Vancouver and buying many opulent mansions.

And from the cash in her own safe and the cash loan from Mailin Chen, Julia Lau said she gave $133,000 cash to Jason Lee on April 30. And Lee set out for Las Vegas again.

But before Jason Lee could board his flight to Las Vegas he was flagged by Canada Border Services agents with the $133,000 in undeclared cash.

In an airport interrogation room, Lee told CBSA agents that the cash they had seized from him included $30,000 from "a loan shark" and $100,000 from Julia Lau. Jason Lee also told the agents he was involved in fraudulent high-end car sales. So he had to leave the airport empty-handed and go back to Julia Lau.

According to Lau, Lee visited her on the night of May 1 to tell her the bad news. Canada had seized $133,000 in cash as proceeds of crime. Julia Lau maintained that Jason Lee had stolen her money, and "the government refused to return the stolen money."

But in 2012, the federal judge said that because Julia Lau had kept the $100,000 in cash that she gave to Jason Lee in her American Security home safe, it "created an undocumented void between a legitimate origin and the seized funds."

And a crude loan document for $30,000 cash written up between Julia Lau and the Guangdong tycoon Mailin Chen raised "as many questions as it answers," the Canadian judge found. There was also the question hanging that Lee said this $30,000 came from a "loan shark."

What happened to Jason Lee from May to mid-June 2010 is also an undocumented void. His death remains a mystery, according to the B.C. Supreme Court judge that handled a separate case. In 2016 the judge ruled that Jason Lee's mother and aunt had to pay a mortgage investment corporation $246,000 because Jason Lee had taken out the fraudulent loan against his family's own real estate assets.

After the *Province* published my story, Julia Lau took strong exception and maintained that she had no connection to any wrongdoing in Jason Lee's case or in Canada's anti-money-laundering action against her.

But there was something else I found in Lau's court file. In 2013 she had sued a real estate broker claiming she didn't receive her full commission for selling a $10-million Burnaby mansion. The buyer was a Chinese construction tycoon and real estate developer named 'YZ'. In September 2017, I found YZ's name on a list of 36 River Rock Casino VIPs investigated by Ross Alderson's team at B.C. Lottery Corp. Alderson had connected these whale gamblers to Paul King Jin's alleged "transnational money-laundering" operation.

So this is the point. In 2015 I had no idea that Julia Lau's clients included Chinese VIP baccarat players such as Mailin Chen and YZ — men involved in major B.C. land deals — and connected to massive suspicious cash transactions at River Rock Casino.

But my September 2015 story about Jason Lee and Julia Lau had all the flags: casinos in B.C. and Las Vegas, undeclared cash, complex transnational deals involving luxury vehicles. Of course, Vancouver mansions, cash lock boxes, and real estate professionals that acted like junket agents for Chinese tycoons. Crude private lender promissory notes, forged banking and mortgage documents. Loan shark death threats, heroin needles and the mysterious death of a transnational money mule with a bad gambling habit and side hustles, including shipping high-end sports cars between Canada, China and the United States. I have to be very clear. Julia Lau stated categorically that she had done nothing wrong in the circumstances: "A story," she wrote, "attempted to link my success to allegations of money-laundering, malpractice and the unfortunate death of a person who the RCMP said committed suicide. These allegations against me are completely untrue with no basis in fact." Indeed. But many of the players and scenes surrounding this case foreshadowed the Vancouver Model, before the Vancouver Model had a name.

My investigative mindset starts with the mode of questioning known as Ockham's Razor. Often the simplest explanation is the right one.

In 2015 Vancouver real estate was skyrocketing. And all indications pointed to capital flight from China. And yet, China had strict export controls of $50,000 per person. Chinese citizens could take no more than $50,000 outside the country each year. So how was all this money ending up in Vancouver? My instinct was to follow the big money and the big players.

In private, big developers told me about 30 cents of every real estate dollar in B.C. came from Mainland China. The realtors in Vancouver were aiming all their marketing at Chinese investors. There was a speculative frenzy. In private, realtors would talk about buyers with suitcases of cash.

But when they were quoted in newspaper stories most B.C. developers and big politicians denied offshore investment was a factor in Vancouver real estate prices. The vehement denials tended to make you think offshore money was actually the primary factor driving prices. You only had to look at a historical price chart for Vancouver homes. Clearly, prices started to curve above trend line in 1988. And they never came back. This was right around the time of Expo 86, when big chunks of downtown Vancouver were sold to the Hong Kong tycoons Stanley Ho, Cheng Yu Tung and Li Ka Shing. At the time, most in Vancouver acted like pennies were raining from heaven.

But a Vancouver professor named Donald Gutstein found the Social Credit government of the day had sold Expo 86 lands for pennies on the dollar. This was about one-sixth of downtown Vancouver. The *Washington Post* did a story called "The New Hongs of Vancouver." The reporters detailed how Canada was courting big money from Asia, and Toronto and Vancouver were being transformed, but in different ways. Toronto was drawing mostly middle-class migrants from Hong Kong. But Vancouver was welcoming Hong Kong's old money. Fortunes that in some cases could be traced all the way back to the days of Jardine and Matheson.

"Foremost among the wealthy arrivals is Li Ka-shing," the *Post* reported, in 1992. "Other big-name Chinese investors in Vancouver include Stanley Ho Hungsun, a Macau gambling and real estate magnate said to be worth $1.2 billion; Cheng Yu-tung, Hong Kong's largest diamond dealer, who owns the sprawling Ramada hotel chain and Vancouver's Meridien and New World Harborside hotels."

This was fine for United States reporters to write. But my *Vancouver Sun* colleague Doug Todd told me that Canadian reporters of the era were called xenophobes or worse for daring to write about Hong Kong money. And the pushback, Todd told me, was directed by Vancouver developers. And it goes without saying. No one was writing about the uncomfortable proximity of Triads and the Chinese state to the New Hongs of Vancouver.

And 25 years later, when I really started drilling down into the story, the money was flowing straight from the river's head: Mainland China. But unlike the Hong Kong tycoons, the Mainland China players had little or no public profile. In order to write about this mystery money, I needed simple and clear evidence: names, faces, bank accounts, and transaction methods.

So Julia Lau had dropped her incredibly lucrative Vancouver real estate licence. But I found she was still very involved with her network of Mainland China clients via a growing shadow market called crowdfunding. According to her own records, Lau had sold $560 million worth of luxury residences in Vancouver from 2009 to 2014. Now she could leverage her pool of ultra-wealthy clients for a new kind of real estate deal. The idea was a multitude of buyers in China could contribute small portions of money for a single land deal in Canada. At least, this is what the crowdfunders claimed in their investment materials. But who each investor was, how much they contributed, and how they exported money into Canada was known only by these crowdfunding networks' directors.

But I was able to identify significant investors by running Julia Lau's name and Vancouver residence through B.C. real estate lending records. The investors had to show their pooled real estate collateral in order to secure funding from small regional banks and murky mortgage-investment corporations.

I found Lau was involved in a Burnaby land assembly deal with a number of Mainland China investors, including Mailin Chen, the Guangdong tycoon who had loaned Julia Lau $50,000 cash in the Jason Lee case.

Mr. Chen had his own wealth-creation story. And it reminded me of others, like Lai Changxing. According to a biography, Chen was a school dropout who was running a failing duck farm before he borrowed money to start a restaurant called the Shangri-La. This restaurant rapidly produced incredible profits. So Mr. Chen redirected these profits into construction, real estate development, and pharmaceutical factories. And somehow, around 2008, Mr. Chen started to export his incredible wealth into Vancouver.

Through land title searches, I found that from 2009 to 2015, Mr. Chen's B.C. landholding company had owned or flipped 13 properties worth close to $100 million. And one of the properties was a $50 million, 17,000-square-foot Italian-style mansion in Vancouver's posh Point Grey neighbourhood.

Another major figure in Julia Lau's crowdfunding network was a mysterious man named Hong Wei Sun, aka Hong Sun, aka Kevin Lin, aka Sun Hongwei, aka Kevin Sun.

By researching lending networks connected to Julia Lau and Mailin Chen, I found that Kevin Sun was the lynchpin between many real estate investors and landholding companies. I made a call to a commercial real estate agent and found that Mr. Sun and his network of Mainland China investors were involved in many B.C. land assembly deals. But I was told the "conglomerate" of Chinese investors didn't speak to reporters in Canada. One of Mr. Sun's primary investment vehicles was the company called Sun Commercial, and Julia Lau was listed as vice-president of SunCrowfunding Holdings Ltd.

I started to put together a network map of the major and minor investors linked to SunCom and its associated companies, which included an oil company that was claimed to have $1 billion invested in the United States and Canada.

But the real estate and oil companies didn't seem to be producing many new homes or barrels of oil. They appeared to be amassing land. From what I could see in Vancouver, Sun's business model was that many residential property owners had aggregated their mansions and condos in pools of collateral. They were using residential real estate to secure loans. And they would use these loans to assemble land for rezoning. Basically, they seemed to be leveraging single-family properties to build condo towers. And for some reason, casinos and cash always revolved around the big players. Sometimes they would sit on assembled land, and sometimes they would flip it to developers from China. By collecting land records into a database, I found that well over $500 million in B.C. property had been bought and sold through companies related to Kevin Sun.

I could see flags surrounding investors by running their names through civil court records, land title records, and lending records. Some names were often spelled with multiple variants in B.C. real estate documents. A big red flag. They could have been attempting to avoid detection from tax and anti-money-laundering authorities. There were so many questions. And why could they not take a call from a reporter to explain their development plans?

After filing a number of stories for the *Province* on various Sun Commercial deals in 2016, I profiled Kevin Sun for Postmedia News and summarized my findings.

"In an era when many B.C. real estate titans seek the media spotlight in person to market their projects, Kevin Sun prefers the shadows ... But after examining many hundreds of pages of corporate, legal and land documents connected to Kevin Sun, a visual metaphor helps to focus the picture. Revolving around Sun are a handful of key people, luxurious homes and Metro Vancouver properties with high-rise potential. The people, homes and land are connected to about 14 investment companies ... in highly fluid relationships where personal names, corporate locations and company names and directorships constantly change."

Some of the properties in my SunCom network map were more interesting than others.

One of the director's addresses, a Tudor-style Vancouver mansion, was bought by Kevin Sun's business partner, a Richmond real estate agent named Denise She, after the previous owner, Big Circle Boys heavyweight Raymond Hong Chao, was executed outside his front gates in 2007. Before his unsolved murder, Raymond Chao had been Betty Yan's boss. He was one of the top heroin, methamphetamine and chemical precursor importers in Canada, with criminal links to China, Hong Kong, the United States and Australia.

Had Chao lived — sources told me — he would now have equivalent status with Big Circle Boys Chi Lop Tse and Kwok Chung Tam.

And there was a $9.5 million gated mansion in Richmond — an opulent rural estate with equestrian quarters — that I found was referred to in B.C. Lottery Corp. investigation records regarding illegal casinos. The records were heavily redacted and didn't explain why investigators were interested in this mansion.

I had more than a few clues to work with. Another tool in my investigative mindset is pattern recognition. When you see enough flags and enough connections, you can make something like an intelligence assessment, which can guide your search for evidence. Is the network you are looking at transparent or totally opaque? What could be the network's primary objectives, secondary objectives, and so on? Why does it exist? Many of the answers follow after you identify the big fish. I had some ideas about Kevin Sun of Richmond, B.C. But there was a huge gap in my knowledge of his background in China.

And Fabian Dawson knew someone that could help me out.

As deputy editor for the *Province*, Dawson was often in the loop on my probes of mystery money from China. He had been following similar files on Hong Kong tycoons since the 1990s. As I continued to probe Vancouver real estate, Dawson informed me that he was handling tense phone calls from two of the most politically connected condo developers in B.C.

These businessmen were angered with my reports questioning real estate investment from China. And they tried to have me sidelined. I was aware they were among the top advertising accounts for Vancouver newspapers. But Dawson knew I was asking the right questions. While I was collecting information on Kevin Sun's business interests in North America, he knew his source, former RCMP international organized crime unit commander Kim Marsh, was simultaneously conducting an international investigation of Sun Hongwei.

* * *

Through his law enforcement sources with access to intelligence in Hong Kong and China, Kim Marsh had learned that Sun Hongwei was connected to investigations of a $500-million banking scandal at Industrial and Commercial Bank of China. And a very familiar pattern had preceded Sun's rise as a tycoon. He was born in Changchun, Jilin, in June 1968. He was a fashionable young hairdresser who plied his trade in Jilin City until 1988. And then, while in his mid-20s, he caught a significant break.

"Reportedly, his life was turned around at this point by a close associate [whose mother] was a senior bank officer of the Jilin branch of the ICBC," an Ipsa International investigation file said. And in the 1990s, Sun somehow rapidly amassed many former state-owned industrial assets in Jilin.

Within a few years, Sun's Jilin conglomerate — including at least 14 companies — had acquired semiconductor plants and various factories as well as pharmaceutical and retail chains. But there were many red flags, according to a Jilin banking loan audit.

I found that in November 2000, the Shenzhen stock exchange announced that Sun Hongwei and the Jilin Pharmaceutical Group were judged by Jilin City People's Court to have violated civil law in a company merger involving the "possession, use and disposal" of a Jilin chemical plant.

And *Caixin*, a Chinese investigative magazine that reportedly has excellent sources with China's national police, reported that Sun was connected to "dubious" venture agreements for a business that "does not exist."

Also, as Kim Marsh's files showed, Sun was powerfully connected in northern China.

"Political exposure: Open source findings determined that Sun Hong Wei, Chairman of Jilin Henghe Enterprise Group Co., was a former representative of the National People's Congress for Jilin City in 2001."

Regardless, in 2001 Sun's Jilin conglomerate was counted among China's top 100 private enterprises.

But around 2000, a nationwide loan audit of ICBC, which is the largest bank in China, allegedly revealed irregularities in the Jilin branch in connection to Sun's many companies.

I reported for Postmedia that according to a statement quoted by Sina Finance, the Industrial and Commercial Bank of China audit commission alleged: "Since 1994, Jilin Heng Enterprise Group Co. Ltd. and 13 affiliates, used a variety of techniques in a conspiracy to defraud banks. By the end of 2002, the Group's total Industrial and Commercial Bank of China provincial branch loans stood at 2.8 billion yuan."

But Sun was not arrested and apparently had already left China.

There was lots of mist surrounding Sun's path to Canada. His residency card indicated he was a Chinese national, and it was marked "04 05 2001 Vancouver." But a social insurance card appeared to have been issued in an Atlantic province, possibly Prince Edward Island.

I talked to several Mandarin speakers who knew the man personally and knew of his business.

"Kevin Sun has been here for a while," one Richmond politician told me. "He is pretty good at staying out of the spotlight."

Another source told me Kevin Sun had arrived in Montreal in 2001 but found it to be "too cold" and settled in south Vancouver before relocating to Richmond.

In Vancouver's Chinese community, it was believed Sun had incredible wealth in China — and he reportedly liked bragging about it. But no one could say how he had transferred this wealth into Canada.

One of Sun's real estate associates told me, though, that Sun was just continuing in B.C. with the methods he used in northern China.

"He is an opportunist. You know, in Jilin, he bought factories very cheap, and he sells it for the real estate value and then leaves," the Vancouver realtor said. "Now he moves very fast from buying farm-land to flipping houses to flipping commercial property. If a developer from China wants to develop in Vancouver, Sun buys the land first and sells it to them. He is very secretive and smart."

The person had another point to make.

"In Vancouver, it is not just Kevin, though. There are hundreds of people similar to him."

This was a statement that all my credible intelligence sources — whether it was law enforcement, real estate development, or underground banking participants — agreed on.

The law enforcement officers I interviewed told us agencies, including the RCMP and Canada Border Services Agency, were aware of investigations in China concerning Kevin Sun and a Sun-Com executive. But despite this, SunCom was incredibly active in B.C. land deals. And I later found through multiple sources with direct knowledge that after B.C.'s government cracked down on offshore investors the Sun network was quickly expanding into Toronto land deals.

And this was the same network that Kim Marsh and I had profiled in July 2016.

"The modus operandi outlined in this case is similar to some of the operations that are using the Canadian real estate market to launder money," Marsh said in the Postmedia News story. "This situation begs many questions, including what happened to the visa vetting process, banking compliance, public company scrutiny and regulators of all sorts."

Mr. Sun did not agree to an interview regarding the July 2016 story's allegations, but responded through his Vancouver lawyer.

"As far as my client knows, there are no 'Chinese police warrants' in China for Kevin Sun (under that or any other name) nor are there any RCMP files in relation to same," lawyer James Carpick stated.

In the aftermath of that story, there were some interesting things that Marsh and his contacts came across.

One source indicated that Kevin Sun was familiar with the Chinese consulate in Vancouver.

Another said Marsh had shared his firm's findings with Chinese banking officials. But for some reason, they showed no interest in repatriating funds in Kevin Sun's case. Meanwhile, my story for Postmedia, "Meet the Mysterious Tycoon at the Centre of Half-a-Billion in B.C. Property Deals", created a lot of interest in Vancouver's real estate markets. In late 2016 the University of B.C. law school invited me to give a presentation on my findings.

Among the crowd of lawyers, casually dressed in jeans and a blazer, was David Eby, the B.C. NDP opposition critic for housing and casinos, and future B.C. attorney general.

There were also several men that I guessed were police officers.

I told the forum that, in my view, B.C.'s crowdfunding real estate market seemed to be growing exponentially, and it was a massive risk for money-laundering.

Land was being traded like shares of stock. Most of the buyers were pretty much anonymous. All kinds of front and side deals involving shadow banking seemed to be connected. And Canadian officials were not tracing the funds.

"There is no way to see who all these land investors are," I said. "When the crowdfunders buy a piece of land, how can you tell whether illegitimate and legitimate funds are getting commingled?"

I could see that Eby, who was seated off to the side of the crowd, was nodding enthusiastically as I said this.

After I finished my presentation and walked from the podium to return to the *Vancouver Sun* newsroom at 200 Granville Street, a man stopped me and asked for a quick word outside. He identified himself as a Canadian intelligence analyst.

"Everything you just said is right on," he said. "Did you know he is involved in gambling? That's my file."

I said no. But if Kevin Sun was involved in gambling, it would make a lot of sense. One of Kevin Sun's associates, a Vancouver realtor, had claimed in a B.C. Supreme Court civil case that after arriving in Vancouver around 2003, Sun had planned to set up a gambling network in B.C., and also a real estate investment network for the Chinese market.

The intelligence analyst didn't say anything more, except that I should keep digging on the file. This type of person helped me understand how targeted freedom of information law requests in B.C. might shed light on a network of Chinese VIPs involved with casino loan sharks in Richmond and Mainland China and Macau.

* * *

So I was starting to learn about the major players and their money. As the legendary U.S. hedge fund manager Paul Tudor Jones put it in the 1987 PBS documentary trader: "The whole world is simply nothing more than a flow chart for capital."

I could visualize that picture, seeing Mainland China as an ocean of money surrounded by a mountainous dam that was riddled with subterranean cavities. Money was flooding out through these underground tunnels and sluicing into a rapidly expanding balloon in Vancouver's residential property market.

But how was the money actually getting into Vancouver real estate? When I talked about this with Marc Cohodes, he said financial systems are basically no different than plumbing. There are pipes and tubes, and valves handling the flow. You had to understand that well-paid professionals — the financial gatekeepers — were manning all of the faucets. So I needed step-by-step evidence in order to explain how the transactions between China and Vancouver occurred. I knew that investors often got involved in B.C. civil court cases revolving around real estate disputes. And lawyers informed me unprecedented numbers of cases involving investors from China were piling up in B.C. courts. I found that when the players fought each other in court, they had to produce confidential records to argue their cases. And sometimes the British Columbia Securities Commission, a regulator usually responsible for probing Vancouver's prolific penny stock scams, got indirectly drawn into these real estate disputes.

That's what happened in 2015 when a Vancouver dentist complained to the commission about getting fleeced in a gold-mining startup scam. But dodgy gold stocks were just a minor money-laundering solution — little pipe connectors — for the industrial-scale fraud at the heart of the case. For me, the case provided the most granular picture of Vancouver Model real estate money-laundering ever reported — minus the casino money-laundering connections that I would later discover.

The dentist, who I and my colleague Dan Fumano agreed not to name in our 2016 *Vancouver Province* story, "Follow the Money", explained his case in hindsight, like this.

"It just unveils a huge, intricate network. It also begets the question of what money fuels the Vancouver real estate industry? And in what light does it show how well the real estate profession is policed in this city?"

UNITED FRONT: PHOTOGRAPHIC AND DOCUMENT RESEARCH

While the Chinese Communist Party vehemently denies interfering in foreign nations through its United Front Work Department, the network is well-documented in People's Republic of China records, and in reports from Western intelligence agencies. The author of *Wilful Blindness* discovered that some suspects in alleged Chinese transnational crime networks investigated by the RCMP, appeared to be well connected to Chinese state officials in Vancouver and Toronto, and also actively engaging Canadian politicians. The selection of photographs and documents displayed in these pages help to demonstrate linkages between tycoons, organized crime suspects, and Canadian and Chinese leaders, who have attended so-called United Front and political fundraising 'cash-for-access' meetings in Canada, according to international experts that reviewed the author's collection of photos and documents. This display starts with a gathering in Burnaby attended by People's Liberation Army hero Rongxiang 'Tiger' Yuan, the Vancouver Chinese consulate's top officials, and leaders from various United Front groups in B.C.

1. E-Pirate target Rongxiang Yuan sits beside Vancouver Chinese consulate officials and community leaders.
Source: Ina Mitchell.

2. Yuana and Consul General Xiaoling Tong confer with United Front leaders at a Chinese state affiliated event in Burnaby in 2019.
Source: Ina Mitchell

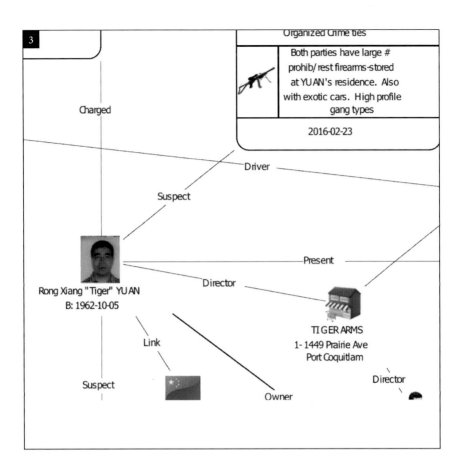

3

Organized Crime ties

Both parties have large # prohib/rest firearms-stored at YUAN's residence. Also with exotic cars. High profile gang types

2016-02-23

Charged

Driver

Suspect

Present

Rong Xiang "Tiger" YUAN
B: 1962-10-05

Director

TIGER ARMS
1- 1449 Prairie Ave
Port Coquitlam

Link

Director

Suspect

Owner

4

3. An RCMP "ProjectWatch" link chart obtained by the author from an RCMP source shows Rongxiang Yuan was targeted by Canadian federal police for organized crime ties and weapons investigations.

4. Liberal MP Joe Peschisolido poses with Tiger Yuan (r) and Paul King Jin (far right) and their associate at a United Front club meeting in Vancouver in 2018. Source: China Hui Club

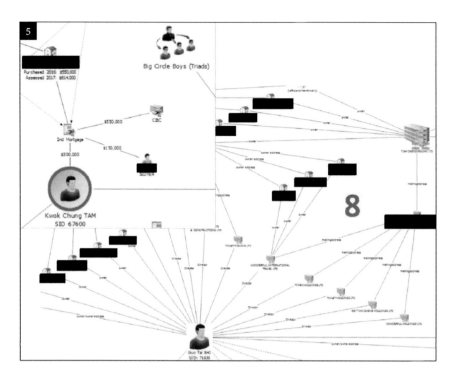

5. BCLC casino money laundering and real estate link charts name Kwok Chung Tam, "Suspect 1" Guo Tai Shi, and the Big Circle Boys.

6. A photo of Canadian Prime Minister and transnational crime suspect Rongxiang Yuan is displayed at Yuan's United Front gala event where Communist Party art groups entertained guests.

7. Burnaby councillor James Wang at Rongxiang Yuan's headtable with community leaders, for Yuan's 2017 United Front event. Source: Lahoo.ca

8/9. Tiger Yuan and RCMP 'Suspect 3' Hongwei Sun (right) pose with friends including Burnaby councillor James Wang (bottom left) at Yuan's United Front gala.
Source: Lahoo.ca

10. Burnaby councillor James Wang (dark blue shirt and sunglasses) stands beside Hongwei Sun, (in white hat) some United Front leaders, and Omni TV broadcaster Ding Guo (sun glasses and light blue shirt on left) at Sun's Richmond mansion.
Source: Facebook

11. A photo of 24-year-old Rongxiang Yuan from his diary of the Sino-Vietnam border conflict, as published in a People's Liberation Army intelligence staff department journal.

12. An Iranian national alleged to be Yuan's "meatshield" sits in an army jeep in Yuan's compound in B.C.'s Fraser Valley.
Source: Facebook

13. Vehicles stored in Rongxiang Yuan's Chilliwack compound.
Source: Chilliwack Progress

14. Burnaby councillor James Wang meets with United Front members and Paul King Jin, back right.
Source: Social Media

15. Tiger Yuan, Liberal MP Joe Peschisolido, Paul King Jin (not pictured) meet with athletes, United Front leaders and others at Jin's Warrior Fighting Dream gym — a Chinese state 'Belt and Road' facility in Richmond, B.C., targeted in a money laundering and illegal casino proceeds case.
Source: Facebook

16. Yuan, Peschisolido, United Front leader Yongtao Chen, BC Liberal Teresa Wat and a Chinese consulate official sing an anthem with United Front members and politicians.
Source: China Hui Club

17. Alleged Big Circle Boys boss Kwok Chung Tam's Chinese passport was seized in a police raid. Tam's name is spelled "Guocong Tan" in the Chinese passport.
Source: Canadian Federal Court files

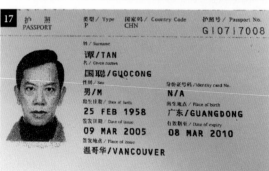

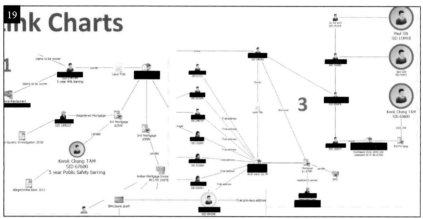

nk Charts

18. Anhui United Front leader Wei Wei's Markham mansion is targeted in a massive illegal casino, weapons and organized crime investigation during the pandemic lockdown in 2020. Criminal intelligence links Paul King Jin's network to Wei Wei's network. Source: York Regional Police.

19. A BCLC link chart connects Big Circle Boys bosses and loan sharks Kwok Chung Tam and Paul King Jin and various real estate lawyers.

20. Paul King Jin holds his face after a shooting at Manzo restaurant in Richmond in September 2020. Jin's business partner Jian Jun Zhu is killed in the targeted shooting and Jin survives. Source: obtained by author

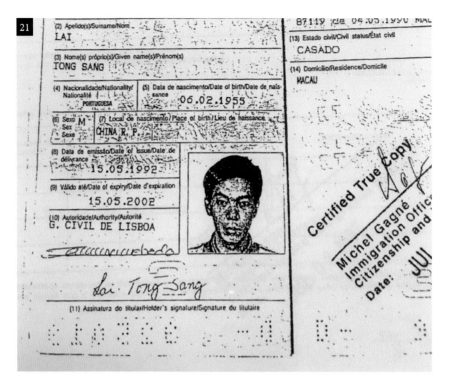

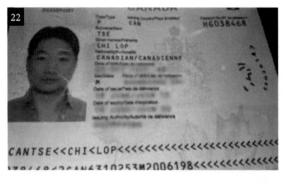

21. Tong Sang Lai, dragonhead of the Macau Water Room Triad, was targeted by the Big Circle Boys and 14K Triad in Vancouver.
Source: Canadian Federal court files.

22. Chi Lop Tse, alleged boss of Chinese state-linked super-cartel "The Company" arrived in Toronto in 1988. Police sources link Tse to crime networks in Markham and Richmond.
Source: Reuters.

23. A polar bear mount and Chinese flag inside Wei Wei's alleged illegal casino mansion, in Markham.
Source: York Regional Police.

24. Anhui United Front leader Wei Wei (on right) attends the inauguration of his Ontario hotel business partner and CACA United Front chairman Yongtao Chen in Vancouver in 2018. Source: Dawa News

25. Yongtao Chen poses with Consul General Tong Xiaoling and Tong's deputy (viewers far left) and the former CACA chairman (viewers right) Source: Dawa News

26. Yongtao Chen poses with Vancouver consul officials that directed the United Front's COVID-19 PPE pandemic supply collections in Canada. Source: 'Canadian Sichuan Association'

27. Wei Wei and CCIA United Front president Bin Zhang donated $1-million to the Trudeau Foundation in 2016. Source: CCIA

28. Justin Trudeau shown with various United Front leaders and Liberal fundraiser Raymond Chan (far right) at a cash-for-access meeting in BC. Source: social media

29. Vancouver United Front leader Yongtao Chen and a number of pro-Beijing community leaders meet with E-Pirate suspect Paul King Jin and a number of athletes in 2019, to announce Jin's boxing gym in Richmond as a People's Republic of China "Belt and Road" facility. Source: Lahoo.ca

30. Tiger Yuan meets a principal of the China Hui club and the club's Chinese state sponsor, a CCIA official. Source: China Hui

31. China Hui club owner meets his sponsor, CCIA president Bin Zhang. Source: Instagram

32. China Hui club owner meets Hong Kong Canadian democracy protesters in front of the Vancouver Chinese consulate in September 2019. Source: Instagram

33. China Hui club owner approaches a Vancouver reporter, as a pro-China mob surrounds a church where Hong Kong Canadians are praying, in September 2019. Source: Bob Mackin-YouTube

34. Rongxiang Yuan and Vancouver United Front leader "Max" meet with Vancouver businessmen and Chinese consulate associates.

35. Vancouver Chinese consulate associates, including Yongtao Chen, are leaders of an election campaign organizing group in British Columbia that supported candidates in 2018 including Burnaby Councillor James Wang.
Source: TheBreaker

36. BC NDP candidate James Wang's 2015 campaign director 'Max' is listed as a leader of the Vancouver pro-Beijing community association called a "controlling level" United Front Work Department group in Canada, by former People's Republic of China diplomat Yonglin Chen.

37. B.C. Lottery Corp. video surveillance records show a B.C. Lottery Corp. casino employee that allegedly worked for Paul King Jin, delivering a bundle of River Rock Casino chips worth $500,000 to a baccarat high-roller that was targeted in RCMP investigations of Jin and a number of mainland China "VIP" gamblers. Source: Cullen Commission exhibits obtained in legal application by Sam Cooper and John Hua.

38. The RCMP seized almost $10-million in suspected drug cash in the October 2015 E-Pirate raids, including bundles of $20 bills stored in this safe located inside "Silver International" in a downtown Richmond office tower. Source: B.C. Supreme Court files

39. An RCMP E-Pirate surveillance record shows locations and vehicles observed by undercover units targeting Paul King Jin in Richmond, B.C., in the summer of 2015 Source: RCMP affidavit filed in Cullen Commission.

40. About a month before Paul King Jin was under investigation in the RCMP E-Pirate probe in 2015, Jin and several River Rock casino "VIP" gamblers are observed in B.C. Lottery Corp. video surveillance meeting with the VIP program managers in the parking lot of New Westminster's Starlight Casino. According to testimony in the Cullen Commission, Jin and VIPs from mainland China were discussing a potential investment in the Starlight Casino facilities, and a casino manager also visited Jin's "Water Cube" massage parlour in order to discuss the potential investment.

EADERS

PRESIDENT
Zhang Bin

VICE PRESIDENT
Zhang Yu
Ma Yun
Yan Bingzhu
Ma Huateng
Hui Ka Yan
Albert Yeung ›
Pan Jianwei

CONSULTANT
Xiong Chengyu
Niu Gensheng

Albert Yeung
- VICE PRESIDENT

Dr. Albert YEUNG, Chairman of Emperor Group and Emperor Entertainment.

Dr. YEUNG opened his own watch shop "Observatory Watch & Jewellery" in 1964. He further expanded his business to jewelry and other ventures. Striving for 50 years, Emperor Group has evolved successfully from a watch shop into a group of listed companies with diverse business interests.

Dr. YEUNG was born in Hong Kong, while his roots are in the Mainland. He sticks with his country through thick and thin. Embracing the mission "From the community, To the community", Dr. YEUNG has established successively Emperor Foundation, Albert Yeung Sau Shing Charity Foundation, and Hong Kong Daily News Foundation, in order to coordinate charitable works. Dr. YEUNG concerns about the provision of hospice service and conducts several Elderly Service Projects in Mainland and in Hong Kong.

News Center | **Open** | **Government**

全站检索·请输入关键字

ent affairs | Cao Yu focus

me> News> Government News >

President of the Canada-China Friendship Promotic Association, Yuan Rongxiang and his entourage came Cao

Publisher: Government Office 2017-04-12 Views: 59   share to:

On April 12, the former President of the Canada-China Friendship Promotion Association ngxiang and his entourage visited Cao, and visited the planning and exhibition center an mber industry park planning and construction. District Chief Liang Zhenjiang met with th legation and made a docking and negotiation on Cao Investment. Liu Tiemin, Zhang Qiang a sponsible comrades of the equipment park participated.

41. Albert Yeung, a controversial Hong Kong tycoon investigated by Canadian officials for alleged Sun Ye On Triad ties in the 1990s "Hong Kong Probe" is VP of Zhang Bin's CCIA group. Yeung strongly denies Triad links.
Source: CCIA

42. In April 2017, shortly after Paul Jin is arrested in the E-Pirate probe, Rongxiang Yuan and Paul Jin visit a port near Beijing for business meetings with CCP officials.
Source: Chinese government affairs

43. United Front official and CCIA president Bin Zhang claims he has built a "high-level international exchange platform, enhancing the global influence (of China) ... he has successively paid visits to key officials ... including Mr. John W. Ashe, President of U.N. General Assembly."
Source: CCIA

EADERS

PRESIDENT
Zhang Bin ›

VICE PRESIDENT
Zhang Yu
Ma Yun
Yan Bingzhu
Ma Huateng
Hui Ka Yan
Albert Yeung
Pan Jianwei

CONSULTANT

Zhang Bin
- PRESIDENT

Mr. Zhang Bin, member of the 12th National Committee of the Chinese People Political Consultative Conference (CPPCC), President of the China Cultural Industry Association (CCIA), Managing Director of the National Animation Game Industry Base Management Committee and Chairman of Millennium Golden Eagle International Media Company.

Since his appointment as the President of China Cultural Industry Association, Mr. Zhang Bin has been taking great initiatives at building high-level international exchange platform, enhancing the global influence and promoting of Chinese culture and leading its drive of going global. He has successively paid courtesy visits to key officials of different international organizations, including Mr. John W. Ashe, President of U.N. General Assembly, Mr. Vijay K. Nambiar, U.N. Under Secretary General, Ms. Irina Bokova, Director General of UNESCO and Mr. Francis Lorenzo, President of the International Organization for South-South Cooperation, etc. Mr. Zhang has therefore won strong supports from the international society.

44

Bottom line – what is going on?

- Real estate is not the only problem

- Demand exists on both sides
  - Organized crime has a lot of cash
  - Need to move it out of Canada
  - Chinese citizens have access to cash
  - Limit of $50k restricts their ability to spend
  - Leads to development of services

44. A Fintrac financial intelligence report explains the symbiotic trade-based money laundering that allows Chinese nationals to export capital and launder money, and Chinese transnational crime underground banks to transfer drug sale proceeds worldwide. Source: Fintrac 2018

45. A Fintrac BC real estate money laundering chart, filed with the Cullen Commission. Source: Cullen Commission

46. A Fintrac "Vancouver Model" money laundering chart shows links between fentanyl trafficking in Canada and China. Source: Cullen Commission

45

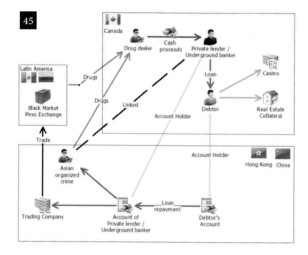

46

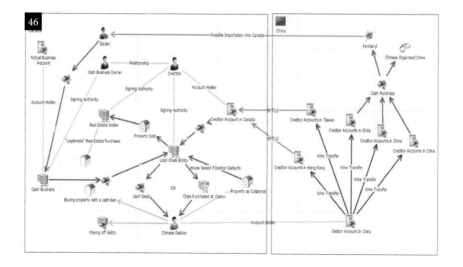

BC Casinos

Dirty Money often includes large quantities of $20 bills

BANK

Bank Note

"Placement"

Individuals deposit bank drafts into own PGF or sell to foreign patrons

Loan Sharks lend cash in exchange for legal title to clean assets for future repayment

Foreign Patrons borrow local cash to skirt foreign capital controls

Bank Note

48

"Layering"

PGF Account

Bank Drafts purchased by foreign patrons are deposited into own PGF

PGF Account

Legitimate Gambling or Minimal Play

Bank Note

"Integration"

"Colour up" smaller quantities of $100 bills

Cheques for winnings or return of funds

Debt incurred by foreign patrons repaid in foreign country

Cheque 01234567890 0123

47/48. A BC casino money laundering chart explains how Chinese transational gangs use B.C. Lottery Corp. casinos and Canadian banks to launder suspected drug money."
Source: GPEB

In simple terms, the case showed that Vancouver fraudsters duped investors into buying fake gold and oil stocks with anonymous bank drafts. And these anonymous bank drafts allowed Mainland Chinese investors to deposit funds in top-tier Canadian banks in order to buy real estate.

The commission did not look at the broader picture but found the dentist was duped into a "complicated transaction [in which the dentist's] bank draft was deposited into the bank account of a woman with whom he had no connection, and in fact, had never heard of." I would later find the anonymous bank draft scam was widely used to launder money into B.C. Lottery Corp. VIP gambler accounts.

In the dentist's case, the linchpin was Richmond casino loan shark Shek-Yin Cheng, a skillful player in Big Circle Boys financial crime cells.

Cheng was a node that connected a large network of stock scammers, Richmond currency exchanges, Mainland China home buyers, Vancouver realtors, and big Canadian banks. Through his hands, three bank drafts totalling $500,000 were deposited into a West Vancouver Bank of Montreal account in December 2014. But whatever his cut of the action was, Cheng didn't live long to enjoy the proceeds. In June 2015, he was found dead in his car in a parking lot outside a temple in Richmond. Witnesses told police a black SUV had pulled up and sprayed Cheng's car with 20 shots and then raced away.

It could have been fallout from any number of money-laundering transactions. Years earlier, Calgary Police's economic crimes unit had caught Cheng working for one of the many cells sent from Vancouver to Alberta to withdraw cash from casino accounts and to buy luxury clothing and electronics using counterfeit credit cards. Alberta police seized 47 fake credit cards from Cheng, eight counterfeit drivers' licences, and $16,000 cash.

I went to my Chinese-Canadian business sources in Vancouver to learn more about Cheng. One woman in the insurance business told me Cheng used Richmond retail stores to sell luxury items stolen from across Canada. She said Cheng also loan sharked and laundered money in the Richmond casino.

She didn't see Cheng as a gangbanger, though.

"He was standing between real business and gangsters," the woman told me. "He wash money and take percentage. He used to say, 'If money can solve the problem — then it is not a problem.'"
In the end, he didn't have enough money to solve his problems. His murder is unsolved. And records showed Cheng still owes Canada $700,000 in back taxes.

In any case, when I boiled it down, it looked like Cheng's primary task for the Big Circle Boys was like priming pumps. Basically, he needed to steal and defraud money from people to create a stock of financial instruments to allow Mainland China investors to deposit funds in B.C. banks. The pools of money could be tied to Canadian investors and professionals. This way, no money actually travelled between China and Canada. Chinese investors could deposit funds to organized crime in China, and they would be paid out with anonymous bank drafts in Canada.

Transcripts from the B.C. Securities Commission investigation showed me that it worked like this.

The Vancouver dentist wanted to make some quick money to buy an investment property for his family. At a party, he met a smooth-talking investment pro who called himself Azim Virani. It was one of the many aliases that Virani used for his many stock-trading scams. He told the dentist a Vancouver gold-mining company was about to go public, and the dentist could make up to 40 percent in two months. All the dentist had to do was give Virani a bank draft for $120,000. And Virani would take care of the rest.

To seal the deal, the dentist met Virani at a steakhouse in the Shangri-La Hotel, a luxury condo tower across the street from the Trump Tower in Coal Harbour.

The dentist was confused about one thing: Why did he have to sign the bank draft for his gold-stock investment in the name of Zhongyun Zhang? He had no idea who this person was.

"Bro, I do this many times and in lots of different ways," Virani explained to the dentist. "It helps me to fly under the radar for tax purposes."

The dentist accepted Virani's excuse and filled out a bank draft on December 17, 2014. And the stock scammer gave the $120,000 bank draft to Shek-Yin Cheng.

The dentist told investigators he never dealt directly with Cheng, but knew him.

"I met him a couple of times. And the way I've described him to friends that I've talked to about him was somebody who'd be able to look you in the eyes and stab you without blinking," the dentist said.

With the Vancouver dentist's bank draft in hand, Cheng now had enough laundered bank drafts in Vancouver to release a single home down payment for a Chinese real estate developer who wanted to step on the first rung of Vancouver's property ladder.

And so, in late December 2014, Vancouver realtor Liang Ming Wei walked into the vast dining hall of Floata, a bustling dim sum restaurant across the street from Sun Yat-Sen gardens in Chinatown.

Wei had been busy for months. In the summer, he opened a bank account in West Vancouver for his client, Zhongyun Zhang, who claimed to be a transportation executive in China. In order to open her Bank of Montreal account, Ms. Zhang had travelled to Vancouver and signed documents claiming that her Canadian address was the Burnaby home of her realtor, Liang Ming Wei. The pair had B.C. land titles adjusted, adding Zhang's name to mortgage documents, on which she claimed to be a "homemaker." And her banking documents claimed she was a Canadian citizen. All of this was false. But it was necessary for Zhongyun Zhang to skirt Canada's money-laundering and tax laws.

As her realtor, Liang Ming Wei had advised Ms. Zhang that Vancouver's property market was skyrocketing. She needed to deposit $500,000 into a Canadian bank right away to fund a down-payment and secure financing.

When investigators asked Wei why "he went through this elaborate transaction to transfer money from China to Canada," he answered matter-of-factly: "The bank in China doesn't provide this kind of service." He didn't explain that a transfer of $500,000 from a Chinese citizen to Canada is ten times greater than the $50,000 annual limit permitted under China's laws.

In corporate records, I also found that Ms. Zhang had set up a Vancouver real estate development company in December 2014, and in March 2015, Liang Ming Wei signed with the company for a lease on a 2014 Rolls-Royce Ghost, which retailed for $360,000.

The main transaction involving Mr. Wei took place in Chinatown. The owner of RTY International currency exchange in Richmond called Mr. Wei and said that Ms. Zhang had deposited three million yuan in a Chinese bank. And now she had $521,470 in Canadian funds ready to be paid out in Richmond. But the currency exchange owner told the realtor it was better not to exchange Ms. Zhang's bank drafts at RTY International. Mr. Wei was directed to meet the Richmond currency exchange owner's brother at a table inside Floata. The busy dining hall would provide cover for an obscure exchange. In Floata, Mr. Wei took three bank drafts totalling $470,000 that were all made out to Zhongyun Zhang, plus a $50,000 cheque. All three of the bank drafts came from separate victims, including the Vancouver dentist.

The funds were deposited in Zhang's West Vancouver bank, and she was ready to buy a home.

There is no record that anyone involved in the real estate transactions faced consequences because the B.C. Securities Commission was not responsible to regulate the business at the heart of the fraud.

But in my story, I made sure to include a transcript of the commission's interview with Ms. Zhang when her BMO account was frozen during the stock fraud investigation. Her answers were ridiculous. But she was smart enough to play dumb.

She was asked why she falsely claimed Canada as her residence when opening a BMO account.

"I don't remember. Perhaps at the time, the bank clerk suggested that to put the Canada down," Ms. Zhang answered.

She was asked why she claimed her realtor's Burnaby address as her own.

"I really don't know. What kind of address is that?" she said.

She couldn't even identify the source of the $470,000 that was deposited into her account on December 30, 2014.

"Where was that money coming from?" the investigator asked, pointing to the banking records and the three bank drafts used to fund the account.

"I don't know."

"It's your account. How is it that you don't know?"

"I cannot recall."

"Is it possible that you might have deposited that money?"

"I cannot recall."

"So, do you know why these three people that you don't know anything about are depositing money into your bank account?"

"I don't know."

While the B.C. Liberal government of the day didn't comment on my story: internal records show that they paid close attention to the apparent organized crime network involved.

For the story, I interviewed the Vancouver NDP MP David Eby, who was paying close attention to my money-laundering investigations and looking at lax regulations for Vancouver realtors. Eby told me that a number of real estate insiders had been visiting his Point Grey office to complain about offshore buyers evidently using realtors' addresses and accounts to purchase homes in Canada. Eby told me he was also looking at a scam in which offshore buyers would purchase homes from Canadian sellers. But their realtor would already have a number of future buyers lined up. And so a single-family home would get bought, and then the purchase contract flipped a number of times to anonymous pools of buyers. It was driving up prices rapidly. But also, as one Vancouver realtor told me, "creating the perfect vehicles for laundering money."

"I was really troubled by the facts in your case," Eby said in an interview. "And I'm concerned this is not a one-off situation, and this could be a systemic, regular practice."

And I found that Eby was right. Not only that. It seemed that by following the money from China, you always ended up with an inter-related network of players. And the bigger the player, the more nodes they are connected to. In the case of Zongyun Zhang, I eventually found that her real estate development company interfaced with several Vancouver real estate developers with direct connections to the Chinese Communist Party.

* * *

So the Shek-Yin Cheng and RTY Financial case was only one real estate transaction. But it pointed to a vast network and a method of skirting China's capital export laws. You have money in China. You want to buy something in another country. So you go to organized crime. The vast underground banks built on heroin money are used to transfer all kinds of money out of China. Much of it is drug and corruption money. But some of it is more or less legitimate income. Whether you are a fentanyl dealer or a computer programmer, it doesn't matter. You make a deposit in China, and you get a credit from the criminal bank. At a later date, the criminals pay you out in the West. And how did you get paid out? The Shek-Yin Cheng case showed me that casinos and currency exchanges were used like ATMs. And my sources in criminal intelligence would talk about the golden mile. It was actually a circle — a couple of blocks surrounding the juncture of No. 3 Road and Westminster Highway in downtown Richmond. My sources said this was the epicentre of Chinese underground banking in North America. Many of the businesses that I flagged in my Vancouver Model maps — RTY Financial, Silver International, Phantom Secure, Guo Law Corporation — all within a five-minute walk. And that must have been very useful for casino gangsters lugging bags of cash and bank drafts.

Some of my best sources knew the Vancouver Model first-hand. Some did shady business with the people I was writing about. Some followed the laws of their professions and resented colleagues that were getting ahead playing dirty. Most of them couldn't speak openly, or they'd be blackballed by their condo-developing colleagues.

The best quote I ever published along these lines came from a Vancouver developer. He told me $300,000 of every $1 million spent in Vancouver real estate comes from Mainland China.

"I own a business, I drive a German sedan, I wear a handmade suit made in Italy, and I drink good wine," he told me. "The people I hang out with, these guys want every floodgate wide open. If we cut off the buyer source, they lose commissions. There is a huge stake for a lot of local people in keeping this thing going."

And I often found that after publishing a story about offshore money, new sources would contact me.

In late 2016 I worked at the *Vancouver Sun* and got a tip from a knowledgeable lawyer about a case involving a Richmond law firm located dead centre of the Golden mile. The Richmond lawyer Hong Guo, a former Chinese government employee who eventually threatened defamation litigation after I wrote six stories about her cases, claimed that her employees had stolen $7.5 million from her trust account. This had impacted conveyancing on a number of home purchases. And many buyers from Mainland China sued the law firm.

Guo claimed her employees had converted some of the funds into bank drafts, which they deposited into VIP gambler accounts at a B.C. Lottery Corp. casino, and then converted to cash. I found that Zixin

Li, the accountant she accused in the case, had actually set up a shell company with Guo shortly before the massive trust account theft. That looked like a flag to me. Next, I found, according to court filings from another of the law firm's employees, Zixin Li had allegedly been running an undeclared cash account at the law firm. That was another big flag for me.

Hong Guo reported her trust fund theft case to the RCMP, claiming that Zixin Li and another employee named Qian Pan had laundered money through B.C. casinos in order to send the funds to Zhuhai. It occurred to me that this Guangdong city connected by bridges to Macau and Hong Kong was reputed to be Asia's supernode of underground banking. It was like the Bermuda Triangle of money-laundering. Uncountable trillions have dropped off the radar of the world's banking system through this black hole of financial crime.

Sources in the RCMP said Hong Guo's story didn't add up. But they were intrigued that she had connections with police officials in China. And one of her employees alleged that Guo claimed her father was a People's Liberation Army official and real estate developer in China. It was a story that more than a few people in Richmond had heard from Guo. All of this was fascinating to my sources. From an intelligence assessment perspective, Guo was well-connected in China and handled massive transfers of funds between China and Canada.

I decided to visit Guo's office and ask some questions myself. My first clue this was a unique legal business was the security camera mounted by the reception desk. A sign with an exclamation mark warned patrons their actions were being recorded.

I sat in Guo's corner office as she leaned forward in a wingback leather chair. A beautiful traditional Chinese landscape painting adorned the wall behind her, and there were jade art pieces and a lovely statue of a long-necked crane. We were planning to do a story, so our long-lens camera specialist, Nick Prokaylo, was posted outside on No. 3 Road. I knew if anyone could get a photo of an unwilling subject, Prokaylo would. I broke the ice with Guo by pointing to a line of photos displayed behind me. There was B.C. premier Christy Clark, former Liberal prime minister Jean Chrétien and future Liberal prime minister Justin Trudeau.

Guo spoke proudly of the pictures and said she had told Christy Clark to welcome more investment from China.

I visited the office several times, and Guo invited Prokaylo to come inside to take pictures. The interviews were progressively strange. Once, in the middle of my line of questions about a case involving tens of millions of mystery funds from China flowing through Guo's legal trust account, she started to cry. She said she feared that some men were taking advantage of her vulnerability. I don't mention this anecdote to make fun of her. It was highly unusual behaviour for a wealthy professional. It seemed like a theatrical flourish aimed at gaining sympathy.

But I was able to collect some interesting answers before our discussions ceased with her personal legal threat letter that included capitalized sentences and exclamation points. Before threatening to sue me, Guo had admitted she had a close relationship with police in Zhuhai. The next time I would see her was late 2017, at a strange press conference in her office, where she announced her investigation with Chinese police had resulted in the arrest of Zixin Li and Qian Pan. Li's family would later reportedly request assistance from Ottawa, claiming he was "refused the recognition of his Canadian citizenship by the Chinese authorities" and that he faced "unfair and inhumane treatment in the Chinese jail."

Meanwhile, in late 2016, a Mandarin-speaking businessman in Richmond contacted me. He said he was following my extensive reporting on Guo's trust fund theft case. His expertise was in brokering subprime financing for real estate development in Richmond. And he quickly got my attention with a stunning allegation. He claimed that he had complained to the B.C. Law Society about Hong Guo. But soon after making the complaint, he was visited by a couple of thugs who severely beat him. He claimed they were associates of a Richmond massage parlour owner named Paul King Jin. Furthermore, he said that he went back to the Law Society and reported the beating allegation. But he told me the Law Society didn't seem to take his allegations very seriously.

So I repeatedly questioned the Law Society about these issues. It was very difficult to get answers.

Finally, in 2020 I got this response, confirming that the subprime mortgage broker, in fact, had complained of a beating.

"The Law Society can confirm it received a complaint," the response said. "The complaint raised several issues, all of which were investigated. The issues that had sufficient information to support disciplinary action were referred to the Discipline Committee, and action was taken."

In 2021, in response to my questions about this case and others, Guo wrote: "I am unaware of any current Law Society investigation regarding me or Guo Law Corp which concerns, directly or indirectly, Mr. Jin or his wife Xiaoqi Wei. I am also unaware of such an investigation of complaints regarding money-laundering, loan sharking or any such criminality ... With respect to the supposed assault upon a person who had made a complaint, your email is the first I had heard of any such thing."

Guo added "I met with Mr. [Peter] German during his [B.C. casino money-laundering] investigation, and more recently with counsel from the Cullen Commission. All were grateful for the small assistance I was able to offer and there was never any suggestion of impropriety on my part."

So late 2016 was the first time I'd heard the name of Paul King Jin. And his name was connected to Guo's Richmond law firm. A business that claimed to be transacting about $700 million per year in residential real estate, mostly for Mainland China investors. They were also involved in numerous commercial deals for Mainland China investors scouring western Canada for ocean ports, freshwater sources, industrial and mining assets, and jade. And they were involved in land assembly for condo developments. Roughly, I estimated they were engaged in about $1 billion of investment per year in B.C.

And Hong Guo's firm was also involved in many civil disputes. The case that intrigued me the most was the one involving the subprime mortgage broker, Hong Guo, and a number of Chinese investors running funds through Hong Kong and the British Virgin Islands. And it involved a currency exchange I had come across before. RTY Financial.

Transcriptions of examinations for discovery — the pre-trial sessions where lawyers grill opposing litigants — provided tantalizing details. They outlined a number of complex transactions that led to a deal for three Richmond development lots in July 2013.

In the run-up to this deal, the Richmond subprime financing specialist, Hong Guo, and Lou Sekora — a former Coquitlam mayor and federal Liberal MP who also worked as a Canadian immigration judge — had been crisscrossing B.C. looking for major land deals. Sekora earned finders' fees for introducing Guo's Mainland China investors to deals that his B.C. municipal politician colleagues were pitching.

In the RTF Financial case, a number of investors from Mainland China were seeking to build condos on Minoru Boulevard in downtown Richmond. They had also acquired a glacier-fed spring near the resort of Whistler and planned to ship bottled water to China. Two men from Beijing were among the major players. There was Mr. Xu, a Chinese national who also had a Belize visa, according to his company documents. And Mr. Li, a Chinese national with entry-exit visas for Macau and Hong Kong.

The men were connected with several Hong Kong companies — Sparkle Long and Double Wealth International. The Panama Papers database showed me Double Wealth was linked to Hong Kong and the British Virgin Islands. I didn't find Sparkle Long in the Panama Papers, but case documents also showed it was registered in the British Virgin Islands.

The Chinese investors had no problem buying land and resources in Canada. Documents showed that tens of millions had been sent into Hong Guo's legal trust to fund the glacier spring and Minoru Boulevard land assembly deal. There was no explanation of how the money got into Canada. But it had been aggregated in Guo's trust accounts.

According to legal filings, the Chinese investors had problems with construction financing and couldn't get funding from big Canadian banks because "the whole transaction looked suspicious."

So they had to seek financing from third-string regional banks. This is where the subprime mortgage broker came in. The Minoru Boulevard deal was about to collapse before he secured lending in July 2013. But he claimed Hong Guo had short-changed his finder's fee, and he sued, triggering a flurry of B.C. Supreme Court claims and counterclaims.

It was a goldmine of records for me.

Legal filings showed the Richmond subprime mortgage broker questioned who really owned $20 million transferred into Hong Guo's legal trust to fund the Minoru Boulevard condo development deal. Guo's client, Mr. Xu of Beijing and Belize, claimed the $20 million was his. But records filed by a third investor, Mr. Yan, said most of the $20 million came from Mr. Li and the Hong Kong companies known as Sparkle Long and Double Wealth International.

"And what was Mr. Li's involvement in any of these companies? Was that your money that was being funnelled through Li?" a lawyer asked Mr. Xu.

"I don't want to answer because I don't want to talk about my money," Mr. Xu answered. "It doesn't matter where it is from. The source is from Hong Kong. That's my business."

"How did you get the $20 million you say that you have invested in this deal, from China to Vancouver?" the lawyer pressed.

"I will not provide you with the documents in China," Mr. Xu answered.

The lawyer tried once more.

"I am asking you if you have anything that can show or corroborate as to where this money came from, how it arrived in Canada. I am asking you if you have documentation, digital or otherwise, other than your testimony, that can explain or show us how that money got to Canada, who gave it to you, who sourced it, how it arrived here?"

"No documents," Mr. Xu insisted.

But other case records showed that Mr. Yan alleged Hong Guo and some investors had cheated him in the Richmond condo development deal. And he was becoming increasingly desperate to pay back his financiers in Mainland China. I found text messages between Mr. Yan and Hong Guo in court files in which Mr. Yan suggested his safety was at risk.

When I questioned Hong Guo about these WeChat texts, she said she believed Mr. Yan had faced severe threats from loan sharks in China.

Other text messages in court files showed that Mr. Yan had tried to resolve his differences in the Minoru Boulevard land deal with Mr. Xu. In January 2016, they discussed meeting in Macau or Hong Kong.

"Mr. Yan … using a third party transferee (you don't have to show your face) so that actual payment will be in cash … the signing can actually take place in Hong Kong," Mr. Xu texted to Mr. Yan. "It's better our future discussions take place either face to face or via WeChat! … If someone out of unfriendly intention complains to the regulatory authority, then it will lead to intervention, delay or termination!"

I had also obtained an extremely interesting snapshot of Hong Guo's trust ledger for the Minoru Boulevard deal. It showed that in July 2013, RTY Financial was paid a fee of $560,000. For a long time, I didn't understand how RTY earned such an enormous sum. This was just a small currency exchange shop. But I did know from the Edwin Shek-Yin Cheng case that RTY Financial had connections to a criminal scheme that facilitated real estate investment from China. Could RTY Financial be an underground banking conduit with connections to Guo's law firm?

Finally, in 2020, when one of Hong Guo's former employees sued her claiming unpaid wages, his court filings showed how RTY Financial fit into the puzzle.

He presented a trust account ledger that showed how dozens of transfers of about $50,000 per transaction had been wired from China into Guo's trust account for the Minoru Boulevard condo deal.

All of the names attached to these transfers appeared to be from Mainland China. Some of the names appeared to match with major Richmond casino VIPs. The Bank of China was listed on some of these transactions. And so was RTY Financial.

Legal instructions from the British Virgin Island company Sparkle Long International said: "I am writing to instruct you to please prepare a cheque to RTY Financial Ltd. in the amount of $560,000 as commission in relation to the purchase of shares" for the Minoru Boulevard condo deal.

The conclusion to me was pretty clear. In the Edwin Shek-Yin Cheng case, RTY facilitated an underground transaction that allowed a Mainland China investor to deposit a $500,000 down payment in a West Vancouver bank account to purchase a Vancouver home.

And in the Minoru Boulevard deal, RTY Financial had facilitated transfers of millions into Hong Guo's legal trust — broken down into $50,000 per transaction — so that Mainland China investors could develop three parcels of land in downtown Richmond.

It looked like RTY Financial was an underground banking node facilitating a blend of smurfing and crowdfunding on a giant scale. Many different people in China provided their names to record a "legal" $50,000 cash export out of China. And the money was aggregated in Canada for Chinese investors involved in condo developments.

I reported on the Minoru Boulevard deal in the *Vancouver Sun*, focusing on the case to highlight broader problems caused by a Supreme Court ruling that excluded Canadian lawyers from reporting suspicious financial transactions to Fintrac.

Adam Ross — author of a 2016 study for *Transparency International Canada* that showed about 50 percent of Vancouver's luxury homes are owned through opaque legal structures — told me Canadian lawyers had failed at "self-policing."

"The law societies claim to have rules in place to prevent money-laundering, but they are weak, non-transparent and almost never enforced," Ross said.

"Unless the law societies demand more of their members and start enforcing those rules, billions of dollars will continue to be washed through lawyers' trust accounts without any consequences."

* * *

Yicheng Jiang pressed his palms together and bowed slightly, and I made the same gesture towards him. He spoke almost no English, and I spoke no Chinese. So we stood steps apart and continued to smile and bow. I could sense he was trying to contain raw emotions. He said thank you and shook his fist as if to say "Keep fighting." And then he walked into the B.C. Securities Commission hearing, where he would testify about losing everything that mattered.

"At times, I wanted to kill myself," Jiang sobbed. He was shaking while on the witness stand. Every sentence of his victim impact statement seemed wrenched from his guts. He was stopping and starting in between violent bursts of tears so that when he could finally speak, it sounded like screaming. I think I've only cried twice while reporting a story. Once at the *Vancouver Province*, I had to cover the funeral of a North Vancouver woman who died with her six-month-old daughter in a floatplane crash off of Saturna Island. On rare occasions, the emotions of a story overwhelm you. And I started to cry taking down notes as Jiang testified in paroxysms of grief.

"It is just because of the two children that I can't die," he cried. "Even my son said to me, 'Didn't you say Canada is a country ruled by law?'"

This was April 2017, eight years after Jiang and many investors from Mainland China had signed up for a British Columbia immigration-investment scheme run by a powerfully connected Vancouver businessman named Paul Se Hui Oei.

It ended badly for all the Chinese investors. But apparently, no one suffered more than Jiang. He said that he had lost his family's life savings, his wife's parents' savings, and his co-investors' money, all because of Paul Oei.

"I don't know how much longer I can live like this," Jiang cried.
He told the adjudicators his wife had lost all hope and attempted suicide. She recovered but insisted on divorcing him, leaving him to raise their children. She told him he had risked it all for a mirage in Canada.

As I sat taking notes that day I was struck by the tragedy of Jiang's life. But I also knew his case proved a crucial piece of my Vancouver Model investigation.

In my efforts to understand how underground bankers in China routed money into Vancouver real estate, by late 2016, I had about 90 percent of the picture. But I was missing testimony from an investor willing to acknowledge using "black market" exchanges and also explain how international banks were involved. And Yicheng Jiang — who had nothing left to lose — had willingly provided that evidence. Not only that, he was motivated to point at the Canadian lawyers, politicians and businesses that had facilitated the Vancouver Model.

The core of the immigration scam involved 64 investment transfers for $13.3 million, routed through several of Oei's Canadian companies and the Richmond law firm of federal Liberal politician Joe Peschisolido. The Mainland China investors were told they would become shareholders in a Vancouver-area recycling business. They claimed they were told not only would they get rich, but they would be fast-tracked for Canadian citizenship because of Oei's high-level political connections.

But the recycling plant was a bust. And Oei ended up diverting at least $5 million of the investor funds for his own personal needs, the commission found. I found the misappropriated funds included political donations to B.C. premier Christy Clark. The commission lawyers said Oei had rubbed elbows with politicians to charm his Chinese investors. Oei also spent investor money on the signifiers of extreme wealth — he and his wife drove Bentleys and Lamborghinis — that helped establish his international reputation. And it worked.

There was more than a little bit of Great Gatsby in Oei's story.

He was featured, very uncritically, in a *New Yorker* magazine profile that called him the financial fixer-of-choice for ultra-rich Chinese fuerdai seeking to invest in North America. The *New Yorker* piece captured Vancouver's decadence but avoided the sordid criminality underlying it. A man named Li Zhao — the father of one of the pretty girls featured in the *New Yorker* piece — ended up shooting and butchering his relative Gang Yuan. Gang Yuan owned tens of millions' worth of mansions in Vancouver and West Vancouver. I also found he was a coal-mining mogul tied to a big corruption case in Yunnan. And I obtained a massive link chart that indicated Gang Yuan was one of the shady tycoons connected to a vast RCMP investigation into international wildlife poaching and casino money-laundering junkets in B.C.

So, Paul Oei's story was just one of many examples where a reporter could scratch the surface on a Vancouver real estate story that made international headlines — and run into underground banking and organized crime.

But not all of Paul Oei's clients were ultra-wealthy.

Yicheng Jiang's case showed me that citizens with relatively modest wealth sometimes took unfortunate risks to spirit their savings out of China. They had to rely on organized crime, and sometimes they got burned. I chose to focus on Jiang among the many other investors because his legal filings included confidential banking records that detailed HSBC wire transfers into Canada. And Jiang provided a ledger that indicated millions of suspicious transactions into the trust account of Joe Peschisolido's law firm.

So with the help of my Mandarin-speaking colleague Chuck Chiang at the *Vancouver Sun*, we got Yicheng Jiang's side of the story.

Jiang told us that when he met Paul Oei in 2009, Oei and his beautiful wife exuded sophistication. They picked Jiang up in a Bentley and drove him to a Richmond office.

Oei showed the Chinese investors clippings from a *What's In* magazine article showing Oei receiving a B.C. Liberal party award from Premier Christy Clark. The article named the immigration and recycling companies that Oei used in his scheme. And it also showed Oei and his wife posing with Donald Trump.

"They mentioned their ties to the government, very clearly," Jiang told us. "[Oei] mentioned the B.C. premier and high-level federal ministers have 'very special' relations with him. He mentioned Christy Clark, and he mentioned some MPs, including Joe Peschisolido."

Other investors later corroborated what Jiang told us.

"[Oei] said this project received strong support from the provincial government, and he showed us a lot of photos with the lady premier," investor Wei Chen testified in the Securities Commission hearing. "He said the B.C. government would use this project to go to China to attract immigrants."

Jiang said the lure was set even deeper one night in Richmond when investors met with Oei and Peschisolido at a Chinese seafood restaurant.

It was the legal trust of Peschisolido and Co., and the Richmond federal politician's stature that provided an extra layer of confidence, Jiang told us. "Paul Oei talked to us about this trust account, and he told us this lawyer is a very famous lawyer in Vancouver and Canada," Jiang said.

The problem was getting $4 million to invest in Oei's recycling plant out of China and into Canada.

Jiang told us he was persuaded to become the point man for six other investors, "like the crowdfunding concept we have in China."

"We talked to Paul [Oei], and he said there's a rush to invest in this project," Jiang told us. "This [underground banking] is very common in China, for real estate buys outside of the country."

So the money gathered from seven investors would be wired to Canada, but under Jiang's name only. And a secret ledger filed in

Jiang's lawsuit against Peschisolido showed the names of the six other hidden investors and the amounts each one contributed.

"We just had to provide a list of the investors involved, then [Oei] would take care of the immigration for us," Jiang said.

This, to me, suggested a very opaque transaction that seemed to bend Canada's anti-money-laundering laws to the breaking point. The only name on international banking records was Yicheng Jiang's. But who were the other six investors behind him? For the sake of argument, what if they were criminals or corrupt officials? The method of transaction would certainly allow officials to launder money into Canada anonymously. And according to a 2020 Radio Free Asia report, Jiang claimed his co-investors indeed were linked to the Chinese Communist Party.

He claimed that after they blamed him for their losses in the Cascade scheme, he and his children were targeted in China's "Fox Hunt" — an illegal covert operation by Chinese security forces that targets citizens accused of transferring assets to foreign countries.

If the transactions running through Peschisilido's law firm, in fact, were meant to facilitate Canadian immigration for Chinese Communist Party members, that would add a whole new angle to the case.

But let's just focus on the underground banking aspect. If such a transaction goes into a Canadian legal trust, but Canadian lawyers are not legally obliged to report to Fintrac, is it illegal?

Yicheng Jiang was only following a secret financial tunnel from China to Canada that was wide open to countless others thanks to a Supreme Court ruling. Plus he said he was induced to complete the transaction by Oei. And he explained to us exactly how it worked.

"Now, it's hard for us to transfer the money out of China individually because of the capital movement limits placed on outbound Chinese capital," Jiang said. "So it's best to concentrate our cash into one place, then to go through an underground bank — which looks for opportunities to transfer funds out to Canada whenever they can."

Jiang said he transferred Chinese currency from himself and the six other investors to "a point-person representing the Chinese underground bank." The underground banker, who Jiang met through a relative, changed the yuan to U.S. dollars at a pre-arranged exchange rate.

"So I transferred [yuan] either to that person directly or to whichever account he wanted us to direct the money to," Jiang explained. "Then, the bank would work their magic — I don't know how — to get the money out of China. U.S. dollar funds would be transferred either to my HSBC account in Hong Kong or in Canada."

The magic touch, other sources informed me, involves underground bankers who have relatives working in Macau casinos and Hong Kong banks who can slip money secretly into accounts.

At times in our interviews with Jiang, it seemed to me he might have been minimizing the seriousness of dealing with what he called "community channel" underground bankers.

But during his B.C. Securities Commission testimony, he made the costs of dealing with organized crime more clear.

"This is equivalent to what the Hong Kong people call the U.S. dollar black market exchange transactions," Jiang told the commission. "This is high risk, and in the beginning, we were not aware of the routes. So after we exchanged a certain amount, the person in the community ran away with the money, so we incurred a loss."

After having some of their funds stolen by underground bankers, Jiang said he learned that "according to the rules in the community," his investment group had to pay "black market insurance" fees of 15 to 25 percent per transaction.

The fee would go up or down according to current market conditions, Jiang said. To me, this suggested that organized crime was making an unreal profit on the trillions sent out of China illegally since the 1990s. But it was Chinese citizens that paid the major fees on these underground transactions. The drug cartels operating in other countries that were almost always the counterparty providing funds for these exchanges outside of China paid almost no fees. So it was easy to understand what my police sources were telling me. The super-criminals at the pinnacle of Chinese underground banking networks wielded tremendous political power inside China and had powerful influence with foreign drug cartels, too. They had to because they controlled so much money.

* * *

So I had learned much from Yicheng Jiang's case about the ways that uncountable sums have been transferred into Canadian real estate from Hong Kong and China since the Five Dragons fled to Canada in the 1980s. Was it tens of billions, hundreds of billions, or more? I can't answer that question. But I can say that whatever the sum, much of the money has flowed through criminal financial plumbing that includes Canadian banks and benefits powerful drug cartels.

I also noted the Securities Commission saw how funds from Chinese investors flowed into the bank accounts of Paul Oei's immigration company, Canadian Manu. And $21,732 of these investor funds went from Canadian Manu accounts to Peschisolido and Co.

Peschisolido has repeatedly denied any wrongdoing in the civil cases involving the Chinese investors, and he was not cited in the Securities Commission case. I kept digging, though.

I found that then-premier Christy Clark and her B.C. Liberals had received $37,888 in political donations that came directly from investor funds for Cascade, Oei's failed recycling plant company.

Line items from Oei's accountant showed a December 1, 2011, transaction for "Premier Christy Clarke [sic] dinner to VIP."

The accountant was questioned by a commission lawyer.

"Well, I know that he knows people in the Liberal party. So I guess it's party's promotions," the account said. "He did tell me, he mentioned that it is for Cascade, for promotion."

So was this political donation funded by money-laundering of an illicit underground banking transfer from China? That wasn't a question for the Securities Commission to answer, but it might be a good question for the Cullen Commission to look into. The BC Liberal Party said it would return the funds, after Oei was cited for fraud in the B.C. Securities Commission case.

There was also testimony from multiple sources pointing to casino flow-through transactions from China and Hong Kong.

For example, one Cascade investor — a "Ms. U Po Chu" of Hong Kong — had provided almost $7 million to Oei "in addition to the Cascade investment."

Accounting showed U Po Chu's investor repayments from Cascade were made in the names of other people and that the payments were made to Las Vegas casinos.

Why were investments for a Vancouver recycling plant flowing through Las Vegas?

"These were money that was paid to Las Vegas," Oei's accountant testified. "It was upon U Po Chu's request because she goes down to Las Vegas quite often. And she wanted the money to go back to Hong Kong. So, she asked Mr. Oei to transfer the money and paid it to Las Vegas."

Records showed that for U Po Chu alone, there was $288,291 in payments made to casino cage depositories at "the Wynn, the Bellagio, the Mirage, and the MGM International."

"Does that, as an accountant, does it raise any red flags for you, where you see hundreds of thousands of dollars of personal payments to Las Vegas casinos purportedly to repay investors?" a commission lawyer asked Oei's accountant.

"Well, I do think about it, but I just left it in Mr. Oei's hands," she answered.

I think about it too. Because I later found that a private real estate lender in Vancouver connected to suspicious transactions in B.C.

Lottery Corp. casinos and Paul Jin's network of loan sharks had also provided a large loan to Paul Oei. Oei told me he was forced to take the B.C. casino VIP loan to cover his legal costs in the Cascade case. The other thing I think about is the access that Paul Oei had to elite Canadian politicians. What does this imply about Canada's democracy? Was Oei trying to buy a favour for his recycling plant project? Was he trying to peddle influence in Canada's investor immigration program? Did politicians flock to Oei because of his political fundraising prowess and his access to major wealth from China? Conversely, did his access to Chinese investors result from his ties with Canadian politicians?

Perhaps all of the above. *Guanxi* all around.

I looked into donation records and found Paul Oei and his wife had donated over $67,000 to the B.C. Liberals. And since 2014, when Justin Trudeau took over the federal Liberals, the couple had shovelled $8,477 into party coffers. Oei had made smaller donations to the Conservatives. And Oei also informed me at least one federal Conservative, Alice Wong, was supportive of the Cascade project. Wong's office, however, strongly denied links to Paul Oei's case.

Also, in July 2015, Oei's company sponsored a pre-election luncheon in Richmond featuring Justin Trudeau. Oei shared the head table with the future prime minister, introduced him to the gathered crowd, and embraced Trudeau. Trudeau's message trumpeting a middle-class voter platform likely missed the mark with the Lamborghini-driving set watching his speech.

Meanwhile, Yicheng Jiang told us that after Trudeau was elected prime minister, Oei sent Jiang messages and photos on WeChat of Oei "hugging Trudeau and all these celebratory photos."

"To me, the intention was obvious; it was to tell me to not mess with him in Canada," Jiang told us. "It was like, 'Look at my relationship with the prime minister. We are like buddies. You are just a Chinese man without even an immigrant status in Canada; don't dare come to Canada to cause trouble.'"

So by the summer of 2017, I had a body of work compiled. To me, the money flooding in from China raised flags of serious corruption, obviously in China but also in Canada. Increasingly I was asked to talk about my findings. And I agreed to attend an anti-money-laundering conference in Victoria to talk about the Yicheng Jiang case.

And for months, sporadically, I had been exchanging emails with Ross Alderson. He had mentioned the names of Paul King Jin and Kwok Chung Tam.

In August 2017, Alderson had pointed me to a B.C. civil forfeiture case involving an RCMP investigation that targeted a massive mansion on a piece of Richmond farmland. Alleged Big Circle Boy heavyweight Peter Lap San Pang was accused of running the Richmond underground casino in connection with Jin's network and Pang's relative from Markham, Ontario. I found that Peter Pang and his crew from Guangdong were ranked up there with Kwok Chung Tam and Chi Lop Tse in the hierarchy of Big Circle Boys with long histories in Canada. It all pointed to a dirty loop of cash, casino chips and Macau VIPs circulating between Lottery Corp. casinos and illegal casinos in Richmond and Markham, with opioids and weapons trafficking and real estate money-laundering all mixed in.

In Victoria, Alderson and I met for coffee before I gave my speech. Among other things, he told me I was doing important reporting for Canada. He talked a little bit about his meetings with Calvin Chrustie. And when I returned to Vancouver, he arranged to transfer the highly confidential Lottery Corp. files that enabled me to pull all of my previous Vancouver Model reporting together. It was the last piece of data I needed to decode Paul King Jin's network.

13
SILVER AND GOLD

"Jin apparently is the biggest client for the law firm,"
Alderson told me. And in Victoria, sitting in the coffee
shop, we talked about something else that blew my
mind. Some investigators in GPEB had lost faith in the
integrity of the B.C. government or possibly a mole in
the RCMP. They believed a raid on Jin's underground
casino in Richmond had been compromised.

For a moment, it looked like *Vancouver Sun* editor-in-chief Harold Munro was going to blow a gasket. I was seated across from Munro and feature story editor Hardip Johal in the *Sun's* editorial board-room. It was September 15, 2017.

I had just rambled through a laundry list of evidence, which must have sounded incredible, to say the least. A vast story had come together very quickly — threads I had been following for years. And I was struggling to explain it all.

In early 2017, I had been guided towards B.C. Gaming Enforcement Branch intelligence documents on a casino-money-laundering net-work involving the Mainland China real estate developers I had been digging into.

And a B.C. government source had sent this email: "Lap Sang Peter Pang is connected to Big Circle Boys. You may also want to look at a guy by the name of Paul King JIN and also Kwok TAM. Big crime figures in Richmond. Suspects in illegal gaming, extortion, loan sharking, drug trafficking and underground banking. Also acquiring real estate."

I had made a number of freedom of information requests based on these tips and I was expecting to receive a massive cache of GPEB documents within days.

But after meeting with Ross Alderson on September 12, I already had a tremendous amount of evidence.

Sitting in a coffee shop near the Hotel Fairmont with a view of Victoria's Inner Harbour, Alderson and I had talked about the RCMP's investigation into Paul Jin. We talked about how Alderson's team had made property ownership maps in Richmond and Vancouver. They found pockets of extreme wealth where the Big Circle Boys and Mainland China VIPs owned lots of land. Mansions sprawled across Richmond farmland were running illegal casinos, according to Alderson's intelligence.

The illegal casinos and B.C. Lottery casino loan sharks were directly connected.

Alderson told me that many millions in high-value casino chips had gone missing from River Rock Casino. This was essentially B.C. government currency that flowed between Richmond illegal casinos and government casinos. It was a store of value for organized crime underground banks in Vancouver and China. And it was much easier to carry a purse with 40 chips worth $5,000 apiece than a hockey bag with $200,000 worth of $20s wrapped in elastic bands.

We discussed how Alderson perceived political connections between Mainland China high-rollers and officials in China.

I also knew that some police believed transnational organized crime had corrupted portions of B.C.'s establishment.

And Alderson told me there was an RCMP intelligence theory that Paul Jin had links to the Chinese Communist Party. He said he found the theory hard to believe at first. But the idea gained credibility in 2017 after Richmond real estate lawyer Hong Guo directed a police "investigation" in Zhuhai that led to arrests of Guo's employees Qian Pan and Zixin Li.

"Jin apparently is the biggest client for the law firm," Alderson told me.

And in Victoria, sitting in the coffee shop, we talked about something else that blew my mind. Some investigators in GPEB had lost faith in the integrity of the B.C. government or possibly a mole in the RCMP. They believed a raid on Jin's underground casino in Richmond had been compromised.

The information we were discussing pointed to a scandal worthy of a public inquiry. So when I returned to Vancouver, Alderson arranged to transfer classified documents. These were official government records about investigations into Paul Jin and the Chinese VIPs. The numbers were massive. The operation was worldwide. It was the story of a lifetime.

Harold Munro had been an investigative reporter before rising to the top editorial position for *Vancouver Sun*. In my experience, Munro loved big, hard-hitting stories. And the bigger the story, the harder his vetting questions. He would come at you like a lawyer, looking for weaknesses. So in this story meeting on September 15, I was trying to boil down incredibly complex information. And Munro seemed to be losing patience. I could imagine what was going through his mind. How the hell can we prove this?

After some cross-examination we were at an impasse. I took a deep breath, pulled a sheet of paper from my binder and shoved it across the table to Munro.

It was a Section 86 report. The legal form must be filed to GPEB whenever Lottery Corp. staff learn of potential crimes. This was Alderson's unredacted July 2015 brief on the Paul Jin "Silver" investigation.

Munro started to read the document with a frown. And I sat waiting. The report was just a few paragraphs. But each sentence was weighty. Within about 30 seconds Munro's mood had brightened considerably. And when he finished reading, he was smiling.

We talked about Alderson's documents and how they would be buttressed by the GPEB records due to arrive any day. Munro told me to drop all my other stories and focus on the B.C. casino files. No one outside of the story meeting knew of the explosive records I had. At the same time, we didn't know B.C.'s government was battling internally over my GPEB disclosure case.

The conflict revolved around an audit of River Rock Casino commissioned by GPEB and completed by the forensic accounting firm MNP.

This was a high-level report on the problems that allowed suspicious cash to flood B.C. casinos. Really, it was an accountant's overview of the RCMP's Jin investigations. For months, I had been negotiating to obtain this report and thousands of related GPEB records.

But for some reason, B.C. attorney general David Eby had decided to release the MNP audit to all media outlets ahead of my legal disclosure request.

And B.C. Lottery Corp. executives panicked.

An email chain I later obtained through freedom of information showed their efforts to "modify" the MNP audit. On Sept. 20 at 5:59 p.m., Lottery Corp. board chair Bud Smith — a former B.C. attorney general — emailed Lottery Corp. CEO Jim Lightbody and chief of compliance Robert Kroeker.

"Colleagues, I just took a call from the Minister's office. Apparently, the FOI process is about to release the MNP on ML [money-laundering]," Smith wrote. "The Minister wants to release it himself and phoned to give a heads up. I said send what is going to be released, and if it's what I think it is, there's an Ernst and Young report, and I believe a Fintrac report that was done around the same time and likely modified some of the MNP conclusions."

Lightbody emailed back: "Bud, the Minister's [assistant] also called me, and it is the MNP audit. It doesn't include our management response, which is a problem. The report is challenging at best. It was commissioned by GPEB."

The email chain shows that Kroeker — River Rock Casino's chief of compliance from 2011 to August 2015 — pushed back on MNP's conclusions.

"The MNP audit covered the period Sept. 2013 to Aug. 31, 2015," Kroeker wrote. "This audit focused on only select transactions at River Rock...

We were not consulted by GPEB prior to the FOI package going to the Minister — certainly I was not given an opportunity to comment on redactions."

Kroeker would later testify in B.C.'s money-laundering inquiry that while he was in charge of compliance at River Rock, feedback from Fintrac on BCLC's money-laundering controls was positive, and Great Canadian "continually endeavoured to improve its controls."

Meanwhile, panicked emails to Eby's staff about MNP's audit continued.

"Sam [Godfrey], I've reviewed the [MNP] document you sent," Lightbody wrote September 20. "We are very concerned that the report does not include our management response that we provided, which is the usual practice and provides balance and perspective."

On Thursday, September 21, I learned that the MNP audit — part of my FOI request — would be released publicly Friday morning. I had been working on the underlying story for months. And now bureaucrats were trying to manage how the information would be disseminated. I had no idea the Lottery Corp. brass was trying to undermine the MNP report. But I was concerned.

I called a government official Thursday evening and complained. There wasn't much I could do. But it was arranged that an embargoed copy of the MNP report came to me that night.

The report was heavily redacted and named no names. But it was obvious why the Lottery Corp. hated it. GPEB had commissioned the MNP audit because an investigation "identified approximately $13.5 million in $20 bills being accepted in River Rock in July 2015."

And MNP's audit tied the funds to the Richmond casino loan sharks and "high-roller Asian VIP clients."

The report said River Rock's staff had "fostered a culture accepting of large bulk cash transactions," and because the VIPs were from China, it was difficult for staff to judge the legitimacy of their wealth.

"Chinese nationals ... comprise the majority of the identified high-risk demographic at River Rock," the audit said. "Interviews have confirmed that VIPs are indeed wealthy non-residents, or business persons with interests in Vancouver and China, coming to Vancouver to gamble. The use of possible underground banking operations using large volumes of unsourced cash have become increasingly common and accepted as a convenience feature for VIP players who may not be able to send funds to Canada."

And it was all about B.C.'s government turning a blind eye to suspicious money.

"Accepting large volumes of cash has been a growing problem in the province for a number of years," the report said. "BCLC is account-able to the province for revenue ... Service providers [are] focusing on revenue."

I broke the MNP audit story Friday morning. But my real work started on Saturday morning. I had documents that named names. I had ultra-confidential Fintrac records. I could connect the Big Circle Boys casino loan sharks and Chinese whales to major real estate lending networks. I could pull back the curtain on a scam that had been covered up for decades. I could tell the story of the largest RCMP money-laundering investigation in Canadian history. And we had a week to pull it together.

The *Vancouver Sun* front page exclusive ran on Saturday, September 30, and I started the story like this.

"On Oct. 15, 2015, a Mountie burst through the front door of an office in Richmond, carrying a battering ram and with a rifle slung on his back. The door swung shut behind him, locking him inside. He was in the lobby of Silver International Investment, a high-end money transfer business, surrounded by bulletproof glass.

"Behind a second glass door, a woman rushed to make a call while hiding several cellphones. Under her desk was a safe stuffed with bundles of cash. The Mountie, a large man, counted seconds anxiously, wondering if the woman would unlock the interior door.

"It was one of 10 police raids in Richmond that day — part of a major investigation that has uncovered massive money-laundering and underground banking networks with links to Mainland China, Macau and B.C. casinos, allege the RCMP's federal organized crime unit and China's national police service.

"Now, the inside story can be told of the investigations that led B.C.'s attorney general last week to order an independent review of casinos overseen by the B.C. Lottery Corp."

The story focused on Paul King Jin. I have never been able to interview him after repeated attempts to reach him through lawyers.

But Jin has left a massive trail of incriminating records. Through dozens of interviews with people in business and law enforcement, and after obtaining and studying many thousands of government, legal and corporate records dating from the early 1990s to 2020, this is what I learned about Paul Jin's background and function in a global criminal network that extends all the way to Beijing.

* * *

Shibao Jia came from a very poor family in the eastern Chinese province of Shandong. It was a hard life.

But boxing saved him. It made him resilient and tough. The gym gave him somewhere to be. And when he had no money, he told people, the coach let him sleep on the floor.

He was a prospect for the Chinese Olympic team in the 1980s.

He didn't quite make the cut. But he learned a lot. He told people that if China had put any money into pro boxing, he might have stayed there. But instead, he came to Canada.

He was in his late 20s when he arrived in the early 1990s. He gave himself an English name: Paul King Jin. Colleagues say he spent some time in Montreal before saving enough money to start the Water Cube, a Richmond massage parlour.

His co-director at the Water Cube was a Triad heavyweight from Guangdong named Lap San Peter Pang. Peter Pang had big interests in illegal casino networks in Richmond and Markham, according to RCMP and GPEB intelligence. His name had come up in a number of 1990s heroin and weapons trafficking investigations in Vancouver.

According to confidential informants Peter Pang was right up there with the likes of Kwok Chung Tam and Chi Lop Tse in Big Circle Boys' hierarchy. He was obviously superior to Paul Jin. An intelligence source told me Pang once roughed Jin up and told him to get his act together when something went sideways in the Richmond illegal casinos.

Jin and his family members — including his wife, mother, father and niece — constantly shuffled Richmond director addresses for Jin's various businesses, including the Water Cube and the Warrior Fighting Dream, his mixed martial arts gym. But other directors listed addresses in Beijing, Qingdao, Guangzhou and Harbin.

After about ten years in Canada, Paul Jin was near the top of Richmond's underworld hierarchy. But there were men high above operators like Paul Jin and Peter Pang, according to my RCMP documents and intelligence sources.

These were the business giants who owned mines and skyscrapers and ships and forests and highways in China. Men well-connected to China's state and military and judicial elite. Men with access to ports in Qingdao, Harbin, Beijing, Shanghai, Guangzhou and Hong Kong. To put it another way, an intelligence source told me, a sort of power shift was playing out in Canada. The southern, Cantonese-speaking cartels may have had more autonomy in the early days of the Vancouver Model. But after 2008, the state-sponsored heavyweights of northern China appeared to gain influence over their networks in Vancouver and Toronto.

So these were the Chinese state actors that Jin served. They were his patrons and bosses.

Business relationships in Canada were formed in playgrounds of vice, Chinese community and RCMP intelligence sources explained to me. It was powerful *guanxi*.

You want to come to my spa in Richmond and play with some girls? No problem. Want to play baccarat in government casinos — even better, lay bets in our own private VIP lounges and cash out winnings at Richmond currency exchange shops? How about a guided safari to kill some black bears? We have "special" relations with some Canadian officials, so don't worry, it's all taken care of. We can even ship polar bear mounts and hunting guns back to you in China.

You'd like to develop some Vancouver real estate? Easy. Mingle with elite Canadian politicians in our China-Canada friendship association fundraisers? Done!

For Jin, this was beyond social networking. He was so connected it would be more appropriate to use the terminology of computer networking. Jin could be called a supernode. He was the intersection — the crucial facilitator — for many people and markets.

According to my documents and a Mandarin speaker in Richmond who knew Paul Jin and saw him in action — Jin had found his true calling in life. A broker of vice for powerful men. And a facilitator for their Chinese state activity in Canada.

And because of this, Shibao Jia became someone in China. He rose from sleeping on gym floors to demanding the best seats in China's most expensive restaurants.

And he acquired assets — a factory, bank accounts, homes, a mine in Mongolia — that proved his *guanxi* with powerful cadres.

So when the RCMP finally questioned Jin about his casino exploits in Richmond, he bragged about his ties to "high level officials."

"In China I'm too important, right? The police officer is a high level, very high. The prime minister is high enough. My classmates are very high-level in China."

And in Richmond, according to the RCMP, he had a stable of high-end cars and multiple condos and an illegal casino mega-mansion and a couple of bodyguards.

The Lottery Corp. even had a file called Project Sienna, named after the fleet of vans he allegedly used to move cash and $13 million worth of missing River Rock Casino chips between legal and illegal casinos.

The RCMP had known long before Shibao Jia arrived in Canada about heroin shipping routes and heavyweights like Kwok Chung Tam in Vancouver. In the 1990s, North American police knew underground banks with vast pools of heroin wealth were massive business.

But for Jin's generation of Big Circle Boys to reach the next level, B.C. Lottery casinos needed the necessary infrastructure.

It was a simple equation. If betting limits for baccarat in Vancouver and Richmond could compete with Macau, B.C. government casinos would become attractive to the transnational whales.

And so, limits were raised exponentially in British Columbia from the late 1990s to 2014. Baccarat bets starting at $25 per hand before 2000, despite many money-laundering warnings, peaked at a devastating $100,000 per hand in 2014. Of course, suspicious cash transactions rose exponentially too.

And Lottery Corp. CEO Michael Graydon loomed over his executives like a taskmaster, his terse emails stinging like a whip.

He ordered his executives to meet revenue and cost targets, or their bonuses would vanish. Was there a financial motive for executives to turn a blind eye to hockey bags stuffed with suspected drug cash?

Around 2007, GPEB started to notice the north China whales coming in. Ripples throughout the industry, indications something big was moving under the surface. Suspicious cash transactions were skyrocketing year-to-year.

But it took a decade before RCMP investigators fully understood the machine behind it.

* * *

Silver International was hiding in plain sight. It was a terribly brazen operation. It was right in your face, down the hall from Richmond law offices.

And that's why the RCMP was able to document such a steady traffic between the cash bank in downtown Richmond and River Rock Casino. All they had to do was follow Paul Jin's fleet of Sienna vans in an incredible beehive of daily activity. From Silver, to Jin's underground casinos, to Hong Guo's law office, to various Chinese restaurants across Richmond, Jin and his bodyguards were always on the move, and sometimes with Jin's child tagging along.

In late 2017, two years after RCMP tactical units raided Silver, in a Vancouver conference room Insp. Bruce Ward briefed a private audience. The crowd included U.S. Secret Service agents, financial professionals and Canadian police. This was information important to the Five Eyes intelligence allies, especially Australia, the U.S. and Canada.

And I obtained a secret audio recording of Ward's presentation. This was the crucial record that took me inside the RCMP's E-Pirate investigation and helped me understand all of the leaked paper records in my cache.

"Silver is an illegal money-laundering service for criminals," Ward said, "and how they were facilitating the purchase and importation of the drugs, by moving the money around the world for drug dealers."

Ward explained to his audience that first, to understand Silver's networks, the RCMP had to understand Asian organized crime in Canada and its connections to China.

"This is not an organized structure with command and control," Ward said. "It is more about business relationships. Because it operates very much parallel to the normal business community."

Through surveillance and confidential informants, RCMP intelligence had learned that narcos, loan sharks, illegal casino operators and B.C. Lottery casino money launderers, lawyers, realtors, mortgage brokers, immigration fraudsters and corrupt politicians all networked for mutually beneficial transactions.

"So you as a member of that community become trusted because, say, you conducted a deal two years ago for some people, and it worked out," Ward said. "So any given gangster, if you want to call them that, businessman, he will have many schemes. And thus many networks."

And as I learned of these networks, I honed my techniques for following the actors. Pictures can be a very important advertisement of *guanxi* between gangsters, politicians and professionals. And these network actors loved to post pictures of themselves raising glasses of red wine at galas attended by Chinese consulate officials and Canadian politicians. The political element would be something I delved into after understanding the narco element.

And the narco network had an ever-present problem in Vancouver: what to do with massive amounts of warehoused drug cash.

"So this networking is what facilitated the business for Silver International," Ward said. "Because they were able to start a profession of money-laundering for their friends in drug dealing, who needed the service of converting cash into bankable instruments."

But Silver first had to collect the cash. A number of businesses clustered into a few downtown Richmond blocks were seen by RCMP intelligence as the geographical supernode of drug-trafficking circuits in North America.

And Silver was in the middle of this heat map, a ten-minute drive from River Rock Casino.

When the RCMP discovered Silver's location in April 2015, undercover teams identified at least 40 different organizations entering a Richmond office tower and ascending to Silver's third-floor office with "suitcases laden with cash."

Most of the organizations were dealing heroin, cocaine and methamphetamines, Ward said. Silver was collecting drug sale deliveries in deposits totalling about $1.5 million per day. The RCMP considered itself lucky that B.C.'s fentanyl crisis was not yet full-blown when they discovered the underground bank and seized over $9 million in cash.

"We broke four money counters in the process," Ward said. "It was fortunate that we seized this money before the fentanyl crisis because that is dangerous dust that comes off the money."

Silver was not Fort Knox. It would have looked no different from a fancy dentist's office with its see-through glass walls and leather couches.

But few people would have known those walls were made of bullet-proof glass, and in the back regions of the office, suitcases of cash were strewn across the floor.

The paper money piling up daily in Silver would have reached the ceiling within a few weeks, unless staff found a way to move it quickly.

And that is where the genius of Silver came into play. In Mainland China each citizen is barred from exporting more than $50,000 per year. There is incredible pent up supply in China's banking system seeking to break that financial wall. And Paul King Jin, Silver International, and some Chinese industrialists had a solution, and a business model called Macau.

* * *

The glittering city on the western shore of the Pearl River delta is called the Las Vegas of China for obvious reasons.

Macau has been a hub of international transactions for centuries, a former colony of Portugal, transformed into an outlet valve for vices banned in Mainland China.

It is a special administrative region for the Chinese Communist Party where casinos are legalized, the majority of GDP is derived from casinos, and the opulent gambling palaces have eclipsed Las Vegas in profitability, producing from $30 to $40 billion USD each year in revenue, at least three times more than the casinos in Nevada. This is where China's 1 percent, elite state figures and Red princelings come to gamble and shop.

In China, it is widely reported that corrupt officials have colluded with Hong Kong and Macau Triads to transfer state funds in and out of Macau through underground gambling junkets.

And the scandals have reached all the way into China's Politburo — the handful of CCP bosses who run the world's second-largest economy — as illustrated by the cases of China's former national security chief, Zhou Yongkang, and Bo Xilai, a north China governor so popular that he was considered a rival to Xi Jinping.
Both leaders were linked in reports to Macau gangs and organized crime junket operators before each was convicted on corruption charges. In the case of Zhou Yongkang, who had control of China's police and security forces, investigators linked his family to a flamboyant real estate and mining tycoon named Liu Han.

Liu Han had amassed a fortune of $6.4 billion and operated mines in Australia and the United States before he was tried and executed in 2015 on allegations that he had risen from "petty thug to billionaire." His mistake had been his brashness and violence; with his fleet of luxury vehicles and mink coats, the facade of an industrialist was easy to see through. And before his death, the public learned he ran a cartel operating illegal casinos in China and laundering money through legal casinos in Macau, as well as trafficking weapons and providing contract-killing services.

Zhou Yongkang, Liu Han and Bo Xilai were all taken down in sweeping corruption probes launched by China's president, Xi Jinping.

In 2015, Macau's GDP fell by 26 percent as fear of Xi's corruption probes expanded.

But even Xi's family has been linked to the vices of corruption, offshore wealth, and foreign casinos. A joint investigation in 2019 by Australian media revealed that Xi's cousin, an official named Ming Chai, was identified as a VIP gambler in Australian casinos, with links to a prominent organized crime junket boss. And these junkets were connected to Chinese foreign influence and espionage networks.

So this is the demographic of VIP gamblers that have helped build Macau's wealth for decades by skimming funds from China's underclasses and making alliances with narcos and loan sharks and spies abroad.

* * *

The Silver network Macau-style money-laundering investigations finally gained focus with B.C. Lottery Corp. surveillance of Paul Jin at River Rock Casino in 2014.
Confidential records that I obtained from Fintrac show that Paul Jin was banned by B.C. Lottery Corp. casinos in 2012 for suspicious transactions and suspected organized crime loan-sharking. One of his associates, according to the Lottery Corp. record, was called "Suspect 1" in an RCMP organized crime target list that called Jin "Suspect 22."

Suspect 1 listed his occupation as shipbuilder. Suspect 2 claimed to be a Chinese restaurant tycoon. And "Suspect 3" was a crowdfunding developer from northern China whom I had been following for a few years.

Anyway, the 2012 Lottery Corp. ban on Jin was meaningless.

"Attached to this email is a collection of the Top-10 money facilitators that work out of the Lower Mainland casinos with the majority devoted to River Rock patrons," a confidential 2014 Lottery Corp. record says. "Of course, Paul JIN is the #1 target and is currently banned but is extremely active and has numerous people working for him."

Paul Jin's Lottery Corp. investigation file says he had tight connections with the VIP baccarat players.

He also frequented Grand Villa Casino in Burnaby and Starlight Casino in New Westminster, the records say. One record produced by Alderson alleged that "several phone calls had been made to Paul JIN originating from the Grand Villa Casino in June 2015."

Records also showed that GPEB investigated the casino's VIP staff for meeting with Jin and discussing an investment in the Starlight's VIP room. Jin was fronting for an unidentified real estate tycoon in China. A lawyer for the casino claimed the meeting was really about a real estate development near the New Westminster casino.

And one of the company's VIP hostesses was investigated for introducing one of Paul King Jin's Chinese whale gamblers, Mr. Fu, to a "known loan shark."

In 2014 one of Alderson's Lottery Corp. colleagues noted: "Most of the players that Jin has supplied cash for are known VIP players with extensive gaming histories and considerable wealth with mostly Asian-based businesses. In almost every instance when Jin has supplied cash for a patron, the cash has been in the form of large amounts of bundled $20 bills."

It would take some time before Calvin Chrustie's federal organized crime unit linked River Rock Casino and Silver's "cash house" in downtown Richmond.

The break came on April 29, 2015.

"We've done four more days of surveillance on our friend, all day shifts, and we have made some interesting observations," a police detective emailed to a Lottery Corp. casino investigator. "I was wondering if you have any new sightings from the last week?"

Within weeks the RCMP would connect the dots: Paul Jin's crew was making cash deliveries to the Chinese VIPs at River Rock Casino; the cash was coming from Silver International; drug trafficking organizations were driving in from across western Canada to Richmond every day with suitcases of cash.

In one case, drug dealers from Alberta were nailed with $1 million cash stuffed into two suitcases.

But where were the casino VIPs coming from, and how was Paul Jin connecting with them?

That would become apparent as the RCMP investigation extended outside Canada. You only had to track Paul Jin's flights out of Vancouver to find the answer.

Bruce Ward explained the international leg of the E-Pirate investigation to his private audience in September 2017.

"The primary target that led us [to Silver International] was a person that is involved in generating whales," Ward said. "Whales are high-end gamblers. So [Paul Jin's] expertise is going over and working in Macau and identifying rich Chinese businessmen that would go to Macau. And he was attracting them to Canada, to gamble."

When Paul Jin met these men of great wealth — such as Jia Gao, a real estate developer who frequented the Venetian Macao — Jin would tell them he was a junket operator in Canada, and that he could take care of them in Richmond.

And it was a neat shell game trick, how they got money out of China and into Canada. In fact, the money never crossed borders. Jin and Silver had pools of drug money sitting in Richmond and China. And the VIP funds were sitting in Chinese banks. The VIP gamblers would arrange a contract with Paul Jin and Silver to deposit funds from their own China bank accounts into China bank accounts controlled by Silver.

This gave them a credit in the underground banking system. And when they flew from China and landed in Richmond, they would call Jin's hotline and arrange to meet his agents in parking lots near River Rock Casino.

All they had to do was lug their bags of cash into the VIP room.

Paul Jin would charge the Macau VIPs from 3 to 5 percent per transaction for the underground service. A $100,000 cash payout in Richmond would coincide with a $105,000 wire transfer from the VIP's Chinese bank to Silver's accounts in China.

"He would use Silver International as a bank account," Ward explained. "He would get that cash, and they would break it up into whatever is the order of the day. They would put $100,000 into a hockey bag, show up at the casino, and give [the whale gambler] $100,000."

Or the transaction could flow the other way.

If the whale was a member of the cartel or an associate with *guanxi* and elevated status in China — like a powerful official — they could travel to Richmond and take out a gambling debt obligation.

The bags of cash used to buy casino chips would be paid back later from the VIP's bank accounts in China into Silver's bank accounts in China.

Or the transactions were run through illegal casinos.

For example, Paul Jin, in his own B.C. Supreme Court filings, said that he carried a large bag holding $2.68 million cash into a Richmond coffee shop and loaned it out to a Chinese real estate developer who is identified in RCMP investigation files. The real estate developer, in turn, said the cash was related to a gambling session at Jin's illegal casino.

Real estate owned by the whale in Richmond and secured by a promissory note was to be used as a transfer of debt in the money-laundering scheme. Lottery Corp. investigators also found that Jin's network was funding River Rock Casino whales with cash provided by currency exchanges in Richmond.

The VIPs could cash their Lottery Corp. casino chips for casino cheques, according to RCMP and GPEB records, and deposit the funds in Canadian banks to buy Vancouver real estate. This was the easiest way for drug cash to seep into luxury homes.

In totality, Silver was incredibly complex because the variety and path of transactions seemed endless. But the core service was incredibly simple.

Credits and debts were adjusted in black market banks separated by thousands of miles, with transactions never recorded on government ledgers.

Ross Alderson would explain it this way, in his September 2015 Lottery Corp. money-laundering report.

"From BCLC investigative interviews conducted with VIP players, BCLC has been able to determine that for a number of players they readily admit to not knowing the source of their cash, and that they pay back in suspicious circumstances using suspicious methods with little or no interest," the document said. "This would indicate transnational money-laundering."

So these VIPs admitted, at least, that they didn't know where Jin's cash came from. But they were not stupid. They knew how the game worked in Macau. Were they narcos themselves? They bet cash like it was going out of style. Like they didn't care whether they won or lost. Like the real point was to keep cash flowing in and out of the casino. Like even when they lost on paper, it was a win. Or just overhead, a cost of doing business. Ward's audience started to laugh when he profiled one notable Chinese industrialist.

"We interviewed one, our primary gambler, over a two-year period, he gambled and lost $57 million" Ward said. "He is living in Canada, but he owns a series of mining conglomerates in China. So his concern about the $57 million is that he didn't tell his wife. Not because she was going to get mad at him, but she would go out and spend $57 million herself, just to pay him back."

This comment was entertaining, but I don't think the RCMP got a straight answer from the miner.

I had found that a coal miner known as the biggest whale in Lottery Corp. records was involved with the Jin group in complex cash and real estate lending through Las Vegas, Vancouver and China. In other words, Vancouver Model underground banking.

What kind of businessman would bet like this?

According to GPEB there were 60 to 80 whales of this magnitude in B.C. at any time; men who bet from $100,000 to $1 million per session. The names would change from month-to-month. Usually a businessman would gamble for a few months, return to China, and come back again.

"The staff at River Rock was allowing this, and B.C. Lottery Corp. wasn't doing anything," a GPEB source said. "I believe it was almost being encouraged. They were flying people in. They were helping people comping rooms. And we said to Fintrac, what are you doing?"

And the RCMP came to similar conclusions.
"If you were able to provide the simplest of excuses or explanations as to where the cash came from, they were happy," Ward said in 2017. "Matter of fact, if they were happy, they would not even fill out a Fintrac report. My example is the B.C. Lottery Corp. had identified in the year leading up to our [E-Pirate] file about $180 million in cash that came into the River Rock Casino. So that is bags of cash. We've talked to the businessmen. It is not cultural. There is no reason in Canada to carry more than you and I carry in cash."

Gaming intelligence documents prepared by Ross Alderson and GPEB Special Constable Scott McGregor painted an even bleaker picture of the whales and their helpers inside B.C. casinos.

"There are likely people in the regulated B.C. Gaming Industry that are involved in facilitating proceeds of crime for players," Alderson wrote in a document prepared for Lottery Corp. management in

2015. "A criminal investigation [could] uncover a criminal element directly linked to B.C. casinos ... there should be a concern that B.C. Lottery Corp. and service provider management will be accused of 'willful blindness.'"

Two years after that assessment, McGregor prepared an 11-page intelligence report for GPEB after a River Rock Casino VIP host was investigated for a suspected money-laundering transaction.

"There was a large third-party buy-in [in late 2017] where a brand new patron walked in with $200,000 in $100 bills and waited to receive chips. Once the chips were delivered, the patron left the casino without any play," MacGregor's report said. "This incident is being investigated for regulatory infractions at the River Rock Casino ... This incident is highly suspect, and the ongoing GPEB investigation into this matter is the first step in identifying the correlation of connections between service provider staff, local patrons, foreign patrons, and illicit activity."

Still, in late 2017, the RCMP had only limited knowledge of who the Silver VIPs were.

"When we take down an elephant, or in this case a whale, we digest one leg at a time," is how a senior RCMP officer put it to me.

But in 2019, when Alderson summed up his findings in notarized filings, he presented a more definitive portrait of the Silver whales.

He wrote that during 2014 and 2015, while B.C.'s fentanyl crisis was evolving into a public health emergency, Lottery Corp. casinos were accepting from $17 to $22 million in suspicious cash transactions per month.

"Being in charge of Lottery Corp. investigative and intelligence groups, I gathered evidence that many of the industry VIP players were involved in criminality, including the drug trade as well as suspected money-laundering in real estate, casinos and other sectors," Alderson wrote. "There was also evidence of political involvement by a number of these individuals.

"And there were indications of government interference in enforcement and possible corruption."

* * *

So on October 15, 2015, Bruce Ward's unit raided ten locations in Richmond, including Silver International Investment, in the office tower on 5811 Cooney Road.

It was an extremely successful raid in most aspects.

Silver was a high-tech operation. The RCMP seized 132 computers and cell phones, transaction ledgers, safes and money counters, over $7 million in cash, and security camera footage that captured massive cash exchanges in cinematic detail.

"We were very lucky because one surveillance team started the file, but they didn't have an understanding of what was going on inside," Ward explained, on my secret audio recording. "We didn't have a chance to use covert teams to see the inside of the business. But they had their own internal security system, and we were able to seize two weeks of their tapes."

And over 1,000 pages of RCMP surveillance and seizure records filed with the Cullen Commission outline the moving pieces of Jin's ops in stunning detail. Police seized many banking records and real estate promissory notes and mortgages from Jin's properties. They also collected legal documents prepared by Hong Guo. These were the legal registration papers that Jin and his wife, Xiaoqi Wei, allegedly used to take collateral against Vancouver mansions for massive cash loans.

One of the real estate documents seized from Jin was a $1.2 million promissory note from one of Jin's River Rock VIPs.
And Jin's wife was interviewed about the lawyer involved.

"So the time that Paul didn't get his money back, did they pay him back eventually?" a Vancouver police detective asked her.

"Not always," Wei answered. "Sometimes, some person just give their house to us."

"So [Hong Guo is] the lawyer that helps facilitate or helps arrange the signing?"

"Yeah," Jin's wife answered.

Surveillance records showed Jin dropping into Guo's office several times, as he made his daily rounds in fleets of vehicles, taking bags in and out of restaurants, withdrawing suitcases of cash from Silver, making drops and exchanges in parking lots, and running in and out of the Water Cube Spa, where Jin's illegal casino clients came to pay when they lost on the credit they drew in his gaming dens.

RCMP also seized "invoices with score sheets" in garbage bags, records from RTY Financial, and receipts from West Coast Hunting. When a police dog searched five vehicles seized from Jin — including a Bentley Continental, a red Porsche 911 and a white Toyota Sienna — all tested postive for narcotics residue. Surveillance records showed that for one complex transaction in a Richmond Costco parking lot, a vehicle registered to YZ — an alleged fentanyl trafficker involved in real estate lending with Jin — appeared to make counter-surveillance manouevres, before a bag was exchanged from the trunk of one of Jin's vehicles.

There was an incredible amount of evidence.

But back in October 2015, already there were troubling signs for an investigation that would ultimately implode.

The underground banking portion of the raid caught staff red-handed, allegedly. But strikes on illegal casinos did not.

"They had two ongoing illegal casinos where the same businessmen who were part of the conspiracy provided non-government gambling for these offshore gamblers," Ward explained while showing images of two luxury properties. "These are some of the illegal casinos he was setting up. Each of these places had significant security cameras and systems. When we did our takedown, one place was closing down."

Four days later, on October 19, Alderson heard from a senior B.C. police officer that the RCMP was concerned that the Lottery Corp. had interviewed whale gamblers in Jin's network ahead of the raid on a sprawling hacienda on 20-plus acres of secluded farmland on No. 4 Road, in south Richmond. It was the city's second-most valuable property, worth about $10 million. The RCMP seemed to be questioning whether the Lottery Corp. had leaked plans to VIPs, who then communicated to Paul Jin about the upcoming raid on the Big Circle Boys casino.

The underground casino on No. 4 Road, complete with tennis courts, swimming pool, and six full bathrooms, had 29 surveillance cameras. And it was hastily abandoned.

"Discussed sensitivity in sharing information as Operation was compromised," Alderson's notes from the meeting with a senior B.C. police officer say. "No. 4 Rd. Location had original warrant date (Oct 14) circled on a calendar. Concerns Govt knew more than Senior Police did."

But it wasn't clear from Alderson's notes who could have leaked the raid plans.

"Talked about how any info Govt had was through RCMP except for the list of players and the locations of gaming houses were given to GPEB," Alderson's notes say. "We were aware of briefing notes written to Minister. Agreed that interviewing players highlighted JIN's involvement, however, locations of Gaming Houses were all provided to GPEB. Agreed that a lot of people had inside knowledge of this operation but reiterated no one (to my knowledge knew of any dates of the operation)."

So, according to Alderson's 2015 records, it looked like a Mainland China drug cartel with possible connections to Chinese officials had accessed the most sensitive police intelligence and operational details held by the RCMP, in Canada's largest-ever transnational money-laundering investigation.

And as far as Alderson knows, there is still no indication of who was responsible.

"After a series of police raids on illegal gaming houses had been conducted in Richmond, B.C., I was party to conversations where there was a belief by some members of law enforcement that the raids had been compromised by a leak," Alderson wrote in 2020. "Possibly within their ranks, or within government."

The fact Big Circle Boys may have access to Canada's most sensitive law enforcement plans is tragic. But considering the sheer scale of Silver's alleged operations and its clientele in China, Mexico and Iran, it is terrifying.

In his 2017 presentation, Bruce Ward explained the opposite arm of Silver's cash lending services for whale gamblers. It had evolved into a financial juggernaut allegedly capable of laundering and moving over $1 billion per year for the import and export of drugs.
All of this emanating from an office tower in downtown Richmond.

While playing video evidence, Ward explained how drug dealers could instantly make their mountains of dirty cash in Canada materialize in bank accounts in China, Mexico, or Peru. It started with a phone call and a visit to the criminal vault. A single woman standing behind a desk with a cellphone and a ledger. That was it — no bodyguards with guns.

"This is a typical event of a drug dealer bringing in cash," Ward said, as a video clip played. "She receives a call, she goes out to receive a trusted customer. There are $100s and $50s. But the vast majority is $20s. The relationship is such, and trusted, that the phone call is made: 'I'm coming in with' — in this case, it was $1.4 million. And the staff will wire transfer the credit for that in China before the cash even comes in the door."

In other words, as Silver recorded a cash transaction in the ledger of its Richmond criminal bank, it would simultaneously send instructions electronically to credit the drug dealer's bank account in China with a fund transfer from one of Silver's bank accounts in China.

Bruce Ward's video clip showed the drug dealer dropping his duffel bag of cash in Silver's Richmond office.

And then "she counts it by hand," Ward said, "writes it down in her ledger, double checks the money is the same that they said by phone. Five minutes later is the end of her shift. And she walks out and locks the door. There is no security because no one would know it is there or dare rob that place."

According to the RCMP's forensic investigation, Silver turned $220 million in drug cash into bankable instruments in Canada in its first year. Most of this was laundered through B.C. casinos and whales. But $20 million of the cash was provided to downtown Richmond currency exchanges. It was an excellent illustration of how the Big Circle Boys have slowly infiltrated banks in Asia by co-mingling clean and dirty money.

"This definitely causes concern, and it is a bigger issue in the future. Because this is a legal business of transferring money on behalf of you and everyone else between countries," Ward said, on my audio recording. "How they do that is they have a safe with cash under the till. Your grandma wires you $30,000 for your birthday. You go into that business and, they could send the $30,000 to your bank electronically. Or, they will give you cash [and give the customer a premium.]"

"So you get $31,000 (cash). So, where do they legally get their cash? From the banks. But where do they illegally get their cash? [From organized crime.] How do we tell the difference?"

So Silver had mastered laundering illegal casino, extortion, prostitution and drug cash through B.C. casinos and real estate, using whales that wanted to invest their Chinese wealth in Canada.

But Silver's move into narco supply chain logistics — also connected to China's biggest whales — appears to have been its highest growth business. When the RCMP took the Richmond underground bank down, it had already set up over 600 bank accounts in China. And the accounts were multiplying exponentially.

"What Silver started to move into is facilitating the purchase and importation of the drugs," Ward said, pointing to transaction records. "So this is a typical request. A direction from Silver International to move money from their own account to a drug dealer's account. And we saw evidence of over 600 accounts in China that were controlled or fed by Silver International. So they would do that on your behalf. They would open up an account in China. You give them $100,000 cash in Richmond, and they wire transfer you $95,000 into your account in China."

Talk about a disruptive innovator. In Vancouver, drug dealers with fentanyl precursor suppliers in Wuhan or Guangzhou could have Silver wire transfer funds to cartel accounts in China. These funds would result in more fentanyl arriving in Vancouver. Drugs would be sold, cash collected, funds wired to China, and the cycle repeated. And if these dealers had cocaine suppliers in Mexico or Peru, they could have Canadian banks wire transfer funds to drug dealer accounts in Latin America.

This way, the trafficker selling in Canada could buy drugs in Latin America or China without assuming the risk of packing cash into a suitcase and boarding a plane. Fake trade invoices from Chinese manufacturers covered the wire transfers. It was the Chinese organized crime variation of what the FBI and DEA call the black market peso exchange.

This is also known as trade-based money-laundering, in which drug shipments are made to look like legitimate products or co-mingled with legitimate products. To the bank it looks like a North America-based importer-exporter is buying something like T-shirts or coffee beans or electronics, when they are really buying cocaine or fentanyl.

"If you work for banks, you are facilitating money-laundering," Ward told his audience while pointing at a Silver wire record. "They are sophisticated enough, they will hide this behind false invoices. I am paying an invoice to somebody from China who supposedly sold me something. And I am paying for it, in this case, to Peru. And then the supplier will release, for transport, the narcotics."

This all meant that Vancouver had become a global tool for buying, selling and shipping cocaine, heroin, methamphetamines and fentanyl, and rinsing the proceeds in local and international real estate. And it wasn't just the Big Circle Boys and Chinese whales using B.C. to operate. My RCMP sources would discover the world's most violent narcos, including Joaquín "El Chapo" Guzmán's Sinaloa cartel, and narco-terrorist networks connected to Iran were multiplying in Vancouver and using Silver's brilliant money-laundering machine.

So, as I broke story after story in late 2017, the RCMP and B.C. government were in a tough position. They had no control over the information. I knew police believed Chinese transnational gangsters had corrupted significant portions of B.C.'s establishment. It wasn't just Lottery Corp. casinos police were worried about.

The RCMP wanted to hold a press conference to inform Canadian citizens what they learned in E-Pirate. But when senior police officials briefed NDP government officials on the plan, the press event was cancelled.

14
KNOWN KNOWNS

*The Ontario Conservative opposition led by Patrick
Brown asked the Ontario Liberal government to hit
the pause button on the Toronto casino contracts, but
the Liberal government pressed forward with Great
Canadian despite the scandal in British Columbia.
Why? Was this another example of wilful blindness?*

Senator Larry Campbell's eyes got big when he saw us approaching
with a TV camera. Since the fall of 2017, when I was with the *Vancouver Sun*, I had repeatedly asked Campbell to comment on his dual role
as a Canadian lawmaker and a highly paid board director for Great
Canadian Gaming, the operator of River Rock Casino.

He wouldn't respond. A year later, I was working for Global News
in Ottawa. So, I waited for the first Senate session of the year and
decided to approach Campbell where he works: Parliament Hill.
As Campbell climbed the steep set of stairs to the Senate chamber,
Global News cameraman Mike Haslett nudged me, and we walked
quickly towards him.

In 2004, Campbell had, as Vancouver mayor, cast the deciding vote
giving Great Canadian Gaming the greenlight to install hundreds of
slot machines at Hastings Race Track.

In 2005 he was made a Liberal senator, and in 2008 he was named
to Great Canadian's board. A massive amount of money-laundering
had occurred since. Based on suspicious transaction records and
interviews with GPEB sources, I estimated that as much as $2 bil-

lion in suspicious funds could have flowed through B.C. Lottery casinos since 2008. Much of this was cash from loan sharks.

But the suspicious funds also included special VIP non-cash accounts funded by anonymous bank drafts and electronic transfers from anonymous bank accounts.

And BCLC's so-called anti-money-laundering VIP accounts were being used almost exclusively by the whale gamblers from China that did business with the Richmond loan sharks at River Rock Casino.

The VIP accounts were supposed to be the lesser of two evils compared to duffel bags of cash. But the loan sharks were funding them through banks and dirty currency exchange shops in Richmond.

So I had shown that B.C. was a big outlier in Canada for casino money-laundering, and River Rock was an outlier in B.C.

All the evidence from RCMP and GPEB showed River Rock's VIP room was the epicentre. And Campbell was chair of Great Canadian Gaming's committee on corporate security and compliance. This meant he was one of those responsible for ensuring that money-laundering did not occur at River Rock Casino. I felt he had to answer for himself. So back in October 2017, as I repeatedly tried to get comments from River Rock Casino executives, including CEO Rod Baker and Campbell, a colleague at the *Vancouver Sun* had given me Campbell's private cell phone number.

Campbell is known to be a jovial and charming interview when he's in the mood to talk with reporters. He answered the phone, but he must have expected another reporter. As soon as I identified myself, there was a brief pause. And then I heard: "I'm sorry, I'm not in Canada, and I can't make out what you are saying."

The line went dead. I called back minutes later, but Campbell didn't answer.

If not for the fact this was a Canadian senator, former RCMP anti-drug unit officer, Vancouver mayor and chief coroner — the phone call would have been comical. But it was Campbell's duty to answer to Canadian citizens. Why did money launderers infiltrate River Rock Casino on his watch? And he was dodging.

September 2018. Now I was in Ottawa with more capacity to question federal politicians. I already knew Canada's casino money-laundering problems went far beyond British Columbia. In May 2018, one of my first stories for Global News probed the awarding of several Toronto-area casino contracts to Great Canadian. This was controversial because the Ontario contracts were issued in 2017 while the company's flagship operation, River Rock Casino, was under a money-laundering review called by B.C. attorney general David Eby.

The Ontario Conservative opposition led by Patrick Brown asked the Ontario Liberal government to hit the pause button on the Toronto casino contracts, but the Liberal government pressed forward with Great Canadian despite the scandal in British Columbia. Why? Was this another example of wilful blindness? It would make another good question for Larry Campbell, a federal Liberal party appointee.

But he just didn't want to meet me.

So, we waited for him.

Campbell reached the top of the stairs and stopped in the grand lobby, where paintings of British royals and eminent legislators are fixed to stone walls below towering columns and vaulted arches.

He had to sign a document before entering the Senate. As he bent to sign the paper, I held my microphone towards him.

"Senator Campbell, I'm sorry to bother you at the moment, we're with Global News. You're a director of compliance at Great Canadian Gaming. Can you tell us any comments about the money-laundering that is occurring at River Rock Casino?"

"I have no idea what you are talking about," Campbell muttered, without looking toward the camera. It appeared that his face was turning red.

"Senator, you serve the Canadian people, but as a director for Great Canadian Gaming, you serve shareholders. Is there a conflict of interest there?"

Campbell finished signing his paperwork without answering and walked across the lobby to the guarded Senate chambers while we followed him with the camera rolling. I could ask only one more question before he walked past the guard.

"Senator, can you tell us how much you earn as a director for Great Canadian Gaming?"

He didn't respond.

On September 18, Global News published my story.

"B.C.'s River Rock Casino has been called the epicentre of money-laundering by international organized crime groups," I wrote. "Throughout the troubles, Sen. Larry Campbell has collected more than $800,000 in cash compensation and about $2.1 million worth of shares as a board director of the company that owns the casino, Great Canadian Gaming."

The story noted that under Canada's laws, senators are permitted to be directors in private corporations and receive compensation.

But was there not a deeper ethical concern?

"As serious public safety and social issues related to casino money-laundering rock B.C., and polling numbers show mounting calls for a public inquiry, could Campbell effectively champion casino reforms that may be called for in B.C. society?" my story asked. "Or would he, like many casino industry spokespersons have over the past year, claim that B.C. casinos are adequately complying with laws currently in place? Would he champion B.C. citizens or Great Canadian shareholders?"

He has yet to answer these ethics questions. As former U.S. defense secretary Don Rumsfeld once put it, in assessing a field of knowledge, there are known knowns. These are the things we have discovered and understand. And there are known unknowns. These are the evasive facts that we know are crucial puzzle pieces to complete our intelligence assessment.

And so — Senator Campbell's knowledge of compliance concerns at River Rock Casino — a big known unknown. Why did Campbell not want to answer my questions?

I had to keep digging for evidence. My sources said B.C.'s government held explosive documents pointing to serious integrity concerns inside River Rock. One source pointed to a 2014 Lottery Corp. report filed by a former Vancouver police officer with in-depth knowledge of Big Circle Boys networks. A source also said various Lottery Corp. records alleged connections between loan-sharking gangsters, VIPs and high-level staff.

For years I made freedom of information requests. But it seemed to me the Lottery Corp. was using every trick in the book to avoid disclosing records that could prove corruption in B.C. casinos.

I kept up the pressure, and in 2020 I requested: "All BCLC reports, notes, player interviews or emails from January 1, 2013–January 1, 2018 related to alleged corruption and direct connections to organized crime involving anyone suspected of being corrupted, bribed, influenced, affiliated to, or facilitating crime connected to BCLC casinos for suspected members of Asian organized crime networks."

I finally got a few highly redacted emails back from the Lottery Corp. But there were just enough clues in the records to prove that my information was credible. And the process also confirmed something obvious for me. The only way names implicated in B.C. casino corruption would come to light was through leaked documents and aggressive investigative journalism.

The government would never disclose this damaging information itself. One 2014 email from Lottery Corp. spokeswoman Laura Piva-Babcock to Lottery Corp. CEO Jim Lightbody said, "FYI. More out-fall from the leaked docs. Mainly calling out Councillor Chang."

The internal Lottery Corp. emails cited a CTV News story about Richard Ching Chang — the Burnaby municipal politician investigated by Ross Alderson at River Rock Casino.

"As a city councillor, Chang is a member of Burnaby's community policing committee, and he recently voted in favour of more slot machines at Burnaby's Grand Villa Casino," the Lottery Corp. emails said. "One of Chang's outings to Richmond's River Rock Casino in 2011 caught the attention of the B.C. Lottery Corporation for what it called suspicious activities. A GPEB investigation found that a casino high roller passed $100,000 in chips to Chang."

The story by CTV investigative reporter Mi-Jung Lee also cited records that said Chang "is believed to be a loan shark" and had an "extensive history ... of chip and cash passing and suspicious transactions."

Lee's story didn't list one more potential conflict. Chang was in a position at Burnaby City Hall to vote on land development plans from groups that included B.C. casino VIPs and RCMP investigation targets. And I know these groups were assembling land in downtown Burnaby while Chang was in office.

But Richard Ching Chang denied the River Rock Casino loan-sharking allegations and has since left B.C. politics. I could not reach him for comment.

Another chain of redacted Lottery Corp. documents pointed to corruption concerns involving high-level staff at River Rock and RCMP investigation targets.

In October 2013, Ross Alderson wrote to a Lottery Corp. casino investigator: "Steve, can you give me the iTrak number regarding that incident you observed outside River Rock Casino Resort involving [redacted identification] and [redacted identification]."

The Lottery Corp. investigator emailed back, explaining that staff had discussed a potential corruption investigation and documented their surveillance observations. But an official Lottery Corp. incident report had not been created "given the sensitivity of the subject matter, and the level of staff involved."

"I called our RCMP contact who was investigating some of these people previously [redacted]," the Lottery Corp. email says. [The RCMP team was] ... busy with other files and the file had been put on the back burner."

Another email released to me says a Lottery Corp. investigator with special knowledge of the Big Circle Boys got information from the "RCMP regarding [redacted] and Richard meeting at [redacted]."

The records suggest corruption involving high-level casino staff, a B.C. politician and transnational organized crime. But because of redactions the records don't have enough information to draw any conclusions.

Similarly, I found a lack of crucial personal and corporate identifiers in the biggest corruption allegation. This was the shocking charge made by Fred Pinnock's former RCMP illegal-gaming unit in 2008, shortly before the unit was disbanded.

It referred to a GPEB employee who allowed a gang associate to buy part of a casino before the employee retired from government and took a job at a casino.

"More specific connections to Asian Organized Crime is/was through a subject, connected to Asian organized crime, who was allowed to buy into a casino," the RCMP report said. "Open source information indicates he is now dead but his casino business associates also have Asian Organized Crime connections."

So, which B.C. casino is referred to? Who is the former government employee? And which B.C. casino company hired them? Who is the Asian organized crime figure "allowed to buy into a casino" and who are his "casino business associates"?

I asked Great Canadian Gaming if River Rock could be the casino referred to in the RCMP's allegation.

"We have no knowledge of the allegation you have suggested, and we would propose you pursue your enquiry of this matter with those that generated the report you are citing from," the company responded. The RCMP also would not comment.

Is it possible that Senator Larry Campbell, who has held a Great Canadian Gaming board seat since 2008, could shed any more light on these questions? He won't respond. So, we don't know.

But here is a huge known known. There is already an audit suggesting systemic compliance concerns under Campbell's watch.

The audit, obtained from GPEB in my 2017 freedom of information request, said from January 1, 2015, to December 31, 2015, several Vancouver-area casinos accepted $6.7 million in "banned cash." River Rock Casino accounted for $5.37 million of that total. The GPEB review found that, "Sites knowingly accepted cash that they acknowledged was obtained from questionable sources ... industry indicators of suspicious activity were present in all incidents which the cage accepted the cash."

And about $4 million of this cash was attributed to Paul King Jin in 2015 — GPEB records showed — while Jin was banned and while the E-Pirate probe continued.

Any way you look at it, this finding seems damning. When I approached Senator Larry Campbell on Parliament Hill, this was the evidence that supported my questions.

But the GPEB audit found something that, for me, was even more intriguing. It suggested "refining" — the money-laundering process narcos use to exchange $20s for $100s and reduce the volume of their warehoused piles of cash — could potentially be occurring systematically inside River Rock Casino.

The GPEB audit said that the Lottery Corps' anti-money-laundering guidance advises that "to prevent a patron from refining bills for the purpose of money-laundering," B.C. casinos should pay gamblers out in the same denomination of currency that they used to buy chips.

But River Rock Casino management held "the view that patrons that buy-in with small-denomination bills can be paid out with big-denomination bills."

So, in order to determine whether refining was occurring at River Rock, GPEB auditors devised an elegant accounting analysis. They looked at funds flowing between the casino VIP room and the casino vault. This is why I think the audit is so important. GPEB data showed me that the River Rock VIP room was both the major revenue generator for B.C. Lottery Corp. casinos, and also the epicentre of money-laundering, via several dozen whale gamblers. So, by isolating the River Rock VIP room, it seems GPEB was examining the precise section of toxic financial plumbing most compromised by B.C.'s dirty money problem.

The auditors looked at cash deposited by VIPs from July 1, 2015, to December 31, 2015. Larry Campbell was elevated to chair of Great Canadian's compliance board in June 2015, meaning he was responsible for overseeing the plumbing examined by GPEB.

The auditors found that VIPs used $40 million worth of $20 bills to buy chips in just six months. And this is the stunner. GPEB says 99 percent of these $20s were sent directly from River Rock VIP cashier windows to the casino's vault. In other words, the $20s were not currency that would be returned to the VIPs. They were only good for buying chips in this micro-economic corner of Canada's economy — the VIP room where Chinese nationals bet up to $100,000 per hand on baccarat. Think about it. The casino's financial plumbing was designed to take the $20s deposited by VIPs out of play automatically and shuttle these bills down to the casino vault. And GPEB believed almost all of these $20s came from Richmond loan sharks. Just like Muriel Labine had believed when she worked in the company's Richmond casino in the 1990s.

And the GPEB auditors found that another $90 million worth of $100 bills was transferred up from the River Rock Casino vault to the River Rock VIP room cashiers.

The auditors also found that VIPs deposited $50 million worth of $100 bills to River Rock Casino VIP cash cages to buy playing chips.

But almost all of these $100 bills stayed in circulation in the VIP room. These $100 bills were not sent down to the casino vault. Recall the U.S. hedge fund manager John Tudor Jones' famous quote: "The whole world is simply nothing more than a flow chart for capital."

And now apply that wisdom to a flow chart of the River Rock VIP room. What the auditors established is that twenty-dollar bills came into the VIP room. And then immediately vanished to the casino vault. And $100s came up from the casino vault for circulation in the VIP room. And $100s that came into the casino with VIPs stayed in circulation. They did not get vacuumed down to the casino vault.

As I wrote for the *Vancouver Sun*: "This suggests that $20 bills not wanted by VIP players at River Rock were taken out of circulation at the casino, and $100 bills that were desired by gamblers were kept in play."

And the auditors concluded: "Our analysis found that nearly all patrons that bought in with $20s were not paid out in this denomination. It is reasonable to conclude that refining is occurring through the high-limit cages at River Rock Casino.

Records show that Great Canadian Gaming and the Lottery Corp. questioned the audit findings. And Great Canadian repeatedly stated to me in emails that the company strictly adheres to Canada's anti-money-laundering regulations.

But the power of this particular allegation can't be overstated. The GPEB audit painted a hell of a picture. And the picture's title could have been something like, *Money-Laundering by Design*.

Sometimes a visual metaphor helps. Imagine the VIP room is literally a coin laundry. The patrons come to this laundromat because they only like to wear bright white shirts. The $100 bills are like white shirts. The patrons come in carrying heavy sacks of mud-splattered shirts. The $20 bills are like muddy shirts. The VIPs drop off their muddy shirts, and they leave with bright white shirts. The coin laundromat exists to turn muddy shirts into white shirts. It is there to turn $20s into $100s.

And this next part of the picture is my imaginary supposition. But it outlines a section of plumbing that needs to be examined. I can visualize the muddy shirts taken down to a big concrete room in the laundromat basement. They are packed into armoured vans and delivered to a bigger concrete room: the Big Five Canadian banks. The armoured vans load up with crisp white shirts and drive back to the coin laundromat. The spotless shirts are delivered to the basement vault and then carted upstairs. And they are handed to the patrons in the VIP room. And everyone is happy and Canada's economy is growing. But at what cost? And who benefited most directly? Who would design such a system?

I eventually learned that Asian organized crime's interest in buying into B.C. casinos wasn't limited to the case cited in 2008 by Fred Pinnock's former RCMP illegal-gaming unit, or the 1990's "Casinogate" scandal, when Kwok Chung Tam may have tried to influence a casino licence application, according to Canadian court files.

Because in 2015, Stone Lee, the Lottery Corp. investigator, reviewed video footage showing Paul King Jin talking with employees of Starlight Casino in New Westminster. The employees told Lee that Jin was asking about an investment proposal for the casino's owner, Gateway. A lawyer for the Starlight Casino later claimed the meeting was actually about real estate development near the casino. Nothing to do with VIP room investments. So, what really transpired? A massive known unknown.

***

Another known unknown is the Ontario casino contracts.

Using freedom of information law, I found that Alcohol and Gaming Commission of Ontario (AGCO) investigators opened an investigation after Ontario's government awarded Great Canadian Gaming contracts, including a major gaming expansion at Toronto's Woodbine casino.

The investigators were specifically interested in an alleged money-laundering transaction in River Rock Casino's VIP room in fall

2017 — involving a VIP host — that I had exposed in reports for the *Vancouver Sun.*

Ontario Provincial Police Det.-Const. Dan MacDonald had emailed to GPEB and said he had to liaise with "RCMP concerning the River Rock Casino [and] any other related investigation.

"As you likely know, Great Canadian Gaming has bought a few casinos here in Ontario … now I am supposed to find out what is going on in B.C.," MacDonald wrote to Kenneth Ackles of B.C.'s anti-gang and anti-illegal gaming unit.

So Ontario's casino regulator was monitoring the investigations in B.C. in connection to Great Canadian Gaming's new casino contracts. Why did the Ontario Liberal government then allow the contracts to proceed?

And why, in late 2017, did the Ontario Progressive Conservative (PC) party stop urging the provincial government to freeze the deals?

As I reported for Global News, under former PC leader Patrick Brown, the party had slammed the Liberals in the legislature.

I obtained party emails that showed former PC party president Rick Dykstra sent out emails titled "Corrupt gaming strategy" and citing the money-laundering probe in B.C.

"We should be going after these guys in the house," Dykstra wrote to Patrick Brown. "We show their process is corrupt, and we can call their whole strategy into question. I just spoke with Duncan Brown, former head of the Ontario Lottery and Gaming Corporation. He said based on this, he would toss Great Canadian Gaming."

My investigation for Global News showed that a Toronto hedge fund with a massive bet on Great Canadian Gaming had repeatedly lobbied the PCs to hit the mute button on their criticism.

The hedge fund, BloombergSen, was powerfully connected and influential, to say the least.

Its board of directors includes significant donors to both the Ontario Liberal and PC parties. Carolyn Mulroney, daughter of former Conservative prime minister Brian Mulroney, was vice-president of BloombergSen before she stepped aside to run for the PCs in 2018.

BloombergSen had at least eight million shares invested in Great Canadian Gaming when it stepped up its lobbying of the PC party in December 2018.

At 8:14 a.m. on December 20, the party campaign chair Walied Soliman received a minimalist email from BloombergSen founder Sanjay Sen. The subject line — "PCs still talking about Great Canadian" — pointed to behind-the-scenes discussions between the hedge fund and the party.

The email included a a link to a December 19 *Globe and Mail* story, which quoted then PC finance critic Vic Fedeli, and said despite ongoing probes in B.C. and Ontario, Great Canadian had been awarded yet another bundle of Ontario contracts, this for several casinos west of Toronto.

On December 20, Soliman forwarded the BloombergSen email to then PC leader Patrick Brown: "So I am continuing to get lobbied on this but have actually changed my view," Soliman wrote. "I think we should attack this … I got some information yesterday … which is very disturbing. Anyhow, the long and short of it, I am not in favour of us pulling back Vic [Fedeli]. I am increasingly thinking there is something bad here."

But the PCs did not continue to attack the Great Canadian Gaming contracts under former leader Patrick Brown or new leader Doug Ford, who was elected premier in June 2018. Carolyn Mulroney also won a seat for the party and was named attorney-general. And as Great Canadian Gaming's stock price surged in late 2017 and early 2018 — boosted by optimism over the company's new Ontario contracts, including the expansion of Toronto's Woodbine casino — as of May 2018, BloombergSen's shares were worth about $420 million.

Did Ontario's government turn a blind eye to evidence of toxicity in Great Canadian Gaming's Macau VIP money machine, that would later come out in Cullen Commission records?

Consider this data point.

With my Global News investigative unit colleagues Brian Hill and Andrew Russell, in January 2020, I reported on a stunning jump in suspicious cash investigations in Ontario casinos in 2018.

The number of potential money-laundering investigations more than doubled, from 945 in 2017 to 2226 in 2018, and those statistics continue to trend higher in 2019, according to statistics obtained in freedom of information from Ontario Provincial Police (OPP).

Chief Supt. Bill Price of the OPP told us the 140 percent increase in his casino investigation unit's suspicious transaction investigations was due, in part, to more gambling in the Toronto region and the OPP's increased scrutiny of that gambling.

"If you turn a slot facility into a full-blown casino with table games, there are larger transactions that automatically occur that should generate suspicious transaction reports," Price said. "Woodbine (casino) itself went from a slot facility to a full-blown casino. That changes the dynamics."

Our data showed that in 2017, there were eight suspicious transactions investigations recorded by the OPP at Woodbine. And in 2018 — after Great Canadian's new contract and expanded gambling operations, there were 58. And from January to August 1, 2019, there were 76 suspicious transactions investigations logged by OPP investigators working at the Woodbine casino.

We asked Great Canadian to respond to the sharp increase in suspicious transactions investigations.

"Fundamentally, our role is to identify and report unusual and large cash transactions," the company said in a statement. "In undertaking this role in Ontario, our obligation is to adhere to all mandated rules and regulations, and even exceed those requirements to ensure a robust [anti-money-laundering] regime is followed."

But Chief Supt. Bill Price told us that the same method of money-laundering seen in B.C. — bulk cash "refining" — is occurring in Ontario casinos.

"A very basic example of currency refining is you walk into the casino with $10,000 ... Very minimal gameplay, you go to the cashier's cage and cash out with $9,000. You've got a casino receipt, and you've just basically laundered $9,000," he said.

And Calvin Chrustie, who retired from the RCMP in 2019, told us the Mainland China narcos had adjusted after B.C. casinos cracked down on dirty money.

"The criminal networks involved haven't been touched, and they are still selling their drugs and making their money," he said. "Money -laundering is like a product of their crime, just like dead kids and corrupt politicians. So that dirty money will find the cracks."

And we heard the same thing from Canada's criminal intelligence service. In 2019, the RCMP had identified a new international money-laundering service based in Ontario and B.C. that used casinos, real estate, underground banks, shell companies, trade-based money-laundering, and straw-buyers. Police believed this elite professional laundering service was washing "upwards of hundreds of millions" each year. To me, it looked like the Ontario-B.C. money-laundering cartel matched the Silver underground bank's modus operandi, precisely.

***

I had started my journey into transnational underground banking without any understanding of how it worked. The concept of an ancient system using credits and debits backed by pools of drug cash worldwide had never crossed my mind when I began evaluating Vancouver's explosive real estate prices. For me, the connection between real estate and casino money-laundering wasn't even a known unknown back in 2013.

But in June 2020, I got the confirmation of what my pattern recognition had been telling me since 2015. By looking at real estate developers and crowdfunders from Mainland China, I had stumbled across the casino whales and loan sharks that defined the Vancouver Model.

A September 16, 2015, email from Lottery Corp. anti-money-laundering investigator Daryl Tottenham to Ross Alderson was 'CCed to Alderson's boss, Brad Desmarais.

The email included a federal court judgement: "Lau vs. Canada's Minister of Public Safety." And it referred to my September 14 story *Vancouver Province* story, Inside the world of B.C.'s top realtor.

"Excellent article got a little bit of everything going on in this story," Tottenham's email said. "Just an FYI a few of the main players in this story are [redacted]."

I had named a number of Julia Lau's real estate clients and crowd-funding associates. This redacted Lottery Corp. record indicated the people I named were VIPs or loan sharks.

While much of Tottenham's email is redacted by the Lottery Corp., there is enough content to prove that Lau and her network were red-flagged by casino investigators. And the email showed that Lottery Corp. brass was warned in 2015 that this prolific Mainland China real estate investor network was involved in suspicious casino transactions.

"The main subject of the article Julia LAU [redacted]," the email says. "However, the 'friend' she got some of the money from [is redacted]."

"Also in Itrak is [redacted] ... Here's another good one: [redacted] ... One other player in this story which is a player with [redacted] ... and is [redacted]"

In my *Province* story, I had reported on Canada's seizure of $133,000 cash from Julia Lau and her contracted agent, Jason Edward Lee, because the source of funds could not be identified. The "friend" referred to in my story and Tottenham's email was Mailin Chen, the former Guangdong duck farmer who had rapidly amassed a fortune in factories and real estate development in southern China before moving to Vancouver and quickly buying some of the most expensive mansions in the city, and then jumping into crowdfunding development and land assembly with Julia Lau and Kevin Sun.

In the "Lau vs. Public Safety Minister" case attachment, there are indications that Tottenham was focused on Mailin Chen.

I have not been able to reach Mailin Chen for comment through his Vancouver development companies, including Global Dingye. Mr. Chen remains an enigma as his real estate development footprint grows in Vancouver. He's developing towers across the city and owns a hotel in downtown Vancouver. Even his son Ding Chen made headlines in the *South China Morning Post* after the young man's Instagram feed revealed he had used Mailin Chen's credit card to buy a $5 million custom Bugatti Chiron. It was a nice addition to the Chen family transportation hangar in Canada, which includes a $50 million Bombardier Challenger jet bearing Ding's name painted in gold.

So what? Is there any concrete reason to question Mailin Chen's riches and associations in Richmond?

Yes, there is. On September 14, 2017, a man parked a silver Mercedes Benz SUV outside River Rock Casino and walked inside with a gray bag containing $200,000 in cash. He was met by Lisa Gao — the River Rock Casino's VIP program manager — and she escorted him to a private cash cage. They ducked inside, and he placed four large bundles of cash on the counter. They were bricks of $100 bills wrapped in elastic bands. This is the way that criminal proceeds are packaged. Banks don't issue $200,000 in elastic bands. The electronic money counter whirred the bills through and registered the total — two thousand $100 bills. The man walked out to a baccarat table, and Lisa Gao brought him a purple velvet River Rock Casino pouch holding 40 casino chips. Each chip was worth $5,000. And the man walked out of the casino with $200,000 worth of River Rock chips without playing a hand.

He was the straw-buyer for Mailin Chen. And Chen was already banned from River Rock Casino. This transaction broke Canada's anti-money-laundering law. But it wasn't that simple. An investigation found Chen planned to distribute these casino chips to several visitors from China. Why? And why did a high-level River Rock Casino employee facilitate this money-laundering transaction for a banned VIP? The Gaming Enforcement Branch investigated and deregistered Gao. But B.C.'s government took no action against Great Canadian Gaming for the serious integrity breach. The money-laundering transaction was reported to the RCMP's Criminal Intelligence Service "for informational purposes only."

There are so many unknowns surrounding the Mailin Chen and Lisa Gao case. But here's a fact we know. This all happened on Sen. Larry Campbell's watch.

***

Our Global News national investigations team met in July 2019. Canada's Public Health Agency had put out brutal new statistics. Opioid overdoses had killed 10,300 Canadians from January 2016 to September 2018. There were almost 4,000 deaths in 2018 alone. Most of the fentanyl overdoses were in B.C., Alberta and Ontario. But Vancouver's Downtown Eastside was the epicentre of this national tragedy. And for the first time in modern history, B.C.'s life expectancy was dropping due to fentanyl overdoses.

My colleague Stewart Bell asked a simple question.

"Who is getting rich selling the fentanyl that's killing Canadians?"

I said I thought we could answer the question. Lots of criminals across Canada were selling fentanyl. The vast majority was coming in from Mainland China. And many shipments arrived in small postal packages. But according to my sources in B.C., at the very top of North

America's fentanyl trade were the same people laundering massive piles of cash in B.C. casinos. It was the network orbiting the Big Circle Boys. The same loose coalition of uber-criminals that had been running heroin loads into Vancouver ports since Expo 86. And they didn't mess around with Canada Post. They were shipping mountains of fentanyl and methamphetamine precursors into Vancouver.

So my sources were saying, if you want to understand fentanyl deaths in North America, visualize a heat map of factories surrounding cities like Wuhan and Guangzhou. And then imagine a multitude of red bands flowing from southern China and landing across the Americas. Sort of like one of those telecommunications network maps.

The tiny bands are landing across North America. And the giant red bands are hitting ports in British Columbia and Mexico. This represents the routes and relative volumes of fentanyl.

I told our team about the criminal intelligence files I had been collecting since 2017. They pointed to the Mainland China industrialists connected to Paul King Jin. Jin was big. He was a River Rock whale. But his friends from China made him look like a minnow.

James Armstrong, managing editor of our national news team, asked me, Stew Bell and our colleague Andrew Russell to work on Bell's question. The objective was to identify the kingpins making a killing on fentanyl.

Now I had a chance to dig deeper into the records that Ross Alderson had entrusted to me, in September 2017. These documents explained what Alderson did in late summer 2015 after Calvin Chrustie dropped the Silver underground bank bombshell on him. Alderson's team mined Lottery Corp. databases for surveillance and suspicious transaction records and combined the information with RCMP organized crime intelligence to draw a circle around the most toxic VIP gamblers active at River Rock Casino. The list included 36 River Rock whales definitively connected to Jin's cash deliveries.

Alderson's report said RCMP suspected Jin's cash supply to the River Rock VIPs was related to "transnational drug trafficking."

And RCMP executed warrants against Jin and his associates in October 2015, on reasonable grounds they were importing and trafficking narcotics, running illegal casinos, and laundering money in legal and illegal casinos.

So the intelligence I had — documents naming the Chinese industrialists in Jin's River Rock VIP network — was extremely sensitive and confidential. But the depth of rot in B.C.'s economy would never have been exposed if Alderson didn't share these records with me. When he argues that he changed the history of B.C. casinos, this is what he means. He gave me the key to exposing the Vancouver Model.

I took the 36 Jin VIP names and ran their I.D.'s through B.C. land title and B.C. Supreme Court databases. I was looking for land ownership patterns, civil forfeiture cases, and disputes between investors. When flags came back connecting whale gamblers to various shell corporations, I could identify company directors and lending arrangements. I could tie in luxury auto leases, criminal record searches, associations with real estate lawyers, and the structure of land assembly and condo development deals.

For example, by matching a Burnaby address used to lease a 2018 BMW XDrive and obtaining banking records, I was able to establish that a B.C. Lottery Corp. casino employee was the director of a shell company used to launder proceeds from a Richmond illegal casino, allegedly run by the Big Circle Boys and Paul King Jin and Lap San Peter Pang.

In simple terms, by cross-referencing open-source records with highly confidential Lottery Corp. records, I could make groundbreaking conclusions.

I found many of the Mainland China whale gamblers who took massive cash deliveries from Jin and committed dozens of suspicious transactions at River Rock also had big land holdings in British Columbia. And they were also receiving strange, gigantic, short-term real estate loans from Paul Jin and his associates.

It took a while to figure out the purpose of these loans because the transactions are complex and meant to confuse.

Basically, the borrowers and lenders were colluding to buy Vancouver mansions like they bought casino chips. Sometimes the loan sharks really acted like loan sharks. They gave a $500,000 cash loan to you, you offered your home as collateral in a promissory note, and you paid the gangsters back in China or gave them bank drafts or cheques in Canada. If you didn't pay, it got violent.

But often, the loan shark and his borrower were in the same gang. They used straw-buyers and straw-sellers to manipulate home sale prices and launder money.

And after the lenders and borrowers conspired to launder drug cash into one mansion, the homeowner would take out more and more private lender cash against the home from the same network of loan sharks. In this way, the gangsters could buy more homes in Vancouver. And they added value — building or renovating mansions and paying contractors drug cash under the table — and flipped homes to bank the proceeds. The lenders and the borrowers and contractors were all parts of the fentanyl trafficking system, looping money repetitively between Vancouver and Mainland China through underground financial plumbing.

They were so brazen that they used B.C. courts to make real estate money-laundering look like legitimate civil law disputes.

And some of the B.C. Supreme Court cases explicitly drew links between B.C. casinos, Macau casinos, prostitution, and enormous pools of real estate wealth in Mainland China.

In order to expose the dark matter core of Vancouver's exploding real estate prices, one B.C. Supreme Court file provided me a goldmine of documents. The case involved a man named Jia Gui Gao. Gao was on Ross Alderson's list of 36 River Rock VIPs. He had 28 suspicious transactions at River Rock Casino.

My criminal intelligence source indicated Gao was a police official in Mainland China. Court files said he had tremendous real estate wealth in China. And he was named on RCMP investigation documents that detailed a massive surveillance operation into a cartel allegedly involved in B.C. casino money-laundering, human trafficking, weapons trafficking and big game hunting junkets. A Canadian banking source also confirmed for me, the primary suspects were making suspicious transnational wire transfers through registered real estate and weapons businesses in Richmond.

Jia Gui Gao was named as "Suspect 19" in the RCMP investigation hierarchy, and Jin was called "Suspect 22."

B.C. Supreme Court records told me Jia Gui Gao had owned at least five mansions in Vancouver. He had sold four of them since 2015, for total proceeds of $48 million.

In the hills of West Vancouver, one of his mansions vividly illustrated the pathology causing Vancouver's overdose crisis.

Gao had taken out $28 million in loans against the property since 2015, to fund Vancouver real estate development. One of the loans from Jin was worth $8 million, court filings said.

In a supposed dispute over repayment terms, Jin's claim alleged he had "advanced monies to Gao for real estate development ... however [Gao] spent the money lent to him on gambling and women."

Court files showed there were many other B.C. and Alberta loan sharks feeding off the West Vancouver property. One was W.Z., who had outstanding loans of $950,000 on Jia Gui Gao's real estate holdings.

He is a Big Circle Boy banned from Lottery Corp. casinos. In 2016 W.Z. was dinged by Vancouver police in a fentanyl trafficking investigation when cops caught him in a Richmond parking lot as he was unloading a suitcase with $513,000 cash from the trunk of his white Range Rover.

His partner Y.Z., another loan shark with $5.3 million in mortgages on Jia Gui Gao's properties, was taken down in the same fentanyl trafficking investigation. And M.H., named as a Paul King Jin associate in Lottery Corp. ban documents, also had $3.2 million in real estate loans on Jia Gui Gao's Vancouver properties.

"They just walked away from this cash like it was nothing," said a senior B.C. police source, about the fentanyl cash forfeiture case. "They said, 'Okay, we'll just take our golf clubs.'"

According to this source, there was total continuity between the Big Circle Boys heroin kingpins who infiltrated Canada in the 1980s and the present-day China fentanyl and methamphetamine cartels, including the narco-billionaires in Asia with Canadian citizenship, like Chi Lop Tse. These narcos don't always identify as Big Circle Boys. But they're all part of the same network. And the drug routes and money-laundering methods haven't changed.

"It has always been the same people involved, and unfortunately, the longer they do it, the more legitimate they look," the source said. "What they do is buy these tear-downs, and they do renovations and build mansions. I know one case, [a Mainland China heroin kingpin] laundered eight of these homes in Vancouver himself."

I found all kinds of B.C. Supreme Court cases and land title records like the fentanyl cash seizure case, cementing the connection between drug trafficking, drug lab houses, drug cash seizures, casino loan sharks, and Vancouver mansion money-laundering.

In one case, B.C. land titles showed me that cartel "Suspect 1" — a shipbuilder in China — had built a number of mega-mansions and resort properties across Richmond and Vancouver. He was I.D.'ed as Jin's loan sharking associate on a Lottery Corp. ban, and also one of the 36 Jin VIPs.

And one more crucial case allowed me to connect the dots between illegal casinos in Richmond and Vancouver real estate lending. The court filings said Paul Jin had loaned a Mainland China hotel tycoon $500,000 to build a home in south Vancouver. The borrower and his Vancouver address were connected to a shell company called the Vancouver International Chinese Association. This was the entity that leased a sprawling mansion on Richmond farmland to start up an underground casino.

The $4.9 million mansion at 8880 Sidaway Road was bought on paper by a Markham woman related to Peter Lap San Pang, police said. The RCMP said the aptly named Mr. Pang and his friends ran the casino and beat loan sharking victims with metal bars, among other blood-soaked crimes. The Lottery Corp. intelligence team told me the casino was a Big Circle Boys venture. And this was the property that, for me, offered clues of leaked police intelligence.

The mansion was bought in October 2015. This was days after the RCMP raided Paul Jin's farmland hacienda in another corner of Richmond, only to find the sophisticated illegal casino abandoned, with the RCMP's warrant date circled on a wall calendar.

I sometimes tell people that when I'm sorting these networks out, it's like building an "FBI target wall" in my mind. You start with a pencil and paper and draw the connections between the players, their businesses, their shell companies, their real estate, their family members, their political donations and affiliations, and their criminal and civil forfeiture court cases. You have big transactions on a timeline. You look at cause and effect.

You have the biggest fish at the top of the map and the network extends downward. It's the people at the bottom more likely to get their hands dirty, and the people up top more likely to look legitimate.

My "FBI wall" had Big Circle Boys loan sharks, River Rock VIPs, Chinese industrialists, police, military and Communist Party officials. Legal casinos. Illegal casinos. B.C. government casino staff connected to Big Circle Boys casinos.

I had fentanyl and ecstasy and methamphetamine traffickers. A gangster associate of Paul Jin was caught in the act of delivering pails of fentanyl precursors to labs in Richmond and Burnaby. I had cash houses and hundreds of bank accounts in China. Fentanyl traffickers caught trafficking guns that they "straw-purchased" from River Rock whale gamblers. I had the megalodon of organized crime in Canada, the Big Circle Boys.

Multiple sources with decades of police experience told me they were the fentanyl kingpins responsible for the warlike opioid death totals in Canada.

But I needed a bigger dataset. How much fentanyl could they be shipping into Canada? And how much money was this network laundering in Vancouver real estate? After a few months working on the file, I got lucky.

**

The secret police intelligence study was stunning. Its methodology was elegant and robust. And its findings were explosive.

The RCMP knew anecdotally that gangs directed from Mainland China dominated Vancouver's luxury real estate market. During the E-Pirate investigation, police analysts began to understand the sheer scale of narco-proceeds looping between Vancouver and China.

But they needed hard data. How could they ask their political masters in Ottawa for more resources to fight money-laundering if they couldn't estimate the size of the problem?

The researchers suspected significant money-laundering was pouring into Vancouver homes in the $1- to $3-million range. But they didn't have the time or resources to study over 20,000 real estate transactions per year. So they focused just on the high-end. They picked one year: 2016. And they examined every Vancouver-area real estate purchase that year valued between $3 million and $35 million.

Now they had a database of about 1,200 property transactions. They had the names of the buyers and their methods of financing.

RCMP researchers cross-referenced these property documents with databases of criminal records and confidential police intelligence regarding ongoing investigations and networks of suspected criminals.

And the results that came back were a blistering indictment of B.C.'s economy.

More than 10 percent of the property sales priced over $3 million in 2016 were tied to buyers with criminal records. And 95 percent of those transactions were believed by police intelligence to be linked to Mainland China crime networks. Many of these purchases were cash. Often the homes were owned in the names of wives and children.

The study concluded that more than $1 billion worth of high-end Vancouver-area property transactions in 2016 were linked to Chinese organized crime. It was a mind-blowing finding. It was a lot more than the tip of the iceberg. But it also suggested much more money-laundering throughout the system.

Remember, the RCMP could only afford to study the high-end.

They were just looking at mansions. But anecdotally, huge money-laundering is happening in the sub-$3-million price range, especially in Vancouver condo units presold and flipped like pancakes offshore.

And consider this. Of the 14 high-level-threat organized crime groups in Canada, according to Canadian police intelligence, there are 10 in B.C. And that includes three cartels offering transnational money-laundering services. That is, more elite organized crime and money-laundering cartels — including Mexican and Middle East crime syndicates — than any other Canadian province.

Add to that list the Hells Angels and violent B.C. dial-a-doper gangs, like the Red Scorpions. All of them were laundering significant criminal funds into homes valued under $3 million.

But the $1 billion in laundered mansions was a conclusive result. And yet, my sources said the RCMP had no resources to investigate this money-laundering criminally. It was just police intelligence. And RCMP officers were not happy having their hands tied due to lack of funding. That is why, I believe, I was given access to study findings in a secure and confidential transfer of information.

And so for my Vancouver Model investigations, the secret police study findings became a known known that would help alter B.C. history.

In order to dig into the study's implications, I obtained a list of the key properties tied to the core of the casino whale network. These were the properties my sources believed were most important for Canadians to read about. They said the mansions were bought with proceeds from fentanyl, methamphetamine and cocaine sales, prostitution, extortion, illegal casinos and financial fraud.

One of the properties on this list — a $22-million home in Shaughnessy — was owned by Jia Gui Gao, the Macau gambler, River Rock VIP, and "Suspect 19" on the RCMP's casino junket-cartel hierarchy chart.

Property records showed that Gao bought this mansion on Matthews Avenue for just $7.5 million in 2011. But after Gao and the network of loan sharks started to run multiple cash loans through the asset, the home was eventually sold in 2016 for $22 million. An obscene $14 million price gain. For me, the price action had broader implications. Some real estate experts told me hot money laundered through a few homes on a high-end Vancouver block can ripple through the whole market, helping to spark speculative frenzy, and pushing benchmark prices for the Vancouver region higher.

Another of the secret police study homes was a $17 million mansion in Shaughnessy. According to study findings, the owner was involved in fentanyl importing and exporting. With the network of names attached to this property, I could do my own international corporate searches and profile the owners.

"Property and lending documents show the owner's family holds at least nine Vancouver-area homes worth over $60 million, in addition to assembling hundreds of acres of residential land in Metro Vancouver since 2014 and also proposing to develop a Vancouver luxury condo tower," we reported for Global News in our November 2018 investigative series "Fentanyl: Making a Killing."

The family were members of the Chinese People's Political Consultative Conference. They were also proposing to develop a residential village in Metro Vancouver. I found the family were connected to Chinese industries — at least on paper — and large-scale construction in Guangdong and Hainan. Their corporations were a spiderweb of offshore banking with Panama Papers and Hong Kong stock market connections. They were patriotic, also. A profile of one of the family's Lamborghini-driving scions — a B.C. student — said the patriarch devoted his international ventures to the "Motherland."

So, with this method — investigating owners of study properties and interviewing sources with knowledge of the E-Pirate investigation — I was able to profile the real estate money-laundering network and detail its modus operandi.

"At the centre of the money-laundering ring is a powerful China-based gang called the Big Circle Boys. Its top-level "kingpins" are the international drug traffickers who are profiting most from Canada's deadly fentanyl crisis," we reported in "Fentanyl: Making a Killing." "The crime network, accoring to police intelligence sources, is a fluid coalition of hundreds of wealthy criminals in Metro Vancouver, including gangsters, industrialists, financial fugitives and corrupt officials from China. The common link among them is an underground banking scheme in which Chinese VIP gamblers and gangster associates secretly transfer money between China and Richmond, B.C., in order to fund fentanyl imports and to traffic in Canada."

But how much fentanyl was the casino-narco cartel running into Richmond ports and warehouses? I needed a big case to understand the scale. So sources pointed me to several related civil forfeiture cases that tied the Chinese cartel to the largest known seizure of fentanyl and methamphetamine precursors in Canadian history.

"Looming behind the purchase of 8880 Sidaway Rd. — a palatial red- and-grey building guarded by black iron gates and ornamental golden lions — was an alleged network of narcos that police would eventually link to an 85-ton shipment of precursors for drugs including fentanyl," we reported in "Fentanyl: Making a Killing."

The civil forfeiture cases described how police raided a chemical research company in Richmond on November 23, 2016, taking down a Canadian businessman allegedly used by the Chinese cartel.

Two days later, police caught another man, Paul King Jin's alleged associate, making runs between labs.

"On November 25, 2016, officers stopped G.W. as he loaded buckets into his Nissan Pathfinder. They arrested him and searched the vehicle, seizing a number of drums containing NPP, a fentanyl precursor produced in China," I reported for Global News.

The forfeiture claim didn't say exactly how much NPP was seized. And RCMP search warrants have been sealed by the courts. But for comparison, according to an unrelated 2017 seizure case in Massachusetts, several containers of NPP weighing 50 kilograms could produce as many as 19 million fentanyl pills. And according to the DEA the pills could be worth US$570 million on the street.

So it is perhaps reasonable to believe that G.W. was caught with a similar amount of NPP. In one single bust.

But the Canadian businessman allegedly working with the Chinese cartel had received 85 tons of precursors from 2014 to 2016, according to the RCMP.

Again, the court records are sealed. So it's impossible to calculate the blend of precursors involved in the seizure. And so, I can't conclude how many fentanyl and methamphetamine pills this mountain of precursors could have pressed in Canada.

But sources with knowledge told me it is safe to say the amount of toxic pills produced had tremendous impact on Canadian society. And not only Canada. We are talking about shipping containers of pills worth more than hundreds of millions on the street. Profits to the Chinese transnational cartel are in the order of billions.

And this cartel is importing precursors from China and exporting pills from Richmond and Markham to countries including Japan, Australia and the United States.

So this brings up a point that Senator Vernon White, a former Canadian police chief, made to me. He sits on Canada's parliamentary national security and intelligence committee, which makes his observation even more significant for me.

He said China's state-controlled fentanyl-producing factories could be shut down if Beijing wanted to act. And Canada should be demanding that China stop the flow or face trade sanctions.

"I have been in policing 33 years and I have never seen anything with the profitability that fentanyl has," White said. "This is a security threat. If terrorists were killing 5-6,000 people per year, we would do something about it."

My sources in national security and intelligence communities said the same thing. If China wanted to stop fentanyl from flooding the West, it could. So for me, this raised a lot of new questions. People in civilian, police, and military intelligence were starting to wonder if China's fentanyl represented hostile state activity. Why were the Big Circle Boys untouchable in China? Why were they enabled to ship deadly toxic opioids worldwide?

So I went back to my sources, who understood both the RCMP money- laundering study and the Big Circle Boys' structure. They told me the Chinese narcos controlled chemical factories and customs with protection from elite Chinese Communist Party officials.

"There are so many players we identified in B.C.," an international policing expert told me. "But this is all directed from inside China. At the very top, they are insulated. It's government officials."

There was a lot going on in our Fentanyl Kingpins series.

My reporting suggests that corruption in China was responsible for Vancouver's housing affordability and fentanyl overdose crises.

Of course there are other factors. Canadian banks and casinos and regulators are implicated. Real estate speculation is a widespread lifestyle in Vancouver with many beneficiaries. But my research shows transnational organized crime directed from China is a driving force. And it's driving home prices higher.

"The [police study] findings come amid Metro Vancouver's housing affordability crisis, in which middle-class families have been priced out of the city," I wrote for Global News, citing the expertise of Andy Yan, a pioneering researcher of offshore money in Vancouver real estate. "Some analysts believe a flood of money from China in recent years forced Metro Vancouver home prices to disconnect from the region's median household wage of $72,000, which ranks among the lowest for Canadian cities, and 50th in North America.)

Yan, director of the City Program at Simon Fraser University, bundled the implications up with this quote: "This is financial fentanyl for our real estate. You have found $1 billion. But it is probably magnified in the banking system, with all of the black money, gray money, and legitimate money cascading through local institutions, to make a toxic sausage. So this is a national security issue. And also a national financial issue."

And in my analysis for Global News, using Ockham's razor, I lined up real estate prices, drug deaths, and suspicious transactions. Correlation doesn't prove causation. But when you see three or four datasets lining up elegantly, it can make a hell of a case.

And this is what I see.

In 2012, when Vancouver real estate price graphs turned vertical, illicit fentanyl overdose death charts started to break upward, according to B.C. coroner data. And fentanyl fatalities rose exponentially from 2014. Money was flooding into real estate, and fentanyl was flooding the Downtown Eastside.

The trends echoed neatly in B.C. casinos.

GPEB data showed suspected drug-money transactions going exponential from 2010. There was $64 million in suspicious cash transactions in Lottery Corp. casinos in 2012. In 2015, the peak year for B.C. casino money-laundering, there was $176 million in suspicious cash transactions, including $136 million in $20 bills. It was a record year for B.C. real estate too.

Vancouver-area home prices surged by more than 30 percent in 2015, and almost 40 percent in some wealthy suburbs. In 2015 it was estimated US$1 trillion escaped China illicitly, more than ever before. Underground narco banks had to be churning at record volumes to facilitate the cross-border financial transfers. And in a microcosm of this dirty money supernova — the River Rock VIP room accepted $13.5 million in $20 bills in July 2015, which triggered a historic GPEB audit.

That brings us back to Paul King Jin and Silver International.

Our police money-laundering study story summed it up like this.

"As the drug kingpins of Vancouver have raked in profits and the city's real estate prices have surged, the fentanyl crisis has spread from its epicentre among addicts in Vancouver's impoverished Downtown Eastside to communities across the country, leaving behind a devastating body count."

A pretty bleak assessment.

But as the law enforcement source that helped me document the hierarchy of E-Pirate targets said, the mansions studied by the RCMP in Shaughnessy were funded by fentanyl deaths in the Downtown Eastside.

"It's a neat circle. Welfare Wednesday spending ultimately enriches those fueling the affordability crisis," he told me.

It's that simple. Deaths at Main and Hastings. Mansions in Shaughnessy and West Vancouver.

In December 2018, after Global News published "Fentanyl: Making a Killing", there was an increasing groundswell of support for a B.C. money-laundering inquiry. Among the influential advocates, the B.C. Government and Service Employees Union, with its 72,000 members, cited our Global News investigations to pressure the NDP government for an inquiry.

And a few days after our RCMP mansion laundering study piece ran, I got a text message from a source. It was one of the police whistleblowers who had stood in front of a steamroller of B.C. casino money-laundering.

"You have an army of supporters," the text said. "An inquiry has to be called."

15

COMPROMISED NODES

Money-laundering was the shared interest in Vancouver. But something else was definitely happening. The Big Circle Boys and Chinese intelligence players had started with casinos. And they moved into real estate and finance, Canada's soft spots for economic infiltration.

My sources had been telling me some things that I couldn't believe until I saw the evidence myself. These were people who understood criminal intelligence and geopolitics. They talked about the convergence of organized crime and state-actors in China and Iran and Mexico and Russia.

They were saying the impacts of the money-laundering that I was uncovering in Canada went a lot deeper than fentanyl deaths and soaring housing prices in Vancouver and Toronto and Montreal.

They were saying transnational money-laundering endangers democracy. It erodes the rule of law. It's a national security threat. But you need to look deeper, they said. Look at who is standing behind the transnational criminals. More to the point, who is standing above them holding a protective umbrella. It was a frustrating situation for the people talking to me. Canada has excellent criminal intelligence. But what the RCMP and CSIS know about the Chinese Communist Party's collusion with the Big Circle Boys and Chi Lop Tse's super cartel never makes it to trial.

What my sources were describing was essentially a modern version of the map laid out 20 years earlier in the controversial Canadian intelligence report, Sidewinder.

And when the people who wrote Sidewinder saw my reporting on E-Pirate and Paul King Jin, it set off alarm bells. Michel Juneau Kat-suya — the former CSIS Asia-Pacific desk chief — recognized the metastasized node he had identified way back in the 1990s. Gangsters, spies and industrialists covertly operating under the Chinese Communist Party.

But there were new convergences.

After 2015, my sources started seeing kingpins of the Chinese underground banking cartel brushing up against state actors from Iranian narco-terrorism networks. For example, E-Pirate surveillance records filed with the Cullen Commission showed a Mideast organized crime suspect was registered to a vehicle used in Paul King Jin's alleged illegal casino and Water Cube spa operation. And Mideast organized crime suspects served as bodyguards for Jin and his superior, these records showed. And the Sinaloa Cartel was also in the mix. But Chinese state actors definitely ran the show, intelligence experts told me.

Money-laundering was the shared interest in Vancouver. But something else was definitely happening. The Big Circle Boys and Chinese intelligence players had started with casinos. And they moved into real estate and finance, Canada's soft spots for economic infiltration. But Beijing has a high-tech long-game. And Vancouver was becoming a global technology node for narcos, state actors and cyber-criminals.

This was fascinating stuff, but I approached it with some caution. It sounded like a spy novel.

Part of it was my innate Canadian sense of insulation. Although I had uncovered lots of money-laundering in B.C. casinos and real estate, I had grown up with a sense that my country was a bastion of uprightness and stability. Corruption and wars and spy plots happened in other countries.

So I would nod with interest when I heard these geopolitical crime tips. But inside, I would think, This is Canada. I'll believe it when I see it. My mind was opening, though. There were major deals happening in Vancouver that made no sense from a national security perspective. In August 2017, I wrote a story with my Postmedia colleague Doug Quan, "How a Murky Company with Ties to the People's Liberation Army Set Up Shop in B.C."

We explained how China Poly — a $95-billion arms trading, real estate and industrial behemoth owned by Red Princeling families — was welcomed with open arms in Vancouver. We reported that China Poly had already been accused of numerous corruption and smuggling cases worldwide. They were deeply involved in Xi Jinping's neo-imperialist Belt and Road infrastructure projects. Their branding depicted the world as a Go board — the ancient Chinese game in which the winner occupies territory to dominate the loser. China Poly often turned up in sketchy dealings with third-world dictators and arms traders. The United States accused them of helping Iran develop its missile program.

In the 1990s, a China Poly agent in California was caught smuggling 2,000 AK-47s into the United States. While that national security probe was underway, one of China Poly's Princelings visited the White House and got implicated in the so-called Chinagate fundraising scandal. Macau casino barons and Triad associates circled around that political influence case. Some of them were familiar names from my research of Lai Changxing's networks. I found the Macau barons and China Poly were like hand and glove. Case in point: Stanley Ho spent millions at auction to hand China Poly an object of tremendous propaganda value.

And this bronze pig head was displayed at Poly Culture's November 2016 "art gallery" opening in Vancouver.

Our *Vancouver Sun* story set the scene like this.

"Under the watchful eye of Vancouver police in tactical gear, attendees admired four rare bronze zodiac heads — a tiger, monkey, ox and pig — that had once adorned the Summer Palace in Beijing.

"It was the first time these cultural relics — looted following the palace's destruction by British and French forces in 1860 — had been displayed outside China since their repatriation.

"The opening of a gallery and North American headquarters here by Poly Culture was the culmination of intense behind-the-scenes courting by local politicians — especially Liberal MLA Teresa Wat, then B.C.'s international trade minister — and was hailed in government documents as a major economic win and 'significant day for British Columbia in its relationship with China.'"

So I could see the shadowy outlines of state actor activity that my sources were talking about. And my instinct was China chose to display the looted relics in Vancouver for propaganda value. It was like Xi's regime was planting a flag in the West. In China, the zodiac heads represent the burning national humiliation of defeat in the Opium Wars.

But now B.C. politicians were quietly rolling out the red carpet for Xi's Belt and Road.

Something else that was hard to believe at first was the connection between China and Mexico that my sources talked about. But I eventually found it was no stretch at all: Chinese actors in fact were merging with the Sinaloa Cartel in North America. And some extremely credible Canadian security intel sources blew my mind with this assessment: the Chinese state seemed to have influence with the Mexican cartels. They had to, one RCMP source told me. Because the Chinese underground bankers were handling almost all of the Latin American narcos' money.

It was trade-based money-laundering on an industrial scale. Chinese merchants moved the Mexican cartel money worldwide by converting drug cash into factory goods. Merchants shipped the goods wherever the cartels needed their funds. The goods were sold. The proceeds banked. Politicians were bribed, weapons were purchased and more drugs were produced and exported. At the same time, Chinese state-controlled factories were shipping mountains of fentanyl precursors into Mexican ports.

As always, it was a textbook case that enabled me to grasp the relationships. I studied U.S. government records on the so-called Chinese-Mexican whale, Zhenli Ye Gon. The Shanghai-born pharmaceutical tycoon — a Chinese national and Mexican citizen — was busted in his Mexico City hacienda in 2007. According to U.S. court records, in a secret room off Ye's master bedroom, police found a stash of military weapons and a two-tonne pile of cash worth US$207 million. Stop for a minute and visualize that. This was a large room with U.S. dollars, Hong Kong dollars, pesos, euros and Canadian dollars neatly stacked halfway to the ceiling. It was the unlaundered proceeds of Ye's crystal meth business. And he looked like a very connected figure in China: educated at East China University of Political Science and Law, a school administered by Beijing's Ministry of Justice.

This was a decade before massive shipments of fentanyl precursors started to land in Vancouver and Manzanillo. But in the early 2000s, Ye was the largest chemical supplier for the Sinaloa Cartel, importing at least 50 tons of meth precursors annually from a Chinese pharmaceutical company. His case had the markers of the Vancouver Model written all over it. He was using Mexican currency exchanges to transfer hundreds of thousands of cash per week into HSBC bank accounts. He was wiring the money into Nevada. In just three years, he gambled at least $125 million in Las Vegas, U.S. court records say, betting $150,000 per hand at baccarat. And Ye was on such good terms with the Venetian Sands — operated by Venetian Macau owner Sheldon Adelson — that the casino comped him a Rolls-Royce, according to the *Wall Street Journal.*

Ye fled to the U.S., where he was arrested and eventually extradited back to Mexico. He denied all charges but Mexico auctioned off his drug mansion in 2019. Ye continues to insist he imported chemicals from China for legitimate purposes, but has also claimed he was operating under corrupt politicians in Mexico who asked him to fund Mexican election campaigns with his cash proceeds. Ye's allegation was vehemently denied by Mexican officials. But the claim made sense to plenty of Mexican citizens. Some reportedly even had licence plates written up: "I believe the Chinaman."

Cases like this — plots that a Hollywood screenwriter couldn't have imagined — showed me that my sources were not out on a limb. They were ahead of the curve.

Meanwhile, I learned the U.S. government had started to pay attention to my reports about China's growing real estate footprint in Vancouver. I was informed that some in the U.S. State Department worried that Chinese transnational crime was establishing a North American beachhead in Vancouver.

But the RCMP and CSIS appeared to be overmatched. Canada had no real counterpunch to answer China's sophisticated financial activities in Vancouver. And so, there was a growing FBI and DEA presence in British Columbia. To me, it seemed like Canada's sovereignty on the west coast was gradually eroding. At least a little bit. And you could see the concern with Xi Jinping's so-called Belt and Road projects, the type of Chinese infrastructure investment deals warmly accepted by tin-pot dictators in underdeveloped nations. I knew these deals were being pitched to B.C. Liberal premier Christy Clark's government in 2016, when Clark and Wat met with Chinese Communist Party officials and real estate tycoons in Guangdong and Hong Kong. And B.C.'s government eventually greenlighted a $190-million Belt and Road import-export centre in 2018. The first of its kind in North America.

This despite the fact the U.S. State Department believes Belt and Road projects are a major vector for Chinese espionage and trade-based money-laundering, according to my Canadian intelligence sources.

In response to questions for this book, Clark, now an adviser with international business law firm Bennett Jones, wrote: "Increasing trade ties with China has been a priority for Canada for many years, including the groundbreaking Team Canada mission led by Prime Minister Chrétien in 1994. Premier Mike Harcourt was part of that mission and every BC Premier since has continued to visit China and worked to strengthen our business relationships there."

So the geopolitical implications of the Vancouver Model were starting to really make sense. But I still had a mental block accepting that
Chinese organized crime and the Chinese Communist Party were on
the same team in Vancouver.

My personal 'This cannot really be happening in Canada but
indisputable evidence says it is' moment came in late 2017. This was
after I started to break E-Pirate stories. Sources I had never heard from
started to contact me. One source told me I should look at a compound
east of Vancouver and near the U.S. border that was filled with stunning
wealth. They said the River Rock Casino whale owned this hacienda in
Chilliwack appeared to be involved in unimaginable money-laundering. In a vast underground bunker, the whale had dozens of high-end
luxury and military vehicles stacked on hoists. There were red Ferraris,
black Rolls-Royces, white Mercedes, green military jeeps. It was a parking lot of horsepower that would have made El Chapo blush. But what
really shocked me was the photos of the River Rock whale's industrial
collection. There was a red and gold fire truck, a big rig truck, and vin-
tage rocket launchers and ground-mount machine guns. (see photos)

A different source with knowledge of RCMP weapons trafficking investigations corroborated the first source's information. RCMP weapons
databases showed the whale owned the largest personal cache of weapons in western Canada, a source said. Dogs and drones patrolled the
compound, and the whale was almost always accompanied by two
young Chinese men who carried weapons. The source said INSET — an
integrated Canadian national security unit including RCMP and CSIS
officers — was watching this compound with interest. And I confirmed
that RCMP headquarters in Ottawa was aware of this Chinese national,
who had arrived in Vancouver on February 15, 2008, and proceeded
to amass extravagant assets in Canada. His passport was from Hong
Kong, and his claimed source of income was a restaurant in China. But
my intelligence sources said he owned aluminum mines in China. And
you don't own mines in China without immaculate *guanxi* in Beijing.

When I ran the whale's personal information through my confidential Lottery Corp. anti-money-laundering record database, a shocking profile emerged. This People's Liberation Army veteran allegedly
cashed in from $200,000 to $300,000 per night at River Rock Casino.

He was Paul King Jin's superior, according to my RCMP source. One of his utility vehicles was a camo Humvee, complete with vanity plates that said TIGER.

I was informed the impressive man — tall, square-jawed and handsome — was called the General by his followers in Vancouver. And indeed, WeChat videos showed that when Rongxiang "Tiger" Yuan relaxed in his compound's karaoke lounge to drink fine liquors and sing odes to the Motherland, he wore his military fatigues.

Despite my efforts to question Tiger Yuan about his many documented ties to Paul King Jin, I have never been able to reach him directly. So I can't ask him why RCMP investigators refer to him as "Suspect 2" in confidential documents that name many alleged River Rock VIP gamblers and loan sharks, including Paul King Jin, who is identified as "Suspect 22."

Through his lawyers, Yuan has denied any involvement in criminality and he sued for defamation after my reports for Global News outlined what my sources and RCMP and B.C. Lottery Corp. investigation records say about him. Yuan says he is a successful businessman who has been an active member of the Chinese-Canadian community for many years, and he meets many individuals.

What I discovered in my own investigations, collecting and assessing photographs and witness accounts, is that Tiger Yuan is evidently so respected in Beijing that he can share a stadium box seat with China's consul-general at state-sponsored events in Vancouver, break bread with Chinese pop stars and Mandarin-language journalists in Vancouver, and even rub shoulders with Prime Minister Justin Trudeau at so-called cash-for-access fundraisers.

This information seemed ridiculously outside the curve of anything in Canadian history.

When you see an elite People's Liberation Army veteran allegedly involved in massive B.C. casino money-laundering and dealing with the most violent of Mainland China narcos and loan sharks in Canada — and very active in Beijing's political influence operations in

Vancouver — to me it suggests problems worth investigating. I knew the RCMP and CSIS were watching The general in B.C. But across the country in Ottawa leaders seemed completely oblivious.

And I had information that screamed for national attention. Sources told me an Iranian national named "Kousha" was the 'meatshield' for Tiger. Canadian deportation records showed this tattooed body-builder had a criminal record. In one case, Kousha was convicted for threatening to kill a Vancouver police officer. He had racially abused the officer and his family, and announced he "hated Jews so much that he smiled at their pain, knowing that he could cause fear."

A confidential RCMP link chart indicated Kousha was an employee of "Kenny" — the young Chinese man who shadowed Tiger in public and stored restricted weapons in Tiger's compound. And photographs from inside Tiger's compound showed Kousha posing with his finger on the trigger of a German MP40 submachine gun.

So why was Rongxiang Yuan surrounded by gun-toting thugs but also tight with Chinese consular leaders? I had to understand what this convergence of state actors and organized crime suspects meant for Canada's security. So I consulted international experts like Jonathan Manthorpe, Alex Joske and Clive Hamilton in Australia, and Professor Anne-Marie Brady in New Zealand to understand President Xi Jinping's so-called magic weapon of espionage and political interference, the United Front Work Department.

By 2020 I had seen enough to eradicate my doubts. My sources were correct. And Canadians had to be informed.

**

I started to hear about problems with the E-Pirate case in late 2018. This was the most significant money-laundering case in Canadian history. Federal charges were laid in September 2017. And the case was scheduled to go to trial in January 2019.

As I had reported for the *Vancouver Sun*, when the RCMP raided Silver's office in downtown Richmond and Jin's Richmond hacienda and luxury condo, they seized 132 computers and cellphones, capturing 30 terabytes of data. If all the digital files were printed on paper, it would have filled three million telephone books. There was a huge forensic accounting element to the case, with transactions traced to 600 bank accounts in China. Evidence was mostly in Mandarin, so the RCMP needed a team of translators working with a small team of federal prosecutors in Ottawa. The file just seemed to drag and drag.

It was a character in Ernest Hemingway's novel *The Sun Also Rises* who described how spectacular busts usually are preceded by myriad paper cuts. The character is asked, How did you go bankrupt?

"Two ways. Gradually, then suddenly."

And that's how E-Pirate imploded. In late November 2018 — the week before Global News ran five stories for our "Fentanyl: Making a Killing series" — I went to a government source and asked for an update on the charges. They said there was a problem with the case. The RCMP and prosecutors had mistakenly exposed a police informant. Some believed the source's life was at risk.

"This could go either way," the source said.

And on November 28 — two days after Global News published our story, "Secret Police Study Finds Crime Networks Could Have Laundered Over $1 Billion Through Vancouver Homes in 2016" — the RCMP dropped its own bombshell.

"E-Pirate charges were stayed for several reasons that materialized during the course of the file; the nature of which will not be discussed," the statement said.

But in B.C. there was incredible public interest to understand how this crucial case had failed. In December 2018, a CBC reporter obtained court files pointing to an evidence disclosure error. And in January 2019, I confirmed what I had been informed of months before.

"A massive RCMP investigation of alleged underground bankers in Richmond, B.C., estimated to be laundering over $1 billion per year collapsed in November because federal prosecutors mistakenly exposed the identity of a police informant who they feared could have been killed if the case proceeded, Global News has learned."

The big problem was Ottawa simply didn't provide the resources to prosecute such an incredible volume of evidence, a source told me. Just translating E-Pirate's Mandarin-language evidence was more than staff could handle. And underlying the spectacular mistake of exposing an informant to the defence lawyer for Paul King Jin is a structural problem. Canada's evidence disclosure requirements are heavily weighted in favour of well-capitalized transnational criminals. Beyond that, to me it's obvious that Canada desperately lacks innovative racketeering laws. It took new legal tools for the FBI to break the Mafia's economic grip on New York City decades ago. But regardless of these systemic legal problems, some officers believed there were more insidious reasons for E-Pirate's failure.

They were thinking back to what had happened in October 2015. When an RCMP tactical unit stormed into an illegal casino in a Richmond farmland hacienda, they had found the operation completely abandoned. Ominously, their original search warrant date was circled on a wall calendar. Senior police in B.C. worried their operational plans were compromised. I only discovered this crucial detail because I obtained Ross Alderson's raw investigative notes. The notes said an experienced GPEB officer on the raid was convinced the RCMP had a serious leak. Someone was giving RCMP plans to well-connected Big Circle Boys.

There was also chatter in policing circles that the E-Pirate raid had been openly discussed by senior officials in Victoria. Could there be deeper political problems for E-Pirate in Ottawa and Victoria?

I can't say definitively. But some sources think so. And there are more questions than answers.

But E-Pirate's failure weakened the NDP government's resistance to a money-laundering inquiry. About 80 percent of B.C. residents wanted an inquiry in late 2018, according to polls. And our reporting at Global News had shown systemic vulnerability in Canada's justice system. Police knew who the money launderers and narcos responsible for Vancouver's fentanyl overdose and housing affordability disaster were. But the criminals couldn't be stopped.

My colleague Jesse Ferreras reported in early 2019 for Global News, "after the collapse of E-Pirate, Premier Horgan said the rule of law had failed in B.C."

And in May 2019, Horgan announced the Cullen Commission inquiry, naming B.C. Supreme Court Justice Austin F. Cullen as the commissioner. For everyone at Global News who worked the B.C. money-laundering file — especially my colleague John Hua, who worked on many TV pieces with me — this was rewarding. Our reporting was credited for accomplishing the highest objectives of investigative journalism in the face of backlash from powerful financial interests.

But I also knew that a national money-laundering inquiry was needed. Reporting from Ottawa, I was finding the Vancouver Model was a Canada-wide problem. Transnational drug cartels running underground banking supernodes in China and the Middle East were deeply intertwined with real estate and trade in Toronto and Montreal as well as Vancouver.

And it was a sprawling DEA investigation that ultimately helped me understand how corruption was enabling organized crime to advance across Canada.

I first learned of the Five Eyes probe of Altaf Khanani and Farzam Mehdizadeh in October 2017. I was waiting to speak to financial professionals about my E-Pirate reporting at a conference in Toronto. Before I was up, Scott Doran, a senior RCMP officer, was delivering his keynote speech on challenges policing big Canadian banks for money-laundering. I was only half awake after tossing and turning all night in my hotel room. A lawyer for Great Canadian Gaming had emailed, warning me not to deliver my speech. I ignored the baseless libel threat. Canadian bankers wanted to hear me talk about a serious threat to the nation. But I have to admit I was a bit distracted. That was until Doran flicked up a slide showing the mug shots of Khanani, a Pakistani national, and Farzam Mehdizadeh, a 57-year-old Toronto currency exchange owner. When Doran said the men were Five Eyes targets I scrambled to turn on my tape recorder. This meant the powerful Western intelligence alliance viewed these men as serious national security threats.

Doran explained that RCMP units had tailed Mehdizadeh driving from Toronto to Montreal and back 81 times in a single year.

The RCMP had been watching Mehdizadeh since at least 2015. Montreal is still superficially dominated by the Italian mafia. But Middle Eastern and Chinese underground bankers increasingly handle the drug money in Montreal, a vital port for narco routes up and down the eastern seaboard.

Mehdizadeh was making about eight trips per month to Laval, where Lebanese drug traffickers warehouse their cash. Every trip, Mehdizadeh would gather about $1.2 million cash, stuff it into his trunk and return to a network of Persian diaspora currency shops clustered in the Steeles Avenue and Yonge Street region of north Toronto. Bricks of cash in elastic bands would be vaulted in back rooms of currency and shops. Massive secret pools of capital in Canada to balance against incalculable sums waiting to be transferred underground out of Iran and Dubai. Banking sanctions levied against Iran in 2010 had only increased the flow in these underground finance networks, a source that ran a Toronto currency shop told me. He said there were only about five Iranian money exchanges in Toronto in 2009. And in 2020 there were over 70. It was an operation very similar to the Richmond cash houses run by the Big Circle Boys.

On March 9, 2016, the RCMP got a warrant to take Mehdizadeh down for international money-laundering. At 10:25 p.m. on April 17, he was speeding back from Montreal on Highway 401 when Ontario Provincial Police pulled him over in Quinte County, near the Sandbanks Provincial Park on Lake Ontario.

He didn't seem very surprised.

"He voluntarily disclosed he has a large sum of money in his possession … in the amount of $1.3 million," an RCMP investigation affidavit says.

Police found bundles of cash beside the gas pedal. They popped the trunk and found a black hockey bag stuffed with 50 bricks of cash, a blue backpack with 21 bricks of cash, and a leather travel bag holding 37 bricks of cash.

A few days later, police searched Mehdizadeh's North York mansion and his Yonge Street currency exchange. They seized numerous banking and ledger documents that showed a spider's web of wire transfers, bank drafts, and substantial loans and transactions with major Canadian banks and numerous Toronto financial businesses.

He faced 16 criminal charges. The RCMP said Mehdizadeh had laundered $100 million in Toronto and Montreal in just one year.

But there was so much more to the case.

I found the RCMP only knew about Mehdizadeh because of brilliant work from the DEA and Australian federal police.

RCMP's intelligence directors were briefed in October 2014 at the DEA's secret headquarters in Chantilly, Virginia. There were dozens of investigators and analysts from the U.S., U.K., Canada, Australia and New Zealand.

Since 2008 DEA had been running undercover agents into Hezbollah narco-launderers' cells in Medellin, Dubai, Panama City. Agents discovered a web of businessmen just like Mehdizdeh collecting drug cash for Iranian state-sponsored criminals in cities worldwide: Toronto, Vancouver, New York, Los Angeles, Sydney, Paris, Melbourne, Miami, London. The DEA broke the case by infiltrating the top of the pyramid. They said Altaf Khanani was the mastermind who washed $16-billion per year for Latin American Cartels, Chinese Triads, Al-Qaeda, the Taliban, Indian narco-terrorist Dawood Ibrahim, and Hezbollah. It was Khanani's ties to Iran and Hezbollah that worried the DEA the most. Police called him the Goldman Sachs of underground banking. Not an exaggeration, considering Khanani's network reportedly handled 40 percent of Pakistan's foreign currency exchange.

So DEA undercovers started chipping away at Khanani's hawala network. They posed as cartel bosses and worked their way up, gaining confidence step by step. Khanani was like a hidden god of the underworld, pushing beads back and forth on a giant abacus. It was all about balancing credits and debits in secret cash houses worldwide. If the Sinaloa Cartel wanted to collect $1 million in cash from a cocaine sale in Montreal, they would call Khanani. Khanani would send his Toronto currency trader to pick it up. And then Khanani would have a currency trader in Mexico pay the funds out in pesos to the Sinaloa Cartel. Minus a 3 percent fee. No money ever crossed borders. At some later date, the Sinaloa Cartel would need funds transferred to Toronto. Maybe to buy weapons or pay off border guards. So Khanani would get them to deposit pesos with his Mexican currency trader. And this time, his Toronto currency agent would pay $1 million cash out to a Mexican cartel agent in North York. Minus a 3 percent fee. An abacus bead slid from Mexico to Canada on a giant scale. It got a lot more complex when Khanani's network mixed wire transfers from Dubai and global textile trading into the mix.

But in simple terms, this was how Khanani used the ancient mercantilist art of hawala to move drugs and weapons across six continents.

The DEA prided itself on non-linear thinking. It was more like a military understanding of supply chain logistics than police running around chasing dial-a-dopers. If you wanted to save lives taken by bombs and guns and opioid overdoses you had to stop the ships carrying the drugs and weapons. And to do that you had to stop the kingpin money launderers financing the trade. So the plan was to take Khanani down by tricking him into moving fake drug cash in Five Eyes cities. And Australian taxpayers fronted over $1 million to seed the undercover operations.

"We were working Khanani around the world, using Australia's money," a U.S. official told me. "We told Khanani we have a certain amount of drug money in Toronto. Do you have someone to pick it up? And they would give us a contact number."

The U.S. source said DEA agents discovered cash laundering contracts in Australia were interconnected with drug transactions in Canada. A cash pickup in Melbourne would send a shipment of cocaine from Vancouver to Toronto. And the investigation proved how Five Eyes partners could disrupt major drug traffickers by taking out their financial masterminds. But the Khanani investigation also revealed something very wrong was happening up high in the RCMP. In retrospect, it seemed to go back to about 2008, my source said. A team of DEA agents had travelled to Ottawa to meet RCMP brass. The DEA had "dirty calls" — wiretaps directing cocaine shipments and cash movements in Canada — from narco-bosses in Colombia to Hezbollah agents in Halifax, Vancouver and Calgary.

The DEA handed the RCMP key targets and solid evidence. But the RCMP didn't want to wire-tap the narco-terror suspects.

"They wouldn't go up on any phones. We were dumbfounded," a U.S. source told me in 2019. "It really bothered me. It was very clear how Canada was a very, very big part of Hezbollah's transnational narco-terrorism. But RCMP made it very clear at that time, they didn't want to bear down on money-laundering and drug trafficking. So when I see what is happening now in Vancouver, I have to think back to what we were seeing."

So it seemed there was a strange reticence in the RCMP to target Iranian state-sponsored crime. Multiple sources confirmed this for me. Ottawa did finally sign onto the sting of Altaf Khanani and Farzam Mehdizadeh. You can't be a Five Eyes partner and decline to investigate a super-criminal believed to be laundering $16 billion annually for the world's worst terrorists and narcos. But it was a hard sell for the U.S. government.

"We really had to push them to drop that cash in Toronto," a U.S. source told me.

And it ultimately blew up.

My colleague Stewart Bell worked the Khanani case with me. And he was informed that Mehdizadeh returned to Iran sometime after he was released on bail in 2016. The RCMP refused to tell me why.

So let's review the record. In Toronto, a key target in a crucial Five Eyes money-laundering investigation just vanishes before trial. And in Vancouver, an even bigger transnational money-laundering case fails weeks before trial.

***

In September 2019, when CSIS agents scoured the Ottawa condo of Cameron Ortis, a civilian RCMP intelligence official, they found dozens of encrypted computers. They also found evidence that Ortis was planning to leak Five Eyes operations plans to Altaf Khanani's network.

So when the RCMP finally announced charges against Ortis, for some officers, there was a burst of relief and then fury.

They called Ortis the Golden Boy, or the Prince, as in Machiavelli. They felt he had been coddled by RCMP brass — the old boy's club.

And in retrospect, for some who worked with Ortis, the RCMP's strange refusal to investigate Hezbollah narco targets finally made sense.

Ortis had the charisma of a cool professor with his tortoiseshell glasses. He looked a bit like Jeremy Irons, but shorter and more muscular. In 2007 the RCMP had recruited him straight out of University of B.C. grad school. He rocketed up to lead a secretive intelligence unit called Operational Results or Operations Research (OR), depending on who you asked. OR was staffed with about ten civilian analysts, just like Ortis. And they pushed the envelope of Canada's justice system by using "high side" intel shared among the Five Eyes.

This was classified information collected from sensitive human sources and intercepted signals. The dangerously exposed human sources could include undercover agents inside Hezbollah or even politically connected tycoons in Mainland China. This Five Eyes intel could rarely be used in Canadian criminal prosecutions. But RCMP Comm. Bob Paulson believed Ortis and his cadre of brilliant academics in OR were skillfully leveraging high side intel to boost the RCMP to the FBI's level.

And in 2016, Paulson and his deputies promoted Ortis, making him director general of RCMP's national intelligence centre. He was the first civilian ever to become the RCMP's gatekeeper for Canada's crown jewel secrets.

Due to Canadian court publication bans, there is some information I can't report. But because of my early knowledge of the Altaf Khanani Five Eyes case, I learned a great deal from Canadian and U.S. sources outside of the courts. And that information I can report. Because it is crucial for Canadians to know how much damage one powerful intelligence analyst could have done.

In the broadest strokes, federal prosecutors' unproven charges allege Ortis has been sharing the RCMP's plans with foreign entities or terrorist organizations since 2015, at least.

Investigators have only started to understand the massive volume of top-secret data that Ortis allegedly stole and encrypted. It includes information that could endanger Canada's national security and sovereignty.

It's not clear from existing allegations whether Ortis was just dealing with state-sponsored gangsters and global money launderers or whether he was working for hostile states. But the information I obtained shows Ortis was allegedly offering to sell the RCMP's tactical plans to currency traders used by Khanani in Toronto. Ortis is charged for contacting Mehdizadeh in 2015 - and offering special operational plans for a fee - while the RCMP was trailing Mehdizadeh driving to Montreal and back to Toronto. And Ortis is charged for twice contacting Mehdizadeh's business associate, Salim Henareh. Henareh is a currency trader involved in major commercial real estate investments in Toronto.

Think about that. Khanani is allegedly a major terror financier, part of a network that literally moves guns and drugs and bombs around the world. And the RCMP is supposed to be protecting Canadians from the harms of money-laundering.

But according to the charges, Ortis - possibly the most influential brain in the RCMP - was offering protection to money launderers.

An RCMP source told me the Toronto currency traders used by Khanani were inter- twined in significant real estate development. On top of that - donation records showed me that Salim Henareh was involved in Liberal party cash-for-access fundraisers and philanthropy. He is also an influential community leader of the Iranian Canadian Congress, according to internal records I obtained.

A lawyer for Henareh sent this to Optimum on the eve of publishing the book:

a) Mr. Henareh has no connection whatsoever to Mr. Khanani or his business dealings whatsoever, illegal or otherwise;

b) Mr. Henareh is not a business partner of Mr. Mehdizadeh. On a few occasions in 2010 and 2011, Mr. Mehdizadeh was a customer of one of Mr. Henareh's cur- rency exchange businesses, like 1000's of others. All transactions processed on behalf of Mr. Mehdizadeh were reported to FINTRAC in the ordinary course and as required by law. Well a er these transactions, in the normal course, Mr. Henareh's businesses were subject to a thorough FINTRAC audit, which covered the periods of 2010 and 2011 and disclosed not a single irregularity;

c) Mr. Henareh is not accused of any wrongdoing whatsoever in relation to Mr. Ortis. Mr. Henareh has never purchased any information, or anything else from Mr. Ortis. Mr. Henareh has cooperated fully with the RCMP in relation to Mr. Ortis' o er to sell information to him.

However, in March 2021, the FBI unsealed a criminal complaint against Henareh, alleging that he and a number of currency traders were part of an interna- tional scheme to make "transactions secretly executed on behalf of Iran."

"During the scheme, the defendants allegedly created and used more than 70 front companies, money service businesses and exchange houses ... in the United States, Iran, Canada, the United Arab Emirates and Hong Kong," the complaint, filed October 2020 in Los Ange-les, said.

In one of the alleged transactions, the FBI said while Henareh was running a Toronto currency exchange in 2012, he used a Hong Kong-based "front company to secretly buy two US $25-million oil tankers on behalf of Iran."

Mr. Henareh's lawyer responded that, *"With respect to the unsealed criminal complaint in the United States naming Mr. Henareh, Mr. Henareh has never been contacted by any US or Canadian authority concerning the matters raised in the complaint. Mr. Henareh denies the allegations contained in the complaint."*

A U.S. source with knowledge of the Five Eyes Khanani probe told me damage in the Ortis case is incalculable.

"The most damning point of this case is it creates distrust in the whole foundation of international intelligence sharing, for fighting terror and crime," he said. "The fact that Ortis was trying to [share Canadian intelligence with] Khanani says it all. You have billions of dollars of money-laundering tied to terrorist organizations that have killed hundreds of thousands of people. People should be saying, 'This is unbelievable. We can never let this happen again.'"

It's not clear what possible motive drove Ortis besides greed. How deep and dark could this be? What could have been compromised, and to who?

Ortis' national intelligence unit was producing reports on cocaine coming from Latin America, transnational gangs based in Macau and China, and weapons trafficking worldwide. Sources said Ortis was a leader on complex investigations focused on China and Iran early in his career. Lots of evidence suggests Ortis was drawn to global money launderers and cybercriminals. But to my mind, exactly who Ortis was working for is a moot point. The cyberworld that he mastered is where criminals and spies and state actors converge to trade secrets.

And I found it incredibly illuminating that Ortis' 2006 UBC graduate thesis explored national security vulnerabilities caused by "compromised nodes" and the "digital black market" that connects gangsters and hackers in Hong Kong and Shenzen, China.

Lines like this one jumped off the page.

"Is transnational organized crime a threat to state security in the digital age?" Ortis wrote. "This chapter introduces that concept of a nexus between two previously distinct, hidden networks: systems intruders and transnational organized crime."

Ironically, Ortis looks like a compromised node himself. But when did he lose his way? I know that investigators have looked all the way back to his studies at UBC. And to me, his graduate research in Asia seems a good place to start. Ortis speaks Mandarin. He was introduced to state sources in Mainland China through his academic research at UBC, the thesis says. And his academic network at the university frequently displays a pro-Beijing message. For example, in 2020, the *Globe and Mail* reported that UBC prof Paul Evans is seen by Huawei Canada as one of the "key opinion leaders" that could help prevent the Chinese telecom giant from being banned from Canada 5G networks. And I found that Evans was Ortis' mentor for the "Compromised Nodes" thesis, which they jointly published.

Evans told me that Ortis had worked with experts in Hong Kong, Taiwan and Mainland China.

"It was a complex and strikingly original thesis that went far beyond the normal bounds of political science and involved conversations with dozens of people in the broad fields of interational [*sic*] relations," Evans wrote to me. "Beyond that, I have nothing more to say in a situation where his case is before the courts."

Ultimately, Ortis' expertise on Chinese transnational crime and cyber-criminals propelled him to the pinnacle of Canadian intelligence, despite his having no operational experience.

And here is something that my sources found very strange.

One of the U.S. State Department's top national security concerns is Chi Lop Tse, the Canadian Big Circle Boy who may have become the world's top narco before Australian federal police nailed him in the Netherlands.

Tse was preparing to fly to Toronto. Australian police apparently felt more confident asking the Dutch to extradite Tse than Canada.

Even though Chi Lop Tse left Canada after 2010, his network in Toronto is very strong. Four of Sam Gor's commanders are Canadian citizens. That fact alone shows how important Canada has become for Chinese transnational gangs. And Tse's associates in Markham appear to have relationships with some staff working in Canadian banks, several RCMP sources informed me. The allegation made sense, because E-Pirate surveillance records showed me that Jin and his associates were observed dealing with various bank staff in Richmond. And an extremely knowledgeable financial crimes investigator told me organized crime almost always cultivates banking staff to obtain instruments such as bank drafts and to complete useful transactions.

So around 2014, the RCMP was informed by Australian federal police that Tse and "The Company" were running a global crystal meth import and export hub in Markham, right under the nose of Canadian police forces. This was embarrassing for Ottawa, to say the least.

And units that Ortis influenced started surveillance on Chi Lop Tse's deputies in Markham and produced intelligence reports for the Five Eyes. Here is an interesting aside. I'm told undercovers who set up at a location in Markham were very surprised to see a senior Canadian elected official in the vicinity of a Chi Lop Tse group meeting. But that undercover observation didn't lead to any deeper investigation.

And here's another mind-bender. Some Canadian and Australian federal police got together in 2015. They concluded that Chi Lop Tse's Toronto network and Paul Jin's Richmond network were of course working together. This all made perfect sense. Chi Lop Tse and Kwok Chung Tam are old comrades.

And think back to Pat Fogarty's stunning wire tap investigations in Vancouver. In the late 1990s Fogarty was listening to Triad commanders calling shots in Macau's bloody war for control of Stanley Ho's baccarat tables.

The Big Circle Boys and the 14K banded together against the Water Room Triad. But these drug cartels were ultimately controlled by Chinese state bosses, who put an end to Triad conflicts.

Many of the Chinese loan sharks and high-rollers identified in Australian intelligence were also identified in Canadian criminal intelligence. Paul Jin recruited his whales in Macau. And Chi Lop Tse bragged of controlling Macau. Kwok Chung Tam was one of Jin's bosses.

So it didn't take a rocket scientist to surmise connectivity between Chi Lop Tse's operation in eastern Canada and Paul King Jin's network on the west coast.

But when Ortis took over the RCMP's national intelligence centre in 2016, suddenly his team had a very different opinion than experts in Australian and Canadian anti-gang units.

Ortis' unit wasn't interested in Chi Lop Tse's connection to E-Pirate. And the RCMP's nascent probe of Sam Gor in Markham fizzled out.

Another crazy occurrence. Abruptly, in 2016, RCMP intelligence-gathering priorities changed. Chinese transnational crime was downgraded as a priority. There are some in the RCMP who wonder if Ortis influenced these strange decisions. And it's not baseless speculation.

There is solid evidence, according to a source, suggesting that Ortis blocked a potential RCMP investigation of EncroChat — an encryptions technology business with links to Vancouver that serviced transnational narcos in the United Kingdom and across Europe, especially.

And that's just one organized crime focused file. Here is a truly scary aspect of the Ortis case.

Sources with knowledge of national security investigations told me Ortis quickly became RCMP Comm. Bob Paulson's most trusted advisor on national security and sensitive political investigations. Ortis and Paulson were so close, sources said, that Paulson treated Ortis almost like an oracle. One source described the influence as "Rasputin-like."

There is a story that seems to highlight the relationship. The claim is that Paulson insisted on bringing Ortis into what was supposed to be a one-on-one meeting in Washington. The alleged meeting — prior to 2014 — was with FBI director Robert Mueller. The FBI would not comment. Paulson also would not comment on my source information for this book. Previously, he acknowledged he was close to Ortis. But he insisted he was never aware of red flags or internal complaints about Ortis before Paulson retired in 2017.

But if Ortis had such influence on Paulson's strategic and tactical priorities, the intangible damage to Canada will be difficult to assess.

A U.S. source familiar with the RCMP's decision-making from 2008 to 2016 said in hindsight, the Ortis case isn't a complete shock.

"There was a lingering feeling, is there an obstruction at the top in Ottawa?" he said. "Overall, operationally we kind of felt there was something in Canada. Like our ops were vulnerable to something like this. So it's really interesting how intelligence analysts like Ortis develop so much power to decide who gets targeted and who doesn't. And it ends up becoming a political thing."

As one Canadian policing executive said, it's terrifying that Ortis had more access to national security secrets than anyone else in the RCMP. It's even more terrifying that he could have enabled hostile state actors to operate in Canada or leaked high side intel to their political masters in China, Russia or Iran.

And even outside his alleged Rasputin-like hold on Paulson, Ortis had enough power himself. Numerous data points from documents and sources say that Ortis was protected from oversight as complaints about his leadership mounted.

So could foreign entities be looking for more than information from someone like Ortis? Could they misdirect Canada's intelligence apparatus by having an agent of influence at the controls? I know some leaders in the RCMP are asking these questions. Because the damage to units that Ortis controlled appears to be deep and lasting.

In September 2019, when the RCMP announced the Ortis arrest, our Global News team started looking for potential damage.

And Global News Ottawa bureau chief Mercedes Stephenson got a huge tip. She pinged me on a secure messaging app and asked if the name Vincent Ramos meant anything to me.

I knew the name well. In late 2018 Ramos and his Richmond encryption technology company, Phantom Secure, was taken down by the FBI. Phantom Secure had sold up to 20,000 untraceable smartphones to elite narcos worldwide, including bosses of the Sinaloa

Cartel, enabling them to evade wiretaps and command drug imports, money-laundering and murders. And Ortis' unit was working Phantom Secure with the FBI and many international forces.

Mercedes Stephenson's tip was that Ortis had contacted Ramos and told him Phantom Secure was under investigation and offered to sell police intelligence. I later learned the opening offer to Ramos allegedly was $20,000. But Ortis wasn't as street smart as he appeared to be in the academic world. When the FBI eventually caught Ramos, they flipped him.

And Ramos had a lot to lose. He had already admitted to undercover DEA agents that his smartphones could be used to geolocate informants. So he gave up Ortis and took an FBI deal. Selling phones to narcos was quite lucrative. But Ramos had to turn over $80 million of his proceeds to the U.S. government.

"Ramos admitted that he and his co-conspirators facilitated the distribution of cocaine, heroin, and methamphetamine to locations around the world, including in the United States, Australia, Mexico, Canada, Thailand and Europe by supplying narcotics traffickers with Phantom Secure encrypted communications devices designed to thwart law enforcement," a U.S. Department of Justice statement says.

Stephenson, Stewart Bell and I worked together to confirm the connection between Ortis and Ramos, and we broke the story.

In the pecking order on transnational crime, Ramos is a non-entity compared to names like Altaf Khanani. But the impact Ortis had on the Phantom Secure case is still enormous. The Five Eyes probe into Ramos had to be rolled up early, and Canada's partners missed opportunities to sting Phantom's most powerful clients, the "ones and twos" of transnational drug cartels. Australia and the United States were "pissed" a source told me.

And the same thing allegedly happened with EncroChat. I was informed that European gangsters were using the service to plan executions. And Ortis blocked Canada's investigations, potentially protecting EncroChat's boss, a man with B.C. roots.

I have repeatedly asked Ortis to respond to my questions but his lawyer has never answered. In early 2020 I called out to Ortis in an Ottawa courtroom, but he turned away. Allegations against him haven't been proven at trial, and he doesn't want to answer my questions.

The question of how many criminal nodes could be connected through high-tech operatives like Vincent Ramos and Cameron Ortis is wide open.

I know some investigators are intrigued by the idea that the networks of Ramos and E-Pirate targets in Richmond could have converged. After all, Silver International and Phantom Secure were located in the same Richmond office building. And a quote from the Phantom Secure CEO's 1993 Richmond high school yearbook only adds to the intrigue.

"Vince's most memorable experience was cruising hardcore and going to JIN's house," text beside Ramos' grinning mugshot says. "His future ambition is to make a lot of money."

***

Brian Hill and I were in the federal court building on Sparks Street. This was one of my favourite places to work, a three-minute walk from our Global News bureau in Ottawa. Whenever I needed a break from reading files I could step into the cobble-stoned street and look north to the Queen's Gate leading up to Canada's Parliament. This view helped me remember the aphorism that motivates investigative reporters: To comfort the afflicted and to afflict the comfortable. But this day I didn't need any motivation. My hands were shaking with adrenaline.

Piles of boxes surrounded us. It was our second day drilling into Kwok Chung Tam's immigration files. The first day is like taking core samples. You dig into a box and get a quick sense of the evidence and move on. Now I had a broad idea of the terrain, and I was focused on RCMP intelligence files and Tam's own financial records. I was amazed at the intelligence from Ottawa that never made it to public trials. I found records that said Kwok Chung Tam had been issued a fraudulent identity record from the Chinese consulate in Vancouver.

Think about that. No one in Canada was informed that the Chinese government issued a fake I.D. to an alleged Big Circle Boy kingpin. Why would they do that?

But I was more interested in Tam's financial records. He was attempting to demonstrate he was a legitimate businessman. There were all kinds of banking assets and real estate investments. When I hit the bare trust file, I stifled a shout.

I understood how controversial bare trusts were in B.C. These legal structures allow wealthy investors to remain completely anonymous on real estate transaction documents. B.C. attorney general David Eby had already travelled to Parliament Hill in 2018 on an anti-money-laundering mission. He told a finance committee that anonymous investors were flooding billions of dollars into B.C. real estate using bare trust loopholes.

The government couldn't learn their identities because only the law firm that constructs the bare trust holds a piece of paper with investor names recorded.

That all sounds a bit academic. But in my hands, I had a bare trust file showing that Kwok Chung Tam — a notorious "drug boss" — had completed a Vancouver condo development deal in 2011 with co-investors, including his sister, another convicted drug trafficker. This file was a huge leap towards explaining how the Big Circle Boys were using lawyers to hide their real estate developments in Canada. But it was the name of the legal company on Tam's bare trust that really mattered to me, because the principal was sitting in the House of Commons. It was Peschisolido and Co., the firm of Liberal MP Joe Peschisolido, an important political fundraiser in Richmond for Prime Minister Justin Trudeau's party. This was exactly the sort of evidence that the Cullen Commission was mandated to examine, on two fronts. Were lawyers facilitating money-laundering, and was political corruption involved in the Vancouver Model?

In our June 2019 story, "Alleged Gang Kingpin May Have Used Liberal MP's Law Firm to Launder Money Through B.C. Condo Deal," we explained that bare trusts are legal in the province. Still, the Tam deal raised all kinds of questions about the role of lawyers in B.C.'s money-laundering crisis.

Peschisolido's firm had enabled Tam's anonymous purchase of a $7.75 million land parcel in 2011, despite many public records gluing Kwok Tam to the Big Circle Boys. Even worse, Peschisolido and Co. completed the deal while Tam was serving a conditional sentence for a 2010 drug trafficking conviction. The *Vancouver Province* had reported on that case and labelled Tam a "drug boss."

I interviewed Kim Marsh, anti-money-laundering expert and former RCMP organized crime unit commander.

"Anybody doing basic due diligence, even basic Google searches, would determine there are huge red flags that these individuals are involved in illicit activities," Marsh said. "So anyone doing business with them is either doing nothing, or it's a case of wilful blindness."

Peschisolido, however, claimed he had nothing to do with the deal.

"While I was practicing at Peschisolido and Associates I never oversaw any bare trust real estate transactions nor did I ever deal with Mr. Tam in any capacity," Peschisolido wrote to Global News.

But when I did a system-wide scan of Canadian legal records, I found yet another Peschisolido and Co. bare trust case. This 2011 deal included a Mainland China construction magnate, Y.Z., who just happened to be one of the 36 River Rock Casino VIPs connected to Paul King Jin's cash delivery network. Furthermore, Y.Z. was a Julia Lau real estate client involved in B.C. real estate developments. This made him a central player in the Vancouver Model networks I was investigating.

We had another scoop for Global News: "Liberal MP Involved in Second Bare Trust Deal with Client Named in 'Transnational Money Laundering' Probe."

Peschisolido claimed again that an associate lawyer at his firm had total responsibility for the file.

But these stories were reverberating in Parliament. Conservative MP Peter Kent grilled Peschisolido and Liberal Public Safety Min. Bill Blair on the allegations exposed by Global News and asked for a Parliamentary ethics commissioner investigation. The commissioner eventually found Peschisolido violated two parts of the conflict of interest code for "chronically failing" to disclose private interests.

And I was getting more information.

A source with direct knowledge confirmed the RCMP had opened a file on Peschisolido because confidential police informants alleged the lawyer had been associating with Chinese organized crime figures through his Richmond practice.

"A source said that during the E-Pirate probe, which was started in 2015, the RCMP 'was hearing' Peschisolido was 'affiliated' with — and involved in 'structuring' investment deals for — some of his law firm's clients that 'he knew' were associated to Asian organized crime," I reported for Global News in July 2019.

Peschisolido strongly denied any involvement in real estate deals involving RCMP organized crime targets or associating with gangsters. There have been no charges against Peschisolido, and a source informed me the RCMP hasn't pursued an investigation on the Peschisolido file.

But having inside sources confirm the RCMP was looking into Peschisolido's associations in Richmond added weight to the interesting things I saw in Vancouver politics. Once, Michel Juneau Katsuya told me evidence of espionage is hidden in plain sight.

And I could see the evidence in WeChat pictures and Zoom group chats and hundreds of photos from Mandarin-language websites linked to the Chinese state. Whether Peschisolido understood it or not, he and many Canadian leaders were players in a social network intertwined with E-Pirate targets and Chinese officials in Vancouver.

This network was nebulous and complicated by design.

It was Beijing's United Front.

This was a totally new area of investigation for me. It was different from the leaked official documents and real estate records and court files I usually worked with. Now I had a large collection of photographs that detailed frequent meetings of Chinese-Canadian political and business associations in Vancouver and Toronto and Montreal and Ottawa. These were mainly 'open source' records stored online and often crowdsourced from a circle of international researchers who mined Chinese state documents for evidence. I found many of these groups in Canada could be connected — through official records in Mainland China — to Xi Jinping's United Front Work Department.

Experts like Juneau Katsuya; Jon Manthorpe, author of *Claws of the Panda*; Clive Hamilton, author of *Hidden Hand*; and Anne-Marie Brady — whose seminal study of the United Front's deep infiltration of New Zealand is cited by CSIS — helped me understand how the United Front's influence campaigns work.

In basic terms, the United Front is "political warfare," Manthorpe said. He said that Beijing had installed United Front agents in all Chinese consulates and embassies worldwide. These agents take orders from Beijing and control United Front groups in cities worldwide. In Canada, United Front agents attempt to infiltrate all levels of government by influencing elected officials, sponsoring candidates for elections, and persuading business and academic elites to adopt the Chinese Communist Party's foreign policy. Equally concerning, Manthorpe said, was the Chinese Communist Party's ideological usage of the United Front in efforts to demand racial loyalty from all Chinese immigrants worldwide. This is despite the fact that the majority of Chinese immigrants in Canada want nothing to do with Xi Jinping's United Front.

Juneau Katsuya told me CSIS investigations showed the United Front is central to the Chinese Communist Party's intellectual property theft in Canada and Chinese intelligence's attempts to spy on, harass and attack Chinese-Canadians who dare to speak out against Beijing. He said CSIS first recognized in the 1990s the United Front was using Chinese organized crime figures to cultivate Canadian politicians on one hand

and to target Chinese dissidents on the other. And this was merely a continuation of the United Front's successful tactics in Hong Kong.
Still, I had a shadow of a doubt. This hidden network had never been proven to exist in Canadian courts. And the Chinese state denied using the United Front on Canadian soil. So I had to look for concrete evidence elsewhere.

The case of Ng Lap Seng — a billionaire Macau casino and real estate tycoon, alleged Triad leader, and United Front Work Department agent — was extremely illuminating.

In August 2019 a U.S. court of appeal affirmed Ng's conviction in an incredibly sophisticated Chinese Communist Party corruption scheme. Ng was indicted for bribing at least two United Nations officials, including former president John William Ashe. Ng's network was funnelling millions to United Nations leaders through NGOs and Chinese spies operating in New York City, Macau, and Antigua. The case deserves a book of its own because it says so much about the Party's global plans. For example, Ng was part of the "China-gate" scandal, donating at least $220,000 to President Bill Clinton's Democratic party in the 1990s. And actors identified by the FBI in Ng's case are central to Beijing's efforts to build telecom and national security infrastructure in Caribbean, South Pacific and African countries. People's Liberation Army intelligence officers circle the case like vultures. And one of the case's many rabbit holes brought me back to the self-acknowledged Chinese intelligence operative Lai Changxing. Patrick Ho, a Hong Kong lawmaker, also convicted of bribery and money-laundering in the case, is intertwined with the very same Chinese oil conglomerate that Lai Changxing ran before he fled to Vancouver.

But I'll just focus on the piece of Ng's indictment that highlights an unexplored node of the Vancouver Model. The implication is that Chinese organized crime networks are not just laundering drug cash through casino junkets. They are also using casinos and real estate investment to produce cash for Chinese Communist Party operations in North America, including political bribes. In intelligence-speak, this would be called threat-financing.

An FBI affidavit explained Ng's scheme like this: "The FBI's investigation has revealed that NG LAP SENG and [Ng's secretary] have concealed consistently ... the true purpose of their importation of more than $4.5 million in United States currency, repeatedly falsely claiming the imported cash was being used for the purchase of art and antiques or real estate, or gambling. The wire that NG LAP SENG caused to be sent to the Casino was not the only wire he has sent or caused to be sent to the United States. NG has wired more than $19 million to bank accounts of entities and/or individuals in the United States."

It means that Ng's network was wiring in funds to bribe United Nations leaders in New York City, all under the cover of Ng's whale casino persona.

But what was happening in Australia gave me even more perspective on the Vancouver Model's clandestine elements.

Sydney Morning Herald investigative reporter Nick McKenzie broke the Crown Resorts scandal in July 2019 with a series of incredible stories. McKenzie wrote that gambling junket operations in Melbourne were linked to Chinese drug and sex trafficking cartels. And the cartel leaders were running gambling junkets that flew in politically connected VIPs from China. But these same organized crime junket players also directed United Front influence-peddling operations in Australia. The officials from China who jetted in to play baccarat and lavish Australian politicians with cash were men worth billions. And they gambled hundreds of millions in Australian casinos each year. All of this mirrored what I was seeing in the Vancouver Model.

I knew Australia had banned a Macau casino junket executive that my sources said was the new boss of the 14k Triad. But related Macau and Hong Kong tycoons were very invested in Vancouver real estate. And I already knew B.C. Lottery Corp. and Australian casinos shared from the same pool of whales and corrupt Chinese officials. In just one example, in June 2018 Henry Tso, the RCMP's top financial crimes investigator, quickly shut down a Chinese official who had set up in a River Rock Casino hotel room.

I heard that Tso — whose family had immigrated to Canada from Hong Kong — had a deep understanding of Chinese transnational crime hierarchies and methodologies.

And Tso decided to hook the Chinese official and have him deported rather than run a sprawling undercover case. The whale was already wanted for laundering $855 million in Australian casinos and various financial crimes in Las Vegas.

But Nick McKenzie's investigation found something totally next level in Australia. Xi Jinping's own cousin — a corruption suspect named Ming Chai — was counted among the Crown Casino VIPs. From 2012 to 2013, Xi's cousin had bet $39 million at Crown Casino, the *Wall Street Journal* reported. McKenzie's reporting tied Ming Chai to an alleged Crown junket crime boss and United Front leader nicknamed Mr. Chinatown.

The biggest player of all seemed to be Huang Xiangmo, an $800-million-per-year Crown high-roller and leader of Guangdong-associated United Front groups in Australia. Huang got his Australian citizenship revoked and ruined Labour Party senator and fundraising rainmaker Sam Dastyari in the process. Dastyari had warned Huang of an Australian counterintelligence investigation against him and the United Front. And he had undermined the Labour Party's criticism of China's military expansion in the South China Sea after Huang threatened to take back a $400,000 political donation.

Alex Joske boiled the issues down in his 2020 report, "The Party Speaks for You: Foreign Interference and the Chinese Communist Party's United Front System."

"In Australia and Taiwan, the Chinese Communist Party has used organized crime groups to carry out United Front work. Several cases suggest that criminal activity may be tolerated by the Chinese Government and even used as leverage in exchange for participation in political influence operations," the report says. "In July 2019, it was reported that two of Xiangmo Huang's [United Front] council members were running illegal gambling junkets for Crown Casino and involved in money-laundering."

And the Huang case demonstrated that the soft spot in Australia's democracy is dark money.

"There is an arms race for donations between the parties," Dastyari said after resigning, according to Joske's report. "And when you've got individuals like Huang who are prepared to fork out millions of dollars they get listened to."

Joske also made fascinating connections that helped explain the increasingly brazen United Front activity I was seeing in Vancouver. This vast espionage network was designed to hide criminality. And it was expanding under Xi Jinping.

"Premier Zhou Enlai, one of the People's Republic of China founding revolutionaries and a pioneer of the Chinese Communist Party's United Front, advocated 'deftly integrating the legal and the illegal,'" Joske wrote. "And Xi Jinping himself spent 15 years climbing the Chinese Communist Party ranks in Fujian Province — a hotbed of the United Front and intelligence work."

This is scary stuff. And in hindsight, I could recognize increased political organization and messaging from the main United Front players I was looking at in Vancouver, from 2018. For example, why did Hong Guo, Paul Jin's lawyer and a denier of human-rights abuses in China, run for mayor in Richmond that year with support from a group that takes direction from Vancouver's Chinese consulate? But I also need to make an important distinction. Unless RCMP or CSIS can prove covert quid pro quo offers taking place when United Front groups met with Canadian politicians, nothing illegal was taking place. Clinking wineglasses and passing the fundraising hat with ultra-wealthy pro-Beijing Chinese nationals isn't a crime for Canadian politicians. And as former CSIS director Ward Elcock told me, proving clandestine United Front political influence is extremely difficult. He added that China is the number one threat in Canada for political interference, but many nations are running similar campaigns, and politicians of all ethnicities are targeted. Here is another important distinction I learned from experts. Not everyone who attends meetings where United Front and Chinese consulate leaders are present is aware of and involved in Xi's interference campaigns. But what I do know from current and former CSIS experts is the more often you see certain community leaders or politicians at gatherings connected to China's United Front Work Department, the more likely these people are involved in United Front activity. And Canadian politicians, community leaders and business leaders need to be aware of the threat of 'elite capture' and espionage, a former senior CSIS officer told me. Because at these United Front events, Chinese consulates will place agents looking for "talent" to cultivate for Xi's foreign interference plans.

***

On August 18, Alice ran into Tenth Church near Vancouver City Hall. She was late to join a meeting of about 70 gathered to pray for peace in Hong Kong. Most were elderly Hong Kong Canadians, but some younger Christians, like Alice (name changed for safety reasons) had protested in front of the Chinese consulate that day. Almost everyone had family members in Hong Kong, a city rupturing with the Chinese Communist Party's expanding national security laws.

The events of July 21 at Yuen Long subway station — mobs of Triad thugs dressed all in white savaged Hong Kong democracy activists with knives and canes — deeply worried Alice's community. They also knew that students at Australia's University of Queensland — including a media-savvy young human-rights activist named Drew Pavlou — had been attacked in late July by pro-Beijing students. And in Vancouver pro-Beijing forces were making similar threats in WeChat groups.

So when Vancouver police entered Tenth Church to announce that about 100 pro-Beijing activists had surrounded the church shouting and waving large red flags, Alice's friends prayed for their own safety.

"It was terrifying. We were trying to figure out how to get out of the church," Alice told me. "Most Canadians don't understand the fear and anxiety we are facing."

Vancouver police escorted the 70 Hong Kong Canadians from the church while agents from the mob moved close to take pictures of their faces. Alice and her friends were shocked. This was Canada. They felt their freedom of religion and expression was being attacked. They felt their identities were being captured for the use of Chinese intelligence services. And this information could be used against family members in Hong Kong or Mainland China.

But because independent Vancouver journalist Bob Mackin was filming outside Tenth Church, the identities of the pro-Beijing mob were also recorded. And this led to a major breakthrough for me. Multiple records and sources confirmed the mob's apparent leader — who I'll call Mr. Ye — is also an elite leader of an umbrella association for about 100 Chinese-Canadian groups. It's a very special association. Former Chinese diplomat Chen Yonglin defined it as the Chinese Communist Party's "controlling level" United Front Work Department group in Canada. Its leaders say they take direction from Chinese consulate United Front officials, records show. And when I ran Mr. Ye through my United Front meeting database, I hit the jackpot.

Mr. Ye showed up frequently with prominent B.C. politicians. He was featured in a Chinese-language report that detailed the grand opening of his Vancouver "China Hui" cultural arts club. Seated beside him at the 2018 opening were Rongxiang Yuan, Liberal MP Joe Peschisolido and Yongtao Chen, a Vancouver real estate developer and then-executive chairman of Canada's controlling level United Front group. B.C. Liberal MLA Teresa Wat and a Chinese consulate official filled out the front row. The crowd was thick with elite Vancouver realtors and alleged Chinese gangsters. After Tiger Yuan and Peschisolido and Yongtao Chen stood to give speeches, Mr. Ye performed an opera solo. Later, Tiger tinkled on a grand piano. Tiger's frequent companion 'Max' — a tattooed leader of Canada's controlling level United Front group — beamed obsequiously over Tiger's shoulder.

While the crowd mingled, Peschisolido posed for multiple pictures with Tiger Yuan and Paul King Jin. It was a stunning demonstration of the connectivity between Chinese organized crime suspects and Canadian political leaders. And China Hui's list of sponsors included the Vancouver Chinese consulate and the China Cultural Industry Association (CCIA).

This indicated a tight relationship between Mr. Ye's arts club and Beijing. And here's the kicker. The CCIA and its president— a United Front official named Bin Zhang — had donated $1 million to Justin Trudeau's family foundation in 2016. This was four years before it emerged another CCIA leader — a real estate tycoon from Markham who met twice with Trudeau and Bin Zhang in connection to the $1 million donation — was also running the largest-ever illegal casino discovered in Canada. And I found one more thing that stunned me. The VP of the CCIA happend to be a Hong Kong tycoon investigated in Canada's 1990s "Hong Kong probe" for his alleged Sun Ye On Triad links, and convicted for running an illegal betting ring. And incredibly, the CCIA's website trumpeted its successful engagement of two UN officials later taken down in the FBI corruption probe, including John Ashe. So the patterns I was seeing seemed to echo some of the plots that emerged in the FBI's investigations of the alleged Macau Triad boss Ng Lap Seng.

Given all these data points, it seems fair to question the $1 million CCIA donation to Trudeau's foundation. Trudeau's office didn't respond to my questions about Bin Zhang and the CCIA. But the federal Liberals said: "Justin Trudeau has been clear that he has not been in any way associated, formally or informally, with the Pierre Elliott Trudeau Foundation in many years — and not in any respect while serving as Prime Minister."

And my photo database showed these types of political gatherings repeated over and over in Vancouver and Toronto. The most illuminating example was a September 2018 photo gallery that showed Peschisolido and Liberal fundraising rainmaker Raymond Chan gathered at the "Warrior Fighting Dream" boxing gym.

My corporate record searches connected Warrior Fighting Dream to alleged illegal casino addresses in Richmond. The gym director's addresses included Tiger Yuan's Richmond home and a number of locations in Beijing and Harbin. Jin and his wife, Xiaoqi Wei, were also listed as directors. The couple had been investigated for drug trafficking and money-laundering in E-Pirate. I found various addresses linked to Warrior Fighting Dream were also connected with the Water Club. This was the Chinese-state "accessory company" run by Paul Jin and various Big Circle Boys, including Peter Lap San Pang.

According to RCMP documents, the Richmond massage parlour was investigated for prostitution involving underaged females from Mainland China. And it was connected to high-level drug traffickers and gun investigations.

So just digest all of that for a minute. The Warrior Fighting Dream is connected — allegedly — to criminal activities that are tearing the social fabric of Vancouver. Illegal casinos. Drug-trafficking. Human trafficking and prostitution of minors. Massive money laundering. Violent loan sharking. Gunplay and weapons trafficking.

But prominent Canadian politicians were lending their names and reputations to Warrior Fighting Dream events! My records showed elite members of Canada's controlling level United Front group also sponsored Warrior Fighting Dream events. For example, Yongtao Chen spoke at a press conference with Paul Jin at the gym in July 2019, where it was announced Warrior Fighting Dream was a Belt and Road project and training centre for the Chinese boxing team. Other members of Chen's group later claimed through a lawyer that they had no idea Paul Jin was to be associated with the press event. But key United Front members stood beside Jin and a B.C. NDP politician at the event for lots of photos, I found.

I wasn't surprised to find Paul Jin's Richmond real estate lawyer, Hong Guo, was also an event sponsor. So was Hongwei 'Kevin' Sun, the Richmond crowdfunding developer.

It was amazing what you could see in these United Front meeting photos. There was a consistent theme. Political fundraising rainmakers and Chinese corruption suspects mingling with prominent Canadian politicians.

Now I could match identities from federal donation records that showed Prime Minister Justin Trudeau, Joe Peschisolido, and Vancouver Liberal MP Joyce Murray held multiple fundraisers and cash-for-access gatherings with the tycoons surrounding Rongxiang Yuan and his many United Front associates in Vancouver. The *Globe and Mail* reported that Miaofei Pan — a former Chinese municipal official now developing real estate in Vancouver

— hosted Trudeau in 2016 for a private fundraiser where he lobbied the prime minister on major Chinese investment proposals. I interviewed Pan, who told me he was close with Rongxiang Yuan in China. In fact, Yuan was the first to call Pan and offer condolences after Pan's $14 million Vancouver mansion was mysteriously torched in an October 2017 blaze, Pan told me. Pan said he knows nothing about RCMP casino money-laundering investigations of Tiger Yuan. And he said Yuan is "a great man of justice."

Back to the federal Liberal cash-for-access meetings. I searched political campaign databases and found Justin Trudeau's Montreal riding association accepted a $1500 donation from Rongxiang Yuan at a Richmond fundraiser in 2016. And I found a large photo of Trudeau and Yuan posing side-by-side and smiling in front of a Canadian flag. The photo was framed and displayed prominently at Yuan's own gala event in 2017. At that dinner, Yuan hosted Kevin Sun and a number of Richmond casino VIPs and United Front leaders. River Rock Casino was a sponsor of the event, according to signage, and the controversial River Rock VIP manager Lisa Gao was there. The photo with Trudeau was great optics for Tiger Yuan, and guests posed to take photos of themselves, using the Trudeau photo as a backdrop. This personal portrait must have suggested to Yuan's network that he was friendly with Canada's head of state. It gave him the look of legitimacy in Canada that he already had in China. There was nothing illegal about Yuan's donation to Trudeau. But how does it look for Canada's leader to receive funds from "Suspect 2" in an RCMP organized crime investigation? The Liberals didn't answer my question about whether Tiger Yuan's donation to Trudeau raised concerns.

"The Liberal Party of Canada fully complies with the Canada Elections Act and all Elections Canada regulations for fundraising," a party spokesman wrote to me. And Yuan has repeatedly denied any wrongdoing or knowledge of RCMP investigations into his activity in Canada. He also sued me for defamation after Global News published a story documenting Yuan's meetings with Peschisolido. And to be clear, there is nothing illegal about being a United Front leader in Canada. But experts in Australia and New Zealand and the United States told me the bar for nefarious United Front activity is met when the action is covert, coercive and corrupt.

And for me, something deeply corrupt occurred on August 18, when Mr. Ye and the mob surrounded a Canadian church and took photographs of citizens gathered to pray for peace in Hong Kong. Alice and her community posted a report saying they have reasons to believe Chinese consular officials directed the pro-Beijing mob. And yet, Alice told me, Canadian governments have done nothing. Not even a word of support. Now the community feels unsafe in their own country. I couldn't understand Ottawa allowing Canadians to be terrorized into silence about Beijing's draconian new national security laws in Hong Kong. Reports from Amnesty International and experts like Alex Joske say this is exactly what the United Front's harassment in the Chinese diaspora aims to do. Silence dissent against the Chinese Communist Party and create a false image of unanimous support for Beijing's policies.

So I decided to compile a dossier of relevant photographs, corporate documents, RCMP investigations hierarchy charts, and United Front Work Department documents. And I shared the brief with Clive Hamilton and Anne-Marie Brady. These are academic experts who have testified to various state councils about United Front networks and activity. I asked them to review my research and come to some conclusions.

I focused on a few key people.

The General, Rongxiang Yuan, describes himself as a political warrior for The Motherland. He made the statements in his official Sino-Vietnam war diary, a collection of writings and photographs of his exploits as a young People's Liberation Army platoon leader. In one diary entry, Tiger Yuan wrote he was "able to stand up to the party's training for me for many years and be worthy of the title of the Communist Party of China ... rushing to victory, and even rushing to death."

These were more than the romantic scribblings of a 24-year-old platoon leader from Liaoning. The diary was published by the military intelligence department of the People's Liberation Army General Staff. And my RCMP sources believed Yuan's connections to Chinese intelligence were significant.

My compilation of records also showed that Tiger Yuan's co-director in his Canada-China Association for Promoting Friendly Relations included a Richmond gun shop owner and real estate developer named Hai Peng Yang, who was probed in RCMP weapons trafficking, illegal hunting junket and suspicious cash transaction investigations. Yang has not responded to my requests for comment.

Another director was "Kenny" — a young Chinese man identified as Suspect 7 in RCMP hierarchy charts. The other directors were Paul King Jin's VIP gamblers. One was also director of a B.C. numbered company connected to the Shandong port city of Qingdao and Jin's Water Cube massage parlour in Richmond.

Tiger Yuan and his friends rubbed shoulders with many politicians. But my dossier focused on a particular politician — Burnaby Coun. James Wang — because Wang appeared so frequently with Vancouver Model suspects. Also, James Wang was a B.C. NDP candidate in 2015. And this fact really blew my mind. His campaign director was "Max" — one of the men often seen at Tiger Yuan's side. I felt this was alarming because Max scored facetime with NDP leader John Horgan while simultaneously leading political operations for Canada's controlling level United Front Work Department group. James Wang is also named as an honorary adviser in the group. The group — which was investigated in 2018 for vote-buying allegations — has funded Wang's campaign. The RCMP did not file charges in the vote-buying case.

My dossier showed that James Wang had corporate ties to Kevin Sun, the Richmond real estate developer identified as "Suspect 3" in RCMP hierarchy charts that name Rongxiang Yuan as "Suspect 2."

And James Wang was pictured repeatedly, in photos that suggest personal relationships, with Rongxiang Yuan, Kevin Sun and Paul King Jin.

To boil it all down, not a very flattering picture. And I found that a number of sources in the Chinese-Canadian political community also had concerns about James Wang.

In one case, an NDP federal candidate alleged that James Wang approached her at a Chinese-Canadian community meeting and promised her campaign staffing and financing. The approach happened shortly after China's consul general expressed interest in her political candidacy, she told me. But there was a condition to James Wang's offer of political support, she said. She needed to pledge support to Beijing on issues such as the persecution of Falun Gong. This proposal looked like a textbook United Front quid pro quo, she told me.

But there was more.

Another B.C. political candidate informed me that James Wang was seen as a fundraising rainmaker for the B.C. NDP. And because of this, James Wang seemed to enjoy favour with the party heavyweights surrounding Premier John Horgan.

This candidate told me of another accusation that fascinated me. It was alleged that Wang told a colleague he was interested in bending farmland zoning protections in order to construct a hotel-mansion. I obtained an email from a credible source that alleged Wang had said he wanted to build such a mansion — with facilities including a private gentleman's club — to accommodate wealthy Chinese officials visiting Vancouver. In the context of the transnational organized crime suspects that James Wang is surrounded by, to my mind, this scenario seemed comparable to a Chicago municipal politician wanting to build a speakeasy in the era of Al Capone.

And I obtained an email from a Chinese-Canadian community source expressing concern about James Wang's interests and his status with the B.C. NDP.

"I just find it incredible that these politicos are always fishing for ways to reach into ethnic blocks, this one being the Mainland Chinese and their $$$, without doing their due diligence & background checks," the source wrote in 2017.

A senior Chinese-Canadian NDP member responded: "It would be our country's undoing if our political parties indiscriminately let such characters into their folds."

James Wang has not responded to many of my detailed questions about these allegations and his documented associations. But in one response, he stated unequivocally, he is not involved in the United Front and does not associate with or have any relationship with criminal suspects. And a lawyer for Kevin Sun said that Sun has no connections to organized crime or Chinese state activity.

So. My dossier curated intelligence and evidence from a wide array of sources. RCMP intel. WeChat group photos. Social media collection. Corporate records. Civil court records. Human sources. Emails. I winnowed it all down to a central node: Rongxiang Yuan; James Wang; Kevin Sun.

And Clive Hamilton provided in-depth comments after reviewing my research. He concluded James Wang is "tightly connected" with Yuan and Sun, and "James Wang is involved in United Front groups that influence Canadian politics, and he meets with consular officials."

"It's been known for some time that the Chinese Communist Party uses criminal gangs to intimidate and beat up pro-democracy protesters, as in Hong Kong recently," Hamilton wrote. "But we are also seeing crooks and gangsters becoming involved in political influence and subversion activities in countries like Canada and Australia. They do this by setting up Chinese Communist Party-endorsed community, arts or business associations, or by being appointed to senior positions in existing organizations."

And Hamilton said he believes that Canada is deeply compromised.

"The fact is that Vancouver politics and business is now riddled with Communist Party agents and informers," he wrote. "And Toronto is not far behind. China's interference in Canada's elections is now far more dangerous than Russia's meddling in U.S. elections."

Anne-Marie Brady reviewed my dossier and replied briefly.

"If the individuals you cite are at such high-profile United Front events, it is for a reason," she wrote. "The information listed is credible and shows United Front organizations."

I remember how mind-blown I was when I listened to Bruce Ward explaining how the RCMP learned Chinese organized crime is networked with legitimate professionals and tycoons. That was September 2017. But Ward had omitted the most stunning fact. The whale in the network is the Chinese Communist Party. And now I had evidence of the network's capacity to harm Canadian citizens.

I found yet another case in September 2019. Turnisa Matsedik-Qira, a Uyghur woman, was protesting in Vancouver against the mass detention of Uyghurs in Xinjiang. She stood holding a placard as Tong Xiaoling and other Chinese consulate leaders and members of Vancouver's controlling level United Front Work Department group celebrated a Chinese arts event at Vancouver Art Gallery.

A Chinese woman approached Turnisa repeatedly and told her to leave.

Turnisa told me she got a call from a man with a strong Mandarin accent about a week later.

"The guy told me I have to stop what I'm doing, stop my activism, or else you have to worry about your family in China," Turnisa told me. "I said, 'Who are you?' and he didn't answer, and then he hung up. I felt extremely shocked because I live in Canada, and I feel alone and unprotected. I felt 100 per cent this call is from the Chinese government."

I'll keep this simple. I obtained photo evidence of the woman confronting Turnisa at the Vancouver art gallery. And I have photos of this same woman monitoring events at the Tenth Church mob. The woman is a 'journalist' for a Vancouver website run by her husband, a former *China Daily* editor, who is also a leader of Vancouver's controlling level United Front group. And photos showed me this woman and a small group of reporters from the Chinese state media meeting privately with Rongxiang Yuan.

Reporters, politicians, tycoons and transnational organized crime suspects. What possible common bond could these people from such divergent backgrounds have? All of my evidence pointed to one factor.

Xi Jinping's magic weapon.

16
STRIKE BACK HARD

*In the story, I also explained the United Front's
methods and ideology in detail. This was
information that CSIS had been trying to raise with
Prime Minister Justin Trudeau's government and
previous federal governments.*

My Personal Protective Equipment story immediately caught the attention of Beijing.

Prior to January 1, 2020, very few people could have predicted PPE would become the world's hottest commodity, and N95 face masks would become life-saving armour. But by mid-January astute observers in supply chain logistics noticed Beijing was scouring the globe for PPE.

In February, my sources were monitoring WeChat and Chinese-language website reports that indicated major PPE ops underway in Vancouver, Toronto, Montreal and Ottawa. It became clear that United Front Work Department groups in Vancouver and Toronto were international leaders in Beijing's PPE logistics. And these United Front operations were replicated worldwide, from Melbourne to Tokyo to Milan to New York to London to Prague. It was all directed from Beijing and run through Chinese consulates. The actors were the same "Chinese overseas" business and community leaders that Xi Jinping uses in normal times to influence politicians in the West.

But from January to March, Xi's tentacles were laser-focused on N95 masks.

On April 30, my story — "United Front Groups in Canada Helped Bejing Stockpile Coronavirus Safety Supplies" — pulled the curtain back on Xi's clandestine PPE op.

In the story, I also explained the United Front's methods and ideology. This was information that CSIS had been trying to raise with Prime Minister Justin Trudeau's government and previous federal governments. But Canada's intelligence on China's subtle attack was ignored by elected officials. And for the first time in Canada, I documented the underground ties between Vancouver's United Front leaders and the E-Pirate money-laundering network. I believe this is what truly enraged Beijing.

The other thing that must have stung: my analysis showed the Chinese Communist Party had covered up pandemic risk while buying back PPE supplies Chinese factories had previously sold to the world. It was like the ultimate case of insider trading.

Conservative party leader Erin O'Toole underlined this point in my Global News story.

"The Communist Party of China willfully withheld information on an outbreak for at least weeks, if not months," O'Toole said. "It not only gave the world less time to respond, it downplayed the potential severity of the threat. Countries did not make decisions with respect to flight bans and [protecting] PPE stores."

And Jorge Guajardo, Mexico's former ambassador to Beijing, told me Beijing acted surreptitiously and left "the world naked with no supply of PPE."

Eventually, Beijing profited by selling stockpiled PPE back to the world at massively inflated prices and with geopolitical strings attached, Guajardo said.

My story used China's own customs data to summarize the scale of the operation. In just six weeks, starting January 24, Beijing imported 2.5 billion pieces of PPE, including over 2 billion safety masks.

And I used United Front Work Department reports and PPE warehousing pictures from inside China, plus WeChat texts and reports in Canadian cities, to show that over 100 tonnes of PPE were gathered in Canada and shipped to China.

I think it's safe to say Beijing's United Front had never been mobilized with such intensity in a condensed time frame. The result was a flood of concrete evidence. It seemed United Front leaders outside of China wanted to prove they had answered Xi Jinping's call. Part of this was nationalistic propaganda. But it also looked like self-interest. Most United Front "overseas" leaders are businessmen who trade on their *guanxi* with Beijing to earn fortunes.

(I eventually found that Vancouver casino tycoons airlifted PPE around the world. Mailin Chen, the Guangdong highroller identified in B.C. Lottery Corp. money-laundering records, had flown his private jet to Papua New Guinea to deliver PPE in June 2020. Chen has been a member of the Chinese People's Political Consultative Congress — a United Front organ. He's also connected to a high-level River Rock Casino employee de-registered after a money-laundering investigation in late 2017.)

Amidst all the evidence sources that documented trailer-loads of PPE delivered to international airports, one report stood out with smoking-gun, end-to-end proof of United Front transactions. The February 2 report from Xinhua, China's state news agency, focused on "overseas Chinese" groups from Fujian, the United Front espionage hotbed where Lai Changxing and Xi Jinping launched their respective careers.

"The menacing epidemic came suddenly. But majestic strength comes from front-line medical staff, party members and cadres, from the people, and from Fujian Chinese and overseas Chinese," says an English-language translation of the Xinhua story. "Fujians from dozens of countries on five continents joined this invisible battle … they travelled day and night and raced against time to send back batches of scarce supplies for the motherland."

The report featured detailed PPE case studies from Japan, United States and Canada. But the Toronto Fuqing Chamber of Commerce's case study was an outlier, with its direct reference to the United Front Work Department's command and control of operations in Canada.

It was also meaningful to me that Xinhua focused on the Toronto Fujian group because I knew this network was important to CSIS.

In 2019 its leaders had attended an anti-Hong Kong democracy rally in Markham, Ont. Photos of the pro-Beijing rally showed the elite of Toronto's United Front Work Department, men who are well-connected to Beijing, according to evidence compiled by Michel Juneau Katsuya.

The Xinhua story said a Toronto Fuqing chamber leader travelled to China in January, and when he recognized the severity of the epidemic in Wuhan, he immediately flew back to Toronto.

According to Xinhua, he raced from the airport in a snowstorm and issued urgent orders sending 200 Fuqing chamber members racing around Ontario buying PPE. And before February 2, many tons of PPE was transferred by Chinese state airlines to receivers that "worked with the United Front Work Department of Fujian, and customs in Fujian" to warehouse "the medical supplies from Canada."

That sentence was all the evidence I needed. Consider the source. Clive Hamilton, author of *Hidden Hand: Exposing how the Chinese Communist Party Is Reshaping the World*, has mapped the United Front's structure. A hierarchy chart published in *Hidden Hand* shows that Xinhua is just a few steps below the Politburo. The Xinhua report established that Beijing used United Front bosses in China, Chinese state-owned airlines, and United Front groups worldwide to vacuum most of the world's PPE in January, before other governments knew what hit them. But I need to make some important distinctions because this is an incredibly complex set of circumstances. There was a big humanitarian element involved in sending PPE to China. Community and government leaders in many countries worked together to answer China's need. Many Chinese-Canadians sent care packages of PPE to family members. At the time, most of the world apparently believed the coronavirus could be contained in China, so it made sense to send medical supplies where the material was needed. This is all good. What is wrong, though, is that Xi Jinping's regime was covering up the outbreak and its severity, leaving the rest of the world in the dark. And in 2021, through my Canadian military and intelligence sources, I have learned more about the outbreak in Wuhan. The evidence dovetails with an increasing number of statements from U.S. intelligence and disease control officials, asserting that a disease matching the nature of the coronavirus was found to be spreading in Wuhan as early as October 2019. About 10,000 soldiers were at the World Military Games in Wuhan in October. And I learned from soldiers at the games that about one-quarter of Canada's team became severely sick in late October, and they flew back to Canada under quarantine. These are extremely fit people. For such a large number of athletes to become sick at once is odd, to say the least. And there are open-source records and accounts from my military and intelligence sources indicating that Wuhan was significantly depopulated during the Military Games, and the Chinese state was engaged in strange behaviours.

"I'm not sure how to explain this," a Canadian soldier wrote to me. The soldier provided a January 22, 2020, letter from the Canadian army's surgeon general regarding reports of sickness among athletes at the Games, which concluded "individual risk of having been exposed to 2019 nCoV during temporary duty in Wuhan City is negligible."

However, a number of the Canadian soldiers don't believe that assessment, multiple intelligence sources informed me. They believe they were infected with the coronavirus in Wuhan.

"Empty highways, no construction workers, 1000's of empty highrise apartments. All empty," the Canadian soldier wrote to me. "Yes, there were a few people you would see, but this was a rarity. The explanation given by the staff at the World Military Games was that the CCP ordered everyone in Wuhan to leave the city to 'make room for the athletes.'"

The soldier informed me his superiors decided "to isolate all the sick in the back of the service flight on the way back. People were all kinds of sick. Myself, I had some weird symptoms and lung difficulties while there. It wasn't until the 12th or 13th of November that I started to get really feverish and terrible coughing fits. From the 15th onwards I was bedridden for about 10 days. I've never been that sick before."

So, my information from Canadian intelligence is some have judged it is highly likely the coronavirus was spreading in Wuhan during the Military Games, and that athletes from a number of nations brought the coronavirus home. Obviously international experts are trying to confirm this information while facing roadblocks from Xi's regime. And the case hasn't been proven. But national security experts in the United States and Canada increasingly believe the coronavirus was racing through Wuhan in October 2019, China knew a dangerous virus was emerging, and Xi's regime covered it up, and collected the world's supply of PPE as the danger mounted in early 2020.

Back to Canada. The Xinhua report proved how important Fujian United Front networks in Ontario were, in China's international PPE ops. And I had equally powerful evidence in Vancouver — provided by United Front websites.

One of the reports said on January 23, Yongtao Chen, the chairman of Vancouver's controlling level United Front group, was ordered by the Chinese consulate to gather PPE desperately needed in Wuhan. WeChat group photos provided supporting evidence. One WeChat photo showed Yongtao Chen standing with the Chinese consulate's top "Overseas Chinese Affairs" United Front official, and consul-general Tong Xiaoling's deputy. Both men are involved in tactical roles for the Chinese consulate, according to my photo evidence. Yongtao Chen's eventual successor — a man also seen standing at Justin Trudeau's elbow in one of my key United Front cash-for-access photos — was with Chen and the consulate bosses in the PPE warehousing photo.

Another report said Yongtao Chen worked with the Canada Chao Shan Association, a United Front group connected to the Guang-dong Overseas Chinese Federation. This was another huge piece of evidence, because the Guangdong Federation has associations in 131 countries. And its leaders in Vancouver are well-known to CSIS agents in B.C., intelligence sources informed me.

An official United Front report in China said that Franco Feng — a prominent Guangdong Federation leader in Vancouver — had facilitated transnational PPE deliveries into China from Vancouver. And he reported to his bosses in China that "local communities actively cooperate with the embassies and consulates to contact all community overseas Chinese groups to prepare various medical supplies."

This was another smoking gun quote directly from an official source in China.

I'll boil down what this all means in very simple terms. The Canada Chao Shan Association had a very important role in Xi Jinping's PPE collection ops. And after China had the coronavirus under control within its borders, the Chao Sha Association was shipping PPE back to Chinese communities worldwide.

I knew from Alex Joske that Huang Xiangmo — the Australian United Front leader and whale gambler — was directly connected to Guangdong United Front leaders in Vancouver.

And the Chao Shan Association had been on my radar since late 2017, because of its direct connection to E-Pirate targets.

Thanks to the Panama Papers leaks, I had the names and addresses of 14 Chao Shan directors. Most of them listed Vancouver addresses. And some listed addresses in China.

One of the Chao Shan directors — a man named Xun Chuang — listed a Panama Papers address that was of incredible importance in my Vancouver Model investigations.

In Vancouver real estate terms, I saw Xun Chuang's property as a code-breaking tool. You have to visualize the East Vancouver property and what lies behind it: a sprawling constellation of B.C. land titles, crudely scribbled promissory notes, and 23 B.C. Supreme Court real estate money-laundering cases that show fentanyl-soaked tentacles stretching from Vancouver to Calgary to Toronto to Macau to Mainland China.

Xun Chuang's home is not distinctive in appearance. He owns a similar one a few doors away on Euclid Avenue. They are strategically located: Vancouver's hotbed of illegal casinos on Kingsway Avenue is two minutes away. And I found that Xun Chuang was sentenced for narcotics production in 2003 and handed a 10-year firearms prohibition. I also found his associates were named in a global smuggling ring linked to China, Hong Kong and Richmond. The connections go on and on. But this is the most important one. I connected Xun Chuang and another owner of the Euclid Avenue Panama Papers address, Li Hua Chen, to a property on Burris Street in Burnaby. I found both men were plaintiffs in a B.C. Supreme Court real estate lending case. That case involved a number of E-Pirate loan sharks and a River Rock Casino VIP.

Stay with me here. We're going down this rabbit hole because Xun Chuang is director of a Panama Papers entity that is central to Xi Jinping's plans.

I found a third man on the land title of the Burris Street property, Mr. Huang, was named along with Paul King in B.C. Lottery Corp. loan-sharking bans.

And the short-list of names on this Lottery Corp. document is extremely important. Because the loan-sharking record names a shipbuilder from China named Guo Tai Shi. And Shi is called RCMP "Suspect 1" in another document that calls Tiger Yuan "Suspect 2" and Paul King Jin "Suspect 22."

Yet another Lottery Corp. record names Guo Tai Shi as one of the 36 River Rock Casino whales funded by Silver International and Paul King Jin.

And RCMP intelligence sources informed me that Guo Tai Shi ran an illegal casino in a massive Richmond farmland mansion that dwarfed similar Richmond properties run by Paul King Jin.

Now back to Mr. Huang and Xun Chuang and their Burris Street property. This home and its owners are connected to fentanyl trafficking. Mr. Huang and Paul King Jin are among the ten "private lenders" involved in the single most important B.C. Supreme Court case for my Vancouver Model investigation.

This was the case where Jin loaned $8 million to Jia Gui Gao — the Macau casino whale — secured against Gao's West Vancouver mansion. Mr. Huang lent Gao $3.2 million. And the two suspects busted in a Vancouver police fentanyl-trafficking investigation in 2016 — W.Z. and Y.Z. — loaned Gao $7 million. The ten private lenders claimed to have loaned a total of $28.8 million to Gao. When I showed these names to one of Canada's most knowledgeable Asian organized crime investigators, he confirmed these are Canada's fentanyl kingpins. These private lenders connected to Xun Chuang are the E-Pirate network.

So let's boil this all the way down to its essence. My investigation, starting with one Panama Papers address in East Vancouver, had connected Canada Chao Shan director Xun Chuang to the fentanyl kingpins.

The suspects connected to Xun Chuang in B.C. land title and real estate and casino lending records were allegedly running fentanyl trafficking and underground banking operations in Richmond, B.C., and mainland China.

And Canada Chao Shan's directors were directly connected to the United Front Work Department and the Chinese Communist Party. These Guangdong United Front officials in Vancouver were pivotal in Beijing's PPE operations. My dossier of photo evidence shows these are men who sit in Beijing and take instructions from Xi Jinping, among hundreds of the most important Overseas Chinese Affairs leaders in Chinese diaspora communities worldwide. And these United Front leaders are not just rubbing shoulders socially with E-Pirate targets in pictures. They are directly connected — with smoking-gun corporate documentation — to underground financing and organized crime targets.

This is what it all means. In one sentence. My PPE story demonstrated the connection between the fentanyl kingpins of Canada and the Chinese Communist Party.

And Beijing struck back immediately.

***

On May 2, a petition demanding the retraction of my United Front PPE story started circulating on WeChat groups across Canada. I had never encountered the petition writer, but I had a few clues about her motivations.

During the fall 2019 Canadian federal election, the Ottawa university professor had spoken out against Canadian politicians voicing support for the Hong Kong democracy movement.

My colleague Jeremy Nuttall — a *Toronto Star* investigative reporter with strong connections in the Chinese-Canadian community — spotted the petition first.

"I'm not going to share this nonsense," Nuttall wrote on Twitter. "But it's a typical tactic from the Chinese Communist Party to try to shut Canadians up when they criticize the regime in Beijing."

The petition and a deluge of similar statements in Chinese-language media claimed my story had lumped all Chinese-Canadians into the United Front PPE mask operation, and this was racist. But Nuttall was right. The petition was nonsense.

My story was based on facts, evidence and direct quotes from official Chinese sources. The story explained that Beijing is trying to control and use all Chinese immigrants. This has been extensively supported by numerous intelligence reports, academic papers and books like *Claws of the Panda* and *Hidden Hand*.

But I had to respond to politically motivated attacks on my story. It wasn't hard to identify the hand of Beijing. Fortunately, I had lots of assistance from sources in the Chinese and Hong Kong Canadian communities. And my sources found the petition and many derivative media posts mirrored statements coming from China's government.

It was so elegantly logical — a perfect circle of United Front activity. The media commentaries and Chinese government statements denouncing my story were published by the same websites that China used in February and March 2020 to publicize the United Front PPE operations in Canada. These were, of course, the very same media websites that I had monitored to document United Front meetings involving E-Pirate money-laundering suspects. The same sites that showed RCMP suspects frequently meeting with Chinese consulate officials and Canadian politicians.

As these waves of media disinformation washed over me day after day in May 2020, one of my sources, a Chinese-Canadian academic, monitored the outlets involved. My source assessed that Beijing was behind the attacks.

The source is studying Chinese Communist Party interference in Canadian media and asked to remain anonymous in order to avoid interference.

The situation was surreal. I was losing sleep. I spent my nights and weekends talking to sources in intelligence and law enforcement. These experts came to the same conclusion as the Chinese-Canadian academic. As reporters, we never want to become part of the story. But I couldn't avoid it. I had poked at Beijing's PPE networks and exposed deep organized crime connections. Now the communications section of this coiled snake was writhing and striking back.

In fact, "strike back hard" was the exact phrase used by a key figure. Aside from his media gig, this broadcaster — Omni TV columnist Ding Guo — leads a society active in lobbying Canadian politicians on issues that align with Beijing's interests in Canada, much like many of Ding Guo's columns.

As an example of the society's activity, one source forwarded screen captures from Ding Guo's May 2020 Zoom chat with a pro-Beijing Canadian senator, in which the senator presented a "not for circulation" insider's analysis of the Canadian government's "response to the COVID-19 health crisis and the politics of COVID-19."

And I had been researching Ding Guo's associations since 2019. My documents suggested links from Ding Guo to Burnaby politician James Wang to Hongwei "Kevin" Sun, the Richmond crowdfunding developer.

Website records showed that Ding Guo and James Wang sat on the board of a Jilin business group run by Hongwei Sun.

But a picture really is sometimes worth a few thousand words. And for me, one photo really demonstrated the intimacy of this trio. It was taken on a warm summer day, and it showed Ding Guo and James Wang celebrating at Kevin Sun's birthday party.

They were in the yard of a Richmond hacienda, a property listed in B.C. Lottery Corp. emails regarding illegal casino investigations. They stood shoulder to shoulder with Kevin Sun and a handful of elite B.C. United Front figures, holding long knives over a nicely charred barbecued hog.

The group included a man — my photo collection shows — who sat in places of honour beside China's consul general Tong Xiaoling and Rongxiang Yuan at important Chinese cultural events in Burnaby. And beside Kevin Sun was Ms. Z, a pharmaceutical business owner in China and a United Front leader in Vancouver.

The photo was reminiscent of another taken at a high-end Chinese restaurant in late 2019, where Ding Guo and Rongxiang Yuan and Ms. Z dined with a famous Chinese actor who also appeared on Ding Guo's TV show.

So I could see the *guanxi* bonding this little network.

And their plotting was revealed in a May 10 Zoom group meeting. It was set up by a Richmond crowdfunding realtor well connected to United Front leaders. About 50 virtual attendees hatched the idea of "crowdfunding" a lawsuit against me by soliciting donations from Chinese diaspora communities across Canada.

Here was another absurd irony. In 2015, I started my journey into the Vancouver Model, writing about Kevin Sun and his murky network of crowdfunding realtors.

Now the very same crowdfunding network was crowdfunding to deter my digging into their crowdfunding.

After the Zoom meeting on May 10, magically, Ding Guo's TV producer emailed me on May 11: "we heard that some people from the Chinese community are planning to file a lawsuit."

And on May 14, members from WeChat and Zoom groups registered a society called MLARA, designed to attack my reporting. I won't name the three frontmen. Two are Vancouver realtors whose boss is identified as a prominent United Front leader who attends meetings in Beijing. His real estate company has corporate links to Rongxiang Yuan, according to my intelligence sources.

So that tells me enough about MLARA.

But the evidence got more blatant. One MLARA director had a direct business relationship with the Chinese state. This real estate agent's shipping company was used in April 2020 to ship boxes of PPE for Vancouver's Chinese consulate!

Meanwhile, as the legal plotting brewed in WeChat discussions, Ding Guo used his Mandarin-language show to disseminate MLARA's disinformation. But he concealed his personal interest.

"He led his audience to the assumption that he was offering objective opinions about MLARA's action," my Chinese-Canadian academic source concluded. "This was noted in a Lahoo.ca report on the first Zoom meeting: 'Ding Guo suggested launching a lawsuit.' And he thinks Chinese Canadians should, in his words, 'strike back hard.' I believe that was also the Chinese government's position."

I asked Ding Guo to comment, but he didn't respond to my messages. And Ding Guo's corporate managers told me they found nothing wrong with his actions.

Meanwhile, many people approached me with the same message. It felt like wrestling an octopus. The tentacles seemed to be guiding me to a place where the struggle would end. If only I would apologize and retract the facts. And that wasn't going to happen. But I took some grim humour from watching the plot unfold. The participants weren't fooling anyone who was watching closely.

"These people are either directly related [to] the United Front Work Department of China or puppets," a source inside their WeChat groups wrote to me. The source asked to remain anonymous for fear their relatives in China could be targeted. "They are coming up with a Gofundme link for collecting donations for (a) lawsuit together with racial attack claims," the source said. "They want to make it an influential Chinese group to lobby and pressure governments, politicians, reporters, institutions and incite national sentiment among Chinese Canadians. [They want to promote] lawsuits against anyone who dares to criticize China. [They also want to] elect more puppets into Canadian governments."

I knew the legal threat against me was frivolous. But I became more concerned when my sources captured WeChat texts showing a ledger of donations for a planned lawsuit against me. The records showed legal advice from a Richmond lawyer well-known to B.C. Law Society misconduct and casino money-laundering investigations.

It was Paul King Jin's real estate lawyer, Hong Guo.

"Hong Guo was invited to give a talk about certain legal matters in the Lahoo.ca WeChat group I am part of," my academic source wrote to me.

And the ledger connected to Hong Guo's WeChat group showed that a Xiaoqi Wei donated $1,000. I recognized the name of Paul King Jin's wife. A "Xiaoqui Wei" was accused in the E-Pirate probe of drug trafficking, money-laundering and tax evasion. I found the same name on corporate records for Warrior Fighting Dream and Water Cube, along with directors in Beijing, Harbin, and Shandong.

The ledger showed that Hong Guo herself donated $500.

And the ledger showed me that Kwok Chung Tam — the name of a man believed by B.C. Lottery Corp. investigators to be superior to Paul King Jin — put up a mere $100. Kwok Chung Tam was known as a spendthrift, though.

So I knew a lot about the crowdfunders. All due to support from Chinese-Canadian sources monitoring WeChat to help me. Regardless, I wasn't writing about the plotting. And then, on May 25, Bob Mackin published a fascinating report. He had discovered a WeChat group post that tied MLARA to Vancouver Liberal MP Joyce Murray.

"A post on the Liberal Minister of Digital Government's group on a China state-censored social media platform is promoting a lawsuit against an investigative journalist who cast a critical eye on China's hoarding of medical supplies during the coronavirus pandemic," Mackin's story for TheBreaker said. "Maria Xu, a member of Vancouver Liberal MP Joyce Murray's WeChat group, posted a notice about the MLARA and a link to the website where it is soliciting donations. Xu was also a participant of a May 19 Zoom meeting hosted … to explore a class action lawsuit against Cooper."

The *Toronto Star* and *Globe and Mail* and CBC quickly followed Bob Mackin's story.

"The situation that had been simmering for weeks boiled over Tuesday after Vancouver news site theBreaker published a report saying federal Liberal MP Joyce Murray had 'promoted' a lawsuit against Global News," Jeremy Nuttall reported for *the Star*.

And Nuttall revealed details of MLARA's Zoom meetings.

"During the May 10 meeting, several ideas were discussed about how to approach Cooper's reporting. Among the suggestions made was to investigate Cooper himself to see if he had ever committed any illegal acts, or if he was behind on his income taxes in a bid to hurt his reputation," Nuttall reported. "Another course of action suggested was to have many people personally file small claims lawsuits against Cooper at the same time. It was suggested that this could exhaust him."

The Conservative party jumped on the story and attacked the Liberals and Murray in parliamentary debates. Murray said the views expressed in the WeChat group run through her office "do not necessarily reflect" her positions. And Prime Minister Trudeau said using WeChat to fund lawsuits against Canadian journalism is "unacceptable."

The WeChat group was not severed from Murray's office, though. It's obviously an important arm for the Liberals into the Mainland Chinese diaspora, and a tool to fundraise and mobilize votes. But, as Alex Joske has reported, WeChat is a vector of Chinese Communist Party influence in the West. So the concern in Canada is obvious to me. Murray, a member of Canada's federal government, is tied up with United Front actors, whether she realizes it or not.

And various WeChat group networks — interwoven through community leaders like the Richmond lawyer Hong Guo and her associate Maria Xu — tried to leverage Murray's credibility in efforts to silence reporting critical of Beijing.

And it gets a lot darker, considering some of the donor names I found recorded on a ledger posted on Hong Guo's WeChat group. As I tried to get my head around all of this, I was reminded of Cameron Ortis's "compromised nodes" thesis. WeChat, a Chinese Communist Party-controlled communications network, is a giant node. It has the capacity to compromise everything it touches in Canadian cyberspace. So here was another perfect irony. WeChat had evidently compromised the office of Joyce Murray, the Liberal Minister of Digital Government. It had latched onto an appendage of Canada's government to attack Canada's free press. This is an attack on democracy.

One person told me, during this media firestorm, that I was experiencing something like psychological warfare. And it was exhausting. My purpose in relating the experience isn't to pose as a victim. Rather, it's to demonstrate how the United Front works. As an expert in Washington once explained to me, it is a Leninist political war tool. The United Front seeks to turn "friends" of Beijing against the Chinese Communist Party's enemies.

United Front leaders in British Columbia lobbied every level of Canadian government seeking allies to attack my PPE story. There were plenty of Zoom meetings and probably many behind the scenes conversations I'm unaware of. The question is, Why did the United Front feel confident that elected Canadian officials would take their side against Canadian journalism? The answer, I suppose, is financial leverage. Political donations win political influence.

Whatever the case, my investigations into organized crime and the United Front continued. And researchers continued to scour Chinese state websites and forward me PPE operation evidence.

This is my best example. When we published the PPE story on April 30, I demonstrated ties between the E-Pirate network and the "controlling level" United Front group in Richmond that worked with Overseas Affairs leaders in the Vancouver Chinese consulate to ship pallets of PPE back to China. At the time, though, I didn't demonstrate that criminal funds were used.

But in November 2020, a Mandarin-language researcher texted me. He shared an official Chinese state report — filed in February 2020 by the Shandong Overseas Chinese Assembly Hall — that said "another batch of donated goods" had arrived from the Canada Shandong Chinese Business Association.

The report — titled "BattleAgainst the 'Epidemic'" — said, "Mr. Paul King Jin of the [Canada] World Champion Club enthusiastically donated CAD $20,000."

So, the self-admitted loan shark, a man convicted of sexual exploitation, an alleged fentanyl kingpin who is tight with People's Liberation Army heavyweights, had paid $20,000 to buy scarce PPE in Canada, for shipment to China, for the benefit of the Motherland.

Paul King Jin's wealth comes from drug trafficking, illegal casino operations, loan sharking, human trafficking and prostitution, and transnational money-laundering, police say.

I'm suggesting that organized crime proceeds from Jin's network could have funded some of Beijing's PPE operations in Canada. And this PPE might have saved some lives in Canadian nursing homes.

Of course, through his lawyers, Jin denies the allegations. He is a legitimate businessman offering boxing lessons to kids.

There is a mountain of evidence against him, though. The evidence says he is a violent money-laundering criminal with ties to the Chinese Communist Party.

So the thought that stays with me, like an alarm ringing louder all the time, like the sound of an echo in reverse, is the pandemic was a crucible for Beijing's amoral methodologies. We saw the United Front's machinery like never before in a compressed time frame with desperate consequences.

For me, in a microcosm, Paul King Jin's United Front PPE contribution shows the Chinese Communist Party's willingness to use any means to survive.

17

AFTERWORD:
INFINITE CONNECTIVITY

"The Party is not squeamish about using any tool.
If they can catch someone doing something illegal,
they will trade off a harsh sentence, perhaps a death
sentence, in exchange for the criminal's compliance,"
Mulroney said. "They hold this over the heads of the
people they are trying to co-opt."

Paul King Jin pulled his black Mercedes van up to Manzo sushi restaurant just after 7 p.m. It was an unusually warm evening for September in Richmond. Jin's party had reserved a private section. Jin walked towards his business partner, 44-year-old Jian Jun Zhu, and greeted him warmly. They had come so far together in Canada — Zhu, the younger man from Hong Kong, and Jin, the boxing hero from Shandong.

While Jin was older — and supremely confident in public — some observers believed Zhu was more powerful. Afterall — on paper at least — Zhu and his wife ran Silver International, the underground bank laundering more than $1 billion annually with Chinese, Latin American, and Iranian drug cartels.

And when Zhu and Jin met each other, the younger man would put his arm on Jin's shoulder, in almost a fatherly way. A hint about who had the clout.

Unlike Paul King Jin — with his boxing gym and stable of illegal casinos in Richmond — Jian Jun Zhu had slipped off the radar after the

E-Pirate raids. Zhu had returned to Hong Kong. And he also spent time in South Africa and Dubai. He finally flew back to Canada in summer 2020, first to Toronto before flying home to Vancouver.

So here they were together again on September 18, 2020. In a party of 12 people preparing to celebrate. It was a formidable array of international criminals. And really, the men gathered in Manzo underlined an improbable fact. Canada had become a command centre for the world's most prolific Chinese transnational narcos. Scrolling over Manzo's location with drone footage would help to illustrate how it happened.

Near the east bank of the Fraser River, Manzo was just a four minute drive from 5811 Cooney Road, the office tower where Silver International had stockpiled drug cash until an RCMP tactical unit rushed through its bulletproof glass doors in October 2015. In this same downtown tower, Vincent Ramos and Phantom Secure had an office, before the FBI busted Ramos in 2018 and flipped him on Cameron Ortis. And at 5811 Cooney Road, Joe Peschisildo's law office was located one door away from the third-floor office that Silver would later occupy. Down at street level — at Cooney Road and Westminster Highway — within a radius of 500 metres, a heat map of currency exchange shops, real estate lawyers and travel agencies to rival the underground banking networks of Shenzhen, Macau and Hong Kong. And who was doing business in the shops on RCMP's radar?

The whose who of transnational narcos and Interpol Red Notice corruption suspects, according to E-Pirate surveillance records. Case in point. One summer morning in 2015, an undercover officer was set up to watch for Silver customers arriving in the parkade of 5811 Cooney. He took note when a black Land Rover pulled in and a man and woman entered the office tower. He ran the licence plate and got a stunning hit. The vehicle was registered to one of Xi Jinping's most-wanted, a politically-connected Vancouver real estate developer of great interest to China's intelligence operatives in British Columbia.

Vancouver International Airport was a seven-minute drive from Manzo, just across the Fraser River. The Water Cube massage club — the business run by Jin's bosses in Beijing and Qingdao and Guangzhou — was a five-minute drive from Manzo. I had found the Water

Cube on a Chinese state online record, that called it a "state accessory" company. But RCMP records documented a constant stream of bags and suitcases full of cash travelling in and out, along with reports of high-level drug traffickers and underage masseuses and illegal casino payments, inside the premises. Two minutes from Manzo was a strip mall with an array of gun shops including West Coast Hunting, a business run by RCMP targets from northern China. This is where the RCMP trailed Jin and one of his bodyguards, an accused drug-trafficker, as they lugged out a gun-safe. That was during E-Pirate. And in a spin-off investigation RCMP followed another of Jin's associates, an accused weapons trafficker later caught with buckets of fentanyl precursors, to the business.

And River Rock Casino — with its luxury hotel rooms where Big Circle Boys stockpiled casino chips for the whales arriving from Hong Kong, Beijing and Macau — was only a three-minute drive from Manzo.

An eight-minute drive east from Manzo into Richmond's farmland would take you past many sprawling mansions with their Roman columns and marble floors and vineyards and spas. Inside Chinese officials could gamble and enjoy young women and dine on shark fin and bear paw soup. Just like they had done in the 1990s, in Lai Changxing's Red Palace in Xiamen.

A seven-minute drive west from Manzo would wind through streets of cookie-cutter iron-gate three-car-garage mansions that concealed innumerable meth and fentanyl labs. These tiny labs with their rotary pill presses were all part of an interconnected machine invisibly ducted into Chinese chemical factories.

And a five-minute drive west from these neighbourhoods of mansion-labs, the dingy warehouses and storage lockers in the blocks on both sides of the Fraser. Buildings that received containers of fake Nikes shipped from the factories of the Pearl River Delta along with piles of chemical precursors. Canada's western port was the trans-shipment point for hundreds of millions of lethal little pills going out to Australia and Japan and coming into North America. And the import-export businesses housed in these river-front streets had capacity to seamlessly recycle all the drug cash into China's industrial production. So if the Sinaloa Cartel wanted their Vancouver cocaine sale proceeds converted to pesos they knew where to go. A quick phone call and cash drop to a Richmond textile merchant would produce a shipload of Gucci suit knockoffs in Guangdong. The clothing would be shipped to Mexico and sold for the cartel. Pesos would be banked. And of course the containers of clothing shipped to Manzanillo would also carry fentanyl and methamphetamine precursors for Sinaloa Cartel labs. My sources in Ottawa said the Chinese underground bankers were charging the Mexican cartels little or nothing for laundering their drug cash. They didn't have to because they were making incalculable sums from the trade-based money-laundering opportunities coming out of drug money-laundering contracts. The implication was obvious. China's mercantilism could not be separated from global drug trafficking and money-laundering.

So this is the dystopia that Canada's leaders are confronted with. What Garry Clement and Brian McAdam and Michel Juneau Katsuya had tried to warn Ottawa of in the 1990s, had come to pass. Canada — specifically Richmond, B.C., and Markham, Ont. — had become a beachhead for Mainland China's opioid cartels.

And the events at Manzo that night demonstrate this frightening truth.

After talking to Zhu for a minute, Jin stood and walked to another table. Zhu's head was inches from a tinted window separating diners from the parking lot outside. Suddenly glass exploded into the restaurant. Six bullets sliced through the window at an angle, rocking Zhu in his seat. It's amazing what can happen when bullets and shards of glass start bouncing around. Jin was hit with shrapnel that ripped through his left cheek and exited near his nose. He crouched over holding his face as his blood dripped to the floor. A bodybuilder in Jin's party snapped a cellphone picture as a woman consoled Jin. Police cars and an ambulance arrived within minutes.

Zhu was rushed to hospital and declared dead. But Jin was released from hospital with no more damage than a hole in his cheek. Within days Jin was seen at Zhu's funeral. Observers counted five bodyguards surrounding him.

Police were stunned by the shooting in many ways. There were families with children dining at Manzo. Children easily could have been hit with ricocheting bullets and glass. But only Zhu died. Was he the only target? Was Jin the intended target? There was much to consider. Jin had arrived and briefly talked to Zhu and then walked away. Just before shots smashed into the restaurant.

Who would dare target Zhu or Jin? There was no question for RCMP experts about who dominated organized crime in Canada. Of course, it was the Chinese transnational cartels. They had the most members in Canada, the underground banking and drug routes, infiltration of trade and protected bases of operation inside China. But make no mistake. RCMP experts saw men like Jian Jun Zhu and Paul King Jin as nothing more than mid-level criminal bankers. Men at their level managed underground drug labs and casinos and piles of chemicals and drug cash. They invested in chemical precursor imports and money-laundering infrastructure — casinos, cash houses, construction and development companies — with their bosses. They were the hands on investors. Their bosses were silent partners. But they all responded to guidance from Beijing. If they didn't they were out of business. And from my sources, I knew that the sensitive and classified reports forwarded to the highest levels of RCMP intelligence in Ottawa assessed that men like Paul King Jin were handled by Chinese intelligence operatives living in British Columbia. Think about that. When people ask why I have chosen to focus on Chinese transnational cartels in Canada, that's the answer. I'm following the money and the power and the greatest threat to Canadian society. It's not that other crime groups — domestic and foreign — get a pass. But I recognize the unique threat posed by state-sponsored crime.

Back to Manzo. I asked my sources what kind of theories were circulating in the RCMP. Who was behind the shooting?

"Probably someone with the blessing of Beijing," one expert said. This was a common theory in federal policing circles. One thing was abundantly obvious. This wasn't the standard tit-for-tat dial-a-doper shootout that periodically rocks Vancouver. This was violence among the fentanyl kingpins, the controllers of the world's chemical narcotics trade.

The fact that someone had put a contract on Zhu or Jin or both was mind-boggling enough. For me it was almost unbelievable. Paul Jin had seemed untouchable. This was September 2020. Three years had passed since September 2017, when I first informed Canadians about E-Pirate and Jin and the Vancouver Model. And for three years, month-by-month, I had learned more about how Jin's loan-sharking network connected with almost every mysterious offshore real estate investor that I had been digging into in Vancouver.

My link charts were expanding all the time. And ever since I had confirmed connections between Jin and RCMP Suspect 2 — Rongxiang "The General" Yuan — I was increasingly seeing a pattern that Canadians needed to hear about.

The E-Pirate network had incredible political connectivity in China and Canada. Sources and documents said they bragged about having special relationships with Canadian officials. But now the extreme violence I had always heard was associated with Paul Jin — despite many politicians and Chinese officials surrounding him — was undeniable. It was as graphic as the photo taken from inside Manzo showing Jin's blood dripping through his hands.

There was a feeling that my investigations had come full circle. Money-laundering in Vancouver equaled violence and death. No one could argue against that now. But I also realized there is no way to end a book like this. Because every drug deal, every shooting, every illegal casino bust highlights new connectivity. I would never stop being shocked.

The Manzo shooting is a perfect example. For experts who construct link charts to decipher the intricate bonds of trust among the Mainland Chinese cartels shipping opioids across six continents — Jin's dinner party guest list was a bit like the Rosetta Stone.

As one well-placed source put it, the list demonstrated "mind-blowing connectivity" between the E-Pirate targets, Sam Gor's commanders, and the United Front Work Department.

Video evidence from inside Manzo showed two men from Markham with Jin.

One of them is the gang boss next in command to Chi Lop Tse. This transnational narco — who has been trafficking drugs in Toronto and Vancouver for decades — is Chi Lop Tse's apparent successor. He has handled Sam Gor's business in Canada since Chi Lop Tse left Markham. Some speculate that with increased media exposure on Chi Lop Tse, the new Markham boss may have assumed active command of the Company. Tse's plans to fly to Toronto in December 2020, before Dutch police nabbed him for extradition to Australia, raise a lot of intriguing questions. Sources who confirmed Chi Lop Tse's deputy was in Jin's party at Manzo asked that his name not be published in this book. He is a top target for the Five Eyes Law Enforcement Group. And along with Chi Lop Tse, he is viewed by the U.S. State Department as a top-tier national security threat, the sources said.

"It would be very easy to surmise that Paul Jin has connectivity to Sam Gor," a source told me. "But we had never seen it. This is the first time we ever saw Jin together with Sam Gor. So what was going on in Manzo that night is totally fitting with the Five Eyes targeting of Sam Gor."

So what was this meeting about? One RCMP theory is celebration of the completion of a major drug trafficking contract. Paul Jin's lawyer didn't respond to my request for comment on the events at Manzo and the totality of current and historic police allegations against him. And the appearance of a second gang boss from Markham at Manzo was another shocking confirmation of connectivity between Richmond and Markham for the RCMP.

This was the Sam Gor associate who had led York Regional police gang units to a 53-bedroom mansion believed to be the largest-ever illegal casino discovered in Canada. An investigation called O Cyber identified this man and wound through a network of underground casinos in north-east Toronto. Finally, on a hot night in July 2020, gang police in tactical gear and pandemic safety masks raided the network's alleged mothership.

The $10-million compound at 5 DeCourcy Court, with its neo-Italianate architecture and terraced restaurant and manicured gardens, looked like a carbon copy of the Richmond farmland casinos run by Paul Jin and his E-Pirate bosses. Only about five times larger.

Police made 45 arrests and seized 11 guns with ammunition and $1-million in cash. The number one target? An associate of the two Sam Gor suspects that had dined with Paul Jin at Manzo.

Wei Wei, a 52-year-old real estate developer from Anhui province with ties to elite Chinese officials, was charged along with his wife for running the operation. Wei Wei owns numerous properties across Canada and controls many real estate holding and development companies, police information and corporate records showed me.

York police said they were stunned by his network's sophistication and brazenness. He appeared to be running a parallel underground economy in broad daylight with absolute disregard for Canada's laws and sovereignty. The polar bear mount displayed beside a large Chinese flag in 5 DeCourcy's grand entrance hall sent a message about the authority that Wei heeded. He also runs a state-connected construction conglomerate in China, I found, which indicates he has blessings in Beijing. And sources told me there were reports of Chinese officials and tycoons flying into Canada and gambling in Wei's mansion of pleasures.

Police alleged all 53 rooms were used for illegal business.

Baccarat tables at 5 DeCourcy took $20,000 maximum bets. Detectives believe young women were trafficked for sex inside the mansion's illegal hotel facilities. Meanwhile — in total breach of COVID-19 restrictions — an unlicenced restaurant complete with maître d', served high-end delicacies such as shark fin soup to families with children.

Police sources told me Wei's businesses were supersized during the coronavirus pandemic, monopolizing the high roller action while Ontario government casinos were forced to close. And police believe the casinos generated huge profits to fund drug deals and human trafficking. There was huge connectivity to B.C. casino money-laundering, sources said. E-Pirate whales travelled to Markham and Toronto whales travelled to Richmond. And Paul Jin's criminal conviction and charge sheet was an excellent map for the underground casino and loan sharking and human trafficking and sexual exploitation loops between B.C. and Ontario and China. Jin has massage spas in Toronto and Richmond, and in 2001 in Markham, he had an assault charge withdrawn. In 2008 in Richmond, he was convicted of sexual assault and sexual exploitation. Back in Toronto, in 2009, he was convicted of aggravated assault. And in Toronto that year, he had an assault with weapon charge withdrawn. Clearly, after 2008, Richmond was the bigger market for Jin's activities.

But Markham's cut of the drug cash laundering had evidently increased in 2018 after B.C. Attorney General David Eby cracked down on the massive cash buy ins flooding B.C. Lottery Corp. casinos.

"That drug cash has to go somewhere," an RCMP source told me.

Wei Wei's political ties were another source of amazement for my sources. He had met with Prime Minister Justin Trudeau at two intimate Chinese-state sponsored events in Toronto. At one of the meetings, Wei Wei represented the China Cultural Industry Association along with an elite Chinese United Front Work Department official who donated $1 million to Trudeau's family foundation. And Wei Wei himself is leader of a Toronto United Front group started by the United Front Work Department in Anhui.

And the United Front ties between Markham and Richmond were just as illuminating as the casino ties. Wei Wei was there in Vancouver in 2018 with Chinese consular officials to celebrate the United Front's promotion of another real estate developer from Anhui, Yongtao Chen. Chen was made chairman of Canada's "controlling level" United Front group with Chinese consul general Tong Xiaoling and her consular United Front officials there to give Beijing's seal of approval. This was two years before Yongtao Chen spearheaded the United Front's PPE collection operation in B.C under Tong Xiaoling and these same consular United Front officials. But my sources were interested in more than the United Front connections between Wei Wei and Yongtao Chen.

Corporate records showed that Wei Wei and his wife and Yongtao Chen were among the directors of an Ontario numbered company that bought two Toronto-area hotels in December 2017, for $75 million. Yongtao Chen did not respond to my questions about these facts and sued for defamation after I reported on his business ties to Wei. And Wei, who faces 21 charges including the illegal operation of a betting house, possession of weapons for a dangerous purpose, possession of a stolen firearm and possession of the proceeds of crime, did not respond either. The RCMP's investigation of Wei continues and York Police allegations have not been proven in court. And I have to be very clear about this. There is no evidence that Yongtao Chen is involved in criminality. And China vehemently denies the United Front operates inside Canada. But what RCMP criminal intelligence reports escalated in Ottawa are concerned with, are the business and politcial connections between men such as Yongtao Chen and Wei Wei. As one source told me, the problem for Canada is that grassroots community associations meant to support Chinese-Canadians have been taken over by Chinese consulate operatives through the United Front. And because of Chinese state interference in Canada, it's very hard to tell where the United Front ends and organized crime starts, a source told me.

There are a few conclusions I take away from the Manzo shooting and the Sam Gor and the Markham casino revelations. Underground banking and trade-based money-laundering run by transnational gangs connected to the Chinese state is the Canada Model, not the Vancouver Model. And opioid cartels from across Mainland China have merged into super cartels run out of Canada. These cartels have support from the Chinese Communist Party. They are key tools in Xi Jinping's magic weapon. What I'm suggesting is that this information warrants a national inquiry in Ottawa. The Cullen Commission was underway when this book was published, and in his first interim report Justice Austin Cullen said he had already seen enough evidence to conclude that money-laundering is tearing the fabric of B.C.'s democratic society. This is an affirmation of the exact point that my sources have been hammering into me for years. The problem is worse than Canadians can imagine. What the commission finds remains to be seen. But as I have written in this book, ultimately elite elected officials in Ottawa need to answer for turning a blind eye to warnings in the 1990s.

Because with the benefit of hindsight, information gathered for Sidewinder — the leaked RCMP and CSIS report that appeared to be buried by senior bureaucrats — has proven largely correct. That's not to say that the draft report didn't contain some flaws. It was far ahead of its time. There may have been some cases of over-reach. But it was visionary. And it predicted the reach of Triads into large swaths of Canadian land.

Here's an example. Part of my advantage in completing this book in 2021 was the ability to look back at Sidewinder's allegations about Chinese tycoons with major real estate development and hotel investment footprints in Vancouver and Toronto. Because offshore investor court battles continue in the byzantine and evolving Vancouver Expo real estate development, I found something interesting in 2019 court filings. One Asian investor outed another alleged hidden Hong Kong investor in one Expo land parcel. I found this alleged hidden investor was a River Rock VIP with a penchant for dating Hong Kong starlets. I ran his information in Hong Kong corporate databases and found many connections to the incredibly convoluted real estate and casino and hotel investment corporations of Cheng Yu Tung and Li Ka Shing.

And I ran this Hong Kong investor's name past Garry Clement. Clement checked in his 1990s Hong Kong dossier. Bingo. The Hong Kong investor had sent his corporate employee — who was also a confirmed Sun Yee On Triad officer according to Clement's files — to Vancouver in the 1990s, seeking real estate and port development deals.

Sidewinder said that tycoons with connections to heroin Triads and the Chinese Communist Party and United Front were gaining a major foothold in Canadian real estate and hotels. And Ottawa's response essentially was to shoot the messengers and ignore their warning. But there is growing recognition from some highly respected former officials that the crime model first exposed in

Sidewinder must be confronted. This isn't just some fringe theory cooked up by spooks with secret dossiers.

I asked David Mulroney, Canada's former ambassador to Beijing, if Sidewinder's core assertions hold up. Is the Chinese Communist Party actually intertwined with transnational gangs and using criminals in the United Front to fulfill the Party's objectives?

"There is no denying the connection," Mulroney told me. "The course of modern Chinese politics, from the earliest days of the Communist Party in Shanghai, has been interrelated with the rise and fall of various crime bosses and triads."

Mulroney told me that when he was a government official, he could not speak out on his knowledge of the party's ties to gangs. But he believes it is now his duty to inform Canadians of what he learned inside China.

"The Party is not squeamish about using any tool. If they can catch someone doing something illegal, they will trade off a vicious sentence, perhaps a death sentence, in exchange for the criminal's compliance," Mulroney said. "They hold this over the heads of the people they are trying to co-opt. There is a very tight, incestuous relationship between organized crime in China and within diaspora communities, and the United Front. Co-opting criminal networks is one of the Party's preferred tools for the infiltration of target organizations and communities and for foreign interference."

So what does this mean? At worst, what does China's infiltration of Canada using criminal networks mean? Is there concrete harm?

Yes, the harm is tangible and increasing. And at worst — according to multiple well-placed sources — it means Beijing is allowing fentanyl to be shipped into Canada. This is another uncomfortable truth. The Chinese Communist Party has used the threat of fentanyl deaths as leverage on Canada's leaders.

Multiple sources with direct knowledge told me that around 2018, Beijing wanted to insert a national security agent into its Vancouver consulate to run Xi Jinping's covert Fox Hunt operations. And these "hunts" for economic fugitives like Lai Changxing are often thinly veiled intelligence operations.

"Before the current frost between us and the CCP, China wanted Canada to accept another police liaison officer but have that position located in Vancouver," a source confirmed. "Canada declined, so CCP were not happy. We knew that their intent is to target ex-pats and other 'economic refugees.' So the CCP held this over us when we went asking for assistance to combat the opioid crisis."

I'm still unpacking the implications of this Machievallian example of China's statecraft. When my sources use words like "narco state" or "opium war in reverse" or "hostile state activity" or "asymmetrical warfare" — these are jarring ideas. It is hard to conceptualize — let alone accept — that China intends to not only profit from fentanyl production but to weaponize it too.

But what the sources are ultimately saying is the Chinese regime is purposefully using fentanyl against other states. And they are saying Canadians need to recognize the ruthlessness of Beijing's compact with opioid cartels. Who are these sources? Some are RCMP criminal intelligence. Some are current and former CSIS agents. Some are from the DEA. Some are from the U.S. national security community. One, a former senior U.S. official with knowledge of global narcos and terror financiers, explained how the DEA believes Hezbollah weaponizes drug-trafficking against enemy states. They want to weaken Western cities by flooding in narcotics, increasing addictions and health care costs, and using the narco-proceeds for guns and bombs. It's profitable for the Iranian regime and deadly for the West. And China's objective with fentanyl seems to be the same, this U.S. source told me. Sources in the RCMP and CSIS agree. Canadian senator Vernon White, of the parliamentary national security and intelligence committee, has a similar perspective. He told me if China wanted to shut down fentanyl production in state-controlled factories, it could easily do it.

"This is a security threat," White said. "If terrorists were killing 5-6,000 people per year, we would do something about it."

But the threat is increasing and Canada appears to be virtually defence-less, the RCMP and CSIS sources I cited in this book say. Transnational cartels are increasingly setting up in Canada because the country has become a weak link in international law enforcement. That's the point that Garry Clement made when I interviewed him about the explosion of growth in Iranian-underground hawalas in Toronto.

"Canada is showing itself to be a weak link," he said. "Because what we are seeing in Toronto is identical to the underground banking we are seeing on the west coast with money-laundering, and how it relates to the regime in China. In Toronto, it relates to the regime in Iran."

And Calvin Chrustie advanced the same argument in his Cullen Commission testimony in March 2021. He described how the world's most powerful narcos — Chinese Triads, Mexican and Colombian cartels, and Middle-Eastern narco-terror operatives — have cooperated to take over Canada's criminal economy. Vancouver has become a high-tech hub for state-sponsored crime facilitated by a proliferation of encryption technology companies servicing gangsters and spies, Chrustie told Commissioner Cullen. Yet Canada is stuck in a 1960s legal framework. The RCMP can't fight transnational crime with Australia, the U.K. and the U.S., because Canadian police have difficulties in sharing sensitive intelligence with allies, using international informants and police agents, and getting phone wiretaps approved. Chrustie gave a few stunning examples. After 2010, Colombian police informed him they were extremely concerned that Latin American narcos were moving incredible amounts of drug money through a Chinese Triad leader in Vancouver. This was years before the E-Pirate investigation. RCMP mounted a big probe but the Triad money launderers simply shut down operations, Chrustie said. He testified that he suspects a leak in the RCMP's leadership could have compromised this crucial investigation. Another source inside the probe of Latin American cartels, Hezbollah and Chinese underground banks, which was code-named Project Scrapyard, told me Chrustie's suspicion is likely accurate. It's believed someone in the RCMP's braintrust was destroying probes of narcos from 2012, the source said.

In his testimony, Chrustie also explained how the major Mexican cartels have set up in Vancouver since 2010, while police watch, almost powerless, because of Canada's welcoming laws. For example, when the DEA informed RCMP that El Chapo had elite Sinaloa Cartel operatives working in Vancouver, Chrustie's legal team rushed to write the court applications needed to secure wiretap warrants. Australian federal police can get approvals to wiretap transnational narcos in several days, Chrustie said. And U.S. police can "go up" on narco phone lines within a week. But after seven months in Canada, the RCMP could not get court approvals to tap the Sinaloa Cartel's communications in Vancouver. In a nutshell, Chrustie testified, this is why Vancouver has become one of the world's most infiltrated narco, money-laundering and foreign intelligence hubs, and why Canada's political and financial institutions are at grave risk of corruption.

He pointed directly at B.C. government casinos, and the RCMP's knowledge of massive floods of $20 bills pouring into River Rock after 2010, to prove his point.

Afterall, Calvin Chrustie was on Barry Baxter's integrated proceeds of crime team, the unit that started to probe Paul King Jin's gang at the Richmond casino in 2010, before brass in Ottawa shut the unit down in 2012, amidst complaints about Baxter by Rich Coleman, and a lack of foresight by RCMP leaders in Ottawa. When Chrustie's federal organized crime unit launched E-Pirate in 2015, he found the problem was much worse. He suggested that people up high in Canadian federal and provincial governments knew how bad it was getting, and they were responsible.

"We are open to corruption by having this illicit money moving through our [financial] systems and our casinos. And our regulatory people having oversight of that, and ministers' offices knowing this," Chrustie testified. "And I was concerned, from 2012 to 2015, what has changed? Why continue to take this money? Because it was somewhat obvious to everybody in 2012 the money was illicitly generated. So I thought the public deserved to know, and everyone deserved to have the transparency of what the police were seeing."

I knew, although Chrustie didn't explicity say it, he was talking about his unit's plans to hold a press conference after they busted Silver International and Jin's underground casinos in October 2015. But for some reason, decisions were made among senior government and police officials, and Chrustie's press conference was cancelled. And yet again, after I exposed the E-Pirate raids for the Vancouver Sun in September 2017, the RCMP planned a press conference. Chrustie and his colleagues wanted the public to know how deep the rot was in B.C. casinos, and how transnational gangs were using B.C.'s economy to traffic fentanyl and launder the proceeds. But again, the press conference was shut down. Powerful people decided the public should be kept in the dark.

And so, in this book, I have tried to shine a light on this roiling pit of vipers. I have tried to show the public what police in Canada know, but can't say.

The problem is big and its complex. How can Canada, a country almost completely naive about the reach of state-sponsored crime networks and narcos with power equals to states, fight back?

Ottawa will need to change national security and foreign interference and criminal prosecution laws. And the RCMP will have to start targeting Beijing's United Front holistically. The RCMP and CSIS need political support and funding to go after the politically connected bosses of men like Paul King Jin. Jin himself, claimed to E-Pirate investigators that he was extremely connected in Beijing! There is no reason to doubt him. He has mines and factories in China. Jin's boxing gym in Richmond is connected to China's Belt and Road project. Elite CCP figures in Vancouver gather at the facility frequently. Meanwhile RCMP and CSIS watch and wait. Canada lacks the legal framework to cast a net over state-sponsored crime. Federal prosecutors need to start making big international cases like their counterparts in other Five Eyes countries. Australia is leading by example and facing harsh backlash from Beijing. Ottawa needs to start carrying its weight. But this will be very heavy lifting, sources say. Because Xi Jinping's United Front has penetrated Canada deeply.

"The tentacles of this thing. We are not talking about an emerging crime problem," a source said. "This is 30 years of a crime trend that has entrenched itself into our upper levels of Canadian society. It's frightening. The connectivity onto our business elites and corridors of power in Ottawa. It will take a long time to turn the tide."

ACKNOWLEDGMENTS

In this book I have described a network of characters involved in underground banking, drug trafficking, and espionage schemes. It seems fitting that I give thanks to my network, fellow journalists, sources, colleagues, and family and friends that assisted and supported my efforts to expose the Vancouver Model. I have chased these stories, essentially, since I returned from Japan with my beautiful wife to be, and enrolled in Langara journalism school in 2004. After enrolling I quickly turned my attention to Vancouver's Downtown Eastside, trying to understand a narco warzone that seemed inconceivable in a first-world economy. Thanks first of all to my wife, who supported me in this period, believing in my dreams and choosing to make a life with me and start a family in Canada. I also thank my children and my mother and father, who taught me public service is the highest calling, and my brother and sisters and their families, for their support and belief in my work. There are many journalists to thank from my time at The Province and Vancouver Sun, so I'll focus on several that I worked with directly on significant investigations that helped illuminate the Vancouver Model for me.

Thanks to Cassidy Olivier, Dan Fumano, Fabian Dawson, and Doug Quan. And at Global News, Stewart Bell, Brian Hill, Andrew Russell, Mercedes Stephenson, and especially John Hua, are to be thanked for important collaborations on stories regarding national security and transnational organized crime and casino money-laundering. I'd also like to tip my hat to Ian Young of the South China Morning Post and Kathy Tomlinson of the Globe and Mail, as well as Jeremy Nuttall and Joanna Chiu of the Toronto Star and Bob Mackin of The Breaker, for writing stories of interest that added to my knowledge.

Specifically, for Wilful Blindness, pre-eminent Canadian journalist Terry Glavin kindly offered to read my early draft. He was a vocal supporter of my reporting and having him on board boosted my confidence. Glavin's wise writing coaching enabled me to amplify my voice and more confidently assert my thoughts, shedding the daily journalism writing mode, and making this story mine alone. Thanks to my publisher Dean Baxendale and to my literary agent Michele Levine, for taking on this book project which has proven to be a complex endeavor. Thanks to Charles Burton for his wise foreword. It is my all-encompassing belief in the public interest, a powerful legal and ethical principle, that guides and sustains me in research that is often fraught with challenges and obstacles. Thanks to my employers for supporting my work and facing legal risks with me. And I will close by thanking my sources for this book, some of whom risked a great deal to share information of crucial importance to Canada. What they have done is in the public's interest, and should never be forgotten.

INDEX

Ackles, Kenneth, 288

Alcohol and Gaming Commission of
Ontario (AGCO), 287

Alderson, Ross: background, 10–11, 12;
BCLC investigation, 213, 264–276,
282–283, 295–296;
BCLC promotion, 1, 24–25;
Chrustie meeting, 1, 15–17, 112;
meeting with author, 10, 248, 250–251;
RCMP meetings, 6–9;
River Rock Casino job, 11–12, 14–15,
20–23, 33, 176–177;
Section 86 report, 26–28;
Tottenham email to, 292–293

Aldeson, Sheldon, 315

Alice (protester), 345, 349–350

Allegiance Capital, 134, 138

Apolinario, Antonio, 76

Armstrong, Jane, 295

Ashe, John William, 341, 347

Australia: Crown Resorts scandal, 342–343;
drug trafficking, 44, 218, 306;
gambling, 263;
money-laundering, 196, 324–326;
Tse extradition case, 166, 199, 331, 379

Avramovic, Proka, 109, 132–134, 137,
138–147, 153–154

Baker, Rod, 24

banking: Chinese underground, 5–6, 30,
242–247;
money-laundering through, 198,
225–230.
See also Silver International

Baxter, Barry, 166–167, 168–169, 171, 387

BCLC. *See* British Columbia Lottery
Corporation

Beeksma, Steve, 24

Bell, Stewart, 294–295, 326, 335

Benger, Bob, 40

"Beyond Social Capital" (Lo), 68–69

Big Circle Boys: Cheng's work for, 225–227;
drug trafficking, 41–45, 140, 193–194,
300–301, 304–309;
financial fraud activities, 194–195;
influence of, 31–32, 34, 36–38, 81;
Labine's records on, 89–100;
Lai's contracts with, 119–122;
Pang's connection to, 248–249, 256;
roots of, 50

Bin Zhang, 346–347

Blair, Bill, 339

Blank, Howard, 168

BloombergSen, 288–291

Bo Xilai, 262–263

Board, Gordon, 110–111

Brady, Anne-Marie, 319, 340, 350, 353

British Columbia Lottery Corporation:
casino money-laundering summit, 2–6;
and GPEB, 147–148, 174, 176, 179–185;
and IIGET, 149–156;
and illegal casinos, 248;
Jin investigation and ban, 263–270;
lack of enforcement in, 169–170, 174;
and large cash transactions, 165–172;

MNP audit, 252–255;
Project Sienna, 258;
raising of baccarat limits, 179–181,
185–186, 258;
River Rock Casino corruption allega-
tions, 277–287
British Columbia Securities
Commission, 224, 226, 244–245
Brown, Duncan, 288
Brown, Patrick, 279, 288, 289

campaign contributions, 347–349
Campbell, Gordon, 65
Campbell, Larry, 204–205, 277–281,
284–285, 294
Canada: Chinese Belt and Road projects in,
314–316;
immigrant investor program, 73, 76;
refugee policies, 30, 37–38
Canada Model, 382
Canadian Border Services Agency, 35
Canadian Security Intelligence Service, 63,
67, 89, 311, 316–319, 327, 340, 344,
356, 385–386
car theft, 79–83
Carpick, James, 222
cartels. See Mexican cartels;
organized crime
Cascade project, 239–247
"Casinogate," 35–36
casinos: Asian organized crime's buying
into, 283–284, 287;
cash flow into, 4–6;
China Sea Discovery, 132, 134–142, 154;
chip-passing, 110–111;
lack of enforcement in, 169–170;
Las Vegas, 83, 155, 156, 210–213, 246,
262, 315;
Macau, 43, 47, 48, 58, 71, 73, 75–77,
80, 106, 117, 119, 121–122, 132,
155–156, 244;
as narco-economies, 31;
O Cyber investigation, 380–381;
Ontario contracts, 287–291;
underground, 149–152, 156–157, 248.
See also British Columbia Lottery
Corporation; gamblers and gambling;
money-laundering; River Rock Casino

CBSA. See Canadian Border
Services Agency
CCIA. See China Cultural Industry
Association
CCP. See Chinese Communist Party
Chai, Ming, 263, 343
Chamberlain, Russ, 97–98
Chan, Kat Hai, 98
Chan, Kwok "Ah Chut," 43
Chan, Kwok "Chester," 43
Chan, Kwok Hung, 43
Chan, Raymond, 38–39, 347
Chand, Vikash, 87
Chang, Richard Ching, 14–15, 281–282
Chao, Raymond Hong, 218
Chao San Association, 360–361
Chen, Billy, 109
Chen, Ding, 293
Chen, Li Hua, 362
Chen, Mailin, 212, 213, 215–216,
293–294, 357
Chen, Wei, 242
Chen Yonglin, 346
Cheng, Muyang "Michael," 39
Cheng, Shek-Yin, 225–227,
230–231, 238
Cheng, Weigao, 39
Cheng Yu Tung, 47, 55, 58, 64, 132,
134–137, 141, 383
Cheung, Po Ho, 158
Chiang, Chuck, 240
China: Belt and Road projects in Canada,
314–316;
COVID-19 outbreak, 355–365;
espionage, 113–115, 126–127;
fentanyl from, 196, 275–276, 294–301,
304–309, 384–386;
gambling in, 3;
Guangzhou, 29–30;
guanxi, 51, 114, 247, 257, 258, 260,
266, 317, 357, 366;
PPE stockpiling, 355–365;
private wealth creation in, 4;
rise of Triads in, 49–51;
underground banking channels, 30,
230–231, 242–247;
United Front Work Department, 68,
319, 339–346, 348–354, 355–365,

380–386;
white gloves system, 125. *See also* Chinese Communist Party; Triads
China Cultural Industry Association, 346–347, 381
China Grain Oil Foods Import-Export, 114
China Light Industrial Products Import-Export, 113–114
China Poly, 313–314
China Sea Discovery (casino), 132, 134–142, 154
"Chinagate" scandal, 313, 341
Chinese Communist Party, 67–68, 243, 262, 341, 343, 353–354, 356, 384–386. *See also* People's Liberation Army; Politburo Standing Committee (CCP); United Front Work Department
Chinese Criminal Entrepreneurs in Canada (Chung), 31
Chinese People's Political Consultative Conference, 357
Ching Men Ky, 59
Chipped Tooth Koi, 76, 80, 86–87
Chow, Mrs. (loan sharking complainant), 39–40
Chow, Simon, 79–82, 84–85, 87
Chow, Stephen, 110
Chrétien, Jean, 32, 61, 65, 73, 316
Chrustie, Calvin, 1, 6, 13, 15–16, 112, 132, 165, 291, 295, 386–388
Chu, U Po, 246
Chu Ming Feng, 157
Chung, Alex, 31
Clark, Christy, 172, 240, 241, 242, 245, 316
Clark, Glen, 35–36, 38, 147
Claws of the Panda (Manthorpe), 340, 364
Clement, Garry, 47–55, 57–59, 63, 64, 67, 70–72, 74, 135, 154, 383, 386
CLEU. *See* Coordinated Law Enforcement Unit
Clinton, Bill, 126, 313, 341
Cohodes, Marc, 207–208, 224
Coleman, Rich, 147–149, 152, 161–162, 169–174, 387
Combined Forces Asian Crime Investigation Unit, 89
community amenities contributions, 200

Coordinated Law Enforcement Unit, 60–61, 79
coronavirus. *See* COVID-19
COVID-19, 356–365, 380–381
Criminal Intelligence Service Canada, 61
crowdfunding: for lawsuit against author, 365–372;
real estate, 215–216, 222, 238, 242, 293
CSIS. *See* Canadian Security Intelligence Service
Cullen, Allen, 163, 322, 382–383
Cullen Commission, 156, 270, 322, 337, 382–383, 386

Dannen, Fredric, 68
Dastyari, Sam, 343–344
Dawson, Fabian, 59–65, 99, 113, 114, 218–219
de Jong, Mike, 6, 25, 179–181
de Vries, Maggie, 202–203
de Vries, Sarah, 202–203
DEA. *See* Drug Enforcement Agency (US)
Delisle, Jean-Paul, 74–75, 76–77
Deng, Mr. (Beijing agent), 118
Deng, Xiaoping, 67
Desmarais, Brad, 5–6, 26, 182–183, 186–187, 292
Dickson, Derek, 165–167
Ding Guo, 365–367
Doran, Scott, 322–323
Dosanjh, Kal, 189–191
Double Wealth International, 235
Doyle, Terrance, 141, 183, 185
Drug Enforcement Agency (US), 108, 193, 275, 305, 316, 322–327, 334, 385
drug trafficking: fentanyl, 44, 108, 177, 196, 206–208, 271, 275–276, 294–301, 304–309, 384–388;
Golden Triangle region, 36–37;
narco-terrorism, 322–329;
and real estate market, 301–309;
Sam Gor syndicate, 196–197;
and trade-based money-laundering, 275–276;
Vancouver Model, 34, 42–45;

Vancouver's Downtown Eastside, 189–196. *See also* money laundering; organized crime

Duff, Rick, 21–22

Dykstra, Rick, 288

Eby, David, 136, 180, 222, 230, 252, 279, 337, 381

Elcock, Ward, 344

EncroChat, 333, 335

E-Pirate investigation, 259–276, 301, 304, 308, 312, 319–322, 331, 386–388

Evans, Paul, 330–331

FBI. *See* Federal Bureau of Investigation (US)

Fedeli, Vic, 289

Federal Bureau of Investigation (US), 127, 275, 300, 313, 316, 321, 333, 334

Feng, Franco, 360–361

fentanyl, 44, 108, 177, 196, 206–208, 271, 275–276, 294–301, 304–309, 384–388

Ferreras, Jesse, 322

Financial Transactions and Reports Analysis Centre of Canada (FINTRAC), 23, 32, 141, 160–163, 167, 170

Five Dragons scandal, 54, 60–61

Five Eyes Law Enforcement Group, 322–329, 331, 379

Fogarty, Patrick, 78–83, 195–201, 332

Fok, Henry, 64, 67

Fok Ying Tung, 58

Fong, Wong Man, 68

Ford, Doug, 289

Four Pacificals, 75

14K Triad, 75–77, 79, 81, 83, 86–87

420 Task Force investigation, 103–106, 112–115

Friesen, Gord, 22, 24

Fu, Gordon, 57, 65

Fumano, Dan, 224

Gagner, Michel, 77

gamblers and gambling: Chinese VIP, 2–3, 8–9, 142–143; Chinese VVIP, 3, 9; Macau Model, 261–263; whales, 10, 15–16, 264–270, 332, 363. *See also* casinos

Gaming Policy and Enforcement Branch, 5, 146–153, 168–169, 172–185, 249–252, 272–273, 284–287

Gang Yuan, 240

gangs. *See* organized crime; Triads

Gao, Jia Gui, 265, 297–298, 303, 363

Gao, Lisa, 293–294, 349

Garrossino, Sandy, 156, 162–163

"George" (hitman), 84–87

German, Peter, 154

Global Financial Integrity, 4

GPEB. *See* Gaming Policy and Enforcement Branch

Graydon, Michael, 179–180, 259

Great Canadian Gaming Corporation, 24, 89, 91, 110, 132–147, 153–154, 277–281, 287–291. *See also* River Rock Casino

Green, Jim, 204–205

Guajardo, Jorge, 356

Guangdong Overseas Chinese Federation, 360–361

Guo, Hong, 231–238, 250–251, 271, 344, 348, 368

Guo, Miles, 127

Guo Wei Liang, 157

Gutstein, Donald, 214

Hamilton, Clive, 319, 340, 350, 353, 358

Harcourt, Mike, 64, 316

Haslett, Mike, 277

Henareh, Salim, 328–329

Heung, Charles, 64, 69

Heung, Jimmy, 69

Hezbollah, 324, 326, 327, 385, 387

Hidden Hand, Exposing how the Chinese Communist Party is Reshaping the World (Hamilton), 340, 358, 364

Hill, Brian, 33, 290, 336

Hiller, Mike, 21–22, 178, 186–187

Hiscox, Bill, 203

Ho, David Kwok, 60

Ho, Patrick, 341

Ho, Stanley, 47–48, 58–59, 64, 86, 132, 136, 313

Hodson, Pete, 190–191

Holland, Wayne, 153

Hon Kwing-shum, 60

Hong Kong: democracy protests, 345–346, 349–350, 353, 358, 364;
drug trafficking, 37, 42–45, 193–194;
immigration to Canada from, 74; Lai's business dealings in, 102–108;
Lai's espionage claims, 117–118; probe, 62–67, 347;
return to Chinese governance, 90;
RTY Financial case, 234–238;
Triads, 47–55, 57–59, 67–70, 75, 81, 262;
underground banking channels, 30, 35
Hong Kong Commission, 47, 52–55, 57–59, 74, 77, 81, 194
Hong Kong Independent Commission Against Corruption, 70–71
Horgan, John, 322, 351, 352
Hua, John, 90–91, 322
Huang Xiangmo, 343, 361–362
human trafficking, 156, 347–348, 380–381

Immigration, Refugees and Citizenship Canada, 58–59, 62, 66–67, 77, 127
Integrated Illegal Gaming Enforcement Team (IIGET), 149–156, 158, 160–163, 170
Integrated Proceeds of Crime (IPOC) team, 166, 168, 175, 176
Ip, Stanley, 50
Iran, 312, 313, 323–327

Jackson, Greg, 111–112
Jardine, William, 49
Ji Shengde, 126–127
Jia Qinglin, 124
Jiang, Yicheng, 239–247
Jiang Zemin, 124
Jin, Paul King: assault charges, 381;
background, 255–259;
BCLC investigation and ban of, 8, 12, 263–270;
Beijing connections, 388;
as a cash runner, 176–178, 181–185;
Gao loan case, 362–363;
Guo law firm connection, 233–234;
Manzo meeting, 373–374, 376–379;
political connections, 346;
PPE operations funding allegations, 371–372;
RCMP investigation into, 250–251,

270–276;
River Rock VIP network, 295–296;
Section 86 report, 27–28;
Tse connection, 331–332;
Warrior Fighting Dream, 347–348;
Water Cube, 115, 256, 271, 347, 374–375;
whale recruitment and funding, 10, 15–16, 265–270, 332, 363
Johal, Hardip, 249
Jones, Paul Tudor, 223, 286
Joske, Alex, 319, 343–344, 350, 361, 370

Kalajdzic, Nebojsa, 144–145
Kamhon, 134, 135
Katsuya, Michel Juneau, 312, 339, 340, 358
Kelly, Patrick, 51
Kendall, Perry, 206–207
Kennard, Edward Trevor, 137
Kent, Peter, 339
Kesi Wei, 182–184
Khanani, Altaf, 322–330
Kousha (Iranian national), 319
Kroeker, Rob, 171–175, 182–183, 252–254
Kwok, Mr. (Triad mediator), 82

Labine, Muriel, 89–100, 145–146, 285
Ladner, Peter, 204
Lai, Tong Sang, 73–78, 80–86
Lai Changxing: bribery investigation, 99, 115–118, 341;
business enterprises, 101–103;
casino bans, 110–112;
deportation, 123;
espionage claims, 117–118, 125–126; 420
Task Force investigation, 103–106, 112–115;
gambling, 108–109;
Gilbert Road casino, 120–122;
money-laundering, 105–108;
PLA's interest in, 126–127;
Red Mansion, 102, 104–105;
refugee case, 114–115, 123;
Thomas's message to, 147
Lai Shui Qiang, 114
Lau, Julia, 210–213, 215–216, 292–293

Law Society of British Columbia, 233–234
Lawrence, Anthony Brian, 137
Lee, Jason Edward, 209–213, 293
Lee, Mi-Jung, 282
Lee, Stone, 24, 111, 287
Lee Shau-Kee, 135
Leung, Lawrence, 54, 66–67, 69–70
Leung, Silvia, 66
Levesque Beaubien Geoffrion, 73
Li, Mr. (real estate investor), 235–236
Li, Peter Sum, 80, 85–86
Li, Rong Lilly, 157
Li, Zixin, 232, 233
Li Jizhou, 116
Li Ka Shing, 64, 67, 383
Li Zhao, 240
Lightbody, Jim, 26, 185–186,
    252–253, 281
Liu Han, 262–263
Liu Huaqing, 126
Lo, Ms. (loan shark), 168
Lo, T. Wing, 68–69
loan sharks, 142–147, 153–154,
    156–159, 175, 297
Lottery Corp.. See British Columbia
    Lottery Corporation
Lui Lok, 53–54

Macau, 47–49, 73–78, 86–87, 90, 106, 117–
    118, 121–122, 132, 137, 155, 197, 263
Macau Model, 139–140, 261–263. See also
    China Sea Discovery (casino)
MacDonald, Dan, 288
Mackin, Bob, 346, 368–369
Manthorpe, Jonathan, 3–4, 319, 340
Manzo (restaurant), 373–374, 376–379
Marsh, Kim, 219–220, 222, 338
Martin, Paul, 205
Matheson, James, 49
Matsedik-Qira, Turnisa, 354
Mazure, John, 179, 184
McAdam, Brian, 53–55, 57–59, 61–63,
    66–67, 70–72, 74, 154
McGregor, Scott, 269
McKenzie, Nick, 342–343
McLeod, Ross, 134, 136–137
Mehdizadeh, Farzam, 322–329
Meilleur, Len, 6, 25, 26–27

Meng, Pretty Boy, 97–100
Meunier, Denis, 163
Mexican cartels, 312, 314–315, 325, 334,
    376, 386–387
Ming, Charles, 134–138, 141
MLARA, 367–369
MNP audit, 252–255
Mok, Sui Hung, 193
money-laundering: BCLC casinos
    summit, 2–6;
    currency refining, 20–23, 95, 291;
    Labine's records on, 89–100;
    NDP's Commission of Inquiry, 91;
    Project Bamboo, 79–83;
    third-party transactions, 141;
    through banks, 198, 225–230;
    through BCLC casinos, 158–159,
    161–163, 165–173;
    through Macau's casinos, 47–48;
    through real estate, 78–79, 198–200,
    296–309;
    through Silver International, 16,
    259–276;
    trade-based, 275–276;
    Vancouver's vulnerability for, 32
Morgenson, Gretchen, 208
Mueller, Robert, 333
Mulroney, Carolyn, 289
Mulroney, David, 384
Mulvenon, James, 125–126
Munro, Harold, 249, 251–252
Murray, Joyce, 348, 369–370

narco-economies, 31, 193, 200
New Democratic Party (Canada),
    90, 91
Ng Lap Seng, 125, 341–342, 347
Ng Yat, 43
Nuttall, Jeremy, 364, 369

O Cyber investigation, 380–381
Oei, Paul Se Hui, 239–247
organized crime: Mexican cartels, 312,
    314–315, 325, 334, 376, 386–387;
    Sam Gor syndicate, 196–197;
    Vancouver Model, 34, 42–45.
    See also Triads
Ortis, Cameron, 327–336

O'Toole, Erin, 356

Pan, Miaofei, 348–349
Pan, Qian, 232, 233
Panama Papers, 361–363
Pang, Peter Lap Sang, 248, 249,
    256, 347
Pappas, Tyson, 191
"Partners in Crime" (Dannen), 68
Paulson, Bob, 327–328, 333
People's Liberation Army, 38, 48, 68, 76,
    102, 118, 125–126, 317–319
personal protective equipment (PPE),
    355–372
Peschisolido, Joe, 240, 242–243, 245,
    337–339, 346, 347, 348–349
Phantom Secure, 334–336
Phillips, Murray, 35
Pickton, Robert, 202–203
Pierre Elliot Trudeau Foundation, 346–347
Ping Ping, 119–120
Pinnock, Fred, 129–132, 142, 149–156,
    161–163, 170, 287
Piva-Babcock, Laura, 281
PLA. See People's Liberation Army
Politburo Standing Committee (CCP),
    123–124
Postmedia News, 217
PPE. See personal protective
    equipment (PPE)
Price, Bill, 290–291
Project Bamboo, 79–81
Project Fallout, 81–87
Project Scrapyard, 387
Project Sidewinder, 63, 67–72, 87, 311–312,
    383–384
Project Sienna, 258
Prokaylo, Nick, 232–233

Quan, Doug, 313
Quartermain, Dave, 40–41, 42

Ramos, Vincent, 334–336
Rankin, Murray, 195
RCMP. See Royal Canadian
    Mounted Police
Read, Robert, 62–63, 67, 72

real estate: author's reporting on, 10,
    217–219, 222–230;
    bare trusts, 336–338;
    Cascade project, 239–247;
    Chinese investment in Vancouver's,
    214–219;
    crowdfunding, 215–216, 222, 238,
    242, 293;
    Minoru Boulevard deal, 235–238;
    money-laundering through, 78–79,
    198–200, 296–309;
    as a narco-economy, 31, 193;
    Richmond market, 2;
    and underground banking, 5–6;
    Vancouver market, 4;
    Vancouver's bubble as sub-crime
    lending, 208
Red Mansion, 102, 104–105
Rideout, Wayne, 6
River Rock Casino: Alderson's job at,
    11–12, 14–15, 20–23, 33, 176–177;
    casino chips missing from, 250, 258;
    corruption allegations, 277–287;
    currency refining at, 20–23;
    diversion of VIP market to, 142–143;
    GPEB audit, 284–287;
    Jin investigation and ban, 8, 263–270;
    Jin's bribing of staffers at, 184–185;
    Kesi Wei conference call, 182–183;
    Labine's records on, 89–100;
    loan sharks at, 175;
    MNP audit, 252–255;
    Tam's banning from, 33;
    VIP players, 3
Ross, Adam, 238
Royal Canadian Mounted Police:
    Casinogate investigation, 35–36;
    E-Pirate investigation, 259–276, 301,
    304, 308, 312, 319–322, 331, 386–388;
    Hong Kong Commission, 52–55,
    57–59; IIGET, 149–156;
    investigation of casino cash flow, 5–6,
    173–174;
    IPOC team, 166, 175;
    Read's bribery investigation, 62–63;
    Silver file investigations, 7–9, 251–252,
    259–276;
    surveillance of Lai, 121

Royal Diamond Casinos, 112
RTY Financial, 228–231, 234–238
Rumsfeld, Don, 280
Russell, Andrew, 290, 295

Sam Gor syndicate, 196, 331–333, 379–380
Schalk, Joe, 166–167, 175–176, 183–184
Section 86 report, 19, 26–28, 251–252
Sekora, Lou, 234–235
Sen, Sanjay, 289
Sha, Li Lin, 11–12, 165–166
Shapka, Cheryl, 36, 39, 81, 87, 119–121
Sharpe, David, 12–13
She, Denise, 218
Shenher, Lorimer, 203
Shi, Guo Tai, 178, 362
Shui Fong Triad, 73–78, 81, 83, 87
Sidewinder. See Project Sidewinder
Sikimic, Boki, 133, 137, 138–139, 140–141,
    143–144
Silver file investigations, 7–9, 251–252,
    259–276
Silver International, 16, 28, 176, 181, 183,
    255, 259
Sinaloa Cartel, 312, 314–315, 325, 334,
    334–335, 376, 387
Smith, Bud, 252
Sociedade de Turismo e Diversões de
    Macau, 47, 58, 74
Soliman, Walied, 289
Soo, Walter, 132–133, 134, 139,
    141, 183
South China Morning Post, 70
Sparkle Long, 235, 237
Spencer, Doug, 34, 35, 38, 109–110, 192–196
Stan (gang member), 190
Starlight Casino, 178, 287
Stephenson, Mercedes, 334–335
Sun, Kevin (Hong Wei Sun/Hong Sun/
    Kevin Lin/Sun Hongwei), 216–223,
    293, 349, 351–353, 365–366
Sun Commercial, 216–217, 221
Sun Yee On Triad, 47, 64–65, 68,
    69, 87
SunCrowfunding Holdings, Inc., 216
Szeto, Madame, 132

Tam, Kwok Chung: bare trust deal,
    336–338;
    and Big Circle Boys, 33–45,
    87, 193;
    casino ban, 33, 184;
    Casinogate, 287;
    Lai connection, 104, 121;
    lawsuit crowdfunding
    donation, 368;
    refugee claims, 29–31
Tenth Church, 345–346, 349
terrorism: narco-, 175, 276, 312, 322–329,
    385, 386–388;
    Silver International financing of,
    16–17, 27
Thatcher, Margaret, 90
Thomas, Adrian, 144, 146
Thomas, Nora, 145
threat-financing, 341
Ting, Henry, 120
"To Get Rich is Unprofessional"
    (Mulvenon), 125–126
Todd, Doug, 215
Tong Xiaoling, 354, 360, 381–382
Top Glory, 113–114, 115
Toronto Fuqing Chamber of
    Commerce, 357–358
Tottenham, Daryl, 181, 292–293
Towns, Terry, 23–24
transnational crime, 329–331.
    See also drug trafficking; money-laun-
    dering; organized crime; terrorism
Triads: Big Circle Boys, 31–32, 34, 36–38,
    40, 41–45, 50, 81, 89–100, 119–122,
    140, 193–195, 225–227, 248–249, 256,
    300–301, 304–309;
    Four Pacificals, 75; 14K, 57–77, 79, 81,
    83, 86–87;
    Hong Kong, 47–55, 57–59, 63–65,
    67–70, 75, 81, 262; rise of, 49–51;
    Shui Fong, 73–78, 81, 83, 87;
    Sun Yee On, 47–48, 64–65, 68, 69, 87
"Triads Entering Canada" report, 63–64
Tricell Forest Products, 113–114, 115
Trudeau, Justin, 247, 318, 346–349, 360,
    369, 381
Trump, Donald, 240
Tse, Chi Lop, 50, 196–197, 199, 331–333, 379

Tso, Henry, 342–343

Unit 61398, 127
United Front Work Department: as
    organized crime front, 380–386;
    political influence campaigns, 68, 319,
    339–346, 348–354;
    PPE stockpiling activities, 355–365
United Nations, 341, 342, 347
United States-Canada Border Drug Threat
    Assessment (2001), 36–37
United World Chinese Association, 59
U.S. Department of Justice, 335
U.S. Library of Congress reports, 32, 37, 105
U.S. State Department, 316, 331

Vancouver, BC: Downtown Eastside drug
    trafficking, 189–196, 204–208;
    as a money-laundering hub, 32;
    real estate market, 4, 208, 215–219,
    222–230, 239–247
Vancouver Model, 34, 42–45, 49–50,
    139–140, 186, 199, 201, 213, 224, 248,
    292, 322, 341, 362–363
Vander Graaf, Larry, 25, 151–152, 183–184
Virani, Azim, 226–227

Wah-keung, Heung, 194
Wai, Market, 86–87
Wall, Bruno, 205
Wang, James, 351–353, 365–366
Wang, Xun Sunny, 33–34
Ward, Bruce, 259–276, 353
Warrior Fighting Dream, 347–348
Wat, Teresa, 314, 316, 346
Water Cube, 115, 256, 271, 347, 374–375
weapons trafficking, 317
WeChat, 16, 22–23, 355, 357, 360, 364,
    367–370
Wei, Liang Ming, 227–228
Wei, Wei, 380–382
Wei, Xiaoqi, 271, 347, 368
Wenezenki-Yolland, Cheryl, 6
whales. See gamblers and gambling
White, Vernon, 306, 385
Wong, Wilson, 79–80, 82, 84
Woodbine Casino, 287, 289–290
World Military Games (2019), 359–360

Xi Jinping, 69, 102, 124, 262–263, 314,
    344, 358, 360
Xi Zhongxun, 102
Xiaopeng, Deng, 51, 101
Xiaoping, Deng, 4
Xu, Maria, 369
Xu, Mr. (real estate investor), 235–237
Xun Chuang, 361–363

Y, Mr. (junket operator), 138–141
Yamamoto, Naomi, 162
Yan, Andy, 307
Yan, Betty "Big Sister," 98–99, 104, 106–
    107, 109–110, 112–115, 119, 122–123
Yan, Mr. (real estate investor), 235–237
Yang, Hai Peng, 351
Yates, Ben, 194, 196
Ye, Mr. (mob leader), 346, 349
Ye Gon, Zhenli, 315
Ye Jianming, 125
Ye Xuanping, 69, 102
Yeung, Albert, 64, 68
Yim, Hoi Sam, 97–98
Yip Hon, 58
Yongtao Chen, 346, 348, 360, 381–382
Yuan, Rongxiang "Tiger," 318–319, 346,
    348–349, 350–351, 353, 354
Yuan Hua Co., 102–103, 113, 125, 126

Z, Mrs. (United Front leader), 366
Zhang, Yu Xiang, 168
Zhang, Zhongyun, 227–230
Zheng, Huo Quin, 40
Zhou Enlai, 344
Zhou Yongkang, 262–263
Zhu, Jian Jun, 373–374, 376–378
Zhu Rongji, 103–104–

APPENDIX A - REFERENCES

Sam Cooper media reports cited in the Cullen Commission Interim Report dated December 10, 2020, and other referenced media reports of significance in Sam Cooper's research.

Since 2015 Sam Cooper has documented dirty money in BC casinos, real estate, luxury cars, cash business enterprises, and numbered corporations set up by Canadian lawyers, with connections to Chinese/Asian business tycoons and organized crime figures.

While it is easy for some to look at all that has been going on in Canada for forty years related to the infiltration of transnational organized crime, money-laundering and wilful blindness by our political class, some have chosen not to. Some have even suggested the author has been on a witch hunt in his pursuit. As history unfolds in British Columbia at the Cullen Commission, it is becoming apparent to the world that links between the Asian underworld and the Chinese Communist Party have created an ecosystem that undermines democracy and the free world. Ultimately the CCP wishes to establish the Law of Rule over the liberal egalitarian order in any country they operate.

This Appendix is a direct transcript from the Cullen Commission interim report and cites the author no less than 47 times. Journalists have played an essential role in exposing many of the criminals, organizations' business practices and politicians who have all contributed to the success of TNOC and the CCP to infiltrate North America via Vancouver.

MEDIA REPORTS

https://cullencommission.ca/files/reports/CullenCommission-InterimReport.pdf

January 4, 2011
'Dirty money' suspected in B.C.
casino deals, *CBC News*

August 10, 2015
Money-laundering accusations are
a raw deal, casinos say Business in
Vancouver

April 1, 2016
Real estate scams need high-tech
attention, say Vancouver
and Canadian experts
Sam Cooper, *The Vancouver Sun*

September 16, 2016
Vancouver real estate used for
money-laundering, international
agency says
Sam Cooper, *The Vancouver Sun*

September 29, 2016
Richmond MP and lawyer named in
fraud lawsuits filed by Chinese immigrant investors
Sam Cooper, *The Vancouver Sun*

December 9, 2016
MP's law firm sued in case involving.
allegations of Chinese underground
banks and missing millions
Sam Cooper and Chuck Chiang,
The Vancouver Sun

February 27, 2017
Battle over lawyers' money-launder-
ing loophole shapes up in B.C.
Sam Cooper, *The Vancouver Sun*

May 25, 2017
Fraser Valley board warns offshore
clients seeking to misuse realtor
bank accounts
Sam Cooper, *The Vancouver Sun*

September 17, 2017
RCMP shelved hundreds of organized
crime cases after terror attacks Colin
Freeze, *The Globe and Mail*

September 26, 2017
Finance minister warned BCLC about
large casino cash transactions
Sam Cooper, *The Vancouver Sun*

September 29, 2017
Exclusive: How B.C. casinos are used
to launder millions in drug cash
Sam Cooper, *The Vancouver Sun*

October 4, 2017
RCMP casino money-laundering
probe uncovered alleged 'terrorist
financing' links
Sam Cooper, *The Vancouver Sun*

October 7, 2017
Organized crime a 'viable threat to
public safety' in B.C. casinos: 2017
gov't report
Sam Cooper, *The Vancouver Sun*

October 11, 2017
Highest proportion of high-rollers at
River Rock Casino are real estate
professionals: internal audit
Sam Cooper, *The Vancouver Sun*

October 16, 2017

B.C. casinos knowingly accepted
'banned' cash: Confidential report
Sam Cooper, *The Vancouver Sun*

October 19, 2017
Charges laid in probe of alleged B.C.
drug-cash money-laundering
Sam Cooper, *The Vancouver Sun*

October 21, 2017
River Rock-BCLC meetings in 2014
show depth of concern over
big-cash gamblers
Sam Cooper, *The Vancouver Sun*

October 24, 2017
Illegal gaming unit killed in 2009 due
to BCLC 'funding pressure'
Sam Cooper, *The Vancouver Sun*

October 30, 2017
Ontario PCs urge halt to Toronto
casino deal during B.C. money-
laundering probe
Allison Jones, *The Globe and Mail*

November 23, 2017
Victoria gives BCLC more teeth to
regulate B.C. casinos
Sam Cooper, *The Vancouver Sun*

November 29, 2017
B.C. attorney general orders ICBC
to investigate claims linked to casino
money-laundering probe
Sam Cooper, *The Vancouver Sun*

December 5, 2017
Richmond lawyer says trust-fund
cash was stolen, laundered through a
B.C.casino and sent to China
Sam Cooper, *The Vancouver Sun*

December 6, 2017
Money-laundering at B.C. casinos:
Review calls for increased reporting
of big cash deposits
Sam Cooper, *The Vancouver Sun*

December 14, 2017
Gang police and 'transaction
assessment team' now operating in
B.C. casinos, documents show
Sam Cooper, *The Vancouver Sun*

December 20, 2017
Documents point to $5,000 chip
problems at River Rock Casino
Sam Cooper, *The Vancouver Sun*

December 21, 2017
B.C.'s top slot machine players rake in
millions in jackpots, review shows
Sam Cooper, *The Vancouver Sun*

January 8, 2018
China's hunt for corrupt officials
could affect BCLC 'whale'
gambler revenue
Sam Cooper, *The Vancouver Sun*

January 12, 2018
Chinese developer took $2.68-million
cash loan in Richmond coffee shop,
legal filings allege
Sam Cooper, *The Vancouver Sun*

January 25, 2018
River Rock VIP host deregistered
after B.C. government probe
Sam Cooper, *The Vancouver Sun*

February 2, 2018
Huge B.C. money-laundering investi-
gation pivots to drugs and guns
Sam Cooper, *The Vancouver Sun*

February 15, 2018
River Rock Casino's top VIP hostess
no longer at the casino following
de-registration
Sam Cooper, *The Vancouver Sun*

February 24, 2018
Police probed calls made from
Burnaby casino to E-Pirate suspect
Paul King Jin
Sam Cooper, *The Vancouver Sun*

March 13, 2018
Massive BCLC casino cheque payouts
were mostly returned funds
Sam Cooper, *The Vancouver Sun*

March 16, 2018
Confidential report: Anti-money-
laundering measures will significantly
reduce BCLC casino revenue
Sam Cooper, *The Vancouver Sun*

April 19, 2018
How Chinese gangs are laundering
drug money through Vancouver
real estate
Sam Cooper, *Global News*

May 30, 2018
EXCLUSIVE: VIP linked to top
Chinese officials, real estate, corrup-
tion allegations, gambled with
$490k at B.C. casino
Sam Cooper, *Global News*

July 24, 2018
Alleged partnership of Canadian
casino company with gambling
tycoon could trigger new
investigation
Sam Cooper, Global News

August 17, 2018
B.C.'s gaming regulator investigating'
deeply concerning allegations' of
sex assault, harassment at River
Rock Casino
Sam Cooper, *Global News*

August 20, 2018
Exclusive: Peter German denies
conflict in B.C. casino probe despite
sitting on board with casino executive
Sam Cooper, *Global News*

August 29, 2018
Exclusive: River Rock Casino warned
employees may have shred large cash
transaction records
Sam Cooper, *Global News*

September 6, 2018
Hidden ownership loopholes make
Canada a 'pawn in global game of
money-laundering' report says
Sam Cooper, *Global News*

October 1, 2018
Former River Rock Casino dealers
caught in raid on suspected illegal
gaming house
Jason Proctor, *CBC News*

September 28, 2018
Exclusive: Documents allege complicity in money-laundering in major investigation of River Rock Casino
Sam Cooper, *Global News*

October 5, 2018
Exclusive: B.C. casino review contractor previously consulted for River Rock Casino
Sam Cooper, *Global News*

November 26, 2018
An introduction to Fentanyl: Making a Killing
Stewart Bell, Sam Cooper, and Andrew Russell, *Global News*

December 3, 2018
If helping China hunt fugitives is the price of stemming deadly fentanyl flow, should Canada pay?
Sam Cooper and Amanda Connolly, *Global News*

January 3, 2019
$20 bills in duffel bags 'obvious' money-laundering, warnings ignored: letter
Jon Woodward, *CTV News*

January 9, 2019
EXCLUSIVE: Crown mistakenly exposed police informant, killing massive B.C. money-laundering probe
Sam Cooper, *Global News*

January 11, 2019
B.C. gaming investigators repeatedly warned bosses of 'horrendous' money-laundering
Eric Rankin, *CBC News*

January 17, 2019
Ontario casino regulator probing whether B.C. casino staff were connected to money-laundering suspects
Sam Cooper, *Global News*

January 18, 2019
B.C. attorney general says money launderers will exploit 'gaps' in information sharing in Canada
Sam Cooper, *Global News*

January 28, 2019
Nearly $2 billion in dirty money may have flowed through B.C. casinos, far more than official estimates
Sam Cooper, *Global News*

January 31, 2019
B.C. casino 'knowingly accepted' millions from banned loan shark, audit alleges
Sam Cooper, *Global News*

February 7, 2019
Justin Trudeau looking for answers but doesn't commit to B.C. casino public inquiry
Sam Cooper, *Global News*

February 7, 2019
'BCLC could have stopped this': Former casino investigators question whether officials unwilling to stop criminal activity
Sam Cooper, *Global News*

February 12, 2019
As RCMP investigated casino money-laundering, police distrust of B.C. government grew
Sam Cooper, *Global News*

February 28, 2019
Toronto man arrested with $1M in cash may have ties to international money launderer. Now, he's allegedly fled Canada
Sam Cooper and Stewart Bell, *Global News*

March 19, 2019
Canada proposes national money-laundering task force in budget 2019
Sam Cooper. *Global News*

March 21, 2019
Toronto's real-estate market risky for money-laundering, with $28B in opaque investments: report
Sam Cooper, *Global News*

March 26, 2019
B.C. Liberal minister intervened to raise betting limits, ignoring money-laundering warnings about Chinese VIPs
Sam Cooper, *Global News*

April 2, 2019
U.S. deems Canada 'major money-laundering country' as gangs exploit weak law enforcement
Sam Cooper, *Global News*

April 10, 2019
It's long been known in B.C. that RCMP not investigating money-laundering, sources reiterate
Sam Cooper, *Global News*

April 15, 2019
B.C. real estate industry recommends amending federal money-laundering laws to improve enforcement
Sam Cooper, *Global News*

May 1, 2019
Former B.C. casino supervisor blows whistle on when Macau-style money-laundering may have exploded
Sam Cooper, *Global News*

May 2, 2019
Whistle-blower warned B.C. casino in 2000 of alleged 'cooperation with organized crime'
Sam Cooper, *Global News*

May 3, 2019
B.C. casino's $18K severance agree-ment prevented public criticism about gangs, former employee claims
Sam Cooper, *Global News*

May 7, 2019
Bag containing $100K allegedly stolen as thieves foil Chinese money 'exchange'
Jason Proctor, *CBC News*

May 16, 2019
Alleged 'heavyweight' gangster could be poster child for B.C.'s public inquiry into money-laundering
Sam Cooper and Brian Hill, *Global News*

May 29, 2019
How Canada's legal system helped an alleged Chinese gangster avoid deportation for decades
Brian Hill and Sam Cooper, *Global News*

June 11, 2019
Alleged gang kingpin may have used
Liberal MP's law firm to launder
money through B.C. condo deal
Sam Cooper and Brian Hill,
Global News

June 17, 2019
Liberal MP involved in second bare
trust deal with client named in 'transnational money-laundering' probe
Sam Cooper, *Global News*

July 9, 2019
B.C. casino regulator received complaint alleging BCLC management
pressured to 'allow dirty money'
Sam Cooper, *Global News*

July 11, 2019
Sources say RCMP opened file on
Liberal MP whose firm facilitated real
estate deals in B.C.
Sam Cooper, *Global News*

OTHER WORKS REFERENCED

June 27 1977
Whoever said 'crime does not pay' never hung out with a Hong
Kong cop
Jack Spackman, Harold Ellithorpe

April 7, 2002
Graft probe a "shock"
Fabian Dawson, *The Province*

November 20 2012
The rise of the Red Mafia in China: a case study of organised
crime and corruption in Chongqing

April 26, 2010
Beyond Social Capital: Triad Organized Crime in Hong Kong
and China

Great Canadian Gaming Corporation
Business Case – River Rock Casino 3rd Floor High Limit Facilities Enhancements
October, 2014

Project Rationale

Immigration and visitation to the GVRD from Mainland China has been on the increase for some time now, resulting in ever increasing levels of higher limit Baccarat play in the marketplace since the beginning of 2013. Current events in Mainland China and Hong Kong are likely to result in even greater inflows of new residents and visitors in the near future.

China's Central Government's anti-corruption and flight capital campaign will continue to escalate in 2015, redirecting VIP Baccarat play to locations other than Macau, such as the GVRD and River Rock Casino Resort in particular. When the investigations have been completed and reports submitted to Beijing it is widely believed that these campaigns will ramp up to compound the aforementioned effects.

The goal of the Chinese campaign is to curb extravagant and conspicuous consumption of premium brand consumer goods purchases, luxury hotel stays and opulent fine dining. Those who currently enjoy this lifestyle will want to maintain low profiles in China, but continue to enjoy the benefits of their wealth, which means in offshore destinations such as Vancouver.

The US government's current campaign to curb money laundering, involving the Justice Department, the Treasury Department and FinCEN, will continue to focus on Las Vegas-based gaming companies that operate in Macau (Wynn, Sands and MGM). VIP residents of the Peoples' Republic will encounter increasing restrictions on access to funds for gaming in Macau and Las Vegas, again making the GVRD a highly desirable gaming destination.

Current protests in Hong Kong against unlimited rule by the Mainland Chinese government will result in much reduced visitation to the city, again diverting tourist traffic to destinations such as the GVRD.

Citizens of the Peoples' Republic who reside in other countries such as Australia, the USA and the UK will be encouraged by the actions and events described above to choose Canada as a travel destination, using 10 year Canadian visitor visas, as opposed to going home for vacations. Similarly, Chinese persons with landed immigrant status in Canada will choose to remain in Canada rather than return to China.

All of the above provide a solid basis for the assumption that prospects for continuing significant increases in VIP, mass VIP and premium play at River Rock are very good.

Purpose and Scope of the Project

The project will have a number of focal points, among which are the following:

- Provide the Salon Prive and Phoenix Room with layouts and décor based on the Macau model, which features brighter lighting, brighter colour schemes and tiered, layered gaming zones, more accommodating to the tastes of the elite VIP player.
- Creation of an 'Inner Sanctum' in the former Surveillance and Security spaces, which will combine private gaming and dining offerings for the first time to greater enhance convenience, privacy and discretion for River Rock's top tier players.

- Create facilities which will be attractive to domestic and international players who visit the area by means of cruise ship operators, Mainland Chinese travel companies and organized golf tour groups who wish to avoid being viewed as 'privileged' in China (golf being viewed as a symbol of extravagance in the homeland). These facilities could well include a redevelopment of the River Rock Marina to create a high-end Chinese private club, members of which are luxury lifestyle seekers who game, sail and golf for pleasure.

Gaming Area Enhancements

The refinished 3rd floor will include:
- 17 additional tables, 7 in the Salon Prive and 10 in the Phoenix Room
- The introduction of smaller Baccarat tables, which accommodate 5 players as opposed to the more conventional 9 seat tables. These tables will facilitate more 'reserved' games which typically seat 1-3 players, resulting in greater productivity in terms of increased hands per hour and more efficient use of available space.
- The introduction of a $25,000 chip/plaque to encourage aspirational play and satisfy the currently unmet demand for a higher bet limit from the VVIP player group.
- The establishment of a $150,000 table aggregate bet limit, pre-approved by BCLC, but deployed at Great Canadian's discretion.
- Increased Executive Host/VIP Host presence in these areas.
- Private cage service in the Phoenix Room.
- Expanded rest room facilities

Player Experience and Entertainment Enhancements

To complement the upgraded gaming facility features, the following would be offered, utilizing the theatre, conference and meeting facilities of the River Rock Resort complex:
- World-class Chinese concerts and variety shows
- Luxury brand lifestyle events
- Chinese economic trade shows and business conferences

In addition, the following would be enhanced or introduced to provide more exclusive VIP privileges and experiences:
- Appreciation dinner parties
- Off-site excursions
- Innovative, customized VIP gifts
- Superior selection and quality of food offerings
- Personalized celebrity meetings

Also, Great Canadian would extend and expand its Chinese community outreach by:
- Increasing its support of impactful Chinese community charities and causes (sponsoring venue and in-kind value for fundraising purposes, for example)
- Developing meaningful, cooperative alliances with Chinese business and social organizations
- Helping to foster relations with governmental agencies that are instrumental in providing opportunities for affluent Chinese to visit the area and utilize the facilities and amenities at River Rock Casino Resort (trade delegations, educational and cultural exchanges, for example)

Project Cost Estimate

The project is currently estimated to cost $3,700,000 all-in.

Assumptions Underlying Incremental EBITDA Projections

Associated incremental revenue projections were based primarily on the estimated utilization of the additional 17 Baccarat tables combined with extrapolations from historical high limit player game duration, average bet, game pace, and hold % data. To project incremental labor costs, projected 'tables opened' data was combined with an estimate of a total time in use per table per day of 10 hours, to produce a forecast of total table operating hours for 2015. Operating hours were then converted to the equivalent labor hours (1.25:1 for dealers and 0.625:1 for supervisors, to account for hourly 15 minute breaks). The estimate of incremental operating expenses was based solely on BCLC's 1% of GGR levy to cover such costs. An additional $10,000 was included to cover the cost of felt replacements.

Summary of Operating Projections

Incremental Revenues from Salon Prive and Phoenix Room	$25,284,376	
Incremental EBITDA	$23,639,388	93.5%
Incremental Cash Flow	$19,922,467*	

*CCA and Income tax expense were estimated using the a flat rate of 20% for the total capex and ½ of the provincial corporate tax rate of 26%, to reflect the impact of the ½ year rule.

Summary of Financial Modeling Results

Given the sizable amount of incremental cash flow relative to the planned capital expenditure over a time span of less than one year, standard ROI computations were not required. A 'simple payback' calculation estimates full recovery of the investment in 2.23 months.

Appendices
1. Renderings and floor plans

2. 2015 high level pro forma schedules (prepared by R. McPherson)

3. 2015 detailed pro forma schedules (prepared by W. Soo)

APPENDIX B - SIDEWINDER

The once top Secret Sidewinder 'report was leaked to the media in 2001

ANDREW MITROVICA in Toronto JEFF SALLOT in Ottawa

The Chinese government and Asian criminal gangs have been working together in drug smuggling, nuclear espionage and other criminal activities that constitute a grave threat to Canadian security, a secret study by federal law-enforcement and intelligence analysts.

"In many ways, China remains one of the greatest ongoing threats to Canada's national security and Canadian industry," the report says.

The study, titled Chinese Intelligence Services and Triads Financial Links in Canada, was prepared in June, 1997 by as many as five analysts from the Royal Canadian Mounted Police and the Canadian Security Intelligence Service who worked for about two years using classified files from both agencies.

Copies of the original draft were destroyed or kept under lock and key until The *Globe and Mail* obtained one this week.

According to sources, the study, known as Project Sidewinder, was considered by some CSIS managers to be so controversial that it was watered down and rewritten before a sanitized version was circulated to other government agencies last year familiar with the history of the document.

The Sidewinder report describes an alliance among the Beijing government and its espionage services, Hong Kong tycoons and Chinese criminal gangs known as triads. The report's ultimate objectives were to alert parliament that Canada was in danger of being overrun by Transnational Organized Crime.

Instead of embracing the findings and taking the appropriate actions, the Prime Minister and key members of his team who had embraced China and the supposed economic benefits for Canadians set out to kill the report and suggest racial bias. While this was going on, it indicated that Global Affairs officials were indeed corrupt and taking bribes and payoffs. Those involved with the investigations were demoted, moved aside or ridden out of town by senior RCMP and CSIS team members. All but destroying the careers of dedicated citizens who were doing what they were hired to do.

But who was exposed? Many, including Jean Chrétien, who since leaving office, has been at the CCP's financial trough earning millions for himself and influencing Global Affairs in the public policy realm. Various Liberal Ministers and Global Affairs have shown a bias and written policy that is favourable to China and not to Canada. That is believed due to monies received by officials from CCP proxy companies.

The report, known originally as Project Sidewinder, was rewritten, watered down and given a new code name, Project Echo because CSIS managers believed its findings constituted a rumour-laced conspiracy theory.

What the report ultimately suggested is our government was deeply infiltrated by the CCP, and criminals were coming to Canada under their watch. As the book has clearly articulated. Now in 2021, we are left with the legacy of inaction and need to reexamine our diplomatic posture and engagement policy with a criminal authoritarian enterprise operating as a government.

The original story broken by the *Globe and Mail* in 2000.

ANDREW MITROVICA AND JEFF SALLOT
TORONTO AND OTTAWA
PUBLISHED APRIL 29, 2000

The Sidewinder report describes an alliance among the Beijing government and its espionage services, Hong Kong tycoons and Chinese criminal gangs known as triads. The ultimate objectives included:

Winning influence with Canadian politicians.

Stealing high-tech secrets.

Laundering money.

Gaining control of Canadian companies in real estate, media and other sectors.

The RCMP and CSIS files revealed only "the tip of the iceberg," the analysts concluded. They recommended expanding their joint task force to include officials from the Department of Foreign Affairs and International Trade, Immigration Canada and Canada Customs.

That recommendation was never followed. Instead, CSIS managers shelved the 1997 report and dismissed its conclusions as a rumour-laced conspiracy theory, with little factual evidence to support its potentially explosive conclusions.

The Security Intelligence Review Committee, an independent watchdog body, is investigating allegations that the original Sidewinder report was suppressed because of political pressure. The committee is expected to complete its investigation and release the results to Parliament within weeks.

Chinese embassy spokeswoman Qin Xin denied that her government is involved in espionage or criminal activities in Canada or poses any threat to Canadian national security. "These kinds of accusations are totally groundless," she said.

Spokesmen for the RCMP and CSIS would not comment on the main conclusion of the study — that China poses a grave threat to Canadian national security.

The Sidewinder study is still classified secret and thus the RCMP can't talk about it, Mountie spokesman Sergeant Andre Guertin said.

CSIS spokesman Dan Lambert said the service does not discuss targets, so it will not confirm or deny whether it considers Chinese activities in Canada a security threat. He did say that CSIS maintains a vigorous counterintelligence program.

Mr. Lambert denied that the original Sidewinder study was watered down and insisted there was no interference from the agency's political bosses.

Both the RCMP and CSIS subjected the 1997 draft to extensive review to make sure the final version, which was produced in 1999, could be supported by facts, he said.

CSIS agents familiar with the 1997 version, however, bristled at Mr. Lambert's version of events and noted that the Liberal government has courted trade and business opportunities with China since coming to office in 1993. Prime Minister Jean Chrétien plans to lead another trade mission to China this year.

The analysts wrote in the foreword of their 23-page study that "this report presents concrete facts, not just ideas or speculation."

The study notes that an earlier RCMP investigation, code-named Project Sunset, turned up evidence that an international food-services company based in Southern Ontario was involved in smuggling heroin into Canada from Hong Kong. The company's chairman was affiliated with a triad. Company managers met regularly with Chinese trade and military representatives in Canada.

The report also says Ontario Hydro believes it was the victim of theft of nuclear technology "by an individual of Chinese origin." The man sent hours worth of material by fax to a telephone number at a Chinese state science and technology commission.

In two other cases the report cited, employees of Chinese origin at Canadian high-tech companies stole proprietary information and sold it to China.

The report says Chinese intelligence services send agents to Canada as part of business and trade delegations.

Chinese intelligence services have set up "front companies" in Canada solely for espionage purposes, including theft of business secrets, the report says. The companies have regular contacts with the triad gangs.

Drawing on intelligence developed by other Western countries, the analysts say there is a well-established relationship between the Communist government in Beijing and the Hong Kong-based triads.
More than 200,000 Hong Kong residents immigrated to Canada during the 1990s. The report says the great majority of these immigrants "were legitimate, [but]Canadian authorities detected a significant presence of Chinese organized crime elements." Some eventually acquired Canadian citizenship.

The study notes that a former Canadian citizenship court judge faces 33 fraud and forgery charges in connection with immigration applications by Hong Kong residents. The RCMP laid the charges in May, 1997, but the case has yet to come to trial.

Some Hong Kong investors and mainland Chinese with ties to the Communist Party leadership and Chinese intelligence services came here using the "entrepreneur" and "investor" categories for Canadian immigration, the report says.

Canadian intelligence indicates that some of these people have worked with the Beijing regime to establish companies that are used as cover for criminal and espionage activities, the report says. "This country is an excellent place to invest in companies to launder the profits derived from criminal activities."

Some companies controlled by Hong Kong executives with ties to the Beijing regime have obtained federal government classified contracts, the report says.

The study also says more than 200 major firms in Canada are influenced or owned by triads, tycoons or Chinese national companies. The Chinese government buys or sets up a legal company in Canada that in turn buys other companies, the report says, creating "an effective domino effect . . . that acts like a well-spun web or network of strategic points."

Initially, the study says, Chinese intelligence agencies acquired firms in so-called soft-sector firms that attracted little attention from CSIS, but then moved to take control of more sensitive companies in high-tech sectors.

Thus, China is quietly but systematically acquiring sensitive Canadian technology, including nuclear information, and is exerting undue influence over Canada's political environment by assuming control of key portions of Canadian industry, the report insists.

The study says there is Chinese "interference" in politics through political donations. It said the U.S. Federal Bureau of Investigation is investigating about 2,000 companies to determine whether they are being used by the Chinese to funnel illegal campaign contributions to U.S. political parties.

In Canada, the study says, the same pattern can be discerned. Companies believed to be controlled by Chinese interests contributed money to the federal Liberal and Progressive Conservative parties between 1991 and 1994.

Prominent former Canadian politicians have been named to boards of Chinese state-owned corporations, the report adds. The report did not identify the politicians by name.

Beijing has a particular interest in Chinese-language media in Canada, the study says. It notes that one Chinese-language cable TV outlet was the target of a takeover bid by a Hong Kong triad figure in

1992. The bid was withdrawn after federal officials notified the Canadian Radio-television and Telecommunications Commission of the bidder's connections to organized crime.

A Chinese-language film-production studio in Ontario was owned by triad figures who were in regular contact with Chinese diplomats posted here, the report says.

The study notes various real-estate purchases, including hotels, in Toronto, Vancouver and other Canadian cities by the owner of a large south Asian gambling casino. The man was put on a Canadian police watch list 10 years ago because of his alleged involvement in organized crime.

THE SIDEWINDER REPORT
PUBLISHER'S NOTE

As you can see from the *Globe* articles some twenty years ago, Sidewinder was controversial, and that Project Echo rebuffed Sidewinder. Key personnel in Global Affairs under Chrétien government officials' direction with close ties with China commissioned Echo. Its purpose was to dispel and discredit the conclusions of Sidewinder. According to sources, no one in the media has seen Echo, but there is yet another still-classified report. One compiled by American intelligence supports the findings in Sidewinder. The Shawinigan Affair involved Chinese tycoon money paid for citizenship directed to PM Chrétien's riding through a Quebec-based investment firm. Still today, Chrétien has close ties to Beijing.

In our estimation, an essential part of the report relates to the infamous meeting between Henry Fok, Li Ka-Shing with Chairman Deng Xiaoping and President Zhao Ziyang in Beijing, as documented in the book Former Prime Minister Thatcher is discussed here. Another critically important fact that speaks to the implicit and complicit relationship with the Triad gangs is as follows. Beijing set up a front company to facilitate legitimate business opportunities for Triad Bosses on the mainland. They would be allowed to continue their illicit criminal business in Hong Kong. This relationship has flourished for close to forty years, giving rise to the world's largest transnational organized crime companies and an effective tool for Beijing's Hybrid War with the free world.

This makes Donald Trump's Quid Pro Quo with Ukraine seem like child's play.

Sidewinder

SECRET

RCMP-CSIS JOINT REVIEW COMMITTEE

DRAFT SUBMISSION

FOREWORD

In May 1996 a joint project was initiated by the RCMP Criminal Analysis Branch and the CSIS Analysis and Production Branch to assess the extent of the threat posed by the acquisition and control of Canadian companies by members or associates of triads with affiliations to the Chinese Intelligence Services. The research team quickly realized that the initial premise was the tip of the iceberg with only a minute portion of a much more complex situation showing. It should be stressed that this report is a prospective document that makes no claim to provide a full survey of the issue; in fact, quite the opposite. (S)

This document does not present theories but indicators of a multifaceted threat to Canada's national security based on concrete facts drawn from the databanks of the two agencies involved, classified reports from allied agencies and various open sources. This study has departed from the conventional and sometimes confining approaches followed by our respective methodologies. Although both organizations have fairly extensive expertise on Chinese matters, it is nevertheless very different. It is clear at the end of this exercise that both organizations have gained from cooperating on this research. When put together, these two bodies of expertise complement each other, providing a broader and more substantial perspective of the Chinese issues. (S)

The scope of the problem found after a few weeks of research dictated that the initial research results had to be presented in the form of case studies. At the moment, we estimate that over 200 Canadian companies are under the direct or indirect control of China. Although it was impossible to do all the research within the parameters initially given; however, sufficient details have been found to reveal the threat. It should be reiterated that this report presents concrete facts, not just ideas or speculation. We trust that we have demonstrated the need to continue the work within a broader and more elaborate framework. (C)

> "Be so subtle that you are invisible.
> Be so mysterious that you are intangible.
> Then you will control your rival's fate"
>
> Sun Tzu
> The Art of War (c. 509 BC)

INTRODUCTION

1. With the announcement of the return of Hong Kong to China in the mid-1980s, Canada witnessed the arrival of a substantial immigration and capital flow from that region. For example, between January 1990 and March 1997, 237,077 Hong Kong residents emigrated to Canada, of whom nearly 70,000[1] were in the "entrepreneur" or "investor" category. This exceeded the "family" category over the same period. Although the great majority of these migrants were legitimate, the Canadian authorities detected a significant presence of Chinese organized crime elements, among them, namely the triads and their associates, some of whom succeeded in obtaining Canadian citizenship.[2] (S)

2. Some wealthy Hong Kong Chinese investors and Chinese from Mainland closely affiliated or related with the country's leadership and the ChIS also took advantage of the "entrepreneur" and "investor" categories to emigrate to and invest in Canada. Few even bought or established companies on Canadian soil through a family member who had obtained Canadian citizenship. Intelligence indicates that these specific individuals with these three groups: triads, Hong Kong investors and people close to China's leadership, have been identified working with concert with the Chinese government to gain influence through some of their "financial ventures" in Canada. Some companies which are also used to conceal criminal or intelligence activities. At the same time, the ChIS use their access to Canadian businesses through exchanges and technical or student visits to steal classified and technological information. They have gone so far as to set up shell companies to pursue their economic and technological information acquisition operations. (S)

3. A new triumvirate was born. This cooperation between Hong Kong Chinese business people, the triads and the Beijing leadership adds a new dimension to the known mass line collection strategy followed by the ChIS. Economic, political and security indicators based on factual data revealed the potential threat and efforts made by the Chinese to obtain Canadian technology, but above all to obtain influence over economic levers and prominent Canadian figures. (S)

BEIJING'S STRATEGIC ALLIANCES, OR THE LESSONS OF SUN TZU

4. When Deng Xiaoping came to power in the late 1970's, he introduced his economic reforms with the slogan "to get rich is glorious". To achieve that end, he had to move China onto the international markets. The isolationism of the former regime, however, handicapped the Chinese leadership. It therefore turned to the richest Chinese business people of Hong Kong, including, among many others, Li Ka-Shing, Henry Fok

---

[1] See Appendixes I and II, tables on immigration from Hong Kong.

[2] See Project Stopover, CID/RCMP.

Ying-Tung, Wang Foon-Shing, Stanley Ho[3] and the man who would eventually be chosen by Beijing to head Hong Kong after the departure of the British, Tung Chee-Wa (C.H. Tung). On 23 May 1982, Li Ka-Shing and Henry Fok met with Deng Xiaoping and Zhao Ziyang in Beijing to discuss the future of the peninsula. Their task would be to advise and educate the Chinese authorities about the basic rules of capitalism. In return, Beijing gave them privileged access to the vast Chinese economic basin. These powerful international financiers played an important role in the preparations for the transfer of Hong Kong. (UC)

5. In 1984, the British Government of Margaret Thatcher announced that it would return Hong Kong to China on 1st July 1997. This was not news to the Chinese or the rest of the world since a treaty signed nearly a century before had stipulated that Hong Kong was to revert to China in 1997. The reality of the impending transfer, however, created insecurity that was strengthened by the tragedy of Tiananmen Square in June 1989. That incident made Beijing realize more than ever that it would have to prepare the ground for its arrival not only with regard to the financial community but also the population. In the late 1980s, Western intelligence services reported the very active presence in Hong Kong of the United Front Work Department (UFW)[4]. For that purpose, the UFW was given the responsibility among other things for building alliance with the triads already affiliated with many business people. As early as 1992, Western intelligence services knew that, Wong Man Fong, formerly Head of the New China News Agency, was instructed to inform the triads bosses that if they agreed not to jeopardize with the transition process and the normal business in Hong Kong, Beijing would assure them that they will be allowed to pursue their illegal activities without interference[5]. The Beijing authorities also created a front company in Hong Kong for Wong Man Fong to facilitate his contacts with the triads and to assist triads groups set up legitimate business in China, particularly in Guangzhou and Shangai[6]. Following these negotiations, Deng Xiaoping himself was speaking of the triads as Chinese "patriotic groups", and the Hong Kong press published a photograph of Charles Heung, a senior officer of the Sun Yee On, conversing with the patriarch's daughter.[7] At the same time, Interior Minister Tao Siji indicated that there were patriotic members among the triads and they were welcome to do business in China. (S)

6. The political class has also been targeted by Beijing's leaders. Without any doubts for the communist masters, it was essential to obtain the cooperation of key elements of influential local personalities. Their collaboration or their resistance to China's requests before July 1st was going to make the difference between the possibility to do business with China after the transition. To achieve this, political and business people

---

[3] In 1996 FORBES magazine estimated the "official" personal fortune of Li Ka-Shing at US$10.5 billion, Henry Fok Ying-Tung at $2.5 billion and Stanley Ho at $3.1 billion. (UC)

[4] The United Front Work Department is one of the five components of the ChIS. See CSIS Report 95-6/13, The Future of Hong Kong: New Dogma, Old Tricks.

[5] In May 1996 the publisher of the Hong Kong tabloid *Surprise Weekly*, Leung Tin-wai, received two individuals at his office at the height of the day. They cut off his arm with a kitchen knife because the newspaper was preparing to publish an article unfavourable to Beijing in relation to Hong Kong's return in July 1997. (UC)

[6] Wong himself recently confirmed this information in a public conference in Hong Kong after defecting to Western authorities.

[7] See Project Sunset, CID/RCMP.

2

APPENDIX C - FATF REPORT

The Financial Action Task Force (FATF) is an independent inter-governmental body that develops and promotes policies to protect the global financial system against money-laundering, terrorist financing and the financing of proliferation of weapons of mass destruction. The FATF Recommendations are recognized as the global anti-money-laundering (AML) and counter-terrorist financing (CFT) standard.

For more information about the FATF, please visit www.fatf-gafi.org

The following pages will provide further clarity regarding the methodology of Money-laundering with references to the Altaf Khanani network and the Vancouver Model

FATF REPORT

Professional
Money Laundering

July 2018

Methodology

This project was co-led by the Russian Federation and the United States and incorporates input from a variety of delegations across the FATF's Global Network. The project team received submissions from Argentina, Australia, Belgium, Canada, China, Germany, Israel, Italy, Malaysia, the Netherlands, the Russian Federation, Singapore, Spain, the United Kingdom, the United States, EAG Members (Belarus, Kazakhstan, Kyrgyzstan, Tajikistan, Uzbekistan), MONEYVAL (Ukraine), MENAFATF (Lebanon), CFATF (Belize) and EUROPOL.

Authorities provided detailed information, including from risk assessments and case examples of various schemes arranged by PMLs, strategic analysis outcomes, information on internal organisational and behavioural aspects of PMLNs and investigative techniques. The report includes select country examples to provide the necessary context.

Input was also gathered at the Middle East and Africa Joint Typologies and Capacity Building Workshop in Rabat, Morocco, from 22-25 January 2018, and input and feedback gathered at the FATF Joint Experts Meeting held in Busan, Republic of Korea, from 1-4 May 2018. The findings of this report also rely on feedback from financial intelligence units (FIUs) and law enforcement agencies (LEAs), based on their experiences in investigating PMLs.

There has been sparse research on this subject. However, the project team did take into consideration previous and ongoing work by the FATF on operational issues, including the 2012 *FATF Guidance on Financial Investigations*, 2013 *FATF Report on ML and TF Vulnerabilities of Legal Professionals* and the 2018 *Joint FATF/Egmont Report on the Vulnerabilities Linked to the Concealment of Beneficial Ownership*.

SECTION II: CHARACTERISTICS OF PROFESSIONAL MONEY LAUNDERING

This section of the report outlines the key characteristics, which make PML unique, and helps to frame the scope of this report. **Section III** then provides a list of specialised services, which include specific roles or functions performed by various individuals. The report has attempted to avoid the use of formal titles (e.g. controller, enabler and facilitator), as multiple and inconsistent terminology is used globally, which leads to confusion when describing these functions. **Section III** provides a business model demonstrating how PMLs generally conduct financial schemes.

Key Characteristics

PML is a subset of third-party ML. The FATF defines third-party ML as the laundering of proceeds by a person who was not involved in the commission of the predicate offence[1]. The main characteristic that makes PML unique is the provision of ML services in exchange for a commission, fee or other type of profit. While the specialisation in providing ML services is a key feature of PMLs, this does not mean that PMLs are not also involved in other activities (including legal businesses).

---

[1] FATF Methodology 2013, footnote to Immediate Outcome 7.

Similarly, this does not mean that they exclusively only launder illicit proceeds. PMLs also use specialised knowledge and expertise to exploit legal loopholes; find opportunities for criminals; and help criminals retain and legitimise the proceeds of crime.

Given that PMLs are third-party launderers, they are often not familiar with the predicate offence (e.g. narcotics or human trafficking) and are generally not concerned with the origins of the money that is moved. Nonetheless, PMLs are aware that the money that they move is not legitimate. The PML is concerned primarily with the destination of the money and the process by which it is moved. They are used by clients in order to create distance between those perpetrating the crimes and the illicit proceeds that they generate as profit, or because the criminal clients do not have the knowledge required to reliably launder the money without law enforcement detection.

Ultimately, PMLs are criminals, who often operate on a large scale and conduct schemes that are transnational in nature. The term "PMLs" is not intended to include unwitting or passive intermediaries who are exploited to facilitate an ML scheme. Other features of PMLs are that they sometimes operate on a large scale and often conduct schemes that are transnational in nature.

Commissions / Fees

A number of different and overlapping factors affect the fee paid to PMLs or the commission they receive for their services. The fee will often depend on the complexity of the scheme, methods used and knowledge of the predicate offence. The rate may change based on the level of risk that PMLs assume. For example, commission rates are often influenced by the countries or regions involved in the scheme, as well as other factors such as:

- the reputation of the individual PML;
- the total amount of funds laundered;
- the denomination (i.e. value) of the banknotes (in cases involving cash);
- the amount of time requested by a client to move or conceal funds (for example, if the laundering needs to be done in a shorter time period, the commission will be higher); and
- the imposition of new regulation(s) or law enforcement activities.

To obtain commission for their services, PMLs may (i) take commission in cash in advance, (ii) transfer a portion of money laundered to their own accounts or (iii) have the commission integrated into the business transaction.

Advertising / Marketing

Advertising and marketing of services can occur in numerous ways. Often, this involves the PMLs actively marketing their services by 'word-of-mouth' (through an informal criminal network). Criminal links and trust developed through previous criminal engagement also strengthens bonds and can encourage further co-operation. Authorities have also identified the use of posted advertisements for PML services on the Dark Web.

Record Keeping (Shadow Accountancy)

Law enforcement has reported that PMLs often keep a shadow accounting system that contains detailed records with code names. These unique accounting systems may use detailed spreadsheets that track clients (using code names); funds laundered; the origin and destination of funds moved; relevant dates; and commissions received. PMLs may either store their records electronically (e.g. a password-protected Excel spreadsheet) or use paper records. These records represent an invaluable resource for investigators.

Individuals, Organisations and Networks

PMLs can belong to one of three categories:

1.   An **individual PML,** who possesses specialised skills or expertise in placing, moving and laundering funds. They specialise in the provision of ML services, which can also be performed while acting in a legitimate, professional occupation. These services can include, but are not limited to, the following: accounting services, financial or legal advice, and the formation of companies and legal arrangements (see *specialised services,* below). Individual PMLs often spread their risks across diverse products, and carry out business activities with several financial specialists and brokers (see examples below).

2.   A **Professional money laundering organisation (PMLO)**, which consists of two or more individuals acting as an autonomous, structured group that specialises in providing services or advice to launder money for criminals or other OCGs. Laundering funds may be the core activity of the organisation, but not necessarily the only activity. Most PMLOs have a strict

hierarchical structure, with each member acting as a specialised professional that is responsible for particular elements of the ML cycle (see **Section III**).

3.   A **Professional money laundering network (PMLN)**, which is a collection of associates or contacts working together to facilitate PML schemes and/or subcontract their services for specific tasks. These networks usually operate globally, and can include two or more PMLOs that work together. They may also operate as informal networks of individuals that provide the criminal client with a range of ML services. These interpersonal relationships are not always organised, and are often flexible in nature.

These extensive PML networks are able to satisfy the demands of the client by opening foreign bank accounts, establishing or buying foreign companies and using the existing infrastructure that is controlled by other PMLs. Collaboration between different PMLs also diversifies the channels through which illicit proceeds may pass, thereby reducing the risk of detection and seizure.

PMLOs work with OCGs of all nationalities, on a global basis or in a specific region, often acting as a global enterprise. The same PML can be used to facilitate ML operations on behalf of several OCGs or criminal affiliates. They are highly skilled and operate in diverse settings, adept at avoiding the attention of law enforcement. One relevant case has been identified demonstrating that the same money launderers provided services to both OCGs and terrorist organisations (see Box 1, below).

Box 1. Khanani Money Laundering Organisation

The Altaf Khanani Money Laundering Organisation (MLO) laundered illicit proceeds for other OCGs, drug trafficking organisations and designated terrorist groups throughout the world. The Khanani MLO was an OCG composed of individuals and entities operating under the supervision of Pakistani national, Altaf Khanani, whom the US Drug Enforcement Administration (DEA) arrested in 2015. The Khanani MLO facilitated illicit money movements between Pakistan, the United Arab Emirates (UAE), the United States, the United Kingdom, Canada, Australia and other countries. It was responsible for laundering billions of dollars in criminal proceeds annually.

The Khanani MLO offered ML services to a diverse clientele, including Chinese, Colombian and Mexican OCGs, as well as individuals associated with a US domestically designated terrorist organisation. The Khanani MLO has also laundered funds for other designated terrorist organisations. Specifically, Altaf Khanani, the head of the Khanani MLO and Al Zarooni Exchange, has been involved in the movement of funds for the Taliban, and Altaf Khanani is known to have had relationships with Lashkar-e-Tayyiba, Dawood Ibrahim, al-Qa'ida and Jaish-e-Mohammed. Furthermore, Khanani was responsible for depositing drug proceeds via bank wires from a foreign business account in an effort to conceal and disguise the nature, source, ownership and control of the funds. Khanani conducted transactions, which involved multiple wire transfers from a number of general trading companies. Khanani's commission to launder funds was 3% of the total value of funds laundered.

The Khanani MLO itself was designated by OFAC in 2015 as a "transnational criminal organisation[1]," pursuant to Executive Order 13581. On the same day, OFAC designated the exchange house utilised by the Khanani MLO, Al Zarooni Exchange. In 2016, the US Treasury's Office of Foreign Assets Control (OFAC) designated four individuals and nine entities associated with the Khanani MLO. On October 26, 2016 Altaf Khanani pleaded guilty to federal ML charges. Approximately USD 46 000 in criminal proceeds was also confiscated from Khanani. In 2017, Altaf Khanani was sentenced to 68 months in prison for conspiracy to commit ML.

Extensive law enforcement co-ordination took place between multiple law enforcement agencies from Australia, Canada and the US who all held a different piece of the puzzle. The designation of Al Zarooni Exchange complements an action taken by the Central Bank of the UAE, with assistance from the AML Unit at Dubai Police General Headquarters, which closely coordinated with the DEA prior to the action taken.

Note: 1. Transnational Criminal Organisation (TCO) is a specific technical term used in the US designation process and is synonymous with organised crime group (OCG), the latter of which is used throughout this report.

Source: United States, Australia, Canada, UAE

OCGs use both outsiders and OCG members to perform ML services on behalf of the group. In cases where there is an in-house component of an OCG that is responsible for ML, these members may receive a portion of the proceeds of the group, rather than a fee or commission. The extent to which PMLs get involved in ML schemes depends on the needs of the criminal group, the complexity of the laundering operation that they wish to execute, as well as the risks and costs associated with such involvement.

When OCGs employ the services of PMLs, they often choose PMLs who are acquainted with persons close to, or within, the OCG network. They can be family members or close contacts. They may also be professionals that previously acted in a legitimate capacity, and who now act as:

- accountants, lawyers, notaries and/or other service providers;
- Trust and Company Service Providers (TCSPs);
- bankers;
- MVTS providers;

- brokers;
- fiscal specialists or tax advisors;
- dealers in precious metals or stones;
- bank owners or insiders;
- payment processor owners or insiders; and
- electronic and cryptocurrency exchanger owners or insiders.

OCGs also make use of external experts on a permanent or ad hoc basis. These experts knowingly operate as entrepreneurs and often have no criminal record, which can aid in avoiding detection. These complicit professionals are increasingly present on the criminal landscape, coming together as service providers to support specific criminal schemes or OCGs (see **Section VI**). PMLs can also provide services to several OCGs or criminal affiliates simultaneously, and are both highly skilled at operating in diverse settings and adept at avoiding the attention of law enforcement.

Compartmentalised relationships also exist, particularly within PMLNs, whereby there may be no direct contact between OCGs and the lead actors responsible for laundering the funds In these instances, transactions are facilitated via several layers of individuals who collect the money (see **Section III**) before funds are handed over to PMLs for laundering.

SECTION III: SPECIALISED SERVICES AND BUSINESS MODELS

PMLs can be involved in one, or all, stages of the ML cycle (i.e. placement, layering and integration), and can provide specialised services to either manage, collect or move funds. PMLOs act in a more sophisticated manner and may provide the entire infrastructure for complex ML schemes or construct a unique scheme, tailored to the specific needs of a client.

There are a number of specialised services that PMLs may provide. These include, but are not limited to:

- consulting and advising;
- registering and maintaining companies or other legal entities;
- serving as nominees for companies and accounts;
- providing false documentation;
- comingling legal and illegal proceeds;
- placing and moving illicit cash;
- purchasing assets;
- obtaining financing;
- identifying investment opportunities;
- indirectly purchasing and holding assets;
- orchestrating lawsuits; and
- recruiting and managing money mules.

Underground Banking and Alternative Banking Platforms

Underground banking is one tool often used by PMLs. This mechanism is used, with the goal of bypassing the regulated financial sector and creating a parallel system of moving and keeping records of transactions and accountancy.

Box 13. Investigation of Massive Underground Banking System

Subject X and his network of associates in British Columbia, Canada, are believed to have operated a PMLO that offered a number of crucial services to Transnational Criminal Organisations including Mexican Cartels, Asian OCGs, and Middle Eastern OCGs. It is estimated that they laundered over CAD 1 billion per year through an underground banking network, involving legal and illegal casinos, MVTSs and asset procurement. One portion of the ML networks illegal activities was the use of drug money, illegal gambling money and money derived from extortion to supply cash to Chinese gamblers in Canada.

Subject X allegedly helped ultra-wealthy gamblers move their money to Canada from China, which has restrictions on the outflow of fiat currency. The Chinese gamblers would transfer funds to accounts controlled by Subject X and his network in exchange for cash in Canada. However, funds were never actually transferred outside of China to Canada; rather, the value of funds was transferred through an Informal Value Transfer System. Subject X received a 3-5% commission on each transaction. Chinese gamblers were provided with a contact, either locally or prior to arriving, in Vancouver. The Chinese gamblers would phone the contact to schedule cash delivery, usually in the casino parking lot, which was then used to buy casino chips. Some gamblers would cash in their chips for a "B.C. casino cheque", which they could then deposit into a Canadian bank account. Some of these funds were used for real estate purchases. The cash given to the high-roller gamblers came from Company X, an unlicensed MVTS provider owned by Subject X. Investigators believe that gangsters or their couriers were delivering suitcases of cash to Company X, allegedly at an average rate of CAD 1.5 million a day. Surveillance identified links to 40 different organisations, including organised groups in Asia that dealt with cocaine, heroin and methamphetamine.

After cash was dropped off at Company X, funds were released offshore by Subject X or his network. Most transactions were held in cash and avoided the tracking that is typical for conventional banking. Subject X charged a 5% fee for the laundering and transfer service. As the ML operation grew, the money transfer abilities of Company X became increasingly sophisticated to the point where it could wire funds to Mexico and Peru, allowing drug dealers to buy narcotics without carrying cash outside Canada in order to cover up the international money transfers with fake trade invoices from China. Investigators have found evidence of over 600 bank accounts in China that were controlled or used by Company X. Chinese police have conducted their own investigation, labelling this as a massive underground banking system.

Source: Canada

An *alternative banking platform (ABP)* is an alternative bank that operates outside the regulated financial system. However, an ABP may use the facilities of the formal banking system, while creating a parallel accountancy and settlement system. ABPs are a form of shadow banking that make use of bespoke online software to provide banking services, without the regulated and audited customer due diligence checks. They are an effective way to transfer the ownership of money anonymously and provide banking services within a bank account across a number of individuals, without being reflected in traditional banking transactions. Usually, it is supported with special software that can encrypt traffic, manage transactions between accounts within the same platform, apply fees and assist with interaction with the outside financial system.

Box 14. Alternative Banking Platforms

An alternative banking platform (ABP) was used to assist organised crime groups (OCGs) in the UK to launder funds from VAT fraud. The ABP had a registered office in one jurisdiction with a holding company in a second jurisdiction and a bank account in a third jurisdiction. It was operated by a PMLN based in a fourth jurisdiction all outside of the UK. The ABP was used for a year with over EUR 400 million moved through it. The ABP was shut down and the creator of the financial software was arrested by international partners, with assistance from Her Majesty's Revenue and Customs (HMRC). The data gathered from the ABP servers was used to identify other ABPs and develop additional cases.

Source: United Kingdom

In some cases, PMLs use specialised software to create an ML scheme to move funds randomly through numerous accounts. This software is generally based on a random data generator principle.

APPENDIX D
CHINESE TRIAD SOCIETIES

A brief history of Chinese Triad Societies and today's gangs and resultant Asian crime syndicates.

CHINESE TRIAD SOCIETY

T. Wing Lo, PhD
Professor and Head, Department of Applied Social Studies, City University of Hong Kong

Sharon Ingrid Kwok, MSc
PhD student, Department of Applied Social Studies, City University of Hong Kong

Introduction

In the seventeenth century, the Chinese triad society, also known as the Hung Mun, Tien Tei Wei (Heaven and Earth Society) or San Hwo Hui (Three United Society), was founded to overthrow the Ch'ing Dynasty and restore the Ming Dynasty in China. Guided by a strong patriotic doctrine, the triad maintained a rigid central control over the behavior and activities of its members, who regarded themselves as blood brothers and were expected to be loyal and righteous. The early triad society still maintained its secret and cultural features, as reflected in its paraphernalia, organizational structure, recruitment mechanism, initiation ceremony, oaths, rituals, secret codes, and communication system. There were clear rules, codes of conduct, and chains of command. In the early 1900s, the Hung Mun gradually disintegrated into many triad societies or gangs that operated independently from each other in different parts of China. With the Chinese Communist Party in power in 1949, many triad members escaped to Hong Kong, Macau, Taiwan and Chinatowns in overseas countries together with thousands of refugees. In the beginning, refugees from the same ethnic groups united themselves to protect their own interest against other ethnic groups in a definite neighborhood. With the infiltration of triad elements, some of these groups were gradually transformed into triad societies (or tongs in Chinatowns overseas) which used violence to protect them in a dominated territory. In postwar decades, Hong Kong was the capital of triads and it was suggested by a police commissioner that one in every six of the 3-million Hong Kong inhabitants was a triad member. Because of their entrenched subculture and cohesion, triads are regarded as effective in enforcing control in local territories, but it is argued that their hierarchical structure is incompatible with the dynamic nature of many forms of transnational organized crime, such as human smuggling. On the other hand, China's open door policy in the 1980s encouraged triads to shift their money-making focus onto mainland China. In view of assistance provided by triads to smuggle out democratic leaders after the Tiananmen crackdown in 1989 and China's resumption of sovereignty of Hong Kong in 1997, China applied a 'united front' tactic to recruit Hong Kong triads to the communist camp. A label of patriotic triad was bestowed on triad leaders, who were able to set foot in China. Triads experienced a process of mainlandization as a result of China's economic growth and rising demand for limited goods and services. They network with Chinese officials and enterprises and forge cooperative relationships with mainland criminal groups, trying to capitalize in the booming underworld. They exchange crime techniques with the Chinese counterparts and import sex workers and dangerous drugs from mainland into Hong Kong. Today, a business approach has developed alongside the traditional triad crime. Triads have been engaged in legitimate businesses and worked with entrepreneurs and professionals to make financial gain in business markets. They are less structurally organized than their patriotic counterparts of the past, and triad rituals are simplified.

General Overviews

Early works on triad societies focused on history and rituals that were based on those used in Hung Mun in ancient times. They described triad myths as the origin of patriotic culture. Among them, Schlegel 1866, Stanton 1900 and Morgan 1960 are authoritative triad literature accepted in the court of Hong Kong. They are often referred to by the police in prosecuting offences related to triad membership. Chu 2000 provides a description of the development of triad societies in Hong Kong. He argued that the emergence of triads in Hong Kong was not a response to local needs, nor a purposive migration of triads from mainland China, but rather a consequence of influx of refugees from mainland to Hong Kong during the post-war and post-communist takeover decades. Chin 1990 found that ordinary street crimes, such as vice, gambling, extortion, and drug dealing, are facilitated by the traditional triad hierarchical structure. Through such structural and subcultural control, triad societies are able to compel their members to run illicit activities. Liu 2001 also provides a comprehensive background of triad history, activities, political involvement, relationships with Chinese officials, and operations in overseas markets. Lo and Kwok 2012 examined the impact of socio-economic changes on triad organized crime in modern times. They contended that triads are abided by the same code of conduct and chain of commands that assure the formation of blood brothers with one solitary aspiration. With such authority and manipulation amid the triad syndicate, this aspiration inevitably results in the running of illicit activities in triad-controlled territories. As a result of socio-economic changes, triads move from localization to mainlandization, triad brotherhood to entrepreneurship, and cohesion to disorganization. Lo and Kwok 2013 suggested that as the intimacy between Hong Kong and China grew deeper, an upsurge of cross-border crime has emerged since the 1990s. Prosperity in China caused a process of mainlandization of triad activities because of an ever-increasing demand of licit and illicit services in Chinese communities. The relationship between triads, tongs and transnational organized crime is examined.

APPENDIX E - WORLD MILITARY GAMES LETTER TO PARTICIPANTS

Surgeon General	Médecin général
Commander Canadian Forces Health Services Group NDHQ Carling Campus 101 Colonel By Drive Ottawa ON K1A 0K2	Commandant Groupe des Services de santé des Forces canadiennes QGDN Complexe Carling 101 Colonel By Promenade Ottawa ON K1A 0K2

6600-01 (CDCP)

22 January 2020

Dear Military World Games 2019 participant,

POTENTIAL EXPOSURE TO 2019 NOVEL CORONAVIRUS DURING 7TH MILITARY WORLD GAMES IN OCTOBER 2019 IN WUHAN, HUBEI PROVINCE CHINA

1. On December 31st, 2019 the World Health Organization (WHO) China Country Office was informed of several cases of pneumonia of an unknown cause in Wuhan, Hubei Province, China. The cause of the illness has since been identified as a novel Coronavirus (2019-nCoV), a virus from the same family as some types of the common cold as well more serious respiratory infections such as Middle Eastern Respiratory Syndrome and Severe Acute Respiratory Syndrome coronaviruses. As of January 20th 2020, more than 200 cases (including five deaths) have been confirmed in Wuhan.

2. At least five cases have been confirmed outside of China – two in Thailand and one in Japan, USA, and South Korea. All of these cases have recent documented travel to Wuhan. Additional cases of pneumonia in travelers returning from Wuhan are being investigated for 2019-nCoV in Hong Kong, South Korea, Taiwan, Vietnam, Nepal, Singapore and other countries that have direct connecting international flights to Wuhan. We are confident that the number of suspected 2019-nCoV cases as well as the number of countries reporting suspected cases will

6600-01 (CDCP)

janvier 2020

Cher participant des jeux mondiaux militaires 2019,

EXPOSITION POTENTIELLE AU NOUVEAU CORONAVIRUS DE 2019 LORS DES 7E JEUX MONDIAUX MILITAIRES TENUS EN OCTOBRE 2019 À WUHAN, DANS LA PROVINCE DE HUBEI, EN CHINE

1. Le 31 décembre 2019, le bureau chinois de l'Organisation mondiale de la santé (OMS) a reçu le signalement de plusieurs cas de pneumonie virale de cause inconnue, survenus à Wuhan, dans la province de Hubei, en Chine. Il a ensuite été établi qu'un nouveau coronavirus (le 2019 nCoV) en était à l'origine. Ce virus fait partie de la même famille que certains types de virus causant le rhume ainsi que de celle des coronavirus causant des infections respiratoires plus graves telles que le syndrome respiratoire du Moyen-Orient et le syndrome respiratoire aigu sévère. En date du 20 janvier 2020, plus de 200 cas (dont 5 décès) ont été confirmés à Wuhan.

2. Au moins cinq cas ont été confirmés à l'extérieur de la Chine – deux en Thaïlande et un chaque au Japon, EUA, et Corée Du Sud. Dans ces cas, les personnes avaient récemment séjourné à Wuhan. D'autres cas de pneumonie chez des voyageurs revenant de Wuhan font l'objet d'une enquête afin d'établir si le 2019-nCoV est présent à Hong Kong, en Corée du Sud, à Taïwan, au Vietnam, au Népal, à Singapour et dans d'autres pays dont les vols internationaux ont une correspondance directe à Wuhan. Nous estimons que le nombre de cas soupçonnés d'infection au 2019-nCoV ainsi

1/3

National Défense
Defence nationale

Canada

increase in the next 30 days. The increasing case count will continue to generate significant media attention and public concern – particularly as travel peaks during the first week of February due to Chinese New Year.

3.   We are not aware of any 2019-nCoV cases among CISM MWG participants. Your individual risk of having been exposed to 2019-nCoV during temporary duty in Wuhan City for the 7th CISM MWG is negligible. This is because of two key reasons. First, all CAF participants left China and returned home well before the virus had begun circulating in Wuhan City. Second, all CAF participants have now been home far longer than the maximum incubation period (12-14 days) between virus exposures and 2019-nCoV symptom development.

4.   DND and its allies are actively monitoring the situation in China. The Directorate of Force Health Protection (DFHP) issued an advisory on January 16th, 2020 to all clinicians, in garrison and on operations, providing information on the virus and advice for managing patients who present with respiratory disease. Domestically, the Public Health Agency of Canada's Health Portfolio Operations Centre (HPOC) is also tracking the evolving situation. The senior leadership of the CAF have been briefed directly on the contents of this communiqué.

5.   **While your risk is assessed negligible, if you are concerned about potential exposure and have had persistent respiratory symptoms including fever and**

que le nombre de pays signalant des cas soupçonnés augmenteront au cours des 30 prochains jours. L'augmentation du nombre de cas continuera de susciter une attention importante des médias et nourrira l'inquiétude du public, plus particulièrement pendant la première semaine de février alors que le Nouvel An chinois donne lieu à de nombreux déplacements.

3.   À notre connaissance, aucun participant aux Jeux mondiaux militaires du Conseil international du sport militaire (CISM) n'a été infecté par le 2019-nCoV. Le risque que vous ayez personnellement été exposé au 2019-nCoV dans le cadre de votre service temporaire à Wuhan à l'occasion des 7e Jeux mondiaux militaires du CISM est jugé négligeable. Deux raisons sous-tendent cette évaluation du risque. Premièrement, tous les participants des Forces armées canadiennes (FAC) avaient quitté la Chine et étaient rentrés chez eux bien avant que le virus ne commence à circuler à Wuhan. Deuxièmement, tous les participants des FAC sont maintenant rentrés depuis une période excédant la période d'incubation maximale (12 à 14 jours) pouvant s'écouler entre l'exposition au virus et la manifestation des symptômes de la maladie causée par le 2019-nCoV.

4.   Le ministère de la Défense nationale et ses alliés surveillent étroitement la situation en Chine. Le 16 janvier 2020, la Direction – Protection de la santé de la Force a diffusé un avis à tous les cliniciens (en garnison et participant à des opérations) afin de leur fournir de l'information sur le virus et sur les façons de prendre en charge les patients présentant des symptômes d'affection respiratoire. Au pays, le Centre des opérations du portefeuille de la Santé de l'Agence de la santé publique du Canada surveille également l'évolution de la situation. Les hauts dirigeants des FAC ont été informés directement du contenu du présent communiqué.

5.   **Le risque auquel vous êtes exposé est jugé négligeable. Toutefois, si vous craignez avoir été exposé au virus et que, depuis votre retour de Wuhan, vous souffrez de**

2/3